D1713474

STUDIES IN COMICS AND CARTOONS
LUCY SHELTON CASWELL AND JARED GARDNER, SERIES EDITORS

À Valérie et Louise, encore et toujours.

REDRAWING FRENCH EMPIRE IN COMICS

MARK McKINNEY

THE OHIO STATE UNIVERSITY PRESS · COLUMBUS

Copyright © 2013 by The Ohio State University.

Library of Congress Cataloging-in-Publication Data

McKinney, Mark, 1961–
Redrawing French empire in comics / Mark McKinney.
p. cm. — (Studies in comics and cartoons)
Includes bibliographical references and index.
ISBN-13: 978-0-8142-1220-2 (cloth : alk. paper)
ISBN-10: 0-8142-1220-4 (cloth : alk. paper)
ISBN-13: 978-0-8142-9321-8 (cd)
1. Comic books, strips, etc.—France—History and criticism. 2. Imperialism in popular
culture—France. 3. France—Colonies—In literature. 4. France—Colonies—History. 5. Algeria—History—1830–1962. 6. Indochina—History. I. Title. II. Series: Studies in comics and
cartoons.
PN6745.M39 2013
741.5'35820971244—dc23
2012043008

Cover design by Laurence J. Nozik
Text design by Juliet Williams
Type set in Adobe Sabon and Formata
Printed by Thomson-Shore, Inc.

∞ The paper used in this publication meets the minimum requirements of the American
National Standard for Information Sciences—Permanence of Paper for Printed Library Materials. ANSI Z39.48–1992.

9 8 7 6 5 4 3 2 1

CONTENTS

ILLUSTRATIONS

ACKNOWLEDGMENTS

I thank my colleagues at Miami University, who have been extremely supportive of my research over the years: Jonathan Strauss, Chair of French and Italian; my other departmental colleagues, who have heard and commented on my presentations of this material in our Irvin works-in-progress series (2000, 2009); Juanita Schrodt, departmental Administrative Assistant; and the university colleagues who awarded me a Hampton Grant in 2006, allowing me to carry out research at the Cité Internationale de la Bande Dessinée et de l'Image, in Angoulême.

Several colleagues read drafts of the manuscript at various points and made invaluable comments on it: Bernard Aresu, Cécile Danehy, Valérie Dhalenne, Ann Miller, Todd Porterfield, Dominic Thomas, Rusty Witek, and two anonymous readers for The Ohio State University Press. I am deeply grateful to all of them for their excellent suggestions and for their kind encouragement.

Colleagues also provided very useful feedback and support when I presented drafts of portions of this study as invited lectures and conference presentations: Peter J. Bloom, Paul Cohen, Anne Donadey, Sylvie Durmelat, Hugo Frey, Laurence Grove, Alec G. Hargreaves, Pascal Lefèvre, Fabrice Leroy, Wendy Michallat, Adrianna M. Paliyenko, Kees Ribbens, Matthew Screech, Vinay Swamy, and Jane Winston. I presented this research at several fora, including: MMLA (Chicago, 1997); France: History and Story (Birmingham, 1999); Faculty Lecture Series, Department of French and

Italian, Miami University (2000); 20th/21st-Century French and Francophone Studies (Urbana, 2003; Tallahassee, 2004); Georgetown University (2004); KFLC (Lexington, 2003, 2008); IBDS (Manchester, 2005, 2011); Technologies of Memory in the Arts (Nijmegen, 2006); Graphic Engagement (West Lafayette, 2010); Florida State University (2012); and the University of Toronto (2012). I much appreciate the efforts of the colleagues who organized these conferences, panels and lectures, and am grateful for the feedback received then.

I assigned comics studied here in several classes at the university, and thank the students who took the courses. They contributed in many ways to my reflection on the meaning and value of the works.

I am grateful to The Ohio State University Press for publishing my study: I especially thank Malcom Litchfield, Director, Sandy Crooms, Senior Editor, as well as Lucy Shelton Caswell and Jared Gardner, Series Editors.

Catherine Ferreyrolle, Jean-Pierre Mercier and Catherine Ternaux at the Cité Internationale de la Bande Dessinée, in Angoulême, and the staff of the Centre Belge de la Bande Dessinée, in Brussels, were most helpful during my research trips there.

Various cartoonists kindly and generously shared their thoughts and sources, and in some cases welcomed me into their studios or homes. For this I am deeply grateful to Yvan Alagbé, Clément Baloup, Baru, Nadjib Berber, Farid Boudjellal, Pierre Christin, Jacques Ferrandez, Frank Giroud, Annie Goetzinger, Kamel Khélif, José Jover, Lax, Leïla Leïz, Larbi Mechkour, Amine Medjdoub, Séra, Slim and Jean-Philippe Stassen.

I put final touches on the manuscript in 2012, as events commemorating the end of the Algerian War and fifty years of Algerian independence unfolded. Azouz Begag, Farid Boudjellal and Alec G. Hargreaves kindly gave me access to pre-publication copies of two comic books scheduled for release on the anniversary.

Cartoonists and publishers very generously granted permission to reproduce the illustrations in this volume. I warmly thank: Yvan Alagbé; David B. and L'Association; Clément Baloup and Mathieu Jiro; Baru; Farid Boudjellal; Rebecca Byers and Editions Plon-Perrin-Presses de la Renaissance; Michel Deligne of 2e Souffle; Jacques Ferrandez and Editions Casterman; Frank Giroud and Lax; Grégory Jarry, Otto T. and Editions FLBLB; and Morvandiau and L'oeil électrique/Maison rouge. I also thank Jeanne Strauss-De Groote and the Public Library of Cincinnati and Hamilton County for assistance with illustrations.

I gratefully acknowledge kind permission granted by the editors of journals that published earlier versions of portions of this study: parts of Chapter 2 appeared in *Modern and Contemporary France*; and parts of Chapter

4 were published in *Etudes Francophones* and the *International Journal of Comic Art*.

My American and French families and friends kindly, generously, and patiently supported my research over the many years that I researched and wrote this book. I gratefully thank Annie Rochard for kindly hosting me in summer 1996 while I interviewed several cartoonists whose work I analyze here. I warmly thank the McKinneys, whose shared interest in French and Belgian comics goes back decades, for their support and inspiration. I am also very grateful to the Dhalennes, who in many generous ways enabled me to bring this project to a conclusion. I thank Valérie and Louise, without whom this book would simply not exist.

1

REDRAWING FRENCH EMPIRE IN COMICS
An Introduction

Redrawing the colonial affrontier

How do French cartoonists redraw French empire in comics? In what ways do they represent its consequences today? In *Jambon-Beur: Les couples mixtes* [Ham-Butter/Arab[1]: Mixed Couples] (1995), by Farid Boudjellal, the painful burden of colonial history has a devastating impact on Charlotte-Badia, the vulnerable young daughter of Patricia Barto and Mahmoud Slimani, a French-Algerian couple. Unmediated, conflicting memories of the Algerian War (1954–62) spark an identity crisis in the child: her French maternal grandfather (Fabien) died in Algeria at the same moment as her mother first opened her eyes at birth, and her Algerian paternal grandfather was wounded in the war.[2] The result is that the three surviving grandparents still harbor pain and resentment, which they communicate to the girl. The cartoonist suggests the weight of the Algerian War in the simple, three-frame opening sequence of the book (5; Figure 1.1). We read first about the birth of Patricia, who first opens her eyes in 1961, towards the end of the war. Then, in a transitional second frame, we see a map of the south of France and the north of Algeria. The third frame informs us that the child's father has just closed his eyes for the last time, having died in the war. This sets up both the continuity or renewal of life and the traumatic, terminal experience of death during the war, which constitute the fundamental socio-historical problem of the comic book: how can those of European-French and Algerian-

Figure 1.1: Birth and death coincide during the Algerian War, creating a legacy of pain and bitterness for future generations in France. From Farid Boudjellal, *Jambon-Beur: Les couples mixtes* [Ham-Butter/Arab: Mixed Couples], articles by Martine Lagardette, colors by Sophie Balland (Toulon: Soleil Productions, 1995), p. 5. © Farid Boudjellal.

French background who were affected by the war, and their descendants, live together peacefully and harmoniously today?

Although one reads these three frames sequentially, the eye also takes them in together and is attuned to the two axes that structure them as a whole: one could draw a horizontal line across the middle, from the child to her father, who are both lying flat, and a vertical line from France to Algeria, in the middle frame. These axes meet in the center frame, in the middle of the Mediterranean Sea, which both unites and separates France and Algeria, Patricia and her father. These imagined, invisible lines redraw what I call the colonial affrontier [l'affrontière coloniale] (McKinney 2007a, 2008c, 2011a), a boundary that here divides and connects France and Algeria, and around which individuals and groups confront each other [ils s'affrontent]—through insulting language [des affronts] or physical confrontation [des affrontements]—or instead seek peace and the effacement of the affrontier, producing an afrontier: a space characterized by freedom of movement and expression. The latter is a post/colonial territory from which colonial confrontation between groups in the present has been eliminated (cf. Hargreaves and McKinney 1997: 22), although the memory of the colonial past may remain. There is also a kind of visual anti-gravitational or centripetal force at work in Boudjellal's page: the head of the child is pointing to the left, whereas the French soldiers carrying her father's body are running toward the right, in the same direction as the helicopters are pointing; while France and Algeria are being pulled apart, and separating into two distinct nations during the war. The old passes in a violent, unnatural way, placing a tragic burden on the new: the affrontier of today is a product of the affront and the confrontations of yesteryear [l'affrontière naît de l'affront-hier, des affrontements d'hier]. It therefore includes a temporal and ontological tension between a dying colonialism, an ill-defined post-colonial present and a post/colonial future.

Other visual correspondences both unite and divide the first and third frames: the black background behind the healthy, pink baby girl in the first frame is echoed by the macabre black silhouettes in the third frame, which stand out against the red background of war, blood and fire—of the sun setting on French Algeria. On the left is the personal dimension, that of individualized history and a new self, represented close-up through the drawing of a human face, while on the right is the larger dimension of national history, seen at a greater distance and depersonalized through the anonymity of the silhouette shapes and the violence of the death-dealing machines hovering above the lifeless body. The two poles are mediated in the middle frame by the formal abstraction of the map, representing the geo-political and natural elements in and through which the personal and the collective meet: the cartoonist draws from the map-maker's symbolism. Through the layout of all these elements, the cartoonist suggests that one of his most important tasks will be the articulation of the individual and the collective, of personal and national histories: the individuation of the historical, making it more comprehensible, real and convincing to readers; and the historicization of the personal. The eye takes in and interprets the simple but profound symbolism of these three frames together as a dynamic whole, while also reading the strip sequentially.[3]

The story then shows Patricia as she grows up, meets and marries Mahmoud, and gives birth to their daughter Charlotte-Badia, who catalyzes the memories of her grandparents about the Algerian War. Faced with the double burden of cultural mixing and family animosities deriving from the war, nine-year-old Charlotte-Badia splits into two separate characters, Charlotte and Badia (Boudjellal 1995: 27; McKinney 1997). In order for the girl to piece together her two halves, her grandparents must be reconciled and their differences laid to rest. This occurs at her birthday party, where the family feud erupts once again, in a complex sequence that weaves together the violence of colonialism (the Algerian War), of the Algerian civil war that erupted in 1992 (and brought back memories of the preceding Algerian conflict for many) and of neo-colonialism (the 1994 genocide in Rwanda, in which the French army has been accused of various types of complicity). Significantly, it is the family matriarchs who open the possibility of healing, of broaching the colonial affrontier, by sadly comparing the pain caused by the death of a loved one. Moreover, they do so in a way that short-circuits the earlier competition between their opposing painful memories of the Algerian War. Instead, they resolve their differences by drawing an equivalence between the painful effacement of self that immigration can bring and the tragic violence of the Algerian War. When Charlotte-Badia's French grandmother mourns the battlefield death of her husband, the girl's Algerian grandmother responds by evoking the loss of her eldest daughter, Latifa, who committed suicide rather than face her father's anger, after she was impregnated by her French boyfriend (Boudjellal 1995: 53). We understand that Charlotte-Badia might once again become whole when we see her two selves looking on at her/their grandmothers, who are embracing for the first time (54). Charlotte-Badia and her French and Algerian families are what Claude Liauzu (2000) designated "passeurs de rives" [shore crossers], and Jean-Robert Henry (1991: 301) called "frontaliers": "individuals and groups living on the symbolic frontier between societies positioned as antagonists or as visibly different. . . . *Marginal* with respect to their society, these individuals are central to the inter-societal conflict, and to zones of common reference constructed by and in spite of this conflict."

In this comic book, the longing and hope for post/colonial vistas no longer plagued by the weight of the colonial past (Hargreaves and McKinney 1997: 22), and for a transformation of the colonial affrontier into an afrontier (a non-frontier) is symbolized by the possibility that Charlotte-Badia may become whole again. Nonetheless, the hyphen in her name remains a fragile link. The comic book's final pages show Mahmoud and Patricia looking at a family tree that Patricia has just made from photographs of four generations of the two families (59–61). The tree's form is symbolic: instead of a trunk representing the family's founding couple, and the branches showing the offspring, here the direction is inverted. In this case, the ancestors are tacked onto the branches, and Charlotte-Badia's portrait is on the tree's base, but it is located on the physical faultline at the center of the double-page (cf. Groensteen 1999: 44–48). This configuration suggests that it is the mixed offspring of France and Algeria who are important today, and not long-departed past generations or ancient quarrels. As Mahmoud gazes at the tree, he admonishes Patricia not to go too far back in their families' histories, lest she encounter unpleasant surprises. Boudjellal suggests here that although one might reexamine colonial history in order to promote the healing of French-Algerian antagonisms, an overvaluation of the past could perpetuate conflict along the French-Algerian affrontier, with negative effects on future generations of Maghrebi-French. Is this an injunction to leave colonial injustices buried in order to facilitate assimilation? For some, the admonishment by Mahmoud would echo eerily with Renan's problematic insistence in "Qu'est-ce qu'une nation?" [What Is a Nation?] (1947; 1993) that a nation must forget historical grievances against minorities in order to survive, intact. However, it has been noted that a major problem with Renan's argument is that it is usually the minority that must hide its historical wounds, not the majority, and that this can have grave consequences for both. *Jambon-Beur* and other graphic narratives by Boudjellal, analyzed below (Chapter 4), demonstrate that the cartoonist is well aware of the risks and benefits, the felt necessity and objective impossibility, of forgetting colonial history and its injustices.

A less pronounced version of the French colonial affrontier can be detected and analyzed today in comics and graphic novels pertaining to other historical contexts and regions, for example, French Indochina, as we shall see (Chapter 3, below). I focus more on French-Algerian relations in this volume because cultural proximity and often violent sharing between French and Algerian cultures—due to many factors, but especially 132 years of French conquest and colonization, and related large population transfers between the two nations—have produced a long, rich, complex and fractured French-Algerian cultural formation, including many French-language comics and graphic novels related to Algeria, drawn and read on both sides of the Mediterranean from before independence to the present. A photograph taken by Pierre Bourdieu (in Bourdieu, Schultheis and Frisinghelli 2003: 186) during the Algerian War and published over four decades later suggests the genesis of French-language Algerian comics and of French comics by cartoonists of Algerian heritage: it shows two Algerian boys standing outside a newsstand in French Algeria and gazing intently through its window at the display of comics inside, which include the French classic *Fantax*.[4] But what appear to interest the children most are the pocket-sized versions of cowboy and Indian comics (referred to in French simply as "pockets"), with titles such as *Totem, Buck John* and *Old Bridger*. Comics such as these helped inspire Algerian cartoonists (Labter 2009: 45–47, 53–55), as well as Algerian-French ones. Here already, the American colonial affrontier appears as a paradigmatic model for the French-Algerian one (cf. Woodhull 1997). And in Boudjellal's "Petit Polio" [Little Polio] series (1998–2002), set in Toulon during the Algerian War, young Mahmoud Slimani admires those same American-themed frontier comics and westerns.[5] That this sharing of a model of remembrance of colonial history was mediated by cartoonists from another country (Italy) may seem stranger still, but exemplifies a recurring feature of cultural memory, according to Ann Rigney (2005: 24): the transfer of "mnemonic technologies and memorial forms" from one group to another. So although I focus here on French imperialism, I am aware that other empires play a role in shaping the colonial affrontier for French comics: for example, it is sometimes figured in comics through references to the American frontier, including the Far West (see below, Chapter 4), while at the other end of North African history stand the Roman empire and then the Ottoman one. These three imperial entities— Roman, Ottoman and American—and their frontiers were already articulated in French colonial visions of its Algerian conquest, to which Algerian novelists Kateb Yacine and Assia Djebar, among others, subsequently responded in their writings.

The frontier is both a hard historical reality and a figure for dividing and connecting cultural, ethnic, linguistic, religious and other entities. To redraw empire therefore involves retracing frontiers still in dispute: that is, affrontiers. Colonialism has produced an unsettling fault line—a kind of frontier—in French-language comics, fracturing the apparently smooth surface and line of pleasant fantasy and artistic style, and running from the present day back through the "ligne claire" [clear line] of Hergé and his studio artists, all the way to the beginnings of the French-language comic book. One might choose, with some justification, to locate the medium's launching in a series of *romans en estampes* [novels of engravings] by Swiss cartoonist Rodolphe Töpffer, including *Histoire de M. Cryptogame* [*Story of Mr. Cryptogame*], whose initial 1830 manuscript version of the book was read and favorably received by Goethe (Kunzle 1990: 29–30, 2007: 49–53; cf. below, Chapter 2). That first draft was drawn during the conquest of Algiers, and expresses European anti-Algerian sentiment of the period, in its representation of merciless Barbary pirates, and of the dey of Algiers as an oriental despot who rules tyranically until he is killed by a captured European woman just added to his harem. Colonialism remains a source of contention in France today, as politicians, pundits and ordinary people debate whether the French colonial occupation of Algeria was essentially a form of exploitation and domination for which France bears responsibility, or was instead mainly a positive outgrowth, expression and even gift of French civilization to North Africa. Much like his presidential predecessors (François Mitterrand, Jacques Chirac),[6] Nicolas Sarkozy often argued that colonialism was at least partly an enterprise for which France should be proud, and that in any case belongs to the past, so does not require apologies ("repentance" is the term often used) or, especially, reparations. However, writing on 18 March 2012, on the occasion of the fifty-year commemoration of the cease-fire of 19 March 1962, historian Benjamin Stora (2012) describes Sarkozy's declaration during a visit to Algeria in December 2007 as a step forward in official French recognition of the injustices of colonialism: "Unjust by nature, it could not have been lived other than as an enterprise of servitude and exploitation" (Sarkozy, quoted by Stora). Perhaps, but the fact remains that Sarkozy's official conduct and language were often neo-colonial in nature; for example when he courted right-wing voters by stigmatizing post-colonial, working-class immigrant minorities in France.

The affrontier is a faultline across and through which national and trans-national identities are constantly being reconstituted. By redrawing empire in comics, cartoonists reenvision identities of the French and of the (formerly) colonized, including people from Vietnam and Algeria, where two of the bloodiest and most protracted modern wars of decolonization were fought. The two wars and the colonial history leading up to them have inspired many French cartoonists in the last few decades. We have already seen some of the iconic figures of the colonial affrontier in French comics: the mixed couple, the *métis/se* [a person of culturally or ethnically mixed descent], the post-colonial immigrant (and family) and the war victim. These exist singly and in various combinations: for example, Abdel, the Algerian grandfather of Charlotte-Badia, is both a post-colonial immigrant and a war victim. Cartoonists who redraw empire often focus on figures who guard the colonial affrontier, challenge it or disregard it: French professional soldiers and conscripts, colonized soldiers in the French army

and nationalist anti-colonial soldiers. Unauthorized crossing of the affrontier constitutes a threat to national identity, so national, ethnic and cultural
betrayal is a key trope of this space and is often personified in army dissent-
ers and deserters, mixed couples and *métis/se* characters. Here too one finds
a concatenation or layering of figures, for example a French soldier falls in
love with a colonized woman, forms a mixed couple and deserts to join an
anti-colonial organization.

In the rest of this chapter I sketch out key dimensions of redrawing French
empire in comics. First I outline the reasons why there has been a return
to colonialism in French popular culture, and specifically in comics, over
the past few decades. Next I explain how genealogy allows cartoonists to
reconnect with the French colonial past. I then describe significant ways
that cartoonists have approached colonial historiography. This leads me to
an exploration of the importance of colonial archives for cartoonists. I then
briefly describe how the medium's specific representational capacities allow
it to depict the colonial past. I conclude by providing an overview of the following chapters of my study.

Returning to colonialism in French popular culture and comics

For the most part, colonial themes fell out of fashion in mainstream French
comics after 1962, when the majority of French colonies had achieved formal independence. With a few significant exceptions, French-language cartoonists did not return to colonial history until a couple of decades after
the end of the Algerian War. They did so then for several important reasons, especially the arrival of post-colonial ethnic minorities as a cultural
and political movement drawing national news coverage in the 1980s (Hargreaves 1995: 142–44; Blatt 1997; Branche and House 2010: 130–31).
Important events in this emergence include, on the political end, the 1983
Marche pour l'égalité et contre le racisme [March for Equality and Against
Racism] and, in the cultural domain, the exhibition of works by "children
of immigrants" at the Centre Pompidou museum of modern art and culture in Paris. Cartoonists participated in these and related events (Mechkour and Boudjellal 2004: 8–9). This new visibility was facilitated by the
election of François Mitterrand to the French presidency in 1981, and the
multicultural initiatives that his government took at the beginning of his
fourteen years in that position. The Minister of Culture, Jack Lang, played
an important role in this opening (Rigby 1991: 182). Another key factor
was the rise of the far right as a political force in the early 1980s, and specifically the electoral breakthroughs of the National Front (FN), then led by

Jean-Marie Le Pen.[7] He helped to resurrect and attempted to rehabilitate a colonial history in which he had played a role personally, by participating as a French soldier in the wars in French Indochina and Algeria, but also as an elected legislator [député] who defended the colonialist cause of *l'Algérie française* [French Algeria] during the Algerian War (Stora 1992: 288–91; 1999: 38–46).

The return to colonial history during this period was in part a continuation of preceding, colonial-era debates and disputes, but conducted more freely, with less censorship, in newspaper articles, films, books, theater and television talk shows (Dine 1994; Stora 1997; Fleury-Vilatte 2000). However, to a certain extent it was taken up by a generation that began to come of age in the 1970s and early 1980s and had been too young to participate directly in France's colonial wars or debates, so was less inhibited by painful personal memories, or feelings of guilt, loss or responsibility: for that generation, engagement with colonial history could even be fashionable or funny. This interest found expression in a variety of popular means of expression, including magazines such as *Actuel,* film and music (for example, the "rock-arabe" of Carte de Séjour and Mounsi; and the songs of the rock group Indochine). Beginning in the late 1970s and early 1980s, exotic adventures in historical comics were published in (now defunct) French magazines such as *Circus* (which serialized François Bourgeon's "Les passagers du vent" [Passengers of the Wind], about the triangular slave trade),[8] *Corto Maltese* (where "Carnets d'Orient" [Oriental Sketchbooks], Jacques Ferrandez's long running series of comic books on the colonization, settlement and decolonization of Algeria, were partly serialized)[9] and *Vécu* [Lived] (which published another series set mainly in colonial Algeria, "Chronique de la Maison Le Quéant" [Chronicle of the Le Quéant Family], by Daniel Bardet and Patrick Jusseaume),[10] whose motto was "L'histoire c'est aussi l'aventure" [History is adventure, too].

The formal independence of most French colonies put pressure on cartoonists to re-evaluate their depiction of colonialism (as epic history), which had long provided them with story material and narrative paradigms, as well as heroic character types (adventurer, missionary, reporter, soldier, settler)[11] and villainous ones (indigenous anti-colonialist leaders, Communist spies, rival imperialists, drug smugglers). Several options were available to them. For example, they could focus on decolonization as a dramatic period in which different groups from colonizing nation(s) were pitted against each other and when Europe was forced to confront the national aspirations of colonized peoples. Pierre Christin, scriptwriter of comics and professor of journalism, described this when I asked him why he chose to focus on decolonization in some of his comics (Christin and Goetzinger 1996):

Quand les choses commencent à se détraquer, c'est ça qui est intéressant. C'est là où il y a des histoires à raconter, parce qu'il y a des déchirements autant politiques que personnels, parce que ça représente un monde disparu ou en train de s'écrouler . . .

[What's interesting is when things begin to go off kilter. That's where there are stories to be told, because there are splits that are political and personal, because it represents a world that has disappeared or is collapsing. . .]

Cartoonists such as Christin attempt to locate the roots of colonialism's failure and retrace the history of its decline and transformation. For example, some have recently depicted a sequence of events that prefigured and helped lead to the Algerian War (Figure 1.2): a nationalist Algerian demonstration in Sétif on 8 May 1945, the immediate violent crackdown by French forces, the ensuing Algerian riot that killed some one hundred Europeans, and the weeks-long retaliatory massacre by the French army, police and *Pieds-Noirs*[12] of untold hundreds and even thousands of Algerians (Horne 1978: 23–28; Abun-Nasr 1990: 339–40; Ruedy 1992: 149–50; Benot 2001: 9–35; Pervillé 2003: 17). Comics that revisit this episode of French colonial history include *Tahya El-Djazaïr: Du sang sur les mains* [Long Live Algeria: Blood on the Hands] (Galando, Dan and Ralenti 2009), *Petite histoire des colonies françaises: La décolonisation* [A Short History of the French Colonies: Decolonization] (Jarry and Otto T. 2009), *Les Z: Sétif-Paris* [The Zs: Sétif-Paris] (Malka and Volante 2011) and *Leçons coloniales* [Colonial Lessons] (Begag and Defali 2012). This last volume, which deplores the French colonial failure to educate Algerians and treat them equally, was scripted by Azouz Begag, former Ministre délégué à la promotion de l'égalité des chances [Under-Secretary for the Promotion of Equal Opportunity] in France. Begag, whose family is from this region of Algeria, and Djillali Defali, who drew the story, researched the event on site.

Christin's statement also suggests that cartoonists may view colonialism's apparent failure in disparate and even conflicting ways. For instance they may portray colonialism as: tragedy, farce, or epic struggle; deeply flawed and doomed to failure from the start or potentially recuperable at key points; a heroic narrative of sacrifice and redemption or a grotesque descent into human depravity; and a closed chapter of history or a force that reaches into the present (for example, as neo-colonialism, uninterrupted colonialism, imperialism, or destruction for which reparation still needs to be made). Moreover, the manner in which artists depict the colonial past always says something about their vision of the present. For example, there may be a nostalgic emphasis on a disappearing colonial society

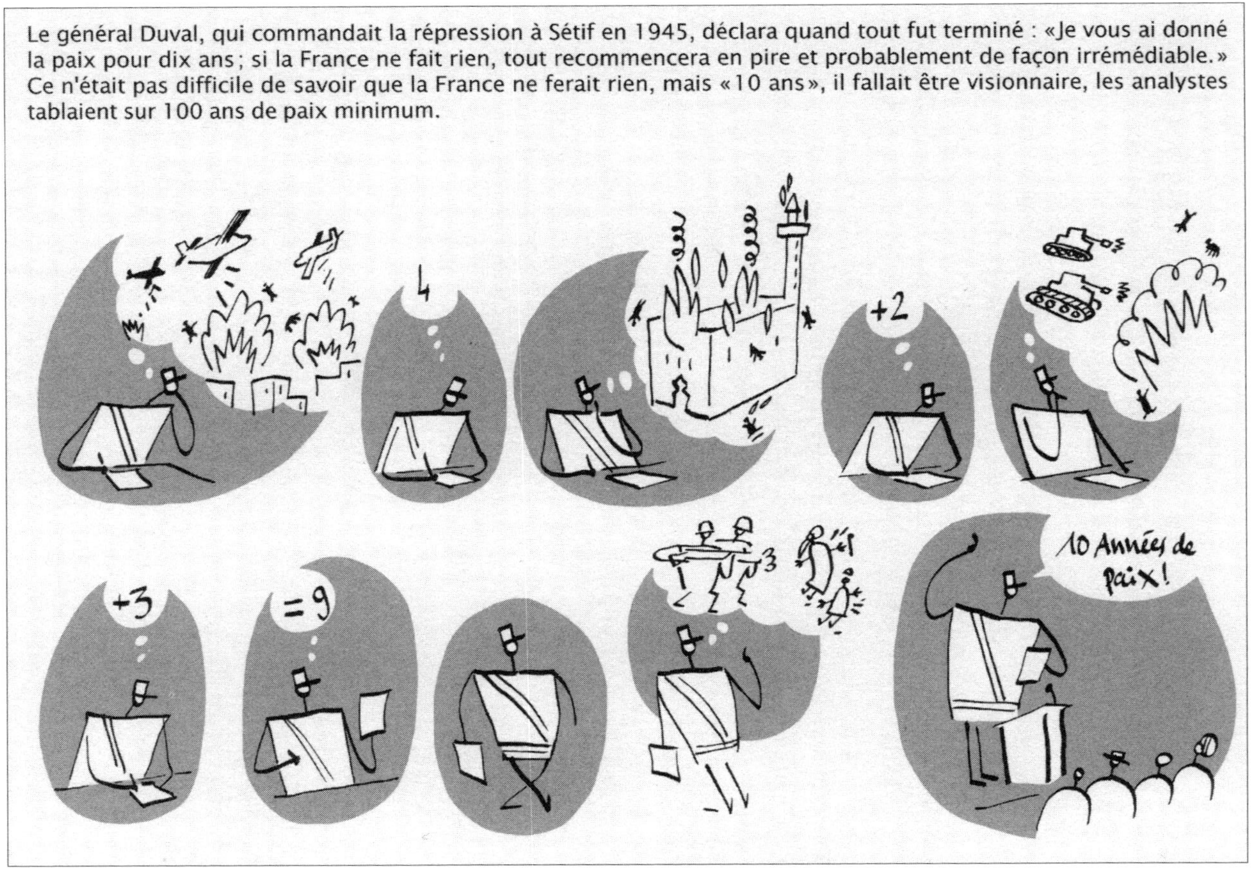

Le général Duval, qui commandait la répression à Sétif en 1945, déclara quand tout fut terminé : «Je vous ai donné la paix pour dix ans ; si la France ne fait rien, tout recommencera en pire et probablement de façon irrémédiable.» Ce n'était pas difficile de savoir que la France ne ferait rien, mais «10 ans», il fallait être visionnaire, les analystes tablaient sur 100 ans de paix minimum.

Figure 1.2: A satirical depiction of the accounting after the massive French repression in Sétif, Algeria, and the surrounding area in 1945. The French general responsible for the massacre proclaims that it has bought ten years of peace for France. The Algerian War began about nine years later. From Grégory Jarry and Otto T., *Petite histoire des colonies françaises*, vol. 3: *La décolonisation* [A Short History of the French Colonies: Decolonization], colors by Lucie Castel and Guillaume Heurtault (Poitiers: FLBLB, 2009), n.p. © Grégory Jarry, Otto T. and Editions FLBLB.

(in Christin's words, "a world that has disappeared or is collapsing") or an anti-colonialist, forward-looking focus on the creation of a new nation by the colonized. In comics that focus on colonial history there always exists, in latent or explicit form, a view of present-day relations between ex-colonizer and ex-colonized, just as comics that focus on the post-colonial multiculturalism of present-day France and on its former colonies incorporate one or more views of colonial history. Here again, comic-book representations of the events in 1945 in the Constantine region provide an excellent example. Whereas the four recent works cited above provide a critical perspective on this infamous example of massive French colonial repression, an earlier work evokes it in vague terms (Tacconi et al. 1978: 1134), a biography of De Gaulle ignores it completely (Saint-Michel, Goutteman and Rufieux 2000), and comics that celebrate French colonial troops either ignore it (Saint-Michel and Le Honzec 1995) or euphemize it as a "une castagne" [a scrap] (Glogowski and Puisaye 2003: 42). This last comic book appeared in a series on the French Foreign Legion (a quintessentially colonial army branch) commissioned by a traditionalist Catholic publisher with ties to the French far right, which suggests how the representation of French colonial history, including in comics, remains a highly politicized struggle. The French state long blocked access to, and even purged, its archives on the event (Rey-Goldzeigueur 2002: 60–61), and it was only in 2005 that the French ambassador to Algeria finally described the French repression as an "unexcusable tragedy" (AFP 2005). Genealogical activity and historical inquiry—such as that of Begag into the uprising and massacre in his parents' home region[13]—provide cartoonists and readers with important ways of reconnecting with French colonial history in comics.

Drawing colonial and imperialist genealogies

Genealogy in relation to colonialism and imperialism in and around French comics takes at least five interconnected forms: familial, ethnic, national, artistic and critical. The potential and problems of genealogy are suggested by the quandry at the end of *Jambon-Beur*: drawing up the family tree may provide self and community with a stable sense of identity and continuity, but when the colonial affrontier traverses it, investing ancestral history with too much authority over the present can create painful divisions. In *Le cimetière des princesses* [The Cemetery of the Princesses] (Ferrandez 1995), Marianne, a *Pied-Noir* art student living in Algiers in 1954, begins to trace back a colonial genealogy to Joseph Constant, an orientalist painter and adventurer who travelled to Algeria in 1832, by reading his "Orien-

Figure 1.3: The reading of an artist's scrapbooks from the Algerian conquest inspires a colonial genealogical search by a *Pied-Noir* art student. From Jacques Ferrandez, *Carnets d'Orient*, vol. 5: *Le cimetière des princesses* [Oriental Sketchbooks: The Cemetery of the Princesses], preface by Louis Gardel (Tournai: Casterman, 1995), p. 24. © Casterman. Reproduced with the kind permission of Jacques Ferrandez and Editions Casterman.

tal sketchbooks" (Figure 1.3): although not a direct descendant, she adopts him as an ancestral figure in quasi-familial and ethnic terms. In many of the comics that I analyze, the familial represents the ethnic (cf. Ferrandez in Buch 2005: 58–59). This comes partly from the generic conventions of historic fiction (family sagas for recounting colonial history, etc.; Tribak-Geoffroy 1997: 124), but is also related to the familial language of nationalism (see below). Marianne's reading spurs her, as it did Captain Haddock in Hergé's *Le secret de la Licorne* [*The Secret of the Unicorn*], to retrace the itinerary of her ancestor (here, Constant) through an initiatory pilgrimage to the *lieux de mémoire* [places of memory] where he was years ago, scattered across Algeria. Today's cartoonists have reworked this theme from earlier colonial comics, such as those of Hergé (McKinney 2011b) to help produce what Rigney (2005: 17, 23–24) calls a working memory. Cartoonists also redraw the genealogy of their own family history as it intertwines with French colonial and imperialist history. Ferrandez has engaged in this type of research on his family's *Pied-Noir* roots in Algeria (Poncet and Morin 1996: 76; Tribak-Geoffroy 1997: 128–29; Buch 2005: e.g., 64–66, 73–77). Marianne is therefore a fictional double of Ferrandez and could also be partly based on Ferrandez's own mother (Poncet and Morin 1996: 76). Marianne's search for her mythical ethnic ancestor (Constant) leads her to interrogate her family history: for example, she learns that her great-grandmother modeled for an orientalist harem painting that Constant made in Nice, just as Marianne models for an Orientalist painter in Algiers decades later.[14] Morvandiau, also of *Pied-Noir* heritage, inserts a drawing of his family tree at the beginning of *D'Algérie* [About/From Algeria] (2007: n.p.), which intertwines his personal and family history with that of French-Algerian relations from the 1830 invasion to the present, to critically examine the connections between his family and the history of colonialism and decolonization. This is also therefore a genealogy of violence and counter-violence, whose erasures still weigh on the present: Morvandiau points out that some events and actions—such as the disappearance of Maurice Audin while in French military custody—remain silenced and taboo for official France (Figure 1.4).

Contemporary cartoonists in France engage therefore in personal and ethnic genealogical inquiries, such as when they reconstitute their family history: fathers and mothers, aunts and uncles, grandparents and others who lived in—or visited—French colonies, including French Indochina and Algeria, arguably the two most significant French colonies of the nineteenth and twentieth centuries. They reconstruct their family history as a genealogical link between themselves and the colonial past, often as a way of situating themselves within strands of history that have not been fully integrated into the dominant French historical narrative, and (or) whose definition is still contested: the colonization of Algeria, which profoundly modified both France and Algeria in palpable ways up to the present (Chapter 2, below); the Indochinese War,[15] which helped launch the process of decolonization across the French empire (Chapter 3, below); and the Algerian War, a bitter and long-lasting colonial conflict that tramautized many Algerians and French (Chapter 4, below). These reconstructed family histories are often related to post-colonial ethnic minorities: for example, presented as symbolic of the history of *Pieds-Noirs,* Algerian Jews, Algerian Muslim immigrants to France or Viet Kieu (expatriate Vietnamese). Others are not: familial stories about French conscript soldiers, for example.

A third form of genealogy, after familial and ethnic versions, is national genealogy. Ferrandez's character Marianne is obviously named after a national symbol of France, suggesting that the recreation of the Algerian past through her involves reinserting Algerian colonial history and memory into the history of France. What is at stake here, therefore, is a coun-

Figure 1.4: On this page of his autobiographical comic book about France and Algeria, Morvandiau interweaves his family history with that of decolonization. Here he redraws a document recalling Maurice Audin—a mathematician and Communist who was born in Tunisia—and overwrites it with text referring to the cover-up of the torture and disappearance of Audin by the French army in Algeria and notes that at the time his own father, a *Pied-Noir* who still believed in "a French Algeria, united and fraternal," read Henri Alleg's *The Question,* which recounts the arrest and torture of Audin and Alleg for their radical activities in Algeria. From Morvandiau, *D'Algérie* [About/From Algeria] (Rennes: L'oeil électrique/Maison Rouge, 2007), n.p. © Morvandiau and L'oeil électrique/Maison Rouge.

ter-memory (Rigney 2005: 23) articulated through an historical fiction, a form of writing and here, of drawing, that helps palliate "the difficulties of using the historiographical genre" (22; cf. Leroy 2011). The latter are compounded when much evidence from the colonial past has been lost for ethnic minorities living in France, at a far remove both temporally and spatially from foundational *lieux de mémoire*.

According to Etienne Balibar (in Balibar and Wallerstein 1991: 101), "in contemporary national societies, except for a few genealogy 'fanatics' and a few who are 'nostalgic' for the days of the aristocracy, genealogy is no longer either a body of theoretical knowledge or an object of oral memory, nor is it recorded and conserved *privately:* today *it is the state which draws up and keeps the archive of filiations and alliances*" (original emphasis). Some cartoonists have become "genealogy 'fanatics,'" or at least devote considerable (though sometimes ambivalent) attention to genealogy, precisely in part because of the ways in which French nationality has been constructed through the nation-state. Balibar argues that the latter produces a fictive ethnicity, which increasingly supercedes other types of kinship structures and identifications (in Balibar and Wallerstein 1991: 49). This creates an "imaginary unity *against* other possible unities," including—in France— groups historically dominated and excluded through colonialism, imperialism, social class and gender. Fictive ethnicity is produced through both language and a notion of race (96): since the linguistic community is inherently open (anyone can learn a national language; 98), it must be closed off through a racial supplement, in the form of the idea that members of the national community all belong to a quasi-family, which is constituted by "the community of 'French,' 'American' or 'Algerian' families" (99–100; cf. Balibar 1998: 83).[16] So for Balibar (in Balibar and Wallerstein 1991: 100; emphasis added):

> The symbolic kernel of the idea of race (and of its demographic and cultural equivalents) is the schema of *genealogy,* that is, quite simply the idea that the filiation of individuals transmits from generation to generation a substance both biological and spiritual and thereby inscribes them in a temporal community known as "kinship."

Genealogies produced in comics about French colonialism tend to reinforce, contest or otherwise rework the racist closing off of French national belonging and, perhaps more rarely, the masculinist gendering of nationalism and national "patrimony" (cf. McClintock 1993; Beaty 2007, 2008), including the colonial heritage of French comics (McKinney 2011b)—the colonial adventure in comics (Miller 2004) was traditionally the preserve of French boys and men, in the stories and among their producers and consumers.

A fourth type of genealogical reconstruction is the search for artistic masters from the past. Marianne also resembles Ferrandez in that her research into the life and work of Constant creates an artistic genealogy (orientalist painting and painters), as well as an ethnic and family one: the references by Ferrandez to Hergé and to Eugène Delacroix as his artistic forebears are transparent here (see above, Figure 1.3, and Chapter 2, below).[17] Another version of this genealogical activity is the field-forming, often institutionalized, search for progenitors of the comics medium, which leads publishers, cartoonists and scholars to consecrate as the founding fathers of comics some cartoonists whose oeuvre is indelibly marked by colonialism and imperialism (cf. McKinney 2011b).[18]

My fifth form of genealogical inquiry in and around comics is the critical investigation into the colonial and imperialist roots of French comics. Here, and in a companion study, *The Colonial Heritage of French Comics* (McKinney 2011b), I engage in this type of investigation, inspired by the methods of Michel Foucault, Balibar, Edward Said, and Rigney, among others. Foucault (1981: 83; quoted in Woodhull 1993: 97), for example, defines genealogy as "the union of erudite knowledge and local memories which allows us to establish a historical knowledge of struggles and to make use of this knowledge tactically today," and archeology as "the appropriate methodology of this analysis of local discursivities" (Foucault 1981: 85; cf. Foucault 1982). However, in *Fast Cars, Clean Bodies: Decolonization and the Reordering of French Culture,* Kristin Ross (1996: 190) argues that "Foucault states that he wants to write about the present; this desire is used to justify the genealogical project, and then he never quite gets to talking about the present." And as Said (1994b: 41) has observed, investigation into European imperialism was mainly absent from Foucault's otherwise powerful and productive genealogical research. By contrast, my critical genealogical project traces colonial ideology and representation up to the present, in a popular medium. And despite its importance for understanding the nature and evolution of present-day French society, popular culture has been mostly ignored by theoreticians and cultural critics such as Said and Foucault, who are otherwise capital to my genealogical investigation.

The reincorporation of colonialism into French history has not happened smoothly or extensively, in part because of the rupture of partial decolonization: the loss of most of the French empire disrupted the national narrative of French grandeur, progress and civilization, which had been instrumental in imperialist expansion and domination (Agulhon 1998: 300). And continuing neo-imperialist relations between France and former colonies also make investigation into colonial history and its aftermath a sensitive subject in France today. A striking example of the resulting blind spot is the often cited and almost complete exclusion of the related histories of colonialism, immigration and slavery from the impressive, multi-volume series on *Les lieux de mémoire* in France, edited by Pierre Nora (1984–92)—this absence has been noted by many commentators (e.g., Noiriel 1992: 18–19; Cottias 2006: 128; Liauzu 2006: 95) and is all the more surprising given his previous research on colonial populations (Nora 1961). Of course the occlusion of colonial history has always been partial: for example, since 1962 there has been much discussion of the ways that it should be viewed and integrated into the national narrative. One illustration is the debate sparked by a law passed by the French parliament on 23 February 2005, which stated that, among other things, in public schooling:[19]

> les programmes scolaires reconnaissent en particulier le rôle positif de la présence française outre-mer, notamment en Afrique du Nord, et accordent à l'histoire et aux sacrifices des combattants de l'armée française issus de ces territoires la place éminente à laquelle ils ont droit.

> [school programs recognize in particular the positive role of the overseas French presence, notably in North Africa, and give to the history and the sacrifices of the French army combatants from those territories the eminent place that is their due.]

Although some found other features of the law objectionable too, this article especially provoked a storm of protest by historians, who argued that their freedom of thought and expression was being unduly restricted (e.g., Liauzu and Manceron 2006). French president Jacques Chirac eventually rescinded the offending article, which had been included in part to satisfy associations of French settlers of Algeria and their descendants.

In the prior decade, one such organization, the Cercle Algérianiste [Algerianist Circle], cited as instrumental in the passing of the 2005 law (Escanglon Morin, Nadiras and Thénault 2005: 41), published a series of five comic books recounting the colonization of Algeria. They exemplify some of the ways in which cartoonists have used genealogy to promote alternative or submerged versions of French history, which reincorporate colonial history viewed through their perspective—in this case, a reactionary, colonialist one. Evelyne Joyaux-Brédy, a teacher and president of the Cercle Algérianiste of Aix-en-Provence, wrote the story for the series, which was published by subscription. She left Algeria in 1961 at age 12 and has explained that her family history helped inspire a prose novel that she published, as well as the comic books (Esteve n.d.). Genealogy is therefore a pertinent category for reading her series: it recounts the fictional(ized?) epic story of a family in Algeria, from 1832 to 1962. The cartoonists include family trees on the title pages of two comic books—they function as both an aid for readers and a visual representation of an ethnic community (the *Pieds-Noirs*) as a family, a nationalist trope (Balibar, in Balibar and Wallerstein 1991; see above) structured by gender (McClintock 1993). In this case it serves both to demarcate a French colonial community and to (re)connect it with the larger national one, beyond the "interruption généalogique" [genealogical interruption][20] caused by the loss of French Algeria. The Algerian War removed the colonizers from their colonial *mère-patrie* [homeland] (their homes, the tombs of their ancestors, etc.) and forcibly (re)inserted them into mainland French society. It also isolated them from French national history, through the temporary suppression or marginalization of its colonialist and imperialist features, whose glorification had previously contributed to French national mythology and history (Dine 1994: 146–77; Agulhon 1998: 300). French comic books and series (but also other narrative forms, including film and prose fiction) such as the Cercle Algérianiste one often recount colonial history via a family saga, and may take the form of fiction, semi-fiction or even straight biography and autobiography (cf. Rigney 2005: 22). This last form of writing has become a dominant one in the alternative comics movement over the last couple of decades (Baetens 2004; Miller 2007: 61–62, 215–41), so it is not surprising that mixtures of autobiography, as well as family, ethnic and national history are found in many comics about French Algeria. The deep settler colonization that occurred there over the 132 years of French occupation (McClintock 1992: 88) has made a significant imprint on French popular culture, including comics.

Drawing on historians and colonial history in comics

What sorts of relationships have existed between, on the one hand, historical and other scholarly research and, on the other hand, (post)colonial comics? This is a leitmotif of my investigation throughout this study, because it helps clarify the meaning and value of these comics and scholarship about them and about colonialism. Throughout this book I highlight the complex and sometimes close links that exist between historical research, (post)colonial studies and comics. Some of the best-known experts on colonialism—including historians, sociologists and anthropologists—have reproduced documents and published research that contemporary cartoonists have drawn on, or redrawn, to create their historical fictions about colonialism

and decolonization. Among the most obvious examples are historical studies that cartoonists quote explicitly, whether within the comic itself (Figure
1.5),[21] in a bibliography at the end,[22] or on an artist's blog.[23] Sometimes one
or more images, stories or texts worked into a comic strongly suggest that a
cartoonist used the work of a particular historian: e.g., some images of colonial-era Algeria found in *L'histoire de l'Algérie en bandes dessinées: L'épopée du Cheikh Bouamama* [The History of Algeria in Comics: The Epic of
Cheikh Boumama] (Bessaih, Bakhti and Masmoudi 1986), *Carnets d'Orient*
(Ferrandez 1994a) and "Le coup de l'éventail" [The Fan Blow/Trick] (Slim
n.d.) were no doubt redrawn from *Villes d'Algérie au XIXe siècle: Estampes*
[Cities of Algeria in the 19th Century: Engravings], edited by Djebar (1984).

In "L'effet d'histoire" [The History Effect], pioneering French comics
critic Pierre Fresnault-Deruelle (1979) argued that historical references in
comics often provide a thin veneer of historical verisimilitude to fictions primarily intended to distract: the historical references help produce an "history effect," much like the "reality effect" theorized by Roland Barthes
(1985) in prose fiction. The four-part model of Fresnault-Deruelle accurately describes the relationship to history and historical research of many
recent comics set in the colonial past: for example, the "Mémoires d'un
aventurier" [Memoirs of an Adventurer] series (Dimberton and Hé 1989–
91), set in colonial Indochina, or the "Chronique de la Maison Le Quéant" series (Bardet and Jusseaume 1985–89), much of which takes place in
colonial Algeria. On the other hand, works by Ferrandez, Lax and Frank
Giroud, Clément Baloup and Mathieu Jiro, Séra, the two Cercle Algérianiste cartoonists (Joyaux-Brédy and Pierre Joux), and comic-book hagiogra-
phies about French colonial soldiers and missionaries commissioned by the
Editions du Triomphe are designed to distract, certainly, but also intervene,
more or less directly, in contemporary debates over the nature of colonial
history and its aftermath. It is not surprising that these and other cartoonists
often take markedly different political and ideological positions on France's
colonial past, given its contentious nature. Contemporary cartoonists may
use historical sources and cite historians with opposing views on colonialism, but some use the same historical evidence and sources in comics whose
historical meanings diverge or even contradict each other. This is especially
obvious in comics about the colonization and decolonization of Algeria, in
part because of the wide variety of comics available in French on this topic,
but also because of the presence in France of several minority groups with
a more or less direct connection to Algeria and the war, and highly contentious public debates about French colonialism in Algeria.

Cartoonists may clearly announce their intention to intervene in historical debates through comics, for example, in published interviews (e.g.,

Figure 1.5: A historian's study that documents a mostly forgotten aspect of the French colonial past in Vietnam—how some French soldiers upheld their ideals by leaving the French army and aiding the Vietnamese nationalists and Communists—is depicted in a comic book partially based on that historical publication. From Lax (art) and Frank Giroud (script), *Les oubliés d'Annam* [The Forgotten Ones from Annam], vol. 1 (Marcinelle: Dupuis, 1990), p. 37. © Lax and Frank Giroud.

Ferrandez, on his publisher's website),[24] in prefatory material or appendices (e.g., *Azrayen'*, vol. 2, by Lax and Giroud [1999]), or by requesting and publishing a preface by a well-known specialist of the history that the comic book retells. The professional credentials of historians[25] can provide cultural capital and legitimation to a medium that has been described as a "paralittérature" (Couégnas 1992) and is often associated with juvenile distractions, not always of the best variety (cf. Beaty 2007, 2008). For example, Belgian historian Louis-Bernard Koch scripted a pro-colonial comic book, *Avec Lyautey de Nancy à Rabat* [With Lyautey from Nancy to Rabat] (Cenci and Koch 2007), published by the Editions du Triomphe, whose cultural and historical agenda is on the far right. As I noted earlier, other historians have prefaced books that deal with episodes from colonial history. Ferrandez invited historians Stora and Michel Pierre to introduce two volumes of his "Carnets d'Orient" (in Ferrandez 1994d, 2005a). Stora, of Jewish Algerian heritage and born in Constantine, is a preeminent historian of Algeria, whereas Pierre has published on the 1931 Paris Colonial Exposition, the *bagnes* [French prison camps] (e.g., in French Guyana), as well as on connections between colonialism and comics. Perhaps inspired by Ferrandez's example, Lax and Giroud sollicited a preface from Stora for the first volume of *Azrayen'* (1998), their two-part comic book about the Algerian War. Stora also prefaced *Octobre noir* [Black October] (Daeninckx and Mako 2011), which recounts the infamously violent police repression in Paris of a peaceful demonstration on 17 October 1961 by Algerians against a curfew imposed on them. An appendix by Jean-Luc Einaudi, whose historical studies have contributed much to public knowledge of the event (e.g., 1991), lists the North Africans who were killed or disappeared in the Paris region in fall 1961. Historian Pascal Blanchard wrote a preface for *Le chemin de Tuan* [Tuan's Way], by Baloup and Jiro (2005), which focuses on anti-colonial activism, including of Vietnamese students in interwar Paris. Blanchard, a co-editor of *Le Paris Asie* [The Paris Asia] (Blanchard and Deroo 2004), has been in the forefront of historical research and debates on French colonial representations, along with Nicolas Bancel, Sandrine Lemaire and other members of ACHAC (Association pour la Connaissance de l'Histoire de l'Afrique Contemporaine [Association for the Knowledge of the History of Contemporary Africa]). And Maximilien Le Roy included an interview with Alain Ruscio, a specialist of French colonialism in Indochina, at the end of *Dans la nuit la liberté nous écoute* [At Night Liberty Listens to Us] (2011), which recounts the real-life story of Albert Clavier during the Vietnamese war of liberation against the French.

These documents constitute, among other things, clear signals that historical publications by these authors helped inspire the cartoonists. As Bart Beaty (2007) has shown, accredited academics and researchers who intervene in comics production and consumption can lend cultural capital to cartoonists attempting to reconfigure their field. This kind of legitimation and support can be especially important to artists and works dealing with issues as contentious as colonial history. This is no doubt part of the reason why Ferrandez and Joann Sfar have sought out other public figures (prose novelists, actors, etc.) associated in some way with the history of Algeria and the Middle East: nine of the ten volumes in Ferrandez's "Carnets d'Orient" have such a preface; as do three of the five original French volumes of Sfar's "Le chat du rabbin" [The Rabbi's Cat] series.[26] Algerian novelist Yasmina Khadra prefaced *Turcos: Le jasmin et la boue* [Turcos: Jasmine and Mud] (Tarek, Payen and Mouellef 2011), about Algerian soldiers fighting in the French army during the First World War. Colonial-era cartoonists and comics publishers also sometimes had recourse to the knowledge of experts, although this is often difficult to ascertain today: for example, Alain Guillemin (2006: 174–75) plausibly speculates that the authors of "Parachutés au Laos" [Parachuted into Laos] (Verdon and Perrin-Houdon 1951–52) may have partially based their comic on a published account (*Parachuté en Indochine* [Parachuted into Indochina], 1947) by Guy de Chezal, a French secret service officer, about his real-life, wartime experiences;[27] and *Bayard,* where the comic was serialized, touts the expertise of Perrin-Houdon, deriving from his status as an officer in the French colonial army ("Parachutés au Laos," no. 274, 2 March 1952, p. 2).

Historians have occasionally been associated with exhibitions of comics related to colonialism and imperialism. They have thereby helped frame how these historical themes are apprehended. For example, in conjunction with an exhibition about comics on the Orient held at the Institut du Monde Arabe [Institute of the Arab World] in Paris, Pierre (1992) published an article about the topic in the French comics magazine (*A Suivre*) [To Be Continued]. More recently, historian Sylvain Venayre curated the exhibition "Le remords de l'homme blanc" [White Man's Remorse], held at the Palais des Beaux-Arts, in Charleroi, Belgium on 12 February–3 April 2005. It focused on European colonialism as represented in the comics of Ferrandez (French), Hugo Pratt (Italian), Jean-Philippe Stassen (Belgian) and Peter Van Dongen (of Dutch and Indonesian heritage). He also wrote most of the exhibition catalog (Pasamonik and Verhoest 2005), providing a useful historical context for, and interpretation of, comic books by the cartoonists.[28] Stassen and Venayre collaborated on an illustrated edition of the French translation of Joseph Conrad's classic colonial text *Heart of Darkness,* published by Futuropolis/Gallimard in 2006. Book reviews by historians and in history periodicals also help draw attention to French-language comics about colonialism and imperialism. The reviewer's reputation and perspective, the choice of books reviewed, and the nature of the publication where the review appears are obviously all significant factors for assessing its potential impact. Pascal Ory, a prominent French historian at the Sorbonne, has a regular column reviewing comics for the generalist, literary magazine *Lire*.[29] He has published short, generally positive reviews there of several recent comics that revisit the colonial past in a more or less critical manner, including *Azrayen'* (Lax and Giroud 1998), *La guerre fantôme* [The Phantom War] (Ferrandez 2002) and *Là-bas* [Down There] (Tronchet and Sibran 2003), which all retell the story of the Algerian War (Chapter 4, below, and McKinney 2011a). Historian Thierry Crépin (2003), who studied with Ory, reviewed two of these same comics in *Vingtième siècle* [Twentieth Century], a French history periodical. One finds, on the far right of the political spectrum, a glowing review of *Les rivages amers: L'Algérie—1920–62* [The Bitter Shores: Algeria—1920–62] (Joyaux-Brédy and Joux n.d.) and the four volumes that preceded it—a colonialist, *Pied-Noir* comic-book series about the creation and loss of French Algeria

(1993–98)—by Dominique Venner (2003), a long-time far-right extremist and the editor of *La nouvelle revue d'histoire* [The New Review of History], a widely disseminated, glossy monthly that provides a regular forum for pro-colonialist accounts of French history by professional historians and others (Chapter 4, below).[30] Venner's review is primarily aimed at an audience that shares his defiantly positive vision of France's colonial presence in Algeria and contests recent, critical assessments of that past by historians such as Stora: "Commence ensuite la guerre d'Algérie à partir de 1954, telle que l'ont vécue les Français d'Algérie et non comme la racontent les historiens" [Then begins the Algerian War, from 1954, in the way that the French of Algeria lived it, and not as historians tell it]. The irony of this statement is that Venner was not only a professional soldier who volunteered to fight in the Algerian War and was imprisoned by the French government for his subversive activity, but he printed this criticism of historians in a journal with historical ambitions. His review of the *Pied-Noir* comic continues his own wartime activities in another way, because he helped publish what were probably the very first comic books about the war—two pro-OAS works, the first of which presents itself as having been drawn in prison during the war (Coral 1962, 1964).[31]

Nonetheless, it is surprising that historians and cultural critics have paid so little attention to imperialism and colonialism in French-language European comics (and to comics in general)—whether Belgian, French or Swiss—given the long and continuing presence of such themes in the medium, and the fact that comics are an ideal place for studying how imperialism and colonialism are embedded in popular culture. It is all the more astonishing because the important anti-imperialist writer and Third World revolutionary Frantz Fanon (1986: 27) once pointed to European colonial-era comics and—more broadly—to popular culture and mass media as a place where colonial racism and imperialist ideology were rife: "Le nègre doit, qu'il le veuille ou non, endosser la livrée que lui a faite le Blanc. Regardez les illustrés pour enfants, les nègres ont tous à la bouche le 'oui Missié' rituel" [The Negro must, whether he wants to or not, don the livery that the white made for him. Look at the illustrated magazines (i.e., magazines containing comics) for children, where Negroes all spout the ritual "yes Mista"] (cf. Fanon 1986: 119; Pigeon 1996: 136; Miller 2007: 172–75).

Drawing on the colonial archives

To some degree there was not a radical break between the new wave of comics with (post-)colonial themes and colonial-era ones. In the past, comics in

France often encouraged positive attitudes towards colonialism and imperialism, despite a long history in France of anti-colonial attitudes, activism, iconography and writings (Biondi and Morin 1993; Liauzu 1993; Girardet 1995). This was due to many factors, including the conservative and reactionary political tendencies of some cartoonists and comics publishers, censorious laws and institutions (Stora 1992: 25–73; Stora 1997: 111–25; Crépin and Groensteen 1999), a paucity of cartoonists or publishers from oppressed groups until recently, the domination of comics publishing by a few large publishers unwilling to take risks with a product directed almost exclusively at children until recent decades, the recycling of formulaic plots and character types in a mass-media form, and the related push to maximize profit through slavish imitation of best-sellers.

Fanon's critical remark quoted above, published in 1952, was directed at racist imagery in colonial-era illustrated children's periodicals ("les illustrés pour enfants" [illustrated magazines for children]) that have by now mostly disappeared from circulation. Jumping forward in time to our period when direct colonial rule by European nations has mostly (but not completely) disappeared, one finds in some comics a longing for a bygone era of colonial adventure and grandeur. In 1993 (46), Laurent Gervereau remarked that French artists had easy access to the archive of colonial representations. Since his observation was published, the availability of colonial-era material has arguably increased greatly, with the transfer of much imagery to the web, but also through the publication—by scholars and collectors—of colonial-era texts and imagery, such as journals, songs, postcards, paintings and comics. Drawing on or mining colonial archives can serve dissimilar and even conflictual purposes.[32] For example, colonial archives may provide material for explaining and critiquing unequal relations today between the dominant majority in France and ethnic minorities from colonized regions. Alternatively, they can be used in attempts to argue that French colonizers treated the colonized well and cohabited peacefully with them. Although both are forms of cultural archeology, their objectives in drawing on the colonial archives are different and even opposed. Critics and publishers have also treated colonial-era comics as a repository of influential graphic styles and techniques, which deserve to be better known because of their artistic qualities and the decisive influence that they have exerted on the comics field and other cartoonists. Some may view the colonial archives simply as a source of income: material retrieved there at low cost can be repackaged and sold today for a tidy profit. Therefore colonial-era comics constitute a multi-faceted colonial inheritance, which is transmitted and redrawn in various ways. For example, stumbling upon a colonial inheritance is still a theme for French cartoonists, some of whom unmistakably borrow the motif from Alain Saint-Ogan or Hergé, both consecrated as founding fathers of French-language comics (McKinney 2011b). In *Le cimetière des princesses* (1995: 22–26), Ferrandez figures the colonial past as an inheritance of his family and ethnic community through the theme of Constant's colonial notebooks, which Marianne and her boyfriend discover in a flea market, just as Tintin discovers a model of the *Unicorn*, the ship of Captain Haddock's ancestor, Sir Francis Hadoque (François de Hadoque; see below, Chapter 2; cf. Tribak-Geoffroy 1997: 124). In post-1962 French comics this colonial heritage has been redrawn at times as a nostalgic story about the loss of the colony, represented, for example, as the disappearance of family possessions in Algeria (Ferrandez 1995: 83–84), or the death of a Vietnamese mistress in French Indochina (Stanislas and Rullier 1992: 40). In such works, all that remains are the visual, textual and oral fragments from which cartoonists and their characters piece together their stories of loss, disappearance, exile, return and remembering: letters, half-remembered family lore, maps and photographs. This is unsurprising given the transition to formal independence of most French colonies, even though France continues to exert considerable political, economic, military and cultural influence on many (former) colonies, helping to arrest their transition, and that of France itself, away from colonialism. In this study I explore the ways in which cartoonists have redrawn colonial material, including history, iconography and adventure stories.

I focus mainly on comics published over the last few decades, including ones originally produced before 1962 and reissued since then. I wish primarily to elucidate how the colonial era has been represented in comics since the majority of French colonies gained formal independence. However, European and other varieties of colonialism and imperialism are clearly by no means finished today. For example, the United States has taken on much of the imperialist role formerly played by Britain and France (Said 1994a). France continues to exert neo-colonial influence over many of the foreign territories that it once ruled directly and openly as colonies (Verschave 2000, 2001). Colonialism and arrested decolonization have left their mark on French comics: one finds both striking continuities and significant differences between those produced at various points in time, so it is important to study their transformation and relationship to history (cf. Nederveen Pieterse 1992). Although French (neo-)colonial influence and activity have not ended, the transition of most French colonies to formal independence created a measurable shift in representations of colonialism in comics. I therefore make a rough distinction between comics published before and after 1962.

Of course most colonial-era comics have not been reprinted in recent years and are now found mostly in specialist libraries, private collections and at rare-book sellers. They are remembered mostly by a few comics specialists, historians and older readers of comics. I refer here to the old stories mainly to make comparisons with newer ones and to reconstruct the genealogy and evolution of important themes and events in comics related to Algeria and French Indochina. On the other hand, those colonial-era comics that are republished today should be analyzed for the ideologies that they transmit, the choices made by publishers and editors (why some colonial-era comics are chosen instead of others) and any justifications given for reissuing the works. Republished colonial-era comics help me interpret the consecration, reworking and contestation of colonial-era paradigms and figures in more recent comics and by cartoonists working today. For example, what remains of the trio once a staple of colonial-era comics: the missionary, colonial administrator and soldier, representing the conjugated might of the church, the government and the army? What did they symbolize in French comics before 1962, the year that France lost formal control over its Algerian colony? What do they represent in today's comics that recreate that epoch? And which characters have supplanted them in other recent publications?

Techniques of redrawing empire in comics and graphic novels

Today cartoonists often represent colonial history in their comics to intervene in debates about contemporary France and its current relationships to its (former) colonies. By their nature and tradition, comics are uniquely configured to participate in these sometimes contentious discussions. Colonialism generated an immense amount of visual imagery and verbal-textual productions—mostly for, but sometimes against, colonialism—much of which can be incorporated into comics today, in one form or another, because comics are generally narratives made of both words and images. Its visual-verbal format allows it to include colonial-era visual representations, and rework or otherwise comment on them, especially through narrative. The dialogical, narrative and visual capacities of comics allow cartoonists to re-view and re-tell the colonial past in ways that are much more difficult, or even impossible, for other sorts of artists: for example, prose novelists and essayists such as Leïla Sebbar (1985) or Djebar (1986)—both authors of Algerian descent who publish in French—usually do not directly *show* readers the orientalist paintings that they critique. Instead they describe them with words, although sometimes there is a reproduction of an orientalist painting on the book's cover. By contrast, cartoonists redraw orientalist paintings in their comics, or use collage techniques to directly insert reproductions into their visual-verbal narratives in ways that are germane to the mixed medium.

Much has been written over the past two or three decades about the visual material left by colonial-era photographers and painters. For French-occupied North Africa, this includes postcards, photographs, paintings, posters, maps and caricatures. These may constitute series, some of which have been reproduced—even many years after they were created—by artists or collectors. For example, Marc Garanger (1982, 1984, 1990) has published books of photographs that he took as a French soldier during the Algerian War, including of Algerian women for mandatory French identity cards, for which they were obliged to unveil. Prefaces by Francis Jeanson, who assisted the Algerian National Liberation Front (FLN) against France during the Algerian War, and by Sebbar help contextualize and interpret Garanger's photographs for us. During the Algerian War Pablo Picasso also famously created a series of paintings entitled "Algerian Women" [*Femmes d'Alger*], after the two well-known paintings bearing the same title that were made by Delacroix in the preceding century (cf. Porterfield 1998: 148–49). Several critics and collectors have published collections of, and interpretive essays on, colonial postcards about North Africa and its peoples. However, these series of photographs, paintings or postcards do not constitute narratives in and of themselves in the same way that comic strips and graphic novels do. Instead, reassembled by producers, collectors and critics, these colonial documents often provide variations on a theme: in postcards, different ethnic types of Algerians (Azoulay 1980), or various colonial monuments in a colonized Algerian city (cf. Prochaska 1990a); a series of Algerian women all photographed in the same place and pose, in Garanger's pictures; or different but related artistic and ideological visions of Algerian women in interior spaces, in paintings by Delacroix, Picasso and Houria Niati (Porterfield 1998: 143–51). By contrast, a comic set in colonial Algeria, for example, does not constitute a series in the same way as the photographs, postcards or paintings do, even when it relies on the latter for documentation. Instead it tells a story.[33]

Moreover, the painters, photographers and printers who created the series of images almost never produced visual narratives about the production or contestation of (neo-)imperialist discourses in the ways that some cartoonists do today in their artwork, through the narrative sequences of images and words that make up most comics. Theoreticians of comics, including Benoît Peeters (2002b: 24–29) and Thierry Groensteen (1999:

5–6), have convincingly shown the radical differences between the ways that paintings and comics usually produce meaning. The capacity of the comic strip or book to narrate in manners that paintings, engravings or photographs cannot is one of the most significant differences between these media. In some comics from the 1980s and 1990s one finds representations of colonial-era visual artists at work, for example: colonial photographers in Morocco, in *Coeurs de sable* [*Hearts of Sand*], by Loustal and Paringaux (1985, 1991), and in Algeria, in *Le centenaire* [The Centennial/ Centenarian], by Ferrandez (1994d; see McKinney 2011b); and orientalist painters and their models in *Carnets d'Orient* (Ferrandez 1994a), *L'année de feu* [The Year of Fire] (Ferrandez 1994b) and *Le cimetière des princesses* (Ferrandez 1995). One already finds colonial-era photography as a motif in *Gringalou en Algérie* [Gringalou in Algeria] (Pinchon and Noé n.d.: 28), serialized in 1947. The artist-within-the-text functions as a reflexive device in comics, as a *mise-en-abîme* of the process of representation, of (re)drawing or representing empire. In some cases this produces a critique of imperialist ways of seeing in the colonial-era imagery used by the cartoonist as documentation for his or her own work. The sequential and narrative capacities of comics can allow cartoonists to represent in detail the production of colonial imagery and reflect on it. Even when there is no artist in the text, cartoonists may use the visual-textual and narrative capacities of the medium to draw attention to the relationships between representation and colonialism or imperialism. Examples of this, which I will analyze in detail in subsequent chapters, include the scrapbook or artist's sketchbook, used throughout Ferrandez's "Carnets d'Orient" series (Chapters 2 and 4, below), and the photo album, found in many French comics about the Indochinese War (Chapter 3, below) and the Algerian War (Chapter 4, below).

There are some similarities between the ways that film and comics function, for example their ability to offer us the visual viewpoint of a character.[34] The spatial layout of sequential frames in the comic strip and on the graphic-novel page, and the separation between them, allow artists to make visual juxtapositions, ellipses between contiguous frames, and other effects that are much more difficult or impossible to achieve in film, whose frames are projected rapidly onto the same space (the screen) and immediately vanish, one after another. Of course the special capacities of the comics medium are double-edged in an important respect that is related to my field of inquiry: they offer unique opportunities to reproduce and perpetuate colonial ideologies, images and discourses, as well as to critique them. The ways and the degree to which they do one or the other tell us a great deal about the place of imperialism and colonialism in French society.

Redrawing French empire in comics: An overview

In this study I focus on the reconstruction of French national and ethnic identities in comics, in reaction to decolonization, and especially the wave of recent works—some by ethnic minority French artists from (former) French colonies—which increasingly provide critical reflection on the historical links between comic books, imperialism and colonialism. My main subject throughout this book is French comics. I chose a national framework for the coherence that it permits: colonial history has national specificities with important effects that continue today—for example, the history of migration flows from (former) French colonies to France, and the resulting constitution of post-colonial ethnic minority groups there. Nonetheless, the book does have a substantial comparative aspect, between the representation of colonialism in French comics about Indochina and Algeria.[35]

This volume is my second on colonialism in French comics. The preceding one, *The Colonial Heritage of French Comics* (McKinney 2011b), focuses on the pervasive but insufficiently acknowledged presence of colonialism within a canon of French comics that has been constructed over roughly the preceding four or five decades. I examine colonialism and imperialism in comics by Hergé, and also especially by Saint-Ogan, who has been given foundational status in French comics by editors, critics and cartoonists, partly because he inspired Hergé, who borrowed ideas freely from the older and—at the outset—more popular French cartoonist (Groensteen 1996). To foreground the colonialism of Saint-Ogan's comics and show how cartoonists have reworked the colonial heritage of French comics over many decades, I analyze two events that have inspired much critical inquiry in recent years: the 1924–25 Croisière noire [Black Journey], a trans-African road trip sponsored by the Citroën car company, which was a massive multi-media event, and the 1931 Paris Colonial Exposition, as well as related events before and after it. I thereby bring into critical dialogue the theoretical and historical analysis of colonialism and that of comics, two fields of research that rarely intersect despite many potential points of engagement. I show how the colonial heritage of French comics continues to exist today, not as something completely stable or unchanging, but instead as an archive of representations that cartoonists redraw, affirm and contest. In the terms that Rigney (2005: 17) borrows from Aleida Assmann, this is the transformation of archival memory into working memory and cultural memory.

Redrawing Empire in French Comics continues that critical inquiry, this time regarding two other important areas of colonial history and comics production. Chapter 2 (below) focuses on Algeria, whose French colonial history extends over more than a century (1830–1962). Although French-language European comics and cartoons representing Algeria have been produced across that entire period and on up to the present, no published study before this one has surveyed the corpus. I show that some French cartoonists who rehearse Algerian colonial history today persist in retelling it from a standpoint of the colonizers. The contradictions inherent in the impossible position of the leftist or liberal colonizer (Memmi 1985: 47–69; 1991: 19–44; Dine 1994: 64–106) are perhaps nowhere more acutely apparent in the post-colonial era than in the case of a descendant of former colonial settlers who critiques colonialism while commemorating the existence and passing of the settler community. My main example is the remarkable comic-book series "Carnets d'Orient," by Ferrandez, born in Algeria during the war but raised in France. His comics elicit positive attention in France far beyond the bounds of comics fandom: for example, several volumes in the series were prefaced by well-known authors, including a leading French authority on the Algerian War (Stora) and a prominent specialist of the Islamic world (Gilles Kepel). By analyzing Ferrandez's use of his source materials, especially nineteenth-century European orientalist paintings and colonialist postcards, I show that the artistic vision contained in his comics remains bound in key ways to the worldviews of French colonial settlers, despite his laudable humanitarian intentions. This chapter engages with important ongoing debates about (post-)colonialism. For example, I document how Ferrandez borrowed erotic images of colonized women from a classic of colonial discourse studies (Alloula 1981, 1986, 2001)—itself forcefully critiqued by feminists (e.g., Woodhull 1991, Bal 1996)—and from erudite studies of orientalist paintings (e.g., Thornton 1985). Following these connections informs us about the degree to which colonial culture and nostalgia survive today in popular culture and the relationships between the latter and scholarly investigation. I analyze Ferrandez's work at length because of its artistic achievement, ideological complexity, and exemplarity as a model for reworking colonial memory in comics. I end the chapter with a brief analysis of other works that strikingly resemble Ferrandez's series: a comic book that three Algerians, B. Bessaih, B. Bakhti and Benattou Masmoudi (1986), published the year that Ferrandez partially serialized the first volume of his "Carnets d'Orient," Joann Sfar's "Le chat du rabbin" [The Rabbi's Cat] series (2003–6), which is far better known internationally but was published later, and Morvandiau's D'Algérie (2007). It is not clear whether Ferrandez was influenced by Bessaih, Bakhti and Masmoudi, or vice versa, but the three Algerian and three French artists draw on, and redraw, some of the same colonial-era historical and artistic sources. Moreover, Ferrandez's series, focused on Catholic

Pieds-Noirs, was clearly a model for Sfar's work, whose main subject is Algerian Jews.

Chapters 3 and 4 study the traces of some of the most violent wars of decolonization in French comics: the French war in Indochina (1946–54) and the Algerian War (1954–62). Their outcome remains especially present and painful for certain groups in France, including the European settler community (*Pieds-Noirs*), the North African communities (Algerian immigrants and *Harkis* [Algerian soldiers in the French colonial army]) and refugees from South-East Asia (especially Vietnamese). To garner votes some political parties (especially the National Front) manipulate resentment over France's loss of prestige from decolonization. This context lends a particular relevance to my analysis of comic-book stories about the wars, in a medium that for generations almost exclusively championed French imperialism and colonialism. Several French artists have a strong personal link to colonization and the bloody wars that brought about its transformation: some are children of the colonized, others of the colonizers, and a few are even former combatants, or their offspring. These artists' depictions of the wars and the preceding colonization of these two regions are often different, sometimes radically so, from the way that comics traditionally presented colonialism, and therefore provide a powerful case-study of the recent transformation of an artistic tradition and of the conflicting positions taken on the divisive issue of France's colonial history.

There are many commonalities between these two wars, including their length (about eight years each), France's ultimate concession and withdrawal, and the fact that many French professional soldiers served in both of them: Raoul Salan and Marcel Bigeard spring to mind. Salan began his military career in French Indochina and later commanded the French war there against the Viet Minh (Ruscio 1992: 185–88), following which he helped direct French fighting during Algerian War, before taking part in the failed putsch of 1961 and then heading the OAS, the French terrorist group, in an attempt to keep Algeria French, even if it required overturning the French government and assassinating President De Gaulle. Bigeard was captured at the battle of Dien Bien Phu (Ruscio 1992: 198), which signaled the end of the Indochinese War, and then went on to take part in the Algerian War—his role included helping to oversee the torture of Algerians during the Battle of Algiers. The war in French Indochina contributed greatly to the determination of many French officers to win the Algerian War at all costs. Several cartoonists explore these connections in their depiction of the Algerian War. However, as Ruscio (1992: 96–97) has pointed out, there were massive differences between the Indochinese War and the Algerian War: for example the much smaller number of French families with a family member who fought in the Indochinese War (all professional soldiers) as compared with the Algerian War, in which virtually all draft-age Frenchmen participated, and the much larger number of French civilians—about one million *Pieds-Noirs*—affected by the Algerian War, by contrast with the some 34,500 French citizens in French Indochina.

Correspondingly, although I point out important similarities between representations of these two wars in comics, I also analyze differences, including a curious, inverse relationship in comics production: during the Indochinese War a few French comics depicted it explicitly in longish stories; by contrast, there was an almost complete blackout on the representation of the Algerian War in comics while it was unfolding. On the other hand, the post-war production of comics about the Indochinese War is generally much thinner than for the Algerian War, both in terms of quantity (number and length of stories) and the array of perspectives represented by the authors and their works. Partly as a consequence, my chapter on the Algerian War is much longer and more detailed than the one about the Indochinese War. Moreover, there are so many French comics on Algeria that I devote separate chapters to those about the colonization of Algeria (Chapter 2) and the Algerian War (Chapter 4).

In my conclusion (Chapter 5) I rework Said's notion of the "voyage in" to outline some of the ways in which new ethnic, post-colonial minorities are complicating the ways that French empire has been drawn in comics. The post-colonial voyage in is the obvious corollary to the colonial voyage out. Both help define the ways in which cartoonists are redrawing French empire in comics.

It should already be clear, but nonetheless bears stating, that my own perspective on colonization and imperialism is that they are violent and reprehensible collective projects and systems, despite the good intentions of many specific individuals who participate in them or any positive effects that result from them, as cultural critics such as Fanon, Albert Memmi and Said have convincingly argued. My goal here is to analyze comic books, especially those drawn or republished after 1962 and the formal independence of most French colonies, as a way of ascertaining whether and how French popular culture is post-colonial: by redrawing empire, are cartoonists buttressing the colonial affrontier or working to move beyond it, toward an afrontier of peaceful, post/colonial relations, no longer characterized by affronts or confrontations [affrontements] linked to colonialism and imperialism? I therefore range widely, examining works ranging from the artistically complex to the rudimentary, and of all political stripes. I am most interested in those that articulate a critical, dialogical vision of the colonial past with skillful artistry. There is an increasing number of them. However,

I also freely recognize that there is no necessary connection between political persuasion, historical vision and artistic accomplishment: what I consider to be bad politics can certainly yield what I believe to be good art and vice versa. I spend considerable space analyzing works despite or even because of their historical or artistic limits.

2
REDRAWING COLONIAL ALGERIA

Redrawing the colonial affrontier in French Algeria

Given the importance of colonial memory to contemporary French politics and national identity (Silverman 1992; Stora 1992), Pierre Nora's editorial decision to more or less neglect colonial sites in his otherwise rich, monumental edited work, *Les lieux de mémoire* [Places of Memory] (1984–92), surprised many people. Many colonial sites *are* places of memory for significant numbers of people in France, even though such sites lack official recognition. Moreover, studies of colonial places of memory within and beyond France's present-day borders would have been ideal candidates for Nora's series since, according to his definition (1984: xxiv), "[l]es lieux de mémoire, ce sont d'abord des restes" [Places of memory are debris, first of all]. His decision to omit them has therefore been criticized.[1] Like prose fiction and film, comics can serve as a *virtual* place of memory for colonial sites, as a substitute for lost or physically inaccessible places of memory. This function is perhaps accentuated for artists whose family members lived in Algeria, including the descendants of the colonized who emigrated to France in search of work and settled there, or of the European settlers who left Algeria. The special status of the Algerian colony for the French,[2] the effects of deep settler colonization there (McClintock 1992: 88), and the nature of decolonization (the Algerian War and its sequels) have meant that the adaptation and assimilation process has been difficult for all the minority groups that once lived in Algeria but now reside in France, whether *Pieds-Noirs*,[3] Algerians, Jews, Muslims or Catholics.

Of course there have been crucial differences for the various groups undergoing this process: people of Algerian, and more generally of North African Arab or Berber, heritage have felt the brunt of neo-colonial racism, sometimes directed at them by some former European settlers and their off-spring, but certainly also by many others in France. *Pieds-Noirs* have also reported mistreatment upon their arrival in mainland France at the end of the Algerian War. Generally speaking, as time passes and assimilation pro-gresses, the links that younger generations from all these groups—but per-haps especially the *Pieds-Noirs*—have to their parents' homeland become more tenuous and are contingent upon an access to the memory of par-ents and grandparents and, increasingly, to historical writing and archives, especially as those with direct memory of Algeria grow old and die. Nora (1984: xxiv) argues that this type of commemorative activity, by minority groups, is in fact exemplary of a more general trend affecting French soci-ety as a whole: "C'est pourquoi la défense par les minorités d'une mémoire réfugiée sur des foyers privilégiés et jalousement gardés ne fait que por-ter à l'incandescence la vérité de tous les lieux de mémoire. Sans vigilance commémorative, l'histoire les balaierait vite" [That is why the defense by minorities of a memory that has taken refuge in privileged hearths that are jealously guarded only brings the truth of all places of memory to incan-descence. Without commemorative vigilance, history would quickly sweep them away].

In this chapter I analyze comics about colonial-era Algeria as a virtual place of memory. I begin by briefly tracing a genealogy of colonial-era rep-resentations in French-language cartoons and comics about Algeria from the initial invasion in 1830 up to formal independence in 1962. I then ana-lyze extensively the first five volumes of the "Carnets d'Orient" [Oriental Sketchbooks or Notebooks] series by French cartoonist Jacques Ferrandez, a cartoonist of *Pied-Noir* heritage. The artistic richness as well as the his-torical and ideological complexity of his work have made it exemplary for other cartoonists working on the subject, including Didier Tronchet and Anne Sibran, in *Là-bas* [Down There] (see below, Chapter 4, and McKinney 2011a), and Joann Sfar, in "Le chat du rabbin" [The Rabbi's Cat] series. I open my analysis of Ferrandez's comics by recalling the importance of what art historian Todd Porterfield (1998) describes as "the allure of empire" in French orientalist painting. I argue that its imperialist allure continues in comics by Ferrandez, even in the sketchbook form that he adopted, partly as a way of producing some critical distance from the orientalist paintings that he redraws in his book. I then analyze in turn the ways that Ferrandez uses three major sources of colonial iconography in his books: conquest-era engravings, orientalist paintings from the nineteenth and twentieth centuries, and postcards. Each of these media are shot through with colonial ideology that Ferrandez negotiates with varying degrees of success, in his project to redraw colonial Algeria as a *Pied-Noir* place of memory. I conclude the chapter by comparing how Ferrandez handles colonial iconography with its treatment in historical comics drawn by Algerian cartoonist Benattou Masmoudi and French cartoonist Sfar. Their shared sources and similar approach indicate that despite the different ethnic and national perspectives that they articulate, the needs and difficulties that they confront are similar, including a desire to produce counter-memory, and a relative scarcity of colonial iconography for nineteenth-century Algeria. However, in the case of Ferrandez and Sfar, the similarities in materials and methods are so close that one can only conclude that the former supplied the memorial model for the latter, suggesting both a scarcity of memorial models and an economy of memorial sites (cf. Rigney 2005). Redrawing empire therefore means both that Masmoudi, Ferrandez and Sfar redraw shared colonial iconographic sources, and that Sfar redraws the model supplied by Ferrandez, adapting it to his own needs.

Masmoudi, Ferrandez and Sfar redraw the colonial affrontier in various ways and for purposes both different and similar. Reproducing it allows Masmoudi to represent an Algerian national identity resisting French colonialism long before the beginning of the Algerian War in 1954. Paradoxically, he does so by repeating colonial artistic gestures while redrawing colonial documents. Ferrandez redraws the colonial affrontier to reconstitute, in historical fiction about the colonial past, a *Pied-Noir* community now assimilating into French society, and also to mourn the historic separation of French colonials and Algerians by the colonial affrontier, because that division—in addition to being violent and unjust (effects which Ferrandez generously condemns)—led to the disappearance of French Algeria and the departure of the *Pieds-Noirs*. This double aim is paradoxical and even contradictory: without the colonial affrontier the settler group that Ferrandez celebrates would not have existed as such, but it was that same affrontier that eventually led to the downfall and departure of the group. By retracing the colonial affrontier Sfar foregrounds Sephardic Algerian Jews, who although already present episodically in Ferrandez's series from virtually beginning to end, had never been the primary focus of a comic-book series. Sfar represents the colonial affrontier as being produced in part by Jewish French Ashkenazim, when they require Algerian Jews to assimilate into French culture as part of a project meant to enlighten them. But here too the reconstruction of the colonial affrontier is paradoxical, insofar as

Sfar also selectively celebrates modernizing, secularizing and Frenchifying aspects of colonial assimilation: this tendency is incarnated by the eponymous cat of the series, but is visible in the transformation of several other characters, including the rabbi and his daughter (cf. Eisenstein 2008; Harris 2008).[4] Taken together, the work of these three artists therefore exhibits some of the most complex and interesting ways that cartoonists redraw empire and retrace the colonial affrontier today.

A genealogy of French Algeria from conquest to tourism in comics and cartoons

The iconographic archives from which cartoonists have borrowed in recent years to create their own comics about French Algeria include comics and caricatures stretching back to the conquest. As we shall see, several French cartoonists, but especially Ferrandez, have demonstrated their familiarity with some of the very earliest material, from the time around the French conquest of Algiers, by pointedly borrowing and redrawing images from it. Some of this historical material has reappeared in print, but even when it has not been republished or otherwise been widely made available again (e.g., on the web), cartoonists can gain access to it through a variety of sources, including the French national library (Bibliothèque nationale) in Paris. This is one of the places where Ferrandez researched material for the first volume of his "Carnets d'Orient" (Ferrandez 1996). Some contemporary cartoonists who have published comics about French colonialism may not have not borrowed from, or even examined, earlier comics on the same theme. In some cases it is impossible to determine with certainty whether they did, for example, by examining their art work. Still, it is still useful to analyze past representations of colonialism in comics and cartoons, because they are part of a cultural formation to which today's comics on the same theme belong: they share images and perspectives with other colonial-era material, including advertising, journalism, photography, prose fiction and film. Most contemporary cartoonists sift through at least some of this material as documentation for their comics with a historical, colonial theme (McKinney 2008b: 163; 2011b). Analyzing earlier texts allows me to create a visual-textual genealogy for post-1962 works. In this chapter I take as my starting point some comics and caricatures that were produced during and after the conquest of Algeria, by important artists in the history of European, especially French-language, caricature and comics. The pre-1962 works I examine here include: cartoons from the 1830 conquest of Algeria that were reproduced in a work published for a colonial exhibition;

an early-nineteenth-century comic book by Swiss artist Rodolphe Töpffer (1799–1846) that was redrawn by French cartoonist Cham (Charles Henri Amédée de Noé; 1818–1879) and serialized in Paris; a cartoon strip by Benjamin Roubaud (1811–1847); a book of cartoons by Cham; and a comic book by French cartoonist and painter Joseph-Porphyre Pinchon (1871–1953), best known as the artist of the Bécassine comics. Some of the works have been republished in recent years (for example, the comic books by Töpffer and Pinchon, and cartoons by Salomon Assus), whereas others have not yet, but all are accessible in one way or another in France today. Taken together with various other materials, they allow me to construct a genealogy for recent French comics about Algeria.

I hasten to say that I am well aware that such genealogies can have pitfalls: even Edward Said's monumental *Orientalism* (1994a), despite its huge impact on cultural and literary studies, has been criticized for presenting an overly homogenized and insufficiently historicized account of cultural attitudes and tropes about the Orient from Greek antiquity to the present (e.g., Rodinson 1989). However, these criticisms do not invalidate the contribution of genealogical research in Said's work, including its ability to produce fundamental insights about imperialist discourse and ideology. Porterfield (1998: 32) quotes Said (1994a: 176) and follows his critical, hermeneutic model in his study of "art in the service of French imperialism" from 1798 to 1836: "This becomes apparent in a close reading of the strategic formation of the imperial discourse, its strategically located, primary texts (the *Description de l'Egypte* [Description of Egypt]), its strategically located witnesses to Egyptian history (Denon, Champollion), and now the diffusion of this ideology, without the slightest resistance, through [what Said calls] the 'citation of antecedent authority.'" My aim in using a genealogical approach in this chapter, and throughout my study, is to trace certain colonialist and imperialist tropes and imagery in (mostly) French comics and cartoons up to the present, to analyze the ways, and assess the extent to which, the field of French comics still remains connected to colonialism and imperialism. As I do this, what interests me most is to understand the manners in which *today*'s cartoonists redraw and rework pre-1962 material, including tropes found in comics and cartoons by Töpffer, Cham and Daumier. I do not analyze the older material at length, as some historians and art historians, on whose work I rely in part, have done (e.g., Bernasconi 1970; Kunzle 1990; Porterfield 1998; Childs 2004).

In many cultural areas the citation of antecedent authority is a key mechanism for cultural production and legitimation, but perhaps especially in a field such as comics, because it is considered by many, including some cartoonists, to be a minor art. As a technique, the citation of antecedent authority is particularly important when the members of an artistic or cultural field wish to increase its prestige and prominence (cf. Boltanski 1975; Beaty 2007, 2008). This activity can take many forms, including manifestoes, visual quotations and other stylistic effects, mentions in interviews of mentors and artistic influences, as well as prefaces, postfaces and bibliographies inserted into comic books (see Chapter 1, above)—their peritexts (Miller 2007: 97). In the comics that are the focus of my study, the issues of positional superiority, strategic location and antecedent authority (Said 1994a; Nader 1989; Nochlin 1989)—which are already important for the reconfiguration of comics as an artistic field—are strongly inflected by the French history of colonial domination and imperialism, including through its imprint on comics and cartoons, images and texts, attitudes and ideas, received from past generations of artists and others. This is perhaps nowhere more striking than in the material that is the subject of this and the next two chapters (3 and 4, below), because of the specifically orientalist and colonialist nature of much of the older material about Algeria and French Indochina on which today's cartoonists rely for documentation—it is very easy to perpetuate orientalist and colonialist paradigms and practices in this way. Paradoxically, this material, even though it is often heavily distorted by colonial and imperialist ideology, is prime source material for cartoonists who are striving for historical and cultural accuracy, in historical comics set in these former colonies. According to Porterfield (1998: 121–22), "the definitive quality of orientalism—reportage," as exemplified by Eugène Delacroix's landmark orientalist and imperialist painting *Femmes d'Alger dans leur appartement* [Women of Algiers in Their Apartment] (1834), allows it to be regarded and passed off as "authentic, true to nature, even scientific." When French cartoonists base their comics on material such as this, they face interpretive obstacles that are very similar to those of historians researching colonial archives for documents to help them create an historical account of the past, turning archival memory into working memory (Rigney 2005: 17–18; cf. Gauthier 1993).

Several caricatures produced on the occasion of the French conquest of Algiers, which began in 1830, were republished in the second of three volumes of the *Iconographie historique de l'Algérie, depuis le XVIe siècle jusqu'à 1871* [Historical Iconography of Algeria, from the 16th Century until 1871], edited by Gabriel Esquer (1929) and published to coincide with the Centenaire de l'Algérie française [Centennial of French Algeria], in 1930. Ferrandez probably consulted this work in preparing his first graphic novel about French Algeria. Six of these caricatures thematize French fascination for women in harems and represent the conquest of Algeria as

either the seduction, kidnapping or rape of Algerian women by French soldiers.[5] "Le sérail en émoi" [The Seraglio in a Flutter] by E. Forest, depicts
six women and one man on a rooftop of a house in the casbah of Algiers,
looking down at the French fleet in the bay. One of the women is peering
through a telescope, no doubt to get a better view of the French soldiers and
sailors on the ships (the phallic and voyeuristic symbolism of the optical
instrument is obvious). The caption of the image suggests that this represents the seraglio of the dey of Algiers.[6] The armed Algerian man in the lithograph, whose baleful look betrays a concern over the interest of the women
in the approaching foreign invaders, could represent the dey himself or perhaps instead a harem bodyguard. In contrast to this image, which depicts a
supposed attraction felt by harem women in Algiers for French men, some
of the other caricatures, such as "Enlèvement de la sultane favorite" [Kid-
napping the Favorite Sultaness] figure the invasion as kidnapping and rape
(Porterfield 1998: 138–40): there, the favorite sultaness is forcibly carried
out of the harem by French soldiers (Figure 2.1). "L'embarras du choix ou le
sens de la hiérarchie" [Too many options, or the sense of hierarchy] suggests
that Algerian women were indeed regarded as spoils of war, to be divided
up among French soldiers according to their rank—here, one French soldier
defers to another, no doubt his superior officer. The soldiers are choosing
between two Algerian women who have begun to undress in preparation
for sex with the Frenchmen. Rape of Algerian women by French soldiers
was no doubt a common occurrence during the conquest, as were a variety
of other brutal practices.[7] However, one of the interesting aspects of some
of these lithographs is the suggestion of consensuality and even eagerness of
the Algerian women to have sex with the French invaders, obviously a case
of wishful thinking. This imagery fits into a long history of French orientalist representations, in both images and written text, of women as prisoners
in the harems of absolutist Muslim rulers—it thereby also participates in fictionalized representations of political power and gender relations in France
itself (cf. Grosrichard 1979; Lowe 1991; Porterfield 1994; Said 1994a;
Porterfield 1998). Figuring harem women as ready to welcome their supposed liberators with open arms, even if the latter are foreign soldiers, can
be a way of celebrating the invasion, or, conversely, satirizing it. In any case,
images of Algerian woman in various states of (un)dress in private spaces
from which outsiders were generally excluded (e.g., homes and, more specifically, harems), and imagery about sexual encounters between French men
and Algerian women (including in bordellos), are common to many French
visual and textual representations, including comics, from the conquest on
up through the present. As with other colonial themes, there has been a

Figure 2.1: Conquering Algiers as a French harem fantasy. A. Menut, "Enlèvement de la sultane favorite" [Kidnapping the Favorite Sultaness], in Gabriel Esquer, *Iconographie historique de l'Algérie, depuis le XVIe siècle jusqu'à 1871* [Historical Iconography of Algeria, from the 16th Century until 1871] (Paris: Plon, 1929), vol. 2, plate CXXIV, no. 286. From the Collection of the Public Library of Cincinnati and Hamilton County.

general neglect, by critics and historians, of this tradition in comics and cartoons,[8] although it has been studied extensively in postcards, painting and prose fiction.

Representations of Algeria have appeared in French-language comics from the conquest through the present. Töpffer, who has been consecrated by several comics critics, historians and institutions as the father of modern French-language comic book,[9] was inspired by the French conquest of Algiers in 1830 for his *Histoire de M. Cryptogame* [*Story of Mr. Cryptogame*]. He modified the story in 1844 or 1845, a year or two before his death, but also arranged for it to be redrawn by Cham and serialized in *L'Illustration,* 25 January–19 April 1845.[10] For art historian and comics specialist David Kunzle, "[t]he earliest manuscript responds to the initial French invasion of Algeria in 1830, and the course of publication of the first, much revised version coincides, with amazing precision, with the massive publicity at the French victory over their tenacious opponent, Abd-el-Kadr, in 1845" (in Töpffer 2007: 640–41). French-language versions of the story have been published repeatedly from the first, serialized, version up to the present (cf. Béra, Denni and Mellot 1996: 207; Töpffer 2007: 641–43). I refer here mainly to a version of the second Töpffer manuscript (from 1844–45), published by Le Seuil (Töpffer 1996) and prefaced by comics theoretician Thierry Groensteen (but cf. Kunzle 1990; 2007; Töpffer 2007).

According to Groensteen (in Töpffer 1996: 9), Töpffer's choice of Algeria in 1830 was motivated by two things: "par la réputation des Algériens, tenus pour les champions de la polygamie, et par la conquête de l'Algérie par la France, en cette même année 1830" [by the reputation of the Algerians, thought to be the champions of polygamy, and by the French conquest of Algeria, in that same year of 1830]. One also finds the following motifs in the comic book: Algerian piracy and cruelty—reasons given by the French for their attack on Algiers (e.g., frames 53–55, 99, 104, 147; cf. Kunzle 1990: 66); the capture, ransoming and enslavement of Christians by Algerians (53–55, 143–56); an allusion to the Spanish Inquisition—some Danish whalers plan to sell Muslim Algerians to Spaniards to burn in autodafés (frames 87–88); despotic oriental rule (frames 136–41); the forcible induction of captured European women into the harems of Muslim men (frames 100–102, 142, 157–58); and Algeria as a wild region where lions roam (frame 165). Many of these motifs return in subsequent French comics and cartoons about Algeria. The original story from 1830, Töpffer's revised manuscript from 1844–45, and Cham's serialized version from 1845 need to be situated with respect to certain contexts, as Kunzle makes clear (1990: 66; cf. 2007: 104–5):

The continuing war to establish French control [in 1845], and the heroic resistance of Abd el-Kadr, kept Algeria and North Africa in the public eye. . . . At the same time, beyond the conquest of Algeria, Arab customs and barbarisms had long been considered exciting subjects, and there existed a historically nonspecific orientalist tradition in the arts, emphasizing harems and the enslavement of Christians.

Kunzle (1990: 66) also argues that we should read at least part of the Algerian episode as a parody by Töpffer of Swiss politics: "In 1844 he added a scene showing the terrible chaos caused by the janissaries' method of choosing a new Dey, meant to mirror the anarchy Töpffer blamed on the electoral agitations of the Genevan radicals" (cf. Töpffer 1996: frame 167). Nonetheless, some of the internecine Algerian violence in Töpffer's story might remind one of the real-life assassinations and plots around the transfer of power in Turkish Algiers, especially in the period preceding the rule of Hussein Dey (Ruedy 1992: 41). In *Histoire de M. Cryptogame*, the Janissaries must choose a new dey because—in order to escape from the harem of the old one, which she had been forced to join—Elvire, the main female character, kills the dey, as Judith killed Holoferne in the Biblical story (frame 158). Kunzle (2007: 103) also mentions as a possible source, and reproduces, *The Virtuous Odalisque*, an orientalist lithograph from 1833, which depicts a nude woman about to stab a clothed man in a harem. Women's violent rebellion against Muslim men who imprison them in harems has long been an orientalist theme in French literature, such as in *Les lettres persanes* [*The Persian Letters*] (1721), the epistolary novel by Montesquieu and, before that, in the play *Bajazet* (1672), by Racine (cf. Kunzle 1990: 66). These works permitted reflection on both France's relationship to rival powers (especially the Ottoman empire) and to foreign cultures, but also to charged power relationships within French society, including male-female ones and royal absolutism (cf. Grosrichard 1979; Childs 2004: 168–70). However, with the French conquest of Algeria, the French fascination with Muslim harems took on new, specific meanings, as we have already seen in the lithographs by E. Forest and others. Malek Alloula (1981, 1986, 2001) has famously analyzed how erotic harem fantasies were depicted and disseminated widely on French postcards during the early twentieth century. Although his work has been critiqued in important ways by feminists, it did provide some fundamental insights into colonialist representation (cf. Porterfield 1998: 207; and below). Among other things, this chapter shows how French cartoonists have reworked the theme of the harem, including attempts to penetrate it by ruse or violence to liberate its women from the despotic grip of their Algerian masters (as in *Histoire de M. Crypto-*

game) and to have sex with them (as was the case with the French conquest lithographs).[11]

Soon after the serialization of *Histoire de M. Cryptogame* in *L'Illustration* was complete, in April 1845, its Parisian publisher (Töpffer's cousin) printed another Algerian story, this time by Roubaud. The artist worked in Paris before moving to Algeria, where he accompanied Théophile Gautier when the latter traveled through the country in 1845 (Gautier 1973: 54; see below). Roubaud, who died in Algiers in 1847, published "Scipion l'Africain" [Scipio the African], a satirical, three-page comic strip about a French dandy's trip to Algeria, in *L'Illustration* (issues of 21 and 28 June 1845). Kunzle (2007: 147) describes the story as "awkward": it "obviously capitalizes on Töpffer's Algerian episode and is interesting only for its audacious indications of sexual promiscuity (Paris or Muslim style?)" (cf. Kunzle 1990: 65). The reference to the Roman general who defeated Hannibal, during a time when the French were conquering Algeria, is satirical. At around the same time, *L'Illustration* was publishing other, propagandistic material on the conquest: for example, engravings including "Attaque du camp français de Sidi-bel-Abbès, par une troupe de fanatiques Arabes, le 30 janvier 1845" [Attack on the French Camp of Sidi-bel-Abbès, by a Troop of Fanatical Arabs, on 30 January 1845] (1 March 1845, p. 4), and a copy of Horace Vernet's *Prise de la Smala d'Abd-el-Kader* [Capture of the Smala of Abd-el-Kader] (15 March 1845, pp. 40–41), a painting then on display in the Salon in Paris; or the sheet music for "Le jeune Arabe à Paris" [The Young Arab in Paris], a song by P. Hédouin and George Bousquet (15 March 1845, pp. 42–43). Roubaud himself contributed a painting entitled *Fête mauresque aux environs d'Alger* [Moorish Party on the Outskirts of Algiers] to the Salon of 1845 (copied in *L'Illustration*, 22 March 1845, p. 56). The satire of Roubaud's "Scipion l'Africain" might be read as directed at himself: like his character, the artist goes to Algeria and indulges in orientalist fantasies, such as the dance scene he depicted in his painting for the Salon. Scipion, dressed in oriental attire and smoking a hookah in a Paris restaurant, is lured to Africa by the account of a "brave officer from Africa." In Algeria, however, his attempt to go native brings him various indignities, including being unceremoniously man-handled by a tailor, a barber, and massagers at the baths, getting kicked in the rear by a French army officer who believes he is an Arab, seeing a ravishing odalisque whom he wishes to marry being taken away by another French officer ("un officier des Zouaves"), being tricked into marrying a less attractive Algerian woman sight unseen, having his horse stolen by his servant, being beaten by a Bedouin, having his wife kidnapped by Algerians, and seven years later, after "many other adventures," finding her again, only to discover that she has had a son with a black man. Here already, as earlier in *Histoire de M. Cryptogame,* where Cryptogame and the Abbé "take the turban" to avoid being killed by the Moorish pirates, the decision by a Frenchman to cross the colonial affrontier and go native is perilous.

A la guerre comme à la guerre [Needs Must When the Devil Drives] (ca. 1846), a collection of thirty lithographs first published in *Le Charivari* [The Shivaree] by French cartoonist Cham, satirizes the conquest of Algeria by depicting the difficulties of French soldiers stuck there, struggling to capture the Algerian leader, Abdelkader:

> But the misfortunes of the soldier extended beyond the worry of possibly being captured. The infantry had to bear the brunt of a war for which "peasants torn from their province to do their seven years" were not the least bit prepared. It was therefore the daily miseries of the footsoldier that satirical drawing strove to represent. PACOT [that is, the average soldier] has the same problems as in 1830: he dreams of his girl in a desert-like place under a burning sun while being stalked by a lion or a panther. Starving, tortured by thirst or stricken by malignant fevers, he cannot avoid forced marches and painfully slogs forward, burdened with sacks, bassins, kindling wood . . . , when he is not stuck up to his waist in desert sand. (Benasconi 1970: 53)

One finds some of the same motifs here as in the conquest engravings and in Töpffer's *Histoire de M. Cryptogame.* For example, lions appear in two of Cham's lithographs, where they symbolize the wild and dangerous conditions that French soldiers faced in Algeria, and the difficulty of their mission.[12] In "Pour faire un bon pot-au-feu" [How to make a good beef stew], a French soldier blithely sets out for a military cook the impossible task of catching, skinning and cooking a lion: "Tu te précipites sur ton lion . . . tu le tue [*sic*] . . . tu l'écorches . . . tu le laisse [*sic*] cuire douze heures, et t'as un bouillon excellent . . . c'est pas plus malin que ça la cuisine . . . " [You jump on your lion . . . you kill it . . . you skin it . . . you let it cook twelve hours, and you have an excellent broth . . . cooking is no trickier than that . . .] (4). In another cartoon (Figure 2.2), entitled "Une visite sous la tente" [A Visit under the Tent], a sleeping soldier is wakened by a ferocious lion that has put its head through the tent opening—the groggy soldier invites the lion in: "Entrez! . . . " [Come in! . . .] (8). If we take the lion as symbolizing Algeria itself (cf. Kunzle 1990: 301), the image suggests a reversal of the aggressor/victim relationship found in the earlier French lithographs (ca. 1830), in which soldiers kidnapped and raped Algerian women as easy spoils of war—here the French soldier, trapped in his tent, is the object of Algerian violence (cf. Sessions 2011: 169–70).

Figure 2.2: Algerian violence in the form of a lion threatens a French soldier during the conquest. Cham [Noé, Charles Henri Amédée de], "Une visite sous la tente" [A Visit under the Tent], *A la guerre comme à la guerre* [Needs Must When the Devil Drives], Paris: Aubert et cie (ca. 1846), p. 8.

From early during the French conquest and colonization of Algeria, the theme of the voyage in, of colonized Algerians traveling to France, responds to the theme of the voyage outward, of the French to Algeria.[13] This is the case in cartoons about French units of colonized soldiers, especially the Turcos (Algerian soldiers). Cham, Daumier and other cartoonists depict French women visiting Turco and Zouave soldiers "under the tent" (and elsewhere) in their military encampment at Saint Maur, in the Bois de Vincennes, on the outskirts of Paris (Cham [n.d.], *Spahis et Turcos;* cf. Childs 2004: 82–91, 228–31).[14] As I argue elsewhere (e.g., McKinney 2011b), the black Turco character in Léonce Petit's *Les mésaventures de M. Bêton* [The Misadventures of Mr. Ninny] (ca. 1868), a comic book no doubt inspired by Töpffer's comics (Kunzle 1990: 152–54; Groensteen in Töpffer 1994: 33), figures the unpredictable violence of the colonized, which is unleashed in the streets of Paris, wreaking bloody havoc in the Parisian capital, in order to produce a form of grotesque, carnivalesque humor (Figure 2.3).

By contrast with Cham's *A la guerre comme à la guerre, Les facéties du sapeur Camember* [The Pranks of Sapeur Camember] (1989: n.p.; first edition 1896), by French cartoonist Christophe (Georges Colomb; 1856–1945), provides its readers with a humorous image of the lot of French soldiers in Algeria, but not a satirical one, Kunzle argues (1990: 186): "*Sapeur Camember* appeared as an attempt to neutralize an increasingly charged topic"—the antimilitarism associated with "socialist, anarchist, and pacifist movements." The book was first published in 1896, at a significant remove in time from the bloody events on which its Algerian episode is based—"la révolte des Flittas" [the Revolt of the Flittas], which sets that portion of Christophe's story in 1864 or thereabouts (cf. Julien 1964: 429–30). The sapeur Camember, a simpleton French soldier of peasant origin with a heart of gold, adopts a child that he saves from the ruins of a burning house in Kabylia, and eventually brings him home to France. The house may have been the home of French settlers; in any case, Camember (re)names the child Victorin, recalling the French victory over the rebellious Algerians. Similarly, the name of his fiancée and wife, Victoire, suggests a hoped-for victory over Germany that would return Alsace and Lorraine to French control (Kunzle 1990: 189).

French comics and cartoons soon incorporated tourism to Algeria as a theme, as part of a general trend in France to create comics about tourist trips and emigration to various places around the world, including French colonies, which Kunzle interprets as an expression of the movement—whether expected or real—of social classes (1990: 84–85, 108, 135–46). The images of Cham's *Les voyages d'agrément* [Pleasure Travels] (1849) were first published in the Parisian satirical daily *Le Charivari.* The booklet

Figure 2.3: When a Turco, an Algerian soldier in the French colonial army, travels to Paris, he imports the potential of danger and wild adventure into the imperial capital. Here he climbs onto an omnibus and beheads several people, including the coachman. From Léonce Petit, *Les mésaventures de M. Béton* [The Misadventures of Mr. Ninny] (Paris: Librairie internationale, ca. 1868), p. 37.

includes eight pages depicting an organized tourist trip to London, followed by seven pages representing scenes from a similar voyage to Algeria. Every page consists of four self-contained drawings, each with a legend printed underneath it. Although the images do not exactly constitute a comic strip, they do form a more or less coherent whole that is based on the structure of the voyage, with a beginning (pre-departure preparations in France, train and sea voyage, and then arrival), middle (various tourist activities and misadventures) and end (return to Algiers and, from there, to France). Kunzle (1990: 85) has suggested that contemporary readers may have read Cham's satire about mishaps of European tourists in Algeria as referring to the tribulations of French soldiers there. This could have been Cham's way of getting around government censors in order to critique the effects of French imperialism on French soldiers, as he had done more directly in *A la guerre comme à la guerre*. Kunzle bases this argument in part on the assumption that there would have been few tourists in Algeria at the time. Nonetheless, *Les voyages d'agrément* does constitute at least an imagined tourist trip to the colony, which draws on contemporary images of the country, and helped inaugurate a theme that would continue over the decades of French rule, in subsequent French comics and cartoons.

In *Les voyages d'agrément* (1849: 11), the voyage out to the colony produces all kinds of identity reversals, beginning with the nature of the voyage itself—upon seeing Algiers from the harbor, a tourist who is on the wrong boat wonders why the city does not resemble London, which he had intended to visit. The transforming nature of the voyage is spoofed by Cham in the following cartoon (Figure 2.4), where "Un voyageur ayant une fâcheuse ressemblance avec Bou-Maza, se voit refuser l'entrée de l'Algérie" [A voyager bearing an unfortunate resemblance to Bou-Maza is refused right of entry into Algeria]. This topical reference alludes, humorously, to a leader of an Algerian rebellion in 1845–47 against French colonial forces (Julien 1964: 201–3; Ruedy 1992: 65, 67). On the next page, Cham has a French tourist voluntarily adopt Biblical identities for himself and his wife (12.4), satirizing the colonialist, romantic trope enunciated by Delacroix, which associated North Africans with classical antiquity, that is, with Europe's pre-history.[15] Cham (1849: 15.4) satirizes another recurring trope from orientalism and the French conquest of Algeria—the association between going native and sexual fraternization with the Algerians: a Frenchman, accompanied by three veiled women, encounters his wife, who exclaims, "Comment, mon scélérat de mari se promène avec trois femmes! . . . " [What, my scoundrel of a husband is walking around with three wives! . . .]; to which he replies, "Ma chère, il faut se faire aux moeurs du pays, la loi du prophète m'autorisait même à en prendre six . . . mais je te

Un voyageur, ayant une fâcheuse ressemblance avec Bou-Maza,
se voit refuser l'entrée de l'Algérie.

Figure 2.4: Cham satirically suggests that European visitors to Algeria confront a colonial otherness that may transform them, sometimes in spite of themselves: here a French tourist resembling Bou-Maza, an anti-colonial Algerian leader, is barred from entering Algeria. From Cham [Noé, Charles Henri Amédée de], *Les voyages d'agrément* [Pleasure Travels] (Paris: Le Charivari, 1849), p. 11.

compte pour trois" [My dear, one must adapt to the local customs, the law of the Prophet even authorized me to take six of them . . . but I'm counting you as three]. No matter that Muslim law has been misquoted here (by mistake or in jest), the Frenchman nonetheless ends up with the reglementary maximum of four wives.[16] This illustrates one of the most common orientalist tropes, seen already in the conquest lithographs: the association in imagery (and in real-life) of conquered North Africa with sexual availability and license that became increasingly standardized, codified and commodified (X 1927; Said 1994a: 184–90; Taraud 2003), as in the series of twentieth-century erotic postcards analyzed by Alloula (1981, 1986, 2001).[17]

The opportunity to change identities thanks to a tourist trip to Algeria also appears in my last example from pre-1962 French comics and cartoons about French Algeria, a comic book titled *Gringalou en Algérie* [Gringa-

lou in Algeria] (n.d.), drawn by Emile-Joseph Porphyre Pinchon (a.k.a.
J.-P. Pinchon), scripted by Jean Noé, and serialized in the Belgian children's
publication *Wrill,* nos. 99–129 (Evrard and Roland 1992: 123), in 1947.[18]
Published approximately a century after Cham's imagined tourist adventures to Algeria, *Gringalou en Algérie* naturally depicts an Algeria that is far
removed in some ways from the country as seen in *Les voyages d'agrément.*
In Algiers, the Parisian tourists, Gringalou (a French boy) and Professor
Cincinnatus, are clearly on French-dominated territory: guided everywhere
by a shoeshine boy named Bab Ouch (cf. *babouche* [slipper]),[19] they walk
down a street (Bab Azoun) that reminds them of the Parisian rue de Rivoli,
view a statue celebrating the conquest (the duc d'Orléans, in the Place du
Gouvernement [Government Square]), see automobiles and ride a bus, sleep
in a comfortable hotel, and board a train at the station (5–8). They visit
Gringalou's cousin, whose wealthy father owns a flourishing orange planta-
tion, for whom Algerians are of course the principal source of labor. On the
other hand, Pinchon and Noé also included (stereo)typical elements found
already in Cham's earlier work: a colorful population of veiled women
and of men wearing fezzes, robes and turbans; an encounter with Muslim
beliefs; a fantasia (25; cf. Cham 1849: 13.4); camels in the desert (28; cf.
Cham 1849: 12.1, 12.4, 16.1); a sandstorm (29; cf. Cham 1849: 13.3); and
various difficulties of tourism in an exotic African locale, including run-ins
with wild animals and arguments with the locals. The perils of late-colonial
tourism are far less severe than in Cham's conquest-era comics: for example,
the wild animals are only mischievous monkeys at a local tourist destination, the Ruisseau des singes [Stream of the Monkeys] in the Gorges de la
Chiffa (11), not the ferocious lions that eat some of Cham's tourists and
carry another away in its mouth (14.2, 15.3); instead of being held by the
forbidding members of a "tribu insoumise qui exige six mille francs pour
votre rançon" [unsubjugated tribe that demands six thousand francs for
your ransom] (Cham 1849: 14.4), Gringalou and his friends are more mun-
danely robbed by a couple of camel drivers in ragged clothes, who demand
a bribe [*bak chich*] before letting the bus that the Parisians are riding cross
a bridge (10)—their lives are never in danger;[20] nor is the health of Cincinnatus seriously compromised by the fatigue caused by their various tourist
excursions, followed by the rigorous workout that he gets in a hammam
(21–22), by contrast with the heavy, sometimes fatal, toll that "les fièvres,
les Arabes, les lions et autres cas de détérioration particuliers au climat
d'Afrique" [the fevers, the Arabs, the lions and other cases of deterioration
specific to the African climate] take on Cham's voyagers (10; cf. 14, 16).
The difference in the tourist experience between the two is obviously due
in part to the transformation of Algeria in the century that elapsed between

the publication of the two works, but no doubt also thanks to the fact that *Les voyages d'agrément* was for adults, one presumes, whereas *Gringalou en Algérie* is a children's book: as a consquence there are no sexual allusions in the latter. On the other hand, *Gringalou en Algérie* does depict its Parisian protagonists indulging in the possibilities for temporarily changing identities that a trip to the colony offers: they don Algerian hats to sell back their earlier purchases in the souk of Algiers (6); and disguise themselves as Algerians to surprise their friends upon their return to Paris (32). In a scene that recalls an earlier visit of the Pieds-Nickelés [Leadfoot Gang] comics characters to West Africa, Cincinnatus is even mistaken for the French Minister of Colonies come to visit Algeria (25).[21] I turn now to a group of post-1962 comics that rework various elements from the comics and cartoons that I have analyzed so far, in their depiction of *l'Algérie française* [French Algeria], from 1830 to 1962.

Post-colonial orientalism and the allure of empire in the "Carnets d'Orient"

Ferrandez is the creator of a well-known series of comic books about Algeria as a French colony. As the *Pied-Noir* community assimilates into the majority, it risks disappearing as a separate group with a distinct identity, which lends urgency to commemorative projects such as that of Ferrandez. His reworking of colonial-era history and representations may be indicative of how *Pieds-Noirs* and their offspring are transforming their past into a version of colonial history more in tune with the cultural and historical sensibility of the French majority (Martini 1997). Indeed, his reworking arguably attempts to inflect mainstream history, but it remains highly problematic when he tries, unwittingly or not, to justify once again the colonial project (cf. Stora 1992: 294–96).

By now, the ongoing debate over the significance and nature of orientalism in literature, film and other arts has generated a substantial body of work. Said's (1994a) provocative, ground-breaking study of orientalism, originally published in 1978, paid scant attention to visual representation. However, the ideological dimension of orientalism (MacKenzie 1995: 45) in visual art has since been studied by critics, who have mostly focused on painting (e.g., Nochlin 1989; MacKenzie 1995; Porterfield 1998; Benjamin 2003a, 2003b), photography (e.g., Graham-Brown 1988), both of these media (e.g., Goldberg 1999), cinema (e.g., Bernstein and Studlar 1997) or postcards (e.g., Alloula 1981, 1986, 2001; Prochaska 1990a, 1990b, 2003; Sebbar and Belorgey 2002). One of my aims in this section is to engage in that debate by analyzing "Carnets d'Orient," Ferrandez's remarkable multi-volume series that chronicles the history of the French colonization of Algeria. Ferrandez borrowed heavily from colonial postcards for his documentation, and produced a re-evaluation of the orientalist tradition in painting (with references to orientalist travel literature as well). I hope that my analysis of this work will shed new light on discussions about orientalism and the visual arts, especially in the relatively neglected area of contemporary popular culture.

One of the most relevant studies of orientalism in visual art is by John MacKenzie (1995).[22] It provides a powerful critique of many shortcomings in Said's work and a fascinating account of ways in which orientalism might be seen as a contradictory, heterogenous and even positive force in European art. Despite his disagreement with many of Said's views about orientalism, MacKenzie (1995: 50–53) nevertheless does concede that the tradition of orientalism in painting was strongly marked by French imperialist incursions into Egypt and Algeria. The extent and nature of this influence have been brilliantly explored by Todd Porterfield (1994, 1998), who sets aside MacKenzie's critique as belonging to "the traditional view of Orientalism" (1998: 155n9) and, instead, convincingly demonstrates that the "allure of empire" motivated French imperialist invasions of Egypt and Algeria, and was embodied as well in artistic projects such as the installation of the obelisk at the Place de la Concorde in Paris, and in French works of art, including *Femmes d'Alger dans leur appartement,* by Delacroix. The main function of empire's allure, Porterfield (1998: 4–5) argues, was to create national unity by acting "as surrogate, mask, and displacement of the [French] Revolution," whose specter haunted France for decades thereafter. We also know that, much later, the Algerian War shook the very foundations of France's "imagined community" (Anderson 1991), provoking a change in government (De Gaulle's return to power and the creation of the Fifth Republic), attempts by the Organisation Armée Secrète [Secret Armed Organization] (OAS) on the life of the French president, and—with the OAS rebellion—the resurrection of imagery from the French Revolution and the Second World War (cf. Stora 1992: 109–13), which had pitted groups of French people against each other. In other words, the apparent end of empire caused a tear in the French national fabric (Stora 1992: 113), one that has not yet disappeared.

Paradoxically, neither has empire's allure vanished; in fact, it is often uncritically recreated in comics that retell the story of French imperialism—specifically here, the colonization of Algeria, from 1830 to 1962. Moreover, it is still available to serve a neo-imperialist purpose, that is to unify the, or some, French people today in a common, nostalgic vision of a glorious colonial past. Not surprisingly, as with the original imperial project, it is the Algerians who are excluded from the alluring dream of empire, and must again pay a price for French national unity when it is founded on that basis. Although I agree with MacKenzie (1995) when he argues, as have others, that orientalist works may exhibit heterogeneity, internal contradictions, and serve counter-hegemonic purposes, I still maintain—with Said, Porterfield and others—that orientalism may, and often does, function as a discourse that ultimately limits criticism—*even when a generously minded critique of colonialism is (also) attempted,* as is the case in Ferrandez's comic books.

Ferrandez is a successful French cartoonist born in Algeria in 1955, but taken to France when his parents moved there a few months after his birth (Poncet and Morin 1996: 69)—in that sense, he is essentially a member of the second generation, that is the offspring of *Pieds-Noirs*. He is the author of a multi-volume comic book series entitled "Carnets d'Orient," which recounts the story of "l'Algérie française" as a national epic.[23] It provides an excellent case study of how comics can function as a virtual place of memory for the *Pied-Noir* community in France. In his series Ferrandez attempts to deal with the vagaries of colonial history in a serious and sustained manner. His project, which necessitated many years of work (published 1986–2009), is complex and has won praise from historians Anne Roche (1990: 526; cf. Ferrandez 1988), Benjamin Stora (according to Ferrandez 1996; cf. Stora in Ferrandez 1994d) and Michel Pierre (in Ferrandez 2005a), among others. Moreover, as part of his extensive documentary research, Ferrandez made use of visual materials that have been the focus of critical debate by scholars: orientalist paintings and French colonial-era photographs, including ones printed on postcards. Indeed, the main character of his first book is an orientalist painter who is partially modeled after Delacroix;[24] other characters are borrowed from photos on postcards.[25] Significantly, one book that Ferrandez used as part of his large corpus of source documents is Alloula's *Le harem colonial: Images d'un sous-érotisme* [The Colonial Harem: Images of a Sub-Eroticism], whose publication in French (1981; 2001) and in English translation (1986) generated considerable discussion and debate in the 1980s and 1990s (e.g., Harlow in Alloula 1986; Woodhull 1991; Apter 1992; Boëtsch 1993; Lazreg 1994; Ferrié and Boëtsch 1995; Bal 1996). This recycling of material (the postcard images) from colonial popular visual culture, through a recent critical work, and back into contemporary popular culture raises interesting questions, which I will investigate later on in this chapter.

By analyzing Ferrandez's approach to some of his sources, I will show the possibilities and problems of his comics as a *Pied-Noir* place of memory.

On the one hand, his reworking of historical material and of visual and print documents allows him to represent and criticize colonial-era attitudes and artistic visions. On the other hand, Ferrandez incorporates this borrowed material into what is finally and most basically a recuperative *commemoration* of French Algeria—this fact fundamentally limits his attempts to diverge from certain aspects of colonial society and the aesthetic movements that it helped to foster. Ferrandez explicitly formulates his commemorative project in his authorial preface to *Les fils du sud* [Sons of the South] (Ferrandez 1994c), the third volume in the series, which is based on his grandfather's boyhood: "Tout cela, je ne voulais pas le laisser perdre" [I did not want to let all of that be lost] (15). I analyze Ferrandez's reconstruction of French Algeria as a place of memory by looking at his reworking of nineteenth-century engravings and paintings about the military conquest, and his reevaluation of orientalist and colonialist visual aesthetics.

Redrawing engravings from the conquest: Documentation and critique

In a book chapter on historical imagery in comics, including *Carnets d'Orient* [Oriental Sketchbooks], Guy Gauthier (1993) analyzes "l'inspiration documentaire" [the documentary inspiration] of cartoonists such as Jacques Martin ("Alix"), Albert Uderzo ("Asterix") and Hugo Pratt ("Corto Maltese"). Both Gauthier and Pierre Fresnault-Deruelle (1979) argue that historical references in many or most historical comics serve mainly as a pretext for creating a fiction that often diverges significantly from historical fact. Fresnault-Deruelle claims that historical documentation, whether visual or textual, serves mainly to "authenticate fiction" and to thereby create an "effet d'histoire" [history effect] (Fresnault-Deruelle 1979: e.g., 101; cf. Tribak-Geoffroy 1997). Fresnault-Deruelle clearly based his argument on Roland Barthes's concept of the "effet de réel" [reality effect] (1985) as a means for understanding nineteenth-century realist prose fiction. In the first book of his series, *Carnets d'Orient* (1994a), Ferrandez used nineteenth-century lithographs and engravings, as well as many other documents, to authenticate his fiction in historical terms and thereby create an "effet d'histoire" (cf. Basfao 1990: 330–31). Gauthier describes Ferrandez's use of orientalist paintings and the notebooks of painter-travelers (specifically, Delacroix) as a "pèlerinage aux sources" [pilgrimage to the sources] of French visual depictions of Algeria. Although Gauthier may have meant to imply as much, he does not explicitly state that this artistic activity is also an ethnic pilgrimage for Ferrandez, insofar as it constitutes a return to the roots of the European colonial settler population of Algeria, in the French conquest (*Carnets d'Orient* is set in the period 1836–46). This adds to the importance of history in Ferrandez's fictional reconstitution: historical authenticity, or faithfulness to history, has an ethnic dimension for Ferrandez, much as it holds a national dimension for Algerian artists, including cartoonists, attempting to exhume the roots of Algerian nation and nationalism in Algerian resistance to the French conquest. French and Algerian artists have borrowed from and reworked many of the same, early documents (limited in number) about colonial Algeria, although not always in the same ways or for the same ends. However, as I argued earlier, comics such as the "Carnets d'Orient" also exceed the limits of the history effect as Fresnault-Deruelle conceives it, insofar as they intervene in debates about French colonial and Algerian national history: instead of history simply authenticating fiction, such fictions contribute to a reevaluation of French colonial history (cf. Witek 1999: 36–45, 58–119).

In an analysis of "imperialist nostalgia," anthropologist Renato Rosaldo (1989) explores the curious phenomenon of "mourning for what one has destroyed," specifically the indigenous, Third World cultures to whose destruction western anthropologists and many others (missionaries, armies) have contributed to varying degrees and in different ways (cf. Branche and House 2010). In her seminal study of "the imaginary Orient" in oriental-ist painting, Linda Nochlin (1989: 50) similarly remarks on the fact that "[t]he same [French] society that was engaged in wiping out local [Algerian] customs and traditional practices was also avid to preserve them in the form of records," including visual ones. The primary feature of "Carnets d'Orient" is mourning for the loss of what French Algeria was and might have become: scenes of dispossession and rituals of mourning are staged repeatedly throughout the series. Are the "Carnets d'Orient" shot through with "imperialist nostalgia"? Despite the fact that Ferrandez himself did not participate in the colonization of Algeria, the short answer is "yes," as I argue below. Still, his approach is complex and nuanced, as can be seen in his redrawing of the visual records of the conquest left by nineteenth-century French artists, such as those we have already seen (above). Ferran-dez does not always "miss [or avoid] their significance as political docu-ments at a time of particularly active military intervention in North Africa" (Nochlin 1989: 56).

From the outset of *Carnets d'Orient,* Ferrandez uses French lithographs and engravings representing colonial Algeria. Several architectural views in "Carnets d'Orient"[26] are based on images collected in *Villes d'Algérie au XIXe siècle* [Cities of Algeria in the 19th Century] (1984), a volume edited by Assia Djebar, the Algerian historian, novelist, essayist and member of the Académie française.[27] These images are important to both Algerians and *Pieds-Noirs,* because they constitute a visual record of Algerian urban and rural topography early in the colonial period and during the preceding, Ottoman period. On the first page of his narrative, Ferrandez (1994a: 11) copied views of Algiers from the sea and of the port (Djebar 1984: 23, 29). This might constitute a relatively neutral or objective use—simply documenting the historical setting accurately (historical verisimilitude)—were it not for the fact that he incorporates these images into a visual-textual narration problematically based on French orientalist and imperialist documents, including Delacroix's notebooks and an illustrated travel narrative by Théophile Gautier (more on this below). Still, on the following two pages, one of Ferrandez's characters, Mario Puzzo, criticizes the French for destroying the Algerian character of the city through construction projects, much as Théophile Gautier (1973: 183–84) and Delacroix did. Ferrandez (1994a: 13) then inserts a panoramic view of the port copied from another conquest-era engraving, but also includes in his comic-strip frame some French soldiers who are rebuilding the city (these are not in the old engraving). This inclusion emphasizes the point just made by Puzzo, that the French are rebuilding the city along European lines, which is a direct outcome of military conquest. By contrast, Puzzo would like to see original local topography preserved instead. The irony is that Puzzo—a parasitic bon vivant who has adopted Algerian ways, including clothing—earns his living by painting portraits of French military officers (this also offers him the opportunity to contract sexual liaisons with their wives; Ferrandez 1994a: 14, 17, 71).[28] In other words, he laments a destruction in which he participates and from which he also benefits, albeit indirectly, as a social parasite. Indeed, he would not be in Algeria were it not for the French conquest. The attitude that Ferrandez gives to his character Puzzo is a form of imperialist nostalgia, which Joseph Constant, the main protagonist, shares by the end of the book. Ferrandez tries to negotiate the contradiction between Puzzo's dependency on the French army and his critical attitude toward the French transformation of Algeria by having him only paint portraits of military and administrative figures [notables] (1994a: 71), thereby producing a documentation of the military conquest.

Moving from topographical engravings and lithographs to military images from the conquest as source material for Ferrandez, we can find examples that he redraws to produce a vision of the conquest that is more critical than that of the original documents, or otherwise shifts their perspective. For example, into one comic-book frame Ferrandez (1994a: 25) copies a well-known print entitled "Nous civiliserons ces gaillards-là . . . " [We'll civilize those fellows], by Auguste Raffet (reproduced in Esquer 1929:

plate CXXXVIII, no. 322), in which French soldiers mock Algerians who carry the regiment's heavy drums and packs (Figure 2.5).[29] Raffet's drawing ridicules the pretensions of the French army and its attempts to justify the conquest: civilizing the Algerians here boils down to exploiting them. A reading of the use that Ferrandez made of the drawing by Raffet must take into account a further level of complexity, especially the fact that France was ultimately forced against its will to withdraw from Algeria and, theoretically, recognize it as a co-equal nation. Algerian independence means that, for many of today's readers, the notion of a French "civilizing mission" in Algeria is now or again problematic.

Moreover, in his image Ferrandez makes explicit a critique of class exploitation in the French conquest that, as we have already seen, also appears in Cham's *A la guerre comme à la guerre:* an awareness of the negative effects of the conquest for the French lower or lower-middle classes (cf. Kunzle 1990: 84–85, 299–300; Sessions 2011: 168–70). The two French soldiers in the foreground of Raffet's drawing are officers—they wear *épaulettes* and have swords—whereas, in the background, soldiers who are not officers carry guns and are accompanied by another officer who is in the middle ground on the left and is more clearly delineated. In the foreground, on the left side of Ferrandez's comic-book frame (Figure 2.6), he inserts two soldiers, visibly from the lower echelons of the army: they are not wearing *épaulettes* or carrying swords, and one has a pack on his back (their facial hair is also less well-groomed than that of the officers). They are complaining that their officers are living the good life in Algeria, while they and their colleagues lead a miserable existence:

> —Tu as vu tout ce beau monde pour le bal du gouverneur?!! . . . Et ces femmes!! . . . Autre-chose que des filles à soldats!! . . .
>> —Ouais. . . . Et pendant ce temps, nous aut' on crève de faim, et on va nu-pieds!! . . .

> [—Have you see all these fancy folks for the governor's ball?!! . . . And these women!! . . . Something else besides soldiers' girls!! . . .
>> —Yeah . . . And meanwhile, the rest of us die of hunger, and go shoeless!! . . .]

In the middle ground on the right side of the frame, we see the two Algerian drum-carriers from Raffet's drawing, surrounded by several French army officers, one of whom says "Allez, avance! . . . " [Come on, get going! . . .], to which another replies "Tu verras qu'on finira par les civiliser, ces gaillards! . . . " [You'll see that we'll end up civilizing them, these fellows! . . .].

Figure 2.5: An 1836 lithograph by Raffet mocks both French soldiers and Algerians: the former view themselves as superior to, and able to civilize, the latter. Auguste Raffet, "Nous civiliserons ces gaillards-là . . . " [We'll civilize those fellows . . .], in Gabriel Esquer, *Iconographie historique de l'Algérie, depuis le XVIe siècle jusqu'à 1871* [Historical Iconography of Algeria, from the 16th Century until 1871] (Paris: Plon, 1929), vol. 2, plate CXXXVIII, no. 322. From the Collection of the Public Library of Cincinnati and Hamilton County.

Ferrandez's critique of classism invites us to side with the exploited, ordinary French soldiers against their hierarchy. Meanwhile, the implicit authorial condemnation of the attitude of racial or civilizational superiority expressed by the French officers, on the right side of the frame, encourages the reader to side with the exploited Algerians pressed into French military service. These two attitudes—of lower-class French resentment (directed at French superior officers) and upper-class French disdain (for ordinary Algerians)—are worked out in the rest of the chapter (25–36), which replays the disastrous first French expedition to conquer Constantine, under the leadership of Clauzel and on the advice of Yussuf (or Yûsuf; cf. Julien 1964: 131–37).

Among other conquest-era imagery that Ferrandez copies, we again find a reworked version of a lithograph by Raffet that—like the previous one—is reproduced in the *Iconographie historique de l'Algérie, depuis le XVIe siècle*

Figure 2.6: Iconography retrieved from the colonial archives is source material for many French cartoonists including Ferrandez, who redraws French empire in Algeria in his comic-book recreation of conquest-era Algeria. Here he glosses Raffet's image captioned "Nous civiliserons ces gaillards-là . . . " [We'll civilize those fellows . . .] (1836). Ferrandez thereby critiques exploitation of, and prejudice against, both poor Algerians and ordinary French soldiers toiling in the colonial army of conquest. From Jacques Ferrandez, *Carnets d'Orient* [Oriental Sketchbooks], vol. 1 (Tournai: Casterman, 1994), p. 25. © Casterman. Reproduced with the kind permission of Jacques Ferrandez and Editions Casterman.

jusqu'à 1871 (Esquer 1929: plate CLXXXIX, no. 447; Ferrandez 1994a: 36, top-left frame). This time, it is a battle scene, to which French historian Annie Rey-Goldzeiguer (1993: 35) apparently refers in the following quote: "Le courage tranquille face aux hordes déchaînées est le message de Raffet dans la retraite de Constantine" [Raffet's message in the retreat from Constantine is calm courage in the face of unleashed hordes]. The lithograph by Raffet depicts a French battalion commanded by Changarnier protecting the retreat of the French army after its disastrous attempt to conquer Constantine in 1836 (Julien 1964: 132–35).[30] However, inserted into Ferrandez's narrative, this image signifies not so much the cool courage of the French and the savage nature of the Algerians, but instead the needless carnage brought on by the foolhardiness of the maréchal Clauzel and his advisor Yussuf. Although in the following frames a French captain cries out "Arrière sauvages!" [Get back, savages!] and "Arrière infidèles. Dieu vous maudisse tous" [Get back, infidels. May God curse all of you], Ferrandez suggests that the French officer is in fact the savage, because he earlier brutalized first an Algerian servant boy in Algiers and then a French soldier named Triard who had revolted against the desperate and unfair (to the enlisted men) conditions of the march on Constantine (27, 31–32). By the end of the episode, the captain has been killed by Triard, who arrived on horseback with the Algerian army, having joined the North African enemy

(36). So in Ferrandez's fictional enactment of the French defeat, the Algerian "hordes déchaînées" [unleashed hordes] that Rey-Goldzeiguer sees in
Raffet's lithography actually include rebellious French soldiers (Constant
as narrator of his "carnets" refers to many of them deserting to join the
Arabs).

In a review article entitled "Un album qui insulte l'Algérie française"
[An album that insults French Algeria], printed in *Présent* (Elbe 1987), a
far-right French newspaper, Ferrandez is copiously insulted as a traitor and
criticized for his visual replication, especially in regards to military uniforms: "Ce dont ne se vante pas l'auteur, c'est du pillage auquel il s'est livré
de notre patrimoine d'imagerie militaire" [What the author does not boast
of, is his pillaging of our patrimony of military imagery] (cf. Poncet and
Morin 1996: 77). This reverses the notion of colonial pillage: for example,
of the French army pillaging Algeria. I think quite the contrary, that Ferrandez's carefulness in this aspect of his visual documentation is entirely to
his credit: it proves that he is a conscientious artist who aims for historical
accuracy. It is true that in some ways in *Carnets d'Orient* Ferrandez clearly
betrays the imperialist spirit of French military sketches and paintings about
Algeria during the conquest, both through his Mario Puzzo character and
by the ways that he redraws some of the colonial imagery that he imports
into his comic books. Throughout his series, Ferrandez tries to maintain a
dual support for working-class Europeans in Algeria and for the Algerians
themselves—he often presents both groups as victims of the larger forces of
French imperialism. However, his *parti-pris* or support for the *Pieds-Noirs*
and their heritage repeatedly tips the balance in favor of the settler community, so that commemoration often curbs his critique of colonialism.

Recuperating the orientalist aesthetic

In *Carnets d'Orient* (1994a), Ferrandez grounds the claims of future generations of European settlers to the right to live in Algeria through a founda-
tion myth (cf. McKinney 1997b): the union of Constant, a French orientalist
painter, and Djemilâh, an Algerian woman, whom he first spies in a harem
in Algiers (Ferrandez 1994a: 19; cf. Tribak-Geoffroy 1997: 120–21), in a
partial reenactment of Delacroix's account of having visited the harem of
the portmaster of Algiers in 1832 and of Léon Roches's story about meeting
Khadidja, the granddaughter of the portmaster, in the same year (Roches
1904: 9–15; cf. Buch 2005: 54). Roches (1809–1901) served as a secretary
for Abdelkader in 1838–39, before becoming an interpreter for, and coun-
selor of, the French General Bugeaud (Julien 1964: 180), and later a French

diplomat (cf. Henry 1991: 304). Ferrandez used Roches as a model for his fictional painter, borrowing extensively from his memoirs, whose historical accuracy was severely compromised, according to French historian Charles-André Julien (1964: 176): "The work, which established his glorious reputation, *Thirty-Two Years across Islam (1832–1864),* had a certain amount of credibility until the day when it was proven to be 'only a novel, a pretty oriental novel,' full of fabulations and falsifications." In *Carnets d'Orient,* the harbor/harem master marries Djemilah to a Kouloughli,[31] from whom Constant is determined to retrieve her (Ferrandez 1994a: 41–42; cf. Roches 1904: 16–31). The male rivalry for the hand of Djemilah symbolizes a struggle between competing Ottoman and French imperialisms in Algeria, and their associated forms of cultural and ethnic *métissage* [mixing] (cf. McKinney 1997b): the negatively connoted *métissage* of both Djemilah's Kouloughli husband and his relationship with Djemilah (one type of mixed couple) are set against the positively marked pairing of her and Constant, a Frenchman. Roches (1904: 12) articulated a colonial-era discourse of national and racial mixing and hierarchy in the description that he provided of Khadidja's origins:

> She is the grand-daughter of the Minister of the Navy who took my husband's place, Mamma Nefissa told me; her mother is a Georgian of princely race whom the sultan of Constantinople gave to him when she was yet a child, and he married her to his son, who was killed at Sidi-Ferruch, fighting the French. Her intelligence is far superior to that of the young Moorish girls. Her mother is equally far above the Algerian women. . . .

Among the many things that Ferrandez borrowed from Roches are the French-Algerian male rivalry over Muslim women, its roots in French imperialism, and language about cultural mixing in Ottoman-era harems in Algiers: "Sa mère était georgienne et *fut capturée* sur les côtes d'Anatolie par le père d'Omar qui la ramena dans son harem. Djemilah est née de cette union. . . . " [Her mother was Georgian and *was captured* on the coast of Anatolia by the father of Omar, who brought her into his harem. Djemilah was born of that union . . .] (Ferrandez 1994a: 22: 12; my emphasis). However, he here also produces or reinforces a violent element that is not more than implicit in Roches' story of pre-colonial mixing—Ferrandez describes Djemilah's mother as having been kidnapped—to lend legitimacy to Constant's attempts to liberate Djemilah from the confines of the harem and marry her. This addition resonates with the racist assertion, found in Roches, that Khadidja and her mother were far more intelligent than Algerian girls and women.

On the other hand, the comic book's visual representation of the harem is primarily based on an orientalist painting by an English artist (see below). Roches (1904) too used the discourse of orientalism, including its visual representations, to describe his infatuation with Khadidja, for example in these two excerpts:

> I had in my bedroom a very lovely illuminated lithograph that represented Greece. It sat close to the head of my bed. The Moorish women, seeing it, exclaimed: "That's Khadidja," and, indeed, there was some similarity between that image and the hair, the clothes and the general appearance of the young Moorish woman. (14)

> This is no longer my little Khadidja of Braham-Reïs. This is the most perfect type of odalisque, about whom one dreams while reading the *Thousand and One Nights*. And her beauty [that of Khadidja, now grown up] was heightened even more by her emotion and her modest attitude. (21)

Moreover, the series title chosen by Ferrandez, "Carnets d'Orient," is itself a transparent reference to the orientalist sketchbooks (usually referred to as *carnets* or *albums*) that Delacroix made during his trip to Morocco, Spain and Algeria (1831–32). They provide the model for Constant's own sketchbook (Ferrandez 1995: 23). Pages from the latter are included at the outset of *Carnets d'Orient* (Ferrandez 1994a: 11) and regularly throughout the rest of the book. Moreover, through page layout and collage, Ferrandez underlines the fact that his multi-volume series is itself a series of "carnets," which rely on many orientalist and colonial-era paintings and other visual source material, as is especially apparent in the first book and in the fifth one, entitled *Le cimetière des princesses* [The Cemetery of the Princesses] (Ferrandez 1995).

Throughout his series, Ferrandez grapples with orientalist and colonialist aesthetics, and with colonial history, in productive but sometimes contradictory and often problematic ways. He also uses orientalist painters and their work in order to lend historical authenticity to his fictional characters, just as he tries to do with his copious documentation about battlefield scenes, military costumes and architecture. Ferrandez attempts a sustained critical evaluation of the orientalist paintings and tradition that he uses as sources for his comic book series, especially in the crucial first and fifth volumes: *Carnets d'Orient* (Ferrandez 1994a) and *Le cimetière des princesses* (Ferrandez 1995). In the latter book a distinction is made between an orientalism that is "boursouflé" [puffy; swollen][32] and one that succeeds in representing "la vie [orientale] telle quelle dans des scènes naturalistes (non dénuées de sensualité, d'ailleurs)" [(oriental) life as it is found in naturalist scenes (not shorn of sensuality, moreover)] (1995: 62)—this last comment refers specifically to Etienne Dinet, whose work is quoted visually by the cartoonist in the same frame.[33] Ferrandez makes clear that the majority of Joseph Constant's orientalist paintings, produced after his return to France, belong in the negatively connoted first category, because of the artificiality imparted to them by his physical and therefore aesthetic distance from his subject matter (Ferrandez 1995: 62). By extension, this judgement on Constant might be read as applying to the orientalist paintings—by Henri Regnault, Jean-Léon Gérôme and others—from which Ferrandez borrows to represent the exotic and grandiose vision of the Orient that Constant creates on canvas after leaving Algeria and returning to France (Ferrandez 1994a: 39–40, 72–74). However, this leaves one wondering how to categorize Ferrandez's own work, based on these same paintings.

The complexity of Ferrandez's approach may be illustrated by an analysis of his insertion into *Carnets d'Orient* (Ferrandez 1994a: 50) of Henri Regnault's orientalist painting *Summary Execution under the Moorish Kings of Grenada* (1870). Ferrandez (1996) points out that Regnault's painting of a decapitation hangs in the Musée d'Orsay. Nochlin (1989: 52–53) describes it as an "irrational spectacle" characteristic of the Orient, according to the norms of orientalist painting. MacKenzie (1995: 46) takes issue with Nochlin's selection of paintings, which he views as representative of ideological distortion, and instead puts (1995: 52) Regnault in a list of painters who represent how "Orientalism celebrates cultural proximity, historical parallelism and religious familiarity rather than true 'Otherness.'" Ferrandez's (1994a: 50) own perspective on this particular painting by Regnault is difficult to ascertain, as we will soon see. One of his main prose sources for *Carnets d'Orient* adds an additional level of complexity to his use of Regnault's painting: the colonial-era description by Roches of beheadings ordered by Abdelkader. The cartoonist first inserts a reworked version of the orientalist painting into a narrative sequence substantially based on a passage by Roches (1904: 91–99) that recounts a battle between Abdelkader's forces and a small group of Kouloughlis allied with the French, the condemnation by Abdelkader of eighteen surviving leaders of the resistance to his authority, the immediate execution of three men, and a pathos-filled conclusion in which the young children of the condemned successfully plead for Abdelkader's mercy for the remaining fifteen, who are led away unharmed. A Muslim, Arab execution as spectacle is obviously the common theme in both Regnault's painting—made in 1870, but depicting a scene set centuries earlier in Moorish Spain—and Roches's prose account of an event purported to take place in 1837 in Algeria. This is surely what led Ferrandez to meld the two in his graphic novel, to show the execution of a captured warrior—who is a Kouloughli and therefore ethnically related to Constant's rival for Djemilah—that was ordered by Abdelkader, trying to assert his authority over various indigenous groups in order to concertedly resist the occupying French army. The particular Kouloughli group to which the condemned man belongs had been allied with the French and had refused to join Abdelkader in his rebellion against the invading Christian nation. After claiming that God is on his side, the defiant Kouloughli chooses death over slavery and is executed. Ferrandez's version of Regnault's painting is indeed "irrational spectacle" (Nochlin 1989: 52), insofar as it represents internecine blood-letting by rival groups of Muslims determined to pursue their specific interests, articulated in terms of a Muslim holy war (Ferrandez 1994a: 47).

Ferrandez sets up a series of contrasts between his French protagonist and the Algerian resistance. Constant is more courageous in battle than the Emir's soldiers whom he helps lead against the Kouloughli group (Ferrandez 1994a: 48), urges clemency for the vanquished (49), and—most importantly—repeatedly encourages Abdelkader to make peace with his rival Algerians and with the French, as the only rational course of action (Ferrandez 1994a: 46, 51–52). According to the comic book's version of Algerian history, the Emir's failure to heed Constant's advice seals his ultimate defeat. This is one in a series of what are presented as missed chances for French-Algerian entente, which—had they been seized—might have ultimately led to the formation of a multicultural nation from which the *Pied-Noirs* would never have been exiled. Despite its generous humanist motivations, this nostalgic reading of history of course downplays, elides or offers shaky solutions to all sorts of very real problems that it raises on several levels. To take just one example, Ferrandez never allows a confrontation between Constant and Djemilah's husband; the closest he gets is through the execution of the Kouloughli, who could be seen as a proxy for Constant's Algerian rival.

Regnault's *Summary Execution under the Moorish Kings of Grenada* is depicted again at the end of the volume (Ferrandez 1994a: 72–73), as one of the problematic paintings that Constant made after his return to France. The transformation of the execution as it was originally witnessed by Constant in Algeria into a studio painting in France symbolizes a detachment of the historical event from its supposedly real context and its insertion into an artificial one, in other words, Constant's later production of orientalist paintings that attempt to show "les mystères et les beautés de l'Orient" [the mysteries and the beauties of the Orient] (Ferrandez 1994a: 74). In fact, Ferrandez's original presentation of the execution, as lived event, incorporates a self-referential gesture designed to disrupt the reality effect (Barthes 1985), or the history effect (Fresnault-Deruelle 1979): the frame depicting the execution is slightly rotated out of alignment with the other frames, and the setting as well as the executioner's clothing are somewhat different from their state in the previous frames. Instead, the beheader's garb corresponds to the clothing worn by the studio model who poses while Constant recreates the scene on canvas in France (Ferrandez 1994a: 72–73). The cartoonist's rotation of the frame, which is the equivalent of a jump cut in a movie, suggests one or both of two things, that: even at the moment it actually occurs in Algeria, the execution is viewed by Constant through orientalist lenses, or the first representation that we see of the event is already a post-event reconstruction by the painter. However, neither of these seriously puts into question the supposedly real existence in the comic book of the execution itself, nor its symbolic value as a spectacle of the "irrational violence" (Nochlin 1989: 52) enacted by one group of Algerians against another one, though it is true that Ferrandez also shows, in a negative light, the irrational violence committed by Frenchmen against each other (Ferrandez 1994a: 30–36) and against Algerians (e.g., Ferrandez 1994a: 27).[34] Ferrandez's (1995) subsequent attempt at resolving the conflict between the two values (accurate historical document versus orientalist fantasy) that he attributes to orientalist art is not wholly convincing. The contradiction between them is most acutely obvious in the manipulation of orientalist paintings, such as Regnault's, that are first integrated into the narrative as depicting or referring to real events in the comic book; it is far less so for the images first inserted as representations of Constant's feverish delirium (Ferrandez 1994a: 39–40) and later transposed onto canvas. In those sequences Ferrandez does not aim to recuperate or reproduce the "attempt at documentary realism" of nineteenth-century orientalism (Rosenthal 1982: 8; quoted in Nochlin 1989: 33; cf. Porterfield 1998); instead, the cartoonist suggests there that orientalist painting was simply a form of self-delusion.

On the other hand, Constant ends up rejecting the "imaginations orientales" embodied in his paintings and comes to believe that his sketchbooks are the only true reflection ("le témoignage authentique" [the authentic testimony]) of his experiences in Algeria (Ferrandez 1995: 77). If we once again extrapolate out from Constant's art to the historical artifacts on which they are based, it is clear that Ferrandez views Delacroix's North African sketchbooks to likewise be an unmediated, authentic reflection of his subject matter. That is why Ferrandez decides to model his own "Carnets d'Orient" after them and to draw a clear contrast within his series, between the unmediated accuracy of Delacroix's vision in his *carnets* and the artificiality of later orientalist paintings, as Ferrandez explained in an interview (1996):

When I stumbled onto it, precisely at the French National Library, there was a facsimile edition of the Sketchbooks [of Delacroix], and I told myself "Well there you have it! My narration is in there." . . . And it was precisely when I saw those books on orientalist painting that I realized, after having seen the Sketchbooks of Delacroix, that there was an *enormous* difference in their way of depicting, and of, finally, what the painters showed of the country, between the fleeting impression, the first impression, which was no doubt very close to reality, and then, after that, this kind of decor from the *Thousand and One Nights*.

According to Ferrandez's account of his series' genesis, the sketchbooks' mixture of text and image appears to provide an ideal model for the hybrid art of the cartoonist. Moreover, Ferrandez describes his desire to find an accurate and non-orientalist vision of North Africa, especially Algeria, in Delacroix's sketchbooks, which he opposes to the "Arabian-Nights decor" of orientalist painting. However, Porterfield (1998: 124–30) has convincingly argued that this widely held view of Delacroix's notebooks is flawed: although Delacroix himself argued for "the documentary nature of his pictures from North Africa," from sketchbook to finished canvas, this claim does not stand up to scrutiny. Neither his North African paintings nor his notebooks can be considered to be free from imperialist ideology and from orientalist techniques of observation and representation. Instead, Delacroix's "documentary stance" and his notebooks belong to a tradition of orientalist observation, sketching and note-taking that evolved in part to justify French imperialist expansion (Porterfield 1998: 66–68). Ferrandez's distinction between Delacroix's notebooks and orientalist painting in general is one of the "authenticating strategies" (Porterfield 1998: 51; cf. Nochlin 1989: 38) that the cartoonist uses throughout the series, to lend ethnographic and historical credibility to his comic-book memorial to the *Pied-Noir* community and *l'Algérie française*. His sollicitation of prefaces by celebrated intellectuals and writers associated with that ethnic group is another such strategy (see Poncet and Morin 1996: 73–74; Buch 2005: 67–73). Of course, Ferrandez's use of Delacroix's sketchbooks as a master model for his own "Carnets d'Orient" also stamps the comics with the cachet of high art.

After Ferrandez has finished separating what he considers to be artificial orientalist chaff from the kernel of authentic artistic perception, the reader is left with a handful of orientalist painters and works that are cited favorably, whether visually or verbally, within the series: the inaugural and innovative Delacroix (Ferrandez 1994a, 1995: 23–26),[35] *Trois Fellahs* [Three Fellahs] (ca. 1835) by Charles Gleyre (1806–1874), the "naturalist"

Alphonse-Etienne Dinet (Ferrandez 1995: 62–63) and the "talented" Henri Matisse (Ferrandez 1995: 14). However, Ferrandez's explicit distinction between authentic and inauthentic orientalist images, and his implied distinction between artistic representations of Algeria that are untainted by imperialism and others that are contaminated, are not entirely consistent—for example, much of Dinet's production is orientalist kitsch,[36] often in an erotic vein[37]—and even break down, especially when subjected to the pressure of Ferrandez's own longing for a lost homeland, *l'Algérie française*.

Despite the negative judgment on most of the paintings made by Constant, which are destroyed when his studio burns down (Ferrandez 1995: 35), his surviving harem painting of Djemilah becomes a *lieu de mémoire* within the comic book series and symbolizes the mythical (even Biblical)[38] origins of the European settler community—symbolically issuing from, or founded upon, the union of Joseph Constant (a renegade French artist) and Djemilah (his Algerian lover) (Ferrandez 1995: 24)—and its dream of possessing Algeria "like a woman" (Ferrandez 1994a: 74), just as Joseph dreamt of uniting with Djemilah after having first seen her in the harem. From the beginning of the comic-book series, Ferrandez's representation of Constant's painting and the art-historical event that inspired it are problematic and can reveal something about the contradictions inherent in the cartoonist's project. Ferrandez's (1994a: 19) representation of the first encounter between Joseph and Djemilah is based on *An Intercepted Correspondence, Cairo* (1869), an orientalist painting by John Frederick Lewis (1805–1875).[39] The narrative conceit of Lewis's painting involves the passing of a message encoded in flowers, sent to a woman in a harem but intercepted by another one, who now shows the missive to the harem's master, whose authority over the women in the harem had been temporarily circumvented by the clandestine message, its author and its intended receiver. From *An Intercepted Correspondence, Cairo* Ferrandez borrows both Lewis's lavishly colorful representation of the harem's sumptuous decor and his ideologically charged allusion to the transgression of domestic oriental despotism (Figure 2.7). He combines Lewis's narrative with Delacroix's story: Joseph Constant, acting here as Delacroix's double, takes on the role of the woman's lover, who is absent from Lewis's painting, although his implied existence is essential to the painting's story and its references to orientalist notions concerning despotic oriental rule, the harem's forced indolence, and the perversions that these produce. To this tale of domestic tyranny Ferrandez (1994a: 40–43) later explicitly attaches the political connotations that the notion of oriental despotism carries: in order to keep Djemilah away from Constant, the harbor master marries her off to a man associated with the Ottoman rulers of Algeria, who had been deposed by the French invaders (as discussed above). This is part of what enables Ferrandez to paradoxically re-frame the motif of a Frenchman's single-minded fascination with, and pursuit of, an Algerian woman as an anti-imperialist act, despite the fact that Constant's (and Delacroix's) initial access to the harem had been facilitated by French imperialism.

My analysis of the way that Ferrandez redraws Lewis's painting and inserts it into his narrative suggests a reply to MacKenzie, who argued that orientalist painting is not generally denigrating, but instead is ambivalent in its depictions of its subjects, and often even quite admiring of the cultures it represents: for example, MacKenzie (1995: 62) sees "a return to craft values" mirrored in orientalist pictorial depictions of various finely wrought objects from the East. Ferrandez's comic books betray a fascination with the colors, objects, landscapes and architectural details of colonial Algeria, but also with orientalist painting. In *Carnets d'Orient,* as in orientalist painting, "[t]iles and wooden lattices, *mashrabiyyah,* are lovingly portrayed" (MacKenzie 1995: 62). Yet the representation of the harem's wooden lattices, in Ferrandez's copy *and* in Lewis's "original" (itself heavily indebted to earlier textual and pictorial descriptions of harems), is part of a eurocentric ideological structure for representing so-called oriental cultures as despotic in domestic and political realms. I am not arguing that eurocentrism is the only representational strategy or value attached to orientalist painting, nor that Ferrandez's "Carnets d'Orient" constitute imperialist propaganda. My point is a subtler one: Ferrandez's choice of this particular harem painting was probably motivated at least as much by the eurocentric narrative about the Orient that it makes explicit, but which is more or less shared by most or all European orientalist harem paintings, as by Lewis's luxuriant depiction of a finely crafted, ornate oriental decor. In borrowing Lewis's painting of what is supposed to be an *Egyptian* harem, Ferrandez was not so much concerned with historical or visual accuracy in depicting an *Algerian* interior as he was in recuperating and reproducing an enduring vision of despotic oriental men and desirable oriental women. Ferrandez loves to portray Algerian women at least as much as he does the *mashrabiyyah* through which Constant longingly gazes at Djemilah (her name means "pretty" in Arabic). The cultural heritage left by orientalist painters is wide open to this particular reinterpretation by Ferrandez, as well as to other ones that would be more critical of the eurocentric strands that exist in orientalist paintings and in the stories that surround them, like the visit said to have inspired Delacroix's *Femmes d'Alger dans leur appartement.*

The transmission of Constant's painting of the moment when he first saw Djemilah, as an inheritance handed down from one generation to the next, also helps to illustrate the settler community's genealogical continuity

Figure 2.7: Ferrandez redraws an orientalist painting from 1869 by an English artist about a harem in Cairo as a replay of a legendary visit by French painter Eugène Delacroix to a harem in Algiers in 1832. From Jacques Ferrandez, *Carnets d'Orient* [Oriental Sketchbooks], vol. 1 (Tournai: Casterman, 1994), p. 19. © Casterman. Reproduced with the kind permission of Jacques Ferrandez and Editions Casterman.

and thereby to legitimate the creation of a settler identity as an ersatz African and Algerian one that, in fact, negates the national identity of the indigenous peoples (Tribak-Geoffroy 1997: 124): as one farmer-settler proclaims, "je suis devenu . . . un Africain, . . . un colon!" [I have become . . . an African, . . . a colonizer!] (Ferrandez 1994c: 74).[40] Marianne, the main protagonist of *Le cimetière des princesses* and a member of the last generation of Europeans to reach adulthood on Algerian soil (that of Ferrandez's parents; cf. Ferrandez in Poncet and Morin 1996: 76), receives a kind of inheritance from Constant when her friend and fiancé-to-be, Sauveur, buys Joseph's sketchbooks at a flea market and gives them to her (Ferrandez 1995: 22–23). She then retraces Constant's itinerary across Algeria in an act of memorial reconstruction that mirrors both Ferrandez's fabrication of a comic-book hommage by sifting through and pasting together colonialism's relics (cf. Fresnault-Deruelle 1979: 103; Certeau 1994: 266–68), and a French reader's experience of his five-volume series as an initiatory voyage back through France's colonial history, presented as a national or ethnic epic, that of the *Pieds-Noirs*. In the fifth book, which closes the first cycle of the series, the apparent destruction of Constant's notebooks in a fire (they miraculously reappear, undamaged, at the beginning of the second cycle of the series, in volume six), and of his harem painting in an earthquake, signals the loss of an artistic legacy and a settler identity memorialized by the comic books (cf. Tribak-Geoffroy 1997: 127–28). However, Ferrandez's recuperation of orientalist and colonialist aesthetics extends to colonial photography and is just as problematic as his treatment of orientalist painting.

Recycling colonial postcards

The cover illustration of the fourth volume, *Le centenaire* (Ferrandez 1994d) conveniently exemplifies some of the possibilities and limits of Ferrandez's series (Figure 2.8). The tableau unites several secondary figures around the main character, and represents the two geographical poles around which the book is structured. Paul (no doubt partly modeled on Albert Camus),[41] is the central, pivotal character who acts as the narrator of the fourth *carnet*. A young reporter for a French newspaper, he returns home to Algeria to write a series of articles on the 1930 centennial celebration of the French conquest of Algeria. On Paul's left side (that is, in the part of the illustration that extends over the back cover) are various European characters, including one who has adopted Algerian dress and costumes, all set against the background of a southern oasis. On his right (on the front cover), against the background of the casbah[42] of Algiers are two women with whom Paul is or was intimately involved: a fully clothed European woman, whom he will eventually marry, and a partially naked Algerian prostitute, Naïma, of whom Paul had previously been an occasional client, during his military service (Ferrandez 1994c: 79; 1994d: 17). The tableau is a complex attempt to represent the strongly gendered geographical, sexual and ethnic-national tensions that structure the volume: the rural south and the desert versus the urban north and the casbah of Algiers; adultery and endogamy (sex with his brother's fiancé, on the left) versus exogamy and prostitution (sex with the Algerian prostitute, on the far right); French versus Algerian women as incarnations of authentic Algerian-ness and its reproduction (cf. Calargé 2010: 114); going native versus French exploitation of the Algerians. As is often the case with comic book covers, this scene occurs nowhere within the covers of *Le centenaire* (Ferrandez 1994d); instead, it is a fantastic one composed by the artist to represent and sell his book.[43]

The right side of the tableau echoes earlier harem and bordello scenes in the series, which were inspired by colonial postcards as well as orientalist paintings and travel accounts. Naïma, who is not veiled and has a breast exposed (cf. Calargé 2010: 114), is an amalgam created by Ferrandez from colonial postcards in Alloula's *Le harem colonial*,[44] two of which are reproduced at the outset of *Le centenaire*'s narrative (Ferrandez 1994d: 12), as part of a collage. The reproduction of the postcards salvaged by Ferrandez via Alloula helps to demonstrate that this volume too is a "carnet d'Orient" into which the author pastes, redraws and rescripts scraps of material from the visual and textual archives of *l'Algérie française*. By redrawing Naïma in a street of the casbah on the front cover of his book, Ferrandez may seem to liberate her from the bordello to which she is relegated within his narrative (Ferrandez 1994d: 17), but the main thrust of the cartoonist's gesture is to expose her for the (male) French reader, just as colonial photographers did by publishing the postcard originals.[45]

Like the photographers, Ferrandez obsessively returned to harem scenes, both within his comic-book series and in at least two other places: (1) in a group show entitled "Bulles d'Eros" [Erotic speech balloons], held from April to May 1993, at Les Larmes d'Eros, a Parisian art gallery, Ferrandez exhibited at least two erotic watercolors, again redrawn from postcards reproduced in Alloula's study,[46] and (2) later in the same year Ferrandez was finally able to imitate Delacroix by helping to produce a contemporary "Album d'Afrique du Nord" [North African Album] on site, when he traveled to Algeria for the first time since his departure while still an infant. He traveled there to produce images for *La colline visitée: La casbah d'Alger* [The Hillside Visited: The Casbah of Algiers] (Mimouni and Ferrandez 1993), a book for which Rachid Mimouni, a well-known Algerian writer who was later forced into exile, wrote the text.

According to Porterfield (1994: 61–63):

> Delacroix's experience of the harem [he visited in Algiers] and his audience's experience of his painting [*Femmes d'Alger dans leur appartement*] were highly mediated . . . [through] many illustrated accounts of the East that Delacroix knew before his trip. . . . This is to say that Delacroix's pre-

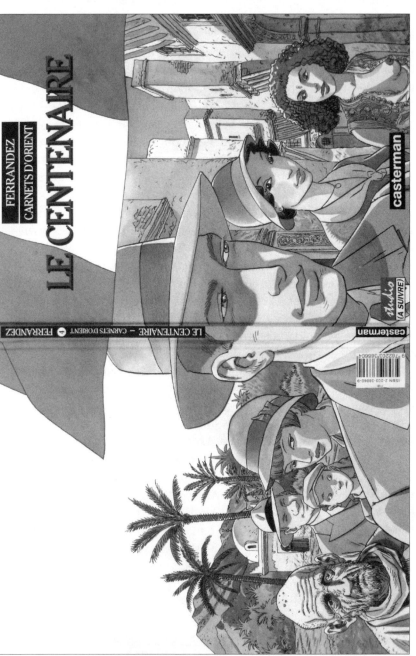

Figure 2.8: Redrawing erotic colonial postcards on a comic-book cover. From Jacques Ferrandez, *Carnets d'Orient*, vol. 4: *Le centenaire* [Oriental Sketchbooks: The Centennial/Centenarian], preface by Benjamin Stora (Tournai: Casterman, 1994), cover. © Casterman. Reproduced with the kind permission of Jacques Ferrandez and Editions Casterman.

vious indoctrination and practice in the culture of Orientalism informed his project. Before going to the Orient, he knew how to paint it.

Similarly, Ferrandez's own visit of discovery to the casbah of Algiers was mediated through his intimate knowledge of Delacroix's North African notebooks and paintings, and more generally through the orientalist tradition in painting, but also by his familiarity with the postcards in Alloula and others (cf. Ferrandez in Poncet and Morin 1996: 76–77). Therefore, it is not surprising to find that to depict Algerian women in *La colline visitée: La casbah d'Alger*,[47] Ferrandez redrew the same colonial postcards from Alloula (respectively 1981: 77 and back cover, 56; 1986: 121, 83), although for this cooperative Algerian-French effort with Mimouni, Ferrandez toned down the eroticism of his reproductions.

Ferrandez's neo-orientalist representation relies on earlier published travel accounts, such as Théophile Gautier's (1973) *Voyage pittoresque en Algérie (1845)* [Picturesque Voyage to Algeria (1845)], whose text and illustrations supplied the cartoonist with much of his anachronistic account of Constant's arrival in Algiers (Ferrandez 1994a: 11–13), which Ferrandez situates on 24 May 1836, approximately nine years before Gautier's actual visit of 1845, and four years after Delacroix's of 1832 (Ferrandez 1994a: 18). Indeed, a significant aspect of Ferrandez's neo-orientalist approach is his heavy reliance on the citation of antecedent authority in order to establish the legitimacy of his project. A perhaps even more telling example of this is Ferrandez's quotation from Flaubert's (1991: 281–88, cf. 70–77, 362–63, 366; 1996: 113–19)[48] infamous description of his encounter with the Egyptian prostitute and dancer Kuchuk Hanem, which Said (1994a: 6, 186–87, 207–8) discusses at length, as a "widely influential model of the Oriental woman" (6). Ferrandez (1994a: 14–15) bases Constant's visit to a bordello in Algiers on Flaubert's influential prototype, going so far as to attribute to Constant, Flaubert's exact words describing his sexual exploits (Buch 2005: 50–51). Here too, Ferrandez appears to have modeled his watercolor and line drawing of a prostitute on one or several postcards in Alloula (1981: 55; 1986: 81).

Clearly, colonial postcards from *l'Algérie française* are a place of memory on which many authors[49] with a personal stake in the colonization and decolonization of Algeria have freely drawn, though not always in a critical manner.[50] My principal criticism of Ferrandez's use, in "Carnets d'Orient," of colonial postcards purporting to depict colonized Algerian women is that he provides little in the way of a critique of the gendered and colonialist visual aesthetic that they emblematize, despite his recognition that the vision embodied in them is quite similar to that of many orientalist paintings (Ferrandez 1996).[51] The most that he accomplishes in this regard is to make explicit the sexist logic that is often implicit in the originals: the women in the cards become prostitutes in his narrative (Ferrandez 1994a: 14–15; 1994d: 12, 17). There is not the type of sustained reflection on the production of colonial-era photographs and postcards that we saw earlier in Ferrandez's treatment of orientalist painting: for example, although an unscrupulous French photographer is criticized, it is because he had manipulated and exploited the image of a French man (a military veteran), not an Algerian woman (Ferrandez 1994d: 72; see McKinney 2011b: 96–99); and there is no equivalent of the explicit critiques that characters make of orientalist painting. Recourse to the colonial archives, especially the visual ones, is a tricky business. A "hermeneutics of suspicion" is necessary, though perhaps not sufficient, to prevent us from participating in a neo-colonial "peepshow" when we look at the "visual exchange that informed colonialism" (Bal 1996: 217, 203, 222).[52]

In "Carnets d'Orient," we can see how the artist's attitude towards the allure of empire—and the aura of orientalism—is expressed through the tropes of mourning and family reconciliation, which renegotiate the boundaries of the French national community and thereby recompose it. The apparent destruction of Constant's sketchbooks in a car crash (Ferrandez 1995: 70–72) permits the reconciliation of two male rivals for Marianne's affection: Sauveur, a settler, and Marnier, an orientalist painter from mainland France. Their reunion symbolizes a mending of the fractures that split the French national community into warring factions during the Algerian War. Indeed, it is at this juncture that the settler figure (Sauveur) definitively supplants the mainlander (Marnier) as Marianne's legitimate suitor; in this way, Ferrandez symbolizes the erasure of the settlers' violent opposition to the French nation, their reintegration into it and even their reincarnation *as* the Republic (Marianne is a settler, but also, obviously, the emblem of republican France, who is courted by her settler savior, Sauveur; cf. Tribak-Geoffroy 1997: 119, 128). So even today, long after the official end of empire, in a work that memorializes the existence and passing of *l'Algérie française,* empire's allure in the form of orientalist art (Constant's sketchbooks and harem painting) plays a role very similar to the one that Porterfield (1998: 4–5) saw it occupying at the outset of France's occupation of Algeria, for example through Delacroix's *Femmes d'Alger dans leur appartement:* creating national unity by displacing the specter of a fratricidal conflict (the French Revolution; the Algerian War) that would otherwise endanger the nation's very existence (the car crash from which Marianne and Marnier escape, by a miracle).

According to Stora (1992: 261), the absence of places of memory (he calls them "espaces de mémoire" [spaces of memory]) is particularly painful for the *Pieds-Noirs:*

> This feeling of going against the current or of having been placed outside of history increases with the disappearance of all the spaces of memory, especially the cemetery of the ancestors. The absence of spaces in France that would offer imaginary, historical reconstructions is painfully felt.

This sheds light on the role of Ferrandez's project. The "Carnets d'Orient" provide a virtual *lieu de mémoire* to replace ones that were lost when the settler community left for France. To create his "sketchbooks," Ferrandez sifts through the flotsam of *l'Algérie française:* colonial postcards, orientalist paintings and writings, history books, old newspapers and the like. Like other generously minded *Pieds-Noirs* (Stora 1992: 240), Ferrandez creates the ideal of a multicultural Algerian society that might have been but never truly was and, in at least one instance, looks forward to France's multicultural society of today (Ferrandez 1994a: 17)—perhaps as a possible substitute for the lost Algerian one. He re-casts the history of France's colonization of Algeria as a national epic, whose untarnished heros were exceptionally generous-minded Frenchmen open to the people and culture of Algeria. He re-frames the road to decolonization as a tragic series of lost chances for French-Algerian reconciliation. Still, I wonder whether his nostalgia-soaked view of history, coupled with the severe limitations to his critique of orientalist and colonialist imagery, which lead him to produce what I have been calling neo-orientalist representation,[53] signal a continuing difficulty in letting go of the myth of *l'Algérie française*. At stake is the possibility of imagining truly equal relations between Europeans and Algerians. It is certainly conceivable that the "Carnets d'Orient" make possible the mourning for a lost homeland, a disappearing imagined community (Anderson 1991) of settlers and an ethnic identity now perhaps vanishing through assimilation of the *Pied-Noir* minority into the French mainstream. Nevertheless, in some ways it may also impede a more critical examination of the historical and aesthetic record, which is necessary for a peaceful resolution today of French-Algerian relations, internally within both France and Algeria, as well as between the two countries. Ferrandez waited several years before beginning to publish books in the second cyle of "Carnets d'Orient," which deals with the Algerian War. It was only in 2002, after the war had once again become a burning topic of debate in France, that the cartoonist finally released *La guerre fantôme* (I analyze that work and subsequent volumes in the "Carnets d'Orient" in Chapter 4, below). Ferrandez's prolonged difficulty in squarely confronting the drama of the Algerian

War—especially its both devastating and empowering effects on Algerians in France and Algeria—within the series could be symbolic or symptomatic of a more widespread limitation that has had negative consequences for the perception of the Maghrebi community in France (cf. Stora 1992: 281–301, 317–21).

Redrawing the French-Algerian affrontier in Algerian and French comics

There is a curious difference between French editions of *La bar-mitsva* [*The Bar Mitsva*], the first volume of Sfar's "Le chat du rabbin" [The Rabbi's Cat] series: an early edition (Sfar 2003a), lacks an indication that appeared in later ones. The cartoonist's belated acknowledgment of a primary source—*Alger et ses peintres, 1830–1960* [Algiers and Its Painters, 1830–1960], a lavishly illustrated study by Marion Vidal-Bué (2000)[54]—explicitly incribes his work in the corpus of French comics about North Africa that I have been analyzing. André Benhaïm (2007: 243; my translation) may be the first and is one of the rare commentators in the United States to point toward the painterly sources of Sfar's art in the series, although he then sets aside this line of inquiry:[55]

> Algeria becomes, in Sfar, a space at once "true" and imaginary, the land of "the 1930s," the land of the father, born in Sétif, and of the paternal grandmother, and a land that the author has only seen in postcards and other orientalist painters, from whom he drew inspiration to illustrate his family stories.

My preceding analysis of Algeria in European, mostly French, comics helps us situate Sfar's project within the general trend or genre of historical comics, and a specific tendency to return to the colonial past in them. It is a shared but conflictual, post-independence, project (cf. Rigney 2005: 22, 24) that dates back to the late 1970s and early 1980s in France, and somewhat earlier in Algeria. The project both follows, and helps produce or inflect, the affrontier (see above, Chapter 1). We can explore this notion further by looking briefly at historical comics about Algeria drawn by Masmoudi (an Algerian)[56] and Sfar (a Frenchman of Sephardic Algerian Jewish heritage on his father's side). They and Ferrandez together represent three major groups that existed in colonial Algeria. Their shared references, sources and practice constitute a model that provides an ideal case study of how the affrontier functions and how cartoonists redraw French empire.

Their memorial model involves cultural mining and recycling, which entails crossing and reworking the affrontier to produce representations of the Algerian past that reflect contemporary concerns in France and Algeria. These cartoonists use comics as one of the available "mnemonic technologies and memorial forms" (Rigney 2005: 24). Comics are one of the "artistic media" that, "[b]y virtue of their aesthetic and fictional properties," can move easily ("they are more 'mobile' and 'exportable'") and serve to help "re-define the borders of imagined memory communities" (25)—here, of the affrontier. Their visual-linguistic and narrative form render them a potentially powerful means for incorporating many types of recovered material from the past, and articulating it as or in a story. To recreate the Algerian past through comics, cartoonists have created a model that is reproducible and exportable (Anderson 1991; Rigney 2005: 25). It allows artists to cross, inflect the contours of, or reinforce the affrontier by sharing techniques and references: Rigney (2005: 24) observes that "models of remembrance may be exchanged among groups with a similarly marginalized position within the public sphere"—here, North African Sephardim and Catholic *Pieds-Noirs* in France, and Algerians in Algeria.[57] Such imitation can involve cross-border raiding and smuggling across the affrontier, a form of cultural *trabendo* (an Algerian term for contraband smuggling). French and Algerian cartoonists are therefore sometimes and to some extent *trabendistes* [smugglers], and their comics a form of *contre-bande-dessinée* [contreband/counter-comics]: ones that traffic in counter-memories and archival material (forms of colonial loot; McKinney 2011b), and disrupt other memorial constructions and identities. Such smuggling is often cross-media or "transmedial" (cf. Rigney 2005: 20–21): cartoonists import imagery from other cultural forms into their art without always naming their specific sources (as in the early French edition of *La bar-mitsva*). It often entails recirculating colonial materials whose original or earlier meanings run counter to or exceed those for which the cartoonist retrieves and rearticulates them.

The artistic-historical model that these artists use involves: redrawing orientalist French paintings, especially by Delacroix or Dinet; using colonial engravings[58] and postcards to produce ethnic authenticity and the historical effect;[59] and inviting prominent historians to write prefaces to comic books, or even drawing ones that historians have scripted.[60] Where did the model come from, and who produced it first? In the material under discussion here (which does not exhaust the available comics, the sources in these comics, or the media either—film, for example),[61] we find it first on the Algerian side, in Masmoudi's work (Bessaih, Bakhti and Masmoudi 1986); and then on the French side, by Ferrandez.[62] By contrast, both far pre-date the series by Sfar, for whom Ferrandez's comics clearly constitute the influential model, even though this fact has been ignored almost completely, especially in the Anglophone world, where Ferrandez's work is still virtually unknown. Although not impossible, it is unlikely that Sfar would have been familiar with Masmoudi's book, because comics published in Algeria are poorly distributed in France.

I have already shown here how Delacroix is the mediating, foundational artist for Ferrandez. This is also true for Sfar: the cartoonist takes Delacroix's North African notebooks and paintings as a first prestigious, painterly contact with the country; and for Sfar, as for Ferrandez, the painter represents the idea of documentary authenticity and reportage in orientalism, a problematic one as we have seen. True, in his use of Delacroix, Sfar draws closer to one kind of authenticity, because he implicitly foregrounds the Jewishness of many of Delacroix's human subjects and settings in North Africa (clothing, furniture, etc.), but the cultural model that Sfar borrows from Delacroix was in part from Morocco, not just Algeria.[63] This produces a detour along the affrontier: both Ferrandez and Sfar go virtually through Morocco to get to Algeria, which exemplifies both the cultural mish-mash of orientalist citation (Porterfield 1998) and the fractal quality of the affrontier (cf. Balibar 1998: 76).[64] Like Ferrandez, Sfar imports material from other famous orientalist painters and paintings into his first comic book about colonial Algeria.[65] In fact, he copies wholesale many orientalist paintings from the single volume by Vidal-Bué mentioned above.[66] Some of these borrowings clearly articulate a Jewish connection to past, either via the subject of the original painting (e.g., the synagogue of the Place Randon [Randon Square]), the ethnicity of the painter (e.g., Armand Assus, Simon Mondzain) or both. However, the range of subjects, the ethnic references and especially the time periods represented in and by the paintings paradoxically obviate any serious or general claim to historical and cultural authenticity in the graphic novel through the copying. Instead, we see once again an ahistorical orientalist practice of unanchored citation of antecedent authority.

Paintings by Dinet are important to both the Algerian cartoonist Masmoudi and the French cartoonist Ferrandez. For historian Claude Liauzu (2000: 38–45), Dinet was an exemplary *passeur de rives* [shore crosser] (cf. Henry 1991: 308; Benjamin 2003a: e.g., 92). He crossed the colonial affrontier, and critiqued certain aspects of it, but without fundamentally questioning French colonialism in Algeria (Pouillon 1997). Dinet furnished official, post-independence Algeria with a problematic model of access to a supposedly authentic cultural and artistic past from the French colonial period (Pouillon 1997; Liauzu 2000: 44–45). For Algerians, recovering and recycling Dinet's paintings has often required evacuating or overlooking the colonial, orientalist eroticism of much of his work, and substituting for it either the cultural authenticity that he was supposedly able to document in his paintings, or the later, pious religious images from after his conversion to Islam. However, this notion of authenticity in Dinet's paintings again rests on the problematic view of orientalist painting as an objective form of reportage that would somehow be substantially unmediated by preexisting artistic or cultural conventions of representation (Porterfield 1998).

For Masmoudi, Dinet's paintings apparently serve as a model repository of cultural authenticity and of an artistic style for depicting the Algerian south (cf. Benjamin 2003a: 96–97). Here, for Masmoudi, Algerian women personify suffering Algeria under French colonialism. The characters in his narrative have been displaced by an attack of French soldiers come to impose the building of a fort, as an advance outpost for the construction of a train track to the desert oasis in southern Algeria. This is problematic, insofar as the historical and cultural authenticity of Dinet's paintings appears to be unverified: Masmoudi uses paintings that the artist made several years after the revolt of Cheikh Bouamama, whose story Masmoudi recounts. Morever, he moves Dinet's women some 600 kilometers southwest, from Bou Saâda to Tiout. In fact one comic-book image (p. 50, third panel) is a redrawn collage of elements from various paintings by Dinet, purporting to represent different scenes of pathos, none of which are connected in any obvious way by Dinet to resistance to French colonialism: a death-watch around a dying patriarch (*Autour d'un mourant* [Around a Dying Man], in Brahimi and Benchikou [1991: 73]); two old women speaking (*Vieilles femmes* [Old Women], in Brahimi and Benchikou [1991: 102]); women at a cemetery (*Le vendredi au cimetière* [Friday at the Cemetery], in Brahimi and Benchikou [1991: 130]); and, perhaps, a repudiated mother and her two children (*La femme répudiée* [The Repudiated Woman], Brahimi and Benchikou [1991: 107]). Dinet's Algerian models may have been prostitutes, and the younger ones, who posed nude for him, were most likely training to become erotic Ouled Naïl dansers in Bou-Saâda, in southern Algeria (Pouillon 1997: 84–90; Benjamin 2003a: 94, 100–101, 165–67). Any shards of cultural authenticity that may have existed in Dinet's paintings have been redrawn and reassembled in a way that is far removed from the originals. Masmoudi also ignores the erotic dimensions of the images, which become more salient when we compare them with other, overtly erotic, paintings by Dinet. What we are left with is kitschy[67] French orientalism of the late nineteenth and early twentieth centuries that the cartoonist has anachronistically placed in the service of (then) consensual Algerian nationalism towards the close of the twentieth century. He thereby helps invent an artistic tradition for Algeria and its comics.[68]

The shared references and materials of Masmoudi, Ferrandez and Sfar are therefore: (1) historical—a shared, conflictual past that simultaneously and alternately unites and divides; (2) cultural—a mutual heritage, with some areas of overlap, for example, the French language; and (3) artistic—most obviously, comics, but also key works and artists that cartoonists use as primary sources for their creations. The communities represented in, and constructed by or through, these works are both imagined and real (cf. Anderson 1991; Balibar, in Balibar and Wallerstein 1991), multiple, and may partially overlap: they include ethnic and national communities, and reading communities. The cartoonists in question create invented tradition/s, in and around comics, which they attach to an appropriate and prestigious historical and artistic past (Hobsbawn and Ranger 1989; Beaty 2008)—especially that of orientalist painting. This involves actively retrieving and reconstituting a historical, cultural and artistic heritage, with the risks, costs and benefits of such activity. The affrontier is therefore a transnational, trans-media phenomenon in comics that involves the in/direct sharing of references, materials, and artistic model and practice. This is paradoxical because the artists are reconstructing perspectives on the past that overlap only partially and, in fact, sometimes confront each other (*elles s'affrontent*), at least virtually or implicitly: whereas Masmoudi and his co-authors provide an Algerian nationalist critique of French colonialism, the primary project of Ferrandez is to commemorate the *Pied-Noir* community in Algeria, while Sfar memorializes North African Jewish culture(s). The cartoonists studied here work to produce collective memory as cultural memory, based on "mediation, textualization and acts of communication" (Rigney 2005: 14) and on a scarcity of materials (16), not on a plenitude/ loss model or a return of the repressed: there are a limited number of materials and models available from the past, a fact that has both productive and limiting effects on the reconstruction of cultural memory.

Connecting the lines from one colonial affrontier to another

The French colonial affrontier is most apparent and divisive with respect to Algeria, to a large extent because of the significant number of *Pieds-Noirs* and Algerians, and descendants of both groups, living in France. The participation of an entire generation of French men as conscripts in the Algerian War also contributes to the sensitivity of that part of colonial history, as does the fact that Algeria won its independence, thereby ending more than a century of French domination. The extreme violence and length of the war, the specific methods used in it, including torture and terrorism, and the long wait for official French recognition of the war and its nature have also helped maintain the colonial affrontier with Algeria. However, the colonial affrontier also exists to a lesser extent with Vietnam. Border conflict along that part of the affrontier flared up in 1991, when French veterans formally accused university professor Georges Boudarel of crimes against humanity, for his actions in a Viet Minh prison camp that held French military captives. In the following chapter I analyze several comics that depict French Indochina and the Indochinese War. Comic books published from wartime to the present bear the trace of the affrontier in French Indochina. As we shall see in Chapters 3 and 4, there are several lines connecting the colonial affrontier from French Indochina to French Algeria: for example, a detective novel in prose about the Algerian War and Vichy France was apparently the model for a comic book about the Indochinese War. The authors of that book then produced a graphic novel about the Algerian War that recycled the same basic detective-story structure. This again supports the observation that memorial models are scarce and therefore are recycled in different contexts (Rigney 2005).

3
THE FALL OF FRENCH INDOCHINA

Returning to Indochina in comics

> Il nous raconta ses trente années passées en Indochine; les temples anna-
> mites, les couchers de soleil sur la baie d'Along, les sampans du delta du
> Mékong, la jungle tonkinoise, les nuits de Cholon . . . . (Stanislas and Rul-
> lier 1990: 10)

> [He told us about the thirty years that he had spent in Indochina; the Anna-
> mite temples, the sunsets over Ha Long Bay, the sampans on the Mekong
> Delta, the Tonkin jungle, the Cholon nights . . . .]

After the loss of an imperial territory, one way of regaining access to it is
vicariously through representation, by redrawing empire and retelling its
myths. It may, for example, be conjured up by a nostalgic colonialist sto-
ryteller, as is the case for the reader-viewer and the fictional characters in
Trafic en Indochine [Trafficking in Indochina], in my epigraph above. The
pleasures and perils of representation are now all the reader risks, the cartoonists suggest in their two volumes on *l'Indochine,* or (French) Indochina,
instead of various colonial-era alternatives presented to the reader, such as
being assassinated by the Viet Minh, receiving a beating from Corsican or
Chinese thugs who control gambling houses and currency trafficking in Saigon, or contracting a venereal disease from a Vietnamese mistress turned

prostitute. However, colonialist and imperialist nostalgia (Rosaldo 1989) does carry risks: becoming stuck in that past can help perpetuate an unequal relationship to the former colony and its people—including those now living in France, often French citizens—as Panivong Norindr suggests, in his study of *Phantasmatic Indochina: French Colonial Ideology in Architecture, Film and Literature* (1996). At least three developments within the comics industry demonstrate a renewed interest in French empire in Indochina.

First there is the republication of colonial-era comics set in Indochina and considered to be classics. For example, "Colonel X en Extrême-Orient" was serialized in 1947–49 and republished in book form in the late 1970s (Marijac and Gloesner 1979). The comic, produced during the French war in Indochina, is permeated with colonialist ideology and contains many of the motifs, images and narrative schema found in later works, as I show below. Similarly, "Bernard Chamblet: En mission au pays jaune," originally serialized in 1949, was republished in book form in 1959 and 1976 (Le Rallic 1976; cf. Gaumer and Moliterni 1994: 61).[1] Republishing these works helps reinscribe the colonial affrontier between France and its former colonies in Southeast Asia.

A second factor, and the one most likely to fundamentally change the representation of French Indochina in the long run, is the appearance of cartoonists of Southeast Asian heritage in France and Belgium, some of whom have begun to actively contest, modify and displace colonialist ideology and imagery. When they redraw French empire in Indochina, they often help produce a counter-memory that works against both colonialist nostalgia and the ideology of authoritarian post-colonial regimes that took control in Vietnam and Cambodia, for example. They include three artists of Vietnamese background (Clément Baloup, Marcelino Truong, and Vink) and two from Cambodia (Séra and Tian).[2] Vink (Vinh Khoa) was born in Da Nang in 1950 and educated at a French *lycée* [high school] before leaving Vietnam in 1969 for Belgium, where he eventually became a cartoonist (Gaumer and Moliterni 1994: 659). Marcelino Truong was born in Manila in 1957 to a Vietnamese father and a French mother, and grew up in Saïgon and then mostly in London, eventually settling in Paris, where he passed the *agrégation* (a French competitive exam for teachers) in English, before becoming a cartoonist (Condé 1991: back cover; Truong 1999). He returned to Vietnam for the first time in 1991, which influenced his vision of the colonial past and the nationalist Vietnamese struggle (Truong 1999: 5–6). Clément Baloup (1978–), a French cartoonist whose father is Vietnamese, studied at an Ecole des arts appliqués [School of Applied Arts], next in the *bande dessinée* [comics] section of the Ecole des beaux arts [School of Fine Arts] of Angoulême, and had an internship at the Ecole des beaux arts of Hanoï

(Baloup 2004).³ Séra was born in June 1961 in Phnom-Penh, Cambodia, to a Cambodian father and a French mother. After the Khmer Rouge captured the capital city, Séra's mother and her children fled to France in May 1975, leaving behind Séra's father, who died at the hands of the Khmer Rouge. Séra studied art in Paris, eventually returning to visit Cambodia several times, beginning in 1993 (Séra 1995: 112–24; Joly and Poncet 2006; Séra 2007: 110–25; Séra 2011; Weeks 2011). Tian, almost fourteen years younger than Séra, was born in Cambodia in April 1975, just after the Khmer Rouge victory, and moved to France with his parents in 1980. He too visited Cambodia years later, in 2001 (Tian 2011: 123). Baloup, Séra and Truong have produced graphic narratives depicting colonial occupation of, and imperialist wars in, their Southeast Asian homelands—Truong and Baloup about Vietnam, and Séra about Cambodia—just as other ethnic minority artists have focused on nationalist struggles and French imperialist wars in Algeria (Boudjellal 1998, 1999) or the French Caribbean (Puisy and Chamoiseau 1981) and Lebanon (Bardet and Klimos 1997). This part of the work of these artists is clearly indebted to felt affiliations related to their family backgrounds and hybrid cultural heritage, and to the fraught history of relations between the French and Southeast Asians: for example, Baloup and Truong include ethnically mixed *métis* characters in various stories—whether the cartoonist himself, in (auto-)biographical comics (Baloup 2004, 2006, 2010, 2012); a figure in a comic set in the colonial past (Truong and Leroi 1991; Baloup and Jiro 2012); or a Viet Kieu interviewee, who left Vietnam and settled in France (Baloup 2006: 41–70; 2010: 43–72). All three have included material in their artwork that either alludes to (in the case of Séra), or graphically depicts (for Truong and Baloup), the history of French colonization in the region. In addition, both Séra and Baloup have published graphic narratives that describe other imperialist occupations of the home countries of their fathers, both the Japanese occupation of Vietnam during the Second World War (Baloup 2006: 41–58; 2010: 5, 43–60; Baloup and Jiro 2007) and the terrible devastation brought by the United States to Southeast Asia during the Vietnam War (e.g., Séra 2003: 17–20, 73–74; Baloup 2004: 17; 2006: 10, 23; 2010: 3–7, 14, 26; 2012: 200–2). The willingness of French publishers to print and distribute autobiographical comics, which the translation of Spiegelman's *Maus* helped to inspire, has opened a space for works by French cartoonists of Southeast Asian heritage who inject an autobiographical element into some of their otherwise fictional stories. A significant difference between the production of French comics on Indochina and Algeria is the fact that there were far fewer French settlers in the former than in the latter. There is a resulting absence of cartoonists who redraw the genealogies of their settler families and ethnic community, as Denis Mérezette, Jacques Ferrandez, Evelyne Joyaux-Brédy, Anne Sibran, Joann Sfar and Morvandiau have done in their comics about colonial Algeria, which are often but not always fictionalized, as I show in Chapters 2 and 4 of this study.[4]

Publishers' interest in (semi-)autobiographical comics about Southeast Asia is therefore one example of a third development within the comics industry over the last few decades that has influenced the production of comics about the region, especially Vietnam and Cambodia: the editorial policies of magazines and comic-book publishers. During the 1980s, *Métal Hurlant Aventure* [Heavy Metal Adventure], renamed *Métal Aventure,* helped reintroduce the theme of *l'Indochine* into French-language comics. In October 1984, the magazine—which generally included a heavy emphasis on comics set in French colonies—published a special issue with a cover illustration drawn by French cartoonist Yves Chaland and bearing a title with a dubious pun: *Indochine 54: L'empire français riz jaune . . .* [Indochina 54: The French Empire Yellow Rice . . .] (cf. "rit jaune" [give a forced laugh]). For the occasion, Jean-Luc Fromental, the editor, gathered together several comics about French colonialism in Indochina, including a story drawn by Truong (Mallet and Truong 1984) and a five-page text-and-photo essay, "Rue Catinat, Saïgon" (Charpier 1984) that recreates Indochina as an erotic and exotic French place of memory structured by key elements and images, including prostitution and gambling in Cholon, the Chinatown of Saïgon; the Continental Palace hotel, a French *lieu de mémoire* [memorial site] in colonial Saïgon, still in existence today; and "le trafic des piastres" [trafficking in piastres], i.e., illicit currency speculation and exchange between mainland France and French Indochina (cf. Ruscio 1992: 127–29). For his article, Charpier contacted and borrowed photographs from Raymond Cauchetier, described as "formerly in charge of the Information Agency of the Airforce in Indochina, until 1956." He also freely quoted and drew information from: "Lucien Bodard, former war correspondant in Indochina" (22) and the author of a series of books about *La guerre d'Indochine* [The Indochinese War] (1963–67); Charles Meyer, at that "time a member of the Institut géographique militaire [Military Geographical Institute], now author and script-writer" (23), who published *La vie quotidienne des Français en Indochine, 1860–1910* [Daily Life of the French in Indochina, 1860–1910] (1985); Charles Baudinat, "who lived for two years in Saigon, first as a soldier and then as a civilian, today editor-in-chief of *Le Point*"; and Jacques Chancel, "correspondent of *Match* in Saigon and local radio announcer."[5] *Métal Aventure* thereby helped to recreate a collective memory of the colonial period. In *Le rendez-vous d'Angkor* [Rendezvous in Angkor], a comic that Fromental scripted and serialized in later issues of the magazine, he went on to recyle many references—to places, people and events—that had been anthologized in "Rue Catinat, Saïgon." Some of these elements reappear in *La nuit de Saigon* [Saigon Night], by Romain Slocombe (1986), who contributed a story about the Algerian War to the Indochina issue of *Métal Aventure* (Fournier and Slocombe 1984). Many related references to *l'Indochine* figure again in two volumes about the Indochinese War, by Stanislas Barthélemy and Laurent Rullier, *Trafic en Indochine* (1990) and *La route de Cao Bang* [The Road to Cao Bang] (1992), which I analyze in detail below. Of course here again, as with comics about colonial-era Algeria, the comic-book form allows cartoonists to redraw empire by copying and quoting colonial-era imagery and text, ranging from maps to photos, prose to song, fiction to reportage. As Ann Miller (2004; 2007: 57–59) has argued, reportage was a typical colonial genre in French-language comics, such as the Tintin series. Comics today about Indochina, including the series by Stanislas and Rullier, often rework that genre in a nostalgic mode.

Other general tendencies in comics publishing that help explain the renewed interest in comics about Indochina include the appearance of so-called adult comics—although they are often read by adolescents—(influenced by so-called underground comics from the United States) and the relative relaxing of censorship of sex and politics in French comics in general. This allowed the recycling into comics of erotic-exotic representations related to Indochina that had appeared during colonial times in prose fiction, painting and photography. Erotic-exotic comics about the colonization and loss of Indochina appeared in *Vécu* [Lived], a magazine of historical fiction from Glénat, a comics publisher based in Grenoble: for example, in 1989 and 1991, *Vécu* serialized portions of "Mémoires d'un aventurier" [Memoirs of an Adventurer] by François Dimberton and Dominique Hé, who eventually produced three books in their series (*Pierre de Saint-Fiacre* [1989]; *Ariane* [1990]; and *Opium* [1991]; Gaumer and Moliterni [1994: 313]). Dimberton and Hé mix historical episodes from the nineteenth-century French conquest, such as the death of Commandant Rivière (Dimberton and Hé 1989: 27–32), with erotic fantasies and exotic fiction. In 1990, *Vécu* published "Une épopée française: Indochine," by Bucquoy and Sels, which subsequently appeared in book form (1990). Set near Cao Bang during the Indochinese War, it features a beautiful Vietnamese villager as a femme fatale who seduces a neophyte French officer and carries out assassinations for the Viet Minh. In 1988, the magazine *Circus* published "Montagne fleurie" [Flowery Mountain], an erotic story by Belgian cartoonists Servais and Dewamme, which thematized pedophilia and incest, in a story about an orphan girl from Indochina who lives in the Belgian city of Bruges.

These trends within the comics industry were closely connected to developments in other cultural domains and in society at large. The publication of autobiographically inflected comics by post-colonial ethnic-minority artists coincided with a wave of interest in various forms of minority expression in France, perhaps most significantly the *Beur* [French North African] movement and Maghrebi-French fiction, whose roots can be traced to the anti-colonialist activism of the preceding generation (Hargreaves 1995, 1997). Moreover, this post-colonial autobiographical vein has no doubt been encouraged by a wider interest in autobiography in France (Lejeune 1985), including in French-language comics (see, for example, *9e art*, no. 1, 1996; Mercier 1999; Baetens 2004; Beaty 2007: 138–70; Miller 2007: 61–62, 165–78, 215–41; McKinney 2011c). Cultural critics have analyzed the renewed interest in Indochina that began in the 1980s and manifested itself in literature (e.g., the fiction of Marguerite Duras and Linda Lê), film and even clothing fashions.[6] To this, one should add music, especially the pop group Indochine (cf. Cooper 2001: 203–4). French historians have played a role in this rediscovery: for example, Benjamin Stora served as historical advisor for Régis Wargnier's *Indochine* (1992), an epic film of historical fiction;[7] and Lax and Giroud relied heavily on Jacques Doyon's *Les soldats blancs de Ho Chi Minh* [The White Soldiers of Ho Chi Minh] (1973), citing it in both their preface (1990: 4) and within the story itself (37; see above, Figure 1.5, p. 21). It is certain that the return to Indochina in French comics was greatly spurred by the release in France of books and movies on *l'Indochine française* and the Indochinese War. Truong (1999: 4), for example, states:

> From adolescence, and even earlier, I read everything I could get my hands on concerning Viêt Nam. I went to see movies. I kept up with the news. I was eleven or twelve. I discovered the Indochinese War in books by Lartéguy and Bodard. A novel by Schoendoerffer inspired me a lot for a composition. In eighth grade [quatrième], I think. We had to describe a striking action. I told the story of a fight in the jungle because I had just read *La 317e section* [The 317th Section].

The return to Indochina in comics was also inspired by American films on the Vietnam War (Stora 1997), as is apparent in Fromental's introduction to the special issue of *Métal Aventure* (1984: 1):

> The war of the French against the shadows from Hanoï was especially complex, painful and emotional. Almost a fratricidal war.
> Then the Americans landed. With their defoliants, their napalm, their

B-52s, their GI junkies and their huge choppers, they gave the world the Hollywood remake (that is, spectacular and dumb) of this conflict, which was atrocious but vibrant with heroic, romantic, or simply human acts. It didn't pay off. They got thrown out too. You can forget Coppola. Our Apocalypse was every bit as good as his.

Fromental paradoxically expresses colonialist nostalgia in anti-imperialist terms, by: (a) depicting the French war as an epic, almost fratricidal—and therefore all the more tragic—struggle, as opposed to the subsequent American war as farce; (b) and implicitly positioning the French as victims of American cultural imperialism, in the form of an invasion of Hollywood movies about Vietnam, specifically Francis Ford Coppola's *Apocalypse Now* (1979).[8] The implication is that French cartoonists must reclaim their historical and fictional territory—France's colonial war in Indochina—from the American artists and culture industry who have colonized it, just as the United States took over France's place in Southeast Asia. This posture of (post-)imperialist rivalry is a classic French move (Marshall 2005: 3). It also exemplifies an aspect of the colonial affrontier mentioned earlier:[9] that groups borrow "mnemonic technologies and memorial forms" from one another (Rigney 2005: 24), and more specifically the importance of representations of American colonialism and imperialism for French memorial constructions of their own colonial history, here with respect to the same colonized others (the Vietnamese). The colonial affrontier of France may therefore intersect with ones of other imperialist powers, including the United States. So one finds French comics that play on rival French and American imperialisms in Asia: for example, *38ème Parallèle* [38th Parallel] (Biard, Bocquet and Rivière 1988), set in 1952 and drawn in a retro *ligne claire* [clear line] drawing style of Hergé and other Belgian and French cartoonists, connects the Korean War with the Indochinese War.

The return to colonial history for dramatic stories, even ones whose protagonists are anti-heroes and apparent losers in the historical sea-change of decolonization, is linked to the continuing allure of the colonialist epic, whose relationship to the anti-colonialist epic I analyze below. The quote from Fromental also exemplifies the erasure that colonialist nostalgia often produces, despite the claim to excavate a past that has been hidden or masked by others: France used napalm in Vietnam, during the Indochinese War, before the massive arrival of American soldiers and the beginning of America's Vietnam War (Ruscio 1992: 152). The use of napalm, the bombing of civilians,[10] and the torture of Vietnamese prisoners[11] were three sorts of war crimes that French forces carried out in Indochina, before using these techniques extensively in the Algerian War. And the French army and police tortured, murdered and unjustly interned suspects in Indochina before the Indochinese War began (Viollis 1935; Ruscio 2003), just as they did in Algeria before 1954 (Vidal-Naquet 1983, 2001; Branche 2001; Liauzu and Liauzu 2003, Thénault 2012). Some post-independence comics depict the torture or summary execution of Vietnamese by the French during the Indochinese War. In *Les oubliés d'Annam* [The Forgotten Ones from Annam] (Lax and Giroud 1991: 48–49), the point is clearly to denounce French war crimes. In that work, redrawing empire is an anti-colonial, anti-imperialist activity that works to renew connections between the French and the Vietnamese people on a more humane and less confrontational basis, thereby breaching the French-Indochinese affrontier and encouraging free passage between former colonizers and colonized. In *La concubine rouge* a *métis* soldier in the French army murders civilians and tortures them through water-boarding (Baloup and Jiro 2012: 41, 44–47). In the torture scene, the cartoonists slipped into the textual narration, in the recitative, some clichés about the propensity of "Orientals" to torture, such as one finds in *Tintin au pays des Soviets* [*Tintin in the Land of the Soviets*] (Hergé 1973: 108–9), and were dismayed when reviewers failed to comment on this racist relic from the past. In two other works—*La nuit de Saïgon* (Slocombe 1986: 13) and *Une épopée française: Indochine* [A French Epic: Indochina] (Bucquoy and Sels 1990: 33–34)—the representation of torture is ambiguous, but in a different, non-ironic way: there, it seems to at least partially serve as a pretext for exhibiting the bound, naked bodies of the colonized (cf. below, p. 180). Since publishing *La nuit de Saïgon*, Slocombe has gone on to produce other sado-masochistic representations of Asian women in prose fiction, film and photography.[12]

In the rest of the chapter, I examine the representation of Indochina in (mostly) French comics from several angles, beginning with an analysis of colonial ideology in comics about the war that were serialized as it unfolded. Although some are skillfully scripted and drawn, including by recognized masters of the medium (e.g., Albert Uderzo, Etienne Le Rallic, Marijac and Gloesner), and are therefore technically impressive, they are by no means dialogical or complex in ideological, historical or artistic terms. Their inability or refusal to imagine or represent the perspective of the colonial subaltern constitutes a failure of creativity and artistic imagination (cf. Johnson in Strömberg 2003: 10–14; McKinney 2011b: 32). Instead, they uncritically supported French colonialism in a manichean fashion at a moment when it was beginning to crumble. At the same time, other French men and women did critique and otherwise resist the colonial mainstream French position. It was therefore possible to imagine and to represent alternatives to colonial domination, including in comics.

I then turn to recent comics about French Indochina and Southeast Asia. Although there are fewer post-colonial French comics about colonial Indochina than about colonial Algeria, there is a significant and growing corpus on the subject. In these comics I first analyze general trends in the French "geographical romance" with Indochina (Norindr 1996: 132), both colonialist and critical ones. This romance features the feminization of Indochina, and its recuperation and reconstruction as an exotic locale with archeological marvels hidden in the jungle, but also sex, drugs and gambling in brothels and opium dens. Its key figures include the *aventurier* [adventurer], colonial and anti-colonial soldiers, the *métis/se,* the reporter who investigates colonial history, and the expatriated exile or emigrant and their descendants. I then focus more specifically on exemplary publications, which rework many of these same tropes: *Le dragon de bambou* [The Bamboo Dragon] (Truong and Leroi 1991), *Trafic en Indochine* and *La route de Cao Bang* (Stanislas and Rullier 1990, 1992), *Les oubliés d'Annam* (Lax and Giroud 1990, 1991), and finally comics by Clément Baloup and his co-author, Mathieu Jiro. Here, as throughout this volume—and in my previous book on colonialism in comics (McKinney 2011b)—one of my primary aims is to determine whether, when, how and to what degree cartoonists critique colonial ideology and representation. Some artists whose work I analyze in this chapter do so through a dialogical orchestration of different perspectives on Indochina: anti-colonial or pro-colonial, mainland French or settler, indigenous or *métis/se,* Communist or non-Communist nationalist. Many others continue to redraw French empire in an uncritical or even celebratory mode, reinscribing and buttressing the colonial affrontier.

Before the fall: French comics published during the war

To help understand how and why ethnic majority and minority artists have depicted the French war in Indochina since the early 1980s, it is useful to return to an earlier period and analyze the way in which the struggle was represented in comics while it was unfolding, in order to show continuities, transformations and breaks in the representations of the war. For this, I analyze four works by French artists: *Colonel X en Extrême-Orient* [Colonel X in the Far East], serialized by Marijac (Jacques Dumas [1908–1994]) and Gloesner (Noël Gloesner [1917–1995]) in the French magazine *Coq hardi* [Brave Rooster] in 1952–53; "Bernard Chamblet: En mission au pays jaune" [Bernard Chamblet: On a Mission in the Yellow Country], by Le Rallic (1891–1968), serialized in the Belgian magazine *Wrill* in 1949—it was later republished as *Bernard Chamblet et l'Indochine* [Bernard Chamblet and Indochina] (Le Rallic 1976); "Parachutés au Laos" [Parachuted into Laos], by Tony Verdon and Perrin-Houdon, serialized in *Bayard* in 1951–52;[13] and a page (published 18 July 1954) from "Valérie André," a four-page story serialized in the women's magazine *Bonnes soirées* by Uderzo (1985), world famous for his best-selling Asterix series, created with René Goscinny.

As I noted in the introduction to this book, there is a remarkable contrast between comics about the Indochinese War and those depicting the Algerian War: during the former, one could find comics that clearly depicted it as it was taking place, whereas in the case of the latter, censorship and self-censorship prevented the publication of any comics openly about the war as it unfolded. As we will see in the next chapter, even though the first full-length comic book about the Algerian War was published in 1962 just after the war's conclusion, it was quickly censored by the French government. Consequently, during and after the Algerian War (and until the loosening of government censorship, especially in the 1970s), cartoonists disguised their allusions to French colonial wars, and other imperialist ones (e.g., the Vietnam War), in order to avoid the censors (Douvrier 1983; 1992: 71–72, 84–85). Earlier, a book republication of "Bernard Chamblet: En mission au pays jaune" was censored by the Commission chargée de la surveillance et du contrôle des publications destinées à la jeunesse et à l'adolescence [Commission Responsible for the Oversight and Control of Publications Meant for Youths and Adolescents], which was set up by the law of 16 July 1949 and is still in effect today. The law was passed in part because of the vigorous efforts of French Communists to keep out American comics, seen as demoralizing (Crépin and Groensteen 1999; Crépin 2001b; Jobs 2003; Grove 2010: 133–36). Comics historian Thierry Crépin (2001a: 141) suggests that this particular act of censorship was pro-Communist:

[French] Communist publications were never censored, contrary to the fears the Communist representatives expressed in 1949. . . . And on the contrary, thanks to the alliance of educators, article 13 of the law [i.e., the article concerning the import and export of prohibited materials] was strictly enforced; the import of foreign comics for the young was submitted to the authorization of the information ministry after the commission had given its green light. Thus, three albums that were hostile to the Communist fighters in Asia could not be imported in[to] France. The first one, "Bernard Chamblet: En mission au pays jaune," which described the war in Indochina, was drawn by Etienne le Rallic, who was a French patriot.[14]

Elsewhere, Crépin (2001b: 322), citing the same Commission meeting minutes, suggests that this decision was due to nationalist considerations: "Political criteria were also introduced by the commissioners, who believed that Belgian publications had no place depicting events in which France was involved, in this case, the Indochinese War." It is true that, although the story was drawn by a French cartoonist, it was published by Gordinne, based in Liège, Belgium (Evrard and Roland 1992). On the other hand, it appears that the story did circulate in France during the war in its preceding, serialized form, in *Wrill*. During the Algerian War there was no equivalent of this or the other serialized Indochinese War comics.

The colonial world of *Colonel X en Extrême-Orient* is starkly manichean, exemplifying the radical division between colonized and colonizer characteristic of the colonial affrontier. Colonel X, a French secret agent, is pitted against Pavot-Jaune, his Vietnamese counterpart and leader of nationalist forces fighting the French. Marijac and Gloesner depict the Asian inhabitants of Indochina (Vietnamese and Chinese) as obsequious (7, 11), sly and treacherous (23, 37), inscrutable (22) and fatalistic (37). The colonized are compared to monkeys (8, 10), water rats (8) and demons (18)—common tropes in colonialist discourses (Fanon 2002 [first ed., 1952]; Spurr 1993). Colonel X's outlook is paranoid: "Tous les hommes ici se ressemblent et une immense conspiration semble les unir" . . . [All the men here look alike and seem to be united in an immense conspiracy . . .] (22). This is apparent in the strict separation of Saigon into safe European and dangerous (for Europeans) indigenous neighborhoods (22–31; cf. Fanon 2002: 42–44; Norindr 1996: 107–30), and in the contrast between coastal Saigon, more or less controlled by the French, and the rebellious interior, where the Viet Minh may gain the upper hand. The constant recourse to maps by the French characters emphasizes the imperialist will to master colonized territories (9, 14, 19, 26, 29, 34). Colonialist paranoia is also expressed in references to potential treachery among Vietnamese soldiers fighting for the French (10, 18). The main antagonist is Pavot-Jaune, who was a staunch ally of the French during the fight against the Japanese, in the Second World War, before turning against France. Pavot-Jaune is clearly modeled on Ho Chi Minh, who helped to direct Vietnamese guerilla fighting against the Japanese before training his sights on the French when they tried to retake Indochina. The comic reproduces other clichéd images from colonialist literature about Indochina: the derogatory name "Pavot-Jaune" [Yellow Poppy] combines references to skin color and, implicitly, to opium use or production (from poppies); the disparaging term "Nha-Qué" [peasant] is freely used to refer to the Vietnamese (4, 10, 14, 39, 41, 43); and *pousse-pousses* (rickshaws) (22–23), water buffalo (40), Buddha statues and a Chinese vase (cover; 42) add local color to the scenery, although the vase is made in France.

The latter, an ironic wink at the pitfalls of an "orientalisme de pacotille" [second-rate orientalism], nonetheless leaves the colonial ideology of the comic undisturbed. This is manifested most profoundly in the conclusion, which finally moves Pavot-Jaune into the role of second-class hero, but only by physically eliminating the nationalist leader and foil to Colonel X. When Colonel X and Sergeant Veyrac (a "titi parisien" [cheeky Parisian lad]; 21), are attacked by Pavot-Jaune and an assistant, Veyrac throws himself on a grenade to save a Vietnamese child playing nearby. Witnessing this gesture, Pavot-Jaune emulates the French hero's self-sacrifice by letting his own grenade explode in his hand instead of throwing it at Colonel X (42–44). The episode represents the French imperialist war against the Vietnamese as disinterested, generous and heroic. Veyrac's attempt to protect an indigenous child from dangerous men puts French imperialism in a paternalistic and disinterested light. Finally, the encounter between two social types—the "titi parisien" and the Indochinese rebel—suggests that the latter's heroism is only imitative and, in any case, leads to his elimination, thereby symbolizing the desired conclusion to the war (the death of Ho Chi Minh and the defeat of the Viet Minh, left without their leader).

"Bernard Chamblet: En mission au pays jaune," my second example of a wartime comic strip, is mostly set in the jungle of French Indochina, where the title character fights with the French Foreign Legion against the Vietnamese guerillas.[15] In preceding episodes, serialized soon after the end of the Second World War, Chamblet participates in the French Resistance against the Nazis. This transition was made by a significant number of French soldiers, and it is represented too in *Les oubliés d'Annam*, published four decades later. Captain Chamblet and Simon, his French subordinate, are accompanied by a young Tonkinese who is mostly referred to simply as "le boy," a patronizing term used in French for an indigenous servant. Here, as in *Colonel X en Extrême-Orient*, French soldiers have difficulty distinguishing between Vietnamese friends and foes: when a group of paratroopers arrives to free Chamblet and Simon, who had been captured by the Vietnamese opposition forces (referred to throughout the comic as "K.O.Y."), one of them captures the Tonkinois and begins to beat him up, before the latter reveals his identity. The apology offered by the French lieutenant is revealing: "Excuse-moi, mais ce n'était pas écrit sur ta figure que tu étais des nôtres!" [Excuse me, but it didn't say on your face that you were on our side!] (21 April 1949). On the one hand this translates the situation of the French army in Vietnam rather well, insofar as every Vietnamese person was potentially an agent of the Viet Minh, in a country where there was widespread popular support for the nationalist forces fighting the occupying colonial power (Ruscio 1992: 163). On the other hand, this kind of comment also suggests the same sort of racistly tinged divide—between "white" French and "yellow" Vietnamese—that is implicit in the title of the episode and has characterized the colonial affrontier.

Similarly, the Vietnamese jungle is presented as exotic and inhospitable. It contains fearsome wild animals—two tigers, a boa and a python—that threaten the French soldiers in the wild or when used by the Vietnamese: the climax of the story occurs when the Vietnamese rebels try to feed Chamblet and Simon to a captured tiger (Figure 3.1). Chamblet, preparing to die, cries out "Vive la France! Vive la Légion!" [Long live France! Long live the Legion!], but the French paratroopers arrive to save them in the nick of time, and Chamblet's Vietnamese assistant sets a python on the tiger before both animals are killed by the French soldiers. The Viet Minh also use elephants in the book. The association between the Vietnamese rebels and these animals produces a representation of an exotic, wild and dangerous country (cf. Delisle 2008: 106–12). When the French paratroopers parachute into the area, which has both jungle and swampland, in order to find and save Chamblet and Simon, they express their disgust and anger at both the country and the rebels: "Quel bled!" "Sale pays. . . . Je vais leur faire payer ça!" ["What a hole!" "Dirty country . . . I'm going to make them pay for that!"]. To combat the savage forces, including wild beasts, afoot in the "dirty land" and "lost country," the French bring a domesticated animal (which embodies a civilized relationship to nature), a dog belonging to one of the lost soldiers: "Nous comptons sur ton flair pour nous guider dans ce pays perdu!" [We're counting on your sense of smell to guide us out of this forsaken country!].

When the French paratroopers find Chamblet and Simon, the latter are being held prisoner in the ruins of an ancient temple hidden in the jungle, which the Viet Minh are using as a fortress and hideout. The dramatic conclusion of the story involves French troops retaking the temple. Its ruins, hidden in the jungle, provide a mysterious and exotic locale for the story, but their symbolism is just as important. Norindr (1996: 4–5, 24–28) argues that Indochina's monumental ruins are key to understanding French perspectives on colonialism. The vestiges were viewed by the French as symbols of their right to don the mantle of empire bequeathed by prestigious indigenous civilizations of the past (much like Roman ruins in North Africa). When the cartoonists associate the Vietnamese fighters with the temple, they suggest that insurgent, anticolonial nationalism is attempting to create a direct link with an earlier, indigenous past, before the arrival of the French

Figure 3.1: Bernard Chamblet and Simon, two French legionaries, are thrown to a tiger by Vietnamese rebels. Proclaiming their allegiance to France and the Legion as they face death, they exemplify the French soldier as courageous colonial hero. From Etienne Le Rallic, *Bernard Chamblet et l'Indochine* [Bernard Chamblet and Indochina] (Brussels: Michel Deligne, 1976), p. 26.

colonizers. The French army then arrives to thwart that link and reclaim the authority that the temple ruins symbolize (Figure 3.2).

"Parachutés au Laos," my third example of a wartime comic, ran in *Bayard* magazine, a Catholic weekly, for over thirteen months, beginning in mid-January 1951. The story had fifty-seven installments of two pages each, for a total of 114 pages, plus—in the issue containing the fourth installment (no. 218, 4 February 1951)—a page (11) with an illustrated map of French Indochina, showing future highlights of the plot and tracing the itinerary of the protagonist. There is also an article in the issue containing the final installment (no. 274, 2 March 1952, p. 2) that favorably compares this and other adventure series published in the magazine to Tarzan and Superman stories, described as unbelievable. The author argues that other Bayard adventures are realistic ("vraisemblable" [believable]), for example, two of them recount "la vie authentique des missionnaires" [the authentic lives of missionaries]. He continues by stating that "Parachutés au Laos" goes even further: "Histoire vraie, aussi, parce qu'elle est construite avec des épisodes vécus par tel ou tel officier. Elle raconte exactement la lutte contre l'occupation japonaise, elle décrit le pays et les moeurs de ses habitants, et le dessinateur [Perrin-Houdon] est un officier des troupes coloniales . . . " [A true story too, because it was put together from episodes lived by one officer or another. It exactly recounts the struggle against the Japanese occupation,

Figure 3.2: Temple ruins provide both exoticism and a symbol of grandeur from past civilizations in Southeast Asia. French soldiers eventually defeat Vietnamese rebels hiding in the ruins, signifying France's imperial right to rule Indochina. From Etienne Le Rallic, *Bernard Chamblet et l'Indochine* [Bernard Chamblet and Indochina] (Brussels: Michel Deligne, 1976), p. 3.

it describes the land and the customs of its inhabitants, and the cartoonist (Perrin-Houdon) is an officer in the colonial troops . . .]. The authors do adhere fairly closely to the main contours of the French military operations from the recent past that they reconstruct. Nonetheless, the result is a form of historical fiction, as are many comics about the war published decades later. However, in its essence "Parachutés au Laos" is propaganda, combining a militant Catholic message of missionary service, including conversion of local populations and French martyrdom (a French priest is killed by the Japanese), with a defense and illustration of French imperialism, as French soldiers fight the Japanese in part one of the series (29 installments) and then turn to the Chinese (briefly) and especially the Vietnamese nationalists in part two (28 installments).[16]

Although its serialization began in early 1951, "Parachutés au Laos" returns its readers to the Japanese occupation during the Second World War and the outbreak of the Indochinese war. The story begins with the announced departure of Henri Natier, a French soldier and the elder son of a family that had lived in Indochina for many years, before the father retired and brought his wife and boys (Henri and Xavier) home to France, along with a Southeast Asian servant. In the first episode, as a member of the Corps Léger d'Intervention [Light Unit of Intervention] (CLI), Henri has just received orders to travel from France to Calcutta, India, where he will begin training with the British army, before being parachuted by them into Laos, from where he and his men will join a larger unit of the French army under surveillance by the Japanese army. This unit, while pretending to do anodyne topographical surveys, is covertly preparing to fight the Japanese, to help liberate French Indochina from them and return it to French control. The first date, 9 March 1945, is given in the installment of 11 March 1951 (no. 223), when a Laotian ally warns the French unit that "[l]es Japs ont attaqué les Français!" [The Japs have attacked the French!] (cf. Ruscio 1992: 33). This signals the beginning of a guerilla combat against the Japanese, during which the French unit will be gradually decimated and the remaining members finally split up, with some captured by the Japanese.

Between parts one and two, the focus shifts from Henri to his younger brother Xavier, a member of the *fusiliers marins* [maritime riflemen] who sails from France to Vietnam in September 1945[17] with the forces of General Leclerc to retake control of French Indochina (cf. Ruscio 1992: 52–57). The reconquest begins in the south—with Saïgon, Cochinchine and Annam—and then moves to Haiphong, Hanoï and the north of Vietnam,[18] and to Cambodia.[19] The narrative is propelled forward in part two by the French reconquest of Southeast Asia and by Xavier's search for his brother, who went missing during the guerilla struggle and cannot be found among either the known dead or the French prisoners eventually freed from the Japanese. In fact he has lost his memory and is being cared for by Vietnamese Christians in the mountains of upper Tonkin. Henri and Xavier help to distinguish this story from the other war-period comics studied here: they are not typical French soldiers because they are intimately acquainted with the colonized country, whose nationalist, anti-colonialist soldiers—characterized simply as "rebels"—they help to fight. As such, they are examples of a pivotal character type found also in post-defeat comics about the Indochinese War,[20] the conquest and colonization of Algeria,[21] and the Algerian War.[22] Alain Guillemin (2006: 175–76) notes that the Natier brothers speak several regional languages: "They speak 'dialects': Henri, Vietnamese and Laotian, and Xavier, Vietnamese, Hmong and Cambodian (his nanny had been Cambodian). They help out their mainland brothers-in-arms by sharing their knowledge of the languages and the customs."

Their knowledge of local languages and customs, and their family contacts, therefore provide them an access to the colony that is denied the Japanese forces, whose rival imperialism in French Indochina is thereby both delegitimized in comparison, and weakened through the material advantage that this confers on the French army: for example, Henri and Xavier inherit the contacts that their father had established with Christianized members of the Méo (i.e., the Hmong, Miao or Montagnard) ethnic minority, on whom the French colonizers (and the American imperialists, later) relied to fight their adversaries, the Japanese and then the Vietnamese Communists and nationalists (no. 222, 4 March 1951). At a banquet for the French leaders of the CLI given by the Méo helping them to gather information against the Japanese, a Méo leader exclaims: "Nous serons toujours attachés aux Français, ils sont bons et justes. S'ils font la guerre, nous la ferons avec eux!" [We will always remain attached to the French, they are good and just. If they make war, we will fight with them!] (no. 222, 4 March 1951). Hao-Ming, another Méo leader,[23] initially mistakes Henri for the soldier's father and later gives Henri money that he will use to buy food throughout his mission in the jungle. In effect, Hao-Ming is helping to pay for the French war effort through a voluntary contribution, no doubt an ideal arrangement from the French perspective. Jean-Ming (the son of Hao-Ming)—who was baptized by the French missionary bishop of the region, bears a Christian name, and wears a Catholic saint's medallion—guides Henri's unit through the jungle, helping them to attack and evade the Japanese. Toward the end of the story he will enable Xavier to reunite with his lost, amnesic brother. Jean-Ming therefore plays a role similar to that of the Vietnamese "boy" who helps the French protagonists in "Bernard Chamblet: En mission au pays jaune." Both are partially assimilated local figures, whose devoted assistance is essential to the success of the French, but play a secondary, subordinate role: when they meet, Jean-Ming pledges to Henri, "Je serai ton oeil et ton oreille!" [I will be your eye and ear!] (no. 222, 4 March 1951). The two indigenous assistants of the French soldiers differ through the special ethnic minority and religious (Christian) characterization of Jean-Ming and his community. Later in "Parachutés au Laos" Xavier also contacts a Vietnamese family friend in Saïgon, who saves his life by shooting at Viet Minh agents attempting to capture him.[24] The cultural entry that Henri and Xavier have into Indochina, and their family connections, enable them to serve as interpreters and intermediaries for other French soldiers in the fiction, as well as for the mainland French children reading "Parachutés au Laos" (cf. Guillemin 2006: 176, 173). As we have seen, Fromental (1984) will later claim this kind of colonial proximity and authority as justification for publishing comics about French Indochina in *Métal Aventure*. The comic-book representation of ties between the Natiers and the Méos is indeed rooted in the history of French colonial penetration and ethnic policies in the region, specifically variations on the divide and conquer strategy: "In Indochina as elsewhere, the colonial system could only function by manipulating intermediary social groups: ethnic minorities against majorities, Catholics against Buddhists, village outcasts against literate elite, by placing them at the interface between white and indigenous societies" (Gantès 2006; cf. Salemink 1999). Several ethnic minorities living in the highlands of Laos and Vietnam feature in post-defeat French comics about French Indochina and contemporary Southeast Asia, where they provide local color (especially through their traditional clothes and jewelry) and—in stories about *l'Indochine française*—sometimes serve as allies of the protagonists, though not always in the service of French colonialism, as we shall see later.[25]

The depiction of wild animals, while still a source of exoticism here, as in the comics analyzed earlier, is also transformed by the colonial claim to local knowledge incarnated in Henri and Xavier. First Xavier correctly identifies a cobra (another soldier called it a python), traps it—thereby saving a sleeping comrade—and defangs it, to give it to the ship's cook to tame and use for catching and eating rats.[26] Later he accurately distinguishes the sound of a wounded wildcat, which had been mistaken for a child's cry, and catches it. It turns out to be a young panther, which he nurses back to health and tames (nos. 254–55, 14–21 October 1951). Xavier's familiarity with the animals of French Indochina enables him to recognize the sound of a charging elephant, allowing him to courageously save himself and an indigenous boy fleeing with his uncle from their animal, which had inexplicably gone mad and attacked them (no. 265, 30 December 1951). The boy in turn saves Xavier's life by helping him escape from the local villagers, who try to kill him because they hate white people. Xavier's mastery over wild animals, and the ways in which the latter threaten certain local people, suggest that he—and, through him, the French in general—has a more legitimate claim on Southeast Asia than do its indigenous inhabitants, at least those who dislike the French.[27] This is especially striking in the case of his panther, which fiercely dislikes and attacks all Asians ("Jaunes" [Yellows], in the comic), both "Annamites" and Chinese, whether or not they serve the French. A sailor suggests that this is because it was wounded by one of them just before Xavier saved it (no. 256, 28 October 1951). The panther, nicknamed Kao (in French, a homophone of K.O. [knock out]), becomes the mascot of Xavier's unit and saves his life during fights with the Viet Minh, by attacking them.[28] French racism against Vietnamese, and the inability to distinguish between allies and foes among them, is naturalized, expressed and justified through the panther (the animal cannot be condemned for its instinctive reactions). Xavier will later regretfully abandon the animal, when the captain of a junk agrees to take him on board: "Ma pauvre Kao, je ne peux t'emmener sur ce bateau où il n'y a que des jaunes. Et puis il vaut mieux que tu retrouves ta liberté" [My poor Kao, I can't bring you on board this boat where there are only Yellows. And it's best that you regain your freedom] (no. 268, 20 January 1952). The abandonment of Kao is one of the ways that the cartoonists attempt to resolve the tension running throughout the comic, between, on the one hand, a manichean, colonial and wartime vision of Southeast Asians, especially Vietnamese, as (potential) enemies and, on the other hand, a Christian message of brotherly love, and a colonial ethnography that foregrounds and explains cultural and religious differences to outsiders in a non-judgmental, though exoticizing, mode (cf. Guillemin 2006: 176–77).

The ancient grandeur of past civilizations figures here as it did in "Bernard Chamblet," but with a twist conferred by the special relationship between the Natiers and French Indochina. The narrator compares Angkor to French cathedrals, thereby diminishing their foreignness: "Le merveilleux temple d'Angkor, maintenant en ruines, a été terminé à l'époque où l'on construisait les cathédrales gothiques en France" [The marvelous temple of Angkor, now in ruins, was completed at the time when gothic cathedrals were being built in France] (no. 270, 3 February 1952). The equivalence between glorious pasts in the two countries is undercut by the state of dilapidation and anarchy of present-day Cambodia: Angkor Wat lies in ruins (whereas many French cathedrals are well maintained) and now houses Cambodian rebels. Here too the ability to speak an indigenous language provides access to information necessary to defeat the rebels, as the French forces reconquer Cambodia from the nationalists. Two officers discuss a lead that Xavier has supplied them: one says, "Excellent, ce renseignement qu'a obtenu Natier . . . " [Excellent, this information that Natier obtained . . .]; to which the other responds, "Ils ont confiance en lui, car il parle bien le cambodgien" [They have confidence in him because he speaks Cambodian well] (no. 270, 3 February 1952). Xavier then tries to win over Cambodians staying at the temple of Angkor Wat: "Nous cherchons les rebelles Issaraks. Il faut qu'ils obéissent à votre roi qui est l'ami de la France" [We're looking for the Issarak rebels. They must obey your king, who is a friend of France] (written in French but meant to be read as though in Cambodian). In the next installment he convinces the rebels hiding in the Bayon temple at Angkor Thom that the French army wants to make peace with them (no. 271, 10 February 1952). Here, as in "Bernard Chamblet: En mission au pays jaune," French soldiers conquer rebel forces hiding in temple ruins. However, in "Parachutés au Laos" Xavier's linguistic abilities and cultural knowledge allow him to transmit the official line in a way that avoids bloodshed. His bloodless mediation at the temple corresponds to French manipulation of Cambodian nationalism and traditional authority, through the figure of Prince Sihanouk (cf. Ruscio 1992: 56–57). In both comics, French forces take on legitimate power and authority through their military success—by fighting or negotiating—in the ruins of past civilizations that previously dominated the region.

By contrast with the preceding stories, which vaunt the exploits of French military men, "Valérie André" dramatically focuses on a real-life French woman who was a military doctor and piloted helicopters during the Indochinese war.[29] Uderzo took care to underscore the fact that André had lost none of her femininity, despite her success in traditionally male occupations (soldier, surgeon) and a violent, masculine context (war): her empathetic and healing nature leads her to nurse even a wounded crow back to health. The *indigènes* exist in the comic as an innocuous peasant with his water buffalo and the unseen rebels who fire bullets at her helicopter as she transports a wounded French soldier. The comic-strip page about André has clear parallels with the photographic representation of the nurse Geneviève de Galard as analyzed by Nicola Cooper (2001: 187–90), minus the sexualized and aristocratic aspects: both represent France's civilizing mission as a courageous attempt to heal the victims of indigenous rebels.

Some important characteristics common to these wartime publications, which distinguish them from later, post-defeat, ones, are their dominant focus on the successful military operations of French soldiers and their portrayal of the French colonial presence in Indochina as not doomed to failure, despite non-negligeable threats to it (cf. Guillemin 2006: 188). This is due to the generally propagandistic nature of these comics and the fact that the French army had not yet been forced to withdraw from Indochina when they were being produced. By contrast, recent, post-war comics about Indochina generally display a perspective marked by (arrested) decolonization, insofar as France's defeat is acknowledged in some way: for example, through a return to the past by a character who reconstructs the story of French colonization, defeat and departure (e.g., Stanislas and Rullier 1990–92; Lax and Giroud 1990–91); through extra-diegetic narrative comments referring to France's impending defeat, even though it is not actually depicted (Raives and Varnauts 1986: 21); and by representing French soldiers as sometimes heroic, but not conquering and, instead, doomed to failure. According to Alain Ruscio (1992: 196), the transition from a language of certain victory to one of heroism in defeat was already a feature of colonial discourse during the Indochinese War, as it became clear that France was going to lose. Given that historical reality, Fromental's call to represent the war—as "this conflict, which was atrocious but vibrant with heroic, romantic, or simply human acts"—is also problematic in its reproduction of a feature of French propaganda during the war (the French combat as heroic). In fact, many post-war comics uncritically replicate a significant amount of French colonial ideology about Indochina, whereas others offer impressive critiques of the myth of *l'Indochine française*.

"Geographical romance":[30] Adventure in Indochina

French Indochina is still a source of masculine adventure in French-language comics, including a few authored by Belgians. In this section I provide an overview of how several cartoonists articulate this adventure through elements they borrow from colonial-era culture, including the feminization of Indochina, the adventurer and emigrant or exile figures, opiate use and trafficking, and archeology. The feminization and sexualization of Indochina is a recurring trope in both colonial-era representations and in recent times (Joyeux 1912; Norindr 1996: e.g., 13, 72–106; Ruscio 1996; Vann and Montague 2008; Vann 2009: 91–95). Examples of it in French and Belgian comics provide an ideal case study for evaluating the relation between colonial and post-colonial imagery. The appearance of Indochina as a seductive woman in comics did not occur until a decade or two after the end of formal colonialism, when this was facilitated by a reduction of the censorship of eroticism and pornography in comics, and the appearance of an adult comics market (by no means limited to erotic or pornographic works). There was then a transfer of colonial eroticism into a medium from which it had mostly been absent during colonial times. At the same time, stories about Indochina were transformed significantly, from heroic narratives of victorious French conquest and civilizing, in colonial-era comics, into romantic epics about the French loss of Indochina, in many post-defeat comics. There, the French loss of Indochina is generally figured through amorous liaisons between Frenchmen and Indochinese women, by contrast with the colonial-era comics, where the French-Asian couple, where it existed, was composed of a French soldier and his Indochinese assistant (Chamblet and his "boy"; the Natier brothers and Jean-Ming). The regular depiction of brothels, situated mostly in Cholon, an indigenous city annexed to the Europeanized Saïgon (cf. Norindr 1996: 127–28), provides one measure of the feminization of Indochina in comics of the last two decades.[31] This principle of representation is stated matter-of-factly in a comic scripted by Fromental: "Il est venu ici pour l'opium et les femmes. Il est de ces blancs qui considèrent l'Asie comme une prostituée . . . " [He came here for the opium and the women. He's one of those whites who takes Asia to be a prostitute . . .] (*Le rendez-vous d'Angkor,* Renard and Fromental [1987: 44]).

The myth of the compliant, exotic Asian lover is carried over from colonial-era culture into post-independence comics such as *Le carrefour de Nâm-Pha* [The Crossroads of Nâm-Pha] (Maltaite and Lapiere 1987: 33, 43) and *Paul* (Raives and Varnauts 1986: 26–31, 47), both set during the Indochinese War. In the latter, a French soldier's encounter with a Vietnamese prostitute provokes a limited reflection on the effects of colonial violence on colonizer and colonized. In the preceding episode (Raives and Varnauts 1985: 25–26), Paul, suspected of murder in Paris, flees to Saigon as a soldier. He then barely escapes from the Viet Minh in the jungle (Raives and Varnauts 1986: 3–7) before returning to Saigon for a bit of rest and relaxation. Paul's realization that he must leave Indochina occurs after he temporarily hallucinates about fighting the Viet Minh, while in a Cholon brothel. In a frenzy, he slashes a Vietnamese prostitute, whose naked body he had just covered with painted ideograms of her name, Tình Yêu (26–31). This suggests the trope of exotic, colonized woman as a blank page—the French agent of imperialism inscribes her identity (her name) onto her body and then tries to efface it, when his paranoid imagination transforms her into the image of an enemy soldier. He subsequently brings her with him back to France, as a sexualized, human example of colonial loot (47–48; cf. McKinney 2011b). The same authors later recycled the image of the sexually available Vietnamese emigrant or exiled woman as a blank page in a different context: this time the male figure is Harold, an author from New York who is writing a story about the American war in Vietnam, and the female figure is Sally, an Asian waitress in London whom he integrates into his fiction before having sex with her in the bathroom of the bar where she works (in "La contortionniste" [The Contortionist], Warnauts and Raives 1997). The apparent self-reflexivity of this second example is just as limited as the first one, in the sense that the eroticizing and exoticizing exploitation of the Asian woman characters by the cartoonists (and their male author character, Harold), as a source of inspiration for a war story, is never seriously questioned. The unexamined incorporation of the trope into comics generally creates an obstacle to serious reflection on the negative effects of French or American imperialism.

The *aventurier* plays a key role in the romantic epic of France's imperialist defeat, just as he did in previous phases of colonization. This figure has been recuperated by contemporary popular culture from earlier, colonial-era cultural productions. For example, the title song of *L'aventurier,* the first album of rock group Indochine, is about Bob Morane, the British protagonist of a best-selling series of novels by Charles Dewisme (alias Henri Vernes), a Belgian author who went on to script a string of very successful comic-book versions of his stories, beginning in 1959.[32] Imperialism's myths of easily acquired riches (called "bonanzas" by Richard Slotkin [1993: 17–18, 30–31, 60, 170, 214] in a study of the American frontier), readily available exotic women, rapid military advancement for soldiers, and masculinist adventure have long helped constitute "the allure of empire" (Porterfield 1998). Norindr (1996: 72–106) perceptively analyzes André Malraux's so-called "aventure indochinoise," during which he played several, apparently contradictory, roles, including entrepreneurial pillager of Indochinese archeological riches and critic of colonialism. The adventurer could undertake these activities and many more, including reporting, spying, exploring, subduing indigenous peoples or defending them. In comics that return to colonialism, one finds instances where an adventurer plays a colonialist role and others where he plays an anti-colonialist one, as Miller (2004) has demonstrated.

Comics about colonial-era adventurers in Indochina often combine a variety of well-worn themes from imperialist fiction, including comics: a search for wealth, knowledge or personal identity; opium-smoking and drug-trafficking; and imperialist wars (cf. Hergé's *Le crabe aux pinces d'or* [*The Crab with the Golden Claws*] [1980, first ed., 1940]). For example, in *Opium* (Dimberton and Hé 1991), the third volume in the "Mémoires d'un aventurier" series, a French doctor, Pierre de Saint-Fiacre, visits Indochina in 1883 and learns the truth about his father, who visited the country years earlier and was given a gold mine by the ruler of Hué. Pierre's discovery of the secret of his identity apparently drives him to become a drug addict.

Similarly, *Le carrefour de Nâm-Pha* (Maltaite and Lapière 1987) mixes references to the war between the French and the Viet Minh with a tale about drug-trafficking and a woman's search for her father. The voyage to Indochina leads to opium-dealing for the lost father and madness for the daughter (41–46). In *Paul* (Raives and Varnauts 1986), the title character pays for his return to Paris by smuggling drugs. In this type of story, the adventurer's concerns are personal, and Indochina serves mainly as a setting for lucrative, usually illicit activities. The theme of the pleasures and dangers of opium-smoking and drug-trafficking, borrowed from colonial-era culture, takes on vaguely counter-cultural connotations in this and many other comics that refer to French Indochina, including *La variante du dragon* [The Dragon Variant] (Golo and Frank 1989). Post-colonial France remains connected to Asia through a conduit of heroin smuggling that reaches into a community of emigrants and their descendants in the Chinatown of Paris in *La variante du dragon* and *L'ombre du triangle* [The Shadow of the Triangle] (Christin and Aymond 1999), which condemns the drug trade.

Cartoonists often mix monuments with opium to represent the French empire in Indochina as a mirage of prestige, wealth, mystery and luxuriance. The association of ancient architectural ruins and splendors (Angkor Wat and Siem Reap; Hué) with opium to create an exoticized image of French Indochina, found already in colonial prose fiction,[33] continues in recent comics about the colonial era[34] and ones about Southeast Asia today.[35] The particular importance of Angkor in the French collective memory of Indochina after the war is prolonged by its redrawing as a topos in comics: for example, it is a mystical destination where worlds collide in *Le rendez-vous d'Angkor* (Renard and Fromental 1987). In *Opium,* which is set entirely elsewhere (Paris, Saigon and Hué), a map of Indochina that situates the action for the reader includes the location of Angkor Wat, as though the story would be incomplete without the site (Dimberton and Hé 1991: 28). The search for treasure, often archeological, in Indochina is integrated into several comics, including *Le rendez-vous d'Angkor* (Renard and Fromental 1987), *Le temple de l'épouvante* [The Temple of Horror] (Chapelle, Marniquet and Chanoinat 2009) and *Le carrefour de Nâm-Pha* (Maltaite and Lapiere 1987: 14). *Le dragon de bambou* (Truong and Leroi 1991: 10, 29) includes references to the trial of André and Clara Malraux for pillaging archeological treasures at Angkor. The two are shown on the cover, with props of Indochinese exoticism: Clara lies naked on a bed, a tea set in front of her, while André, sitting next to her, prepares to light an opium pipe. However, the book depicts them primarily not as temple thieves or drug addicts—the latter a common Orientalist image in comics since at least *Tintin et le lotus bleu* [*Tintin and the Blue Lotus*] (Hergé 1979, first ed., 1934)—but as sympathizers of Vietnamese nationalists. We follow them not on a trip across French Indochina to loot ancient archeological sites (as depicted in *La voie royale,* a semi-autobiographical novel by André Malraux [1962: 75–88]), but instead on a cross-country trip to learn more about Vietnam and to obtain a printing press for publishing a newspaper that critiques certain aspects of French colonialism (see below).[36]

The French debacle in Indochina is illustrated in *Une épopée française: Indochine* (Bucqouy and Sels 1990: 44–45), when a French unit fleeing Communist nationalists seeks refuge for the night in the ruins of an ancient temple. It turns into a trap when a captive Viet Minh agent manages to kill the French soldier guarding her and escapes into the surrounding jungle. In *Les oubliés d'Annam* (Lax and Giroud 1991: 32), a French reporter discovers debris from a French army encampment, where Viet Minh soldiers had been tortured and killed, in the ruins of a Cham temple site, suggesting a critique of the myth that the French colonizers were the legitimate successors of former indigenous empires.[37] By contrast, in *L'ombre du triangle* Christin and Aymond (1999: 25–28) house a modern drug-traffickers' laboratory in the ruins of a temple on the border between post-independence Vietnam and Laos. *La colonne* [The Column] (Martin and Simon 2001), in the Guy Lefranc comics series, similarly incorporates references to temples in a story about modern-day drug production in the Cambodian jungle. The exotic, iconic value of ancient Southeast Asian sculpture and architecture is exemplified by the use of such imagery in cover illustrations for several recent comic books: *L'ombre du triangle* (Christin and Aymond 1999), *La colonne* (Martin and Simon 2001), *L'affaire Sirben* [The Sirben Affair] (Bardet and Boutel 2002), *Le sourire de Bouddha* [The Smile of Buddha] (Warnauts and Raives 2003) and *Le temple de l'épouvante* (Chapelle, Marniquet and Chanoinat 2009). I turn now to *Le dragon de bambou,* whose story refers to and historically comes after the episode of colonial trafficking by André Malraux, and which figures the mixed couple as well as the *métis.*

Le dragon de bambou, or, the *métis* in the middle

Although it has received very little attention from academics who study French Indochina but may be unfamiliar with French graphic novels and comics,[38] *Le dragon de bambou,* by Truong and Leroi (1991), is a fascinating comic book that deals with issues central to several debates about the representation and memory of French Indochina. The publication of *Le dragon de bambou* preceded an event that generated considerable media coverage and public interest: the release of Régis Wargnier's film *Indochine* (1992) which is largely set during the same time period and deals with similar material. Moreover, *Le dragon de bambou* provides a more critical perspective than the film on the same events and structural inequalities of colonialism. Another reason why *Le dragon de bambou* merits close scrutiny is for the way in which it revisits the so-called Indochinese adventure and the writings of André Malraux, which have been the object of debate by critics.[39] Third, it raises the important question of how ethnic minority artists present a colonial past that informs their own position in France today. In this respect, *Le dragon de bambou* and two other, shorter comics by Truong provide a useful counterpoint to the ways that ethnic majority cartoonists have usually represented the French colonization of Vietnam.

Le dragon de bambou recreates colonized Vietnam in the *années folles* [the roaring Twenties]—its narrative begins in 1925—with a stylized drawing style evocative of the era, but which is also indebted to the *ligne claire* drawing style (cf. Truong 1999). The colonial ideological baggage that is attached to the *ligne claire* style is consequential, as Miller (2004) has argued in a perceptive article on the role of the *aventurier* in postcolonial comics about Asia. Truong's style is ambivalent: on the one hand, he mines its nostalgic and exotic connotations in his return to the colonial past through comics and in his illustrations, often for books about Southeast Asia; on the other hand, in "Sur le Fleuve Rouge" (Truong 1984) and *Le dragon de bambou* (Truong and Leroi 1991), he turns colonial nostalgia against itself, as it were, by using his art to depict a brutal, racist and highly stratified colonial society in French Indochina. The list of places and themes in *Le dragon de bambou* that constitute colonial *lieux de mémoire* is long, and includes the bordellos of Cholon (15–17), as well as the Cercle sportif (25–26) and the Continental Hotel (21) of Saïgon. However, one of the most interesting aspects of the graphic novel is the displaced perspective from which these *lieux de mémoire* are presented: that of the *métis*, who is simultaneously attached to and detached from Vietnamese and French cultures. His "double vision" (Gilroy 1993: 126–27) allows him to focus a critique of French colonial culture from inside and outside. Truong and Leroi represent the French-Vietnamese *métis* Clément-Rivière as being torn between the capricious and condescending Yvonne Beauprée, who is part of the French high society in Saïgon (her father is the director of the Chamber of Commerce of Saïgon; 15), and Liên, a young Vietnamese woman who faithfully waits for him to return to Hongay, on the Baie d'Along, where his mother was from and is buried (42, 47–48). His attraction for the two women, on opposite ends of the colonial hierarchy, overlays the oppositions of class, culture, ethnicity and geographical location. When Yvonne disdainfully mistreats him as a pretentious and lowly *métis,* Clément-Rivière finds temporary consolation with a prostitute from his mother's region, whom his godmother, who runs a brothel in Cholon, procures for him (15–17). The construction of this fictional perspective on *métissage* [ethnic or cultural mixing] by the cartoonists, although based on historical documentation and colonial myths, can also be read figuratively as a comment on the situation in which ethnically mixed people such as Truong find themselves in France today: with ethnic and cultural attachments to groups on both sides of the colonial affrontier. The artists encourage the reader to make this connection through two fundamental attributes of their fictional protagonist: his name, *Marcel* Clément-Rivière, recalls that of *Marcel*ino Truong; and Clément-Rivière (or Clem) works as a visual artist whose drawings serve to critique French colonialism in Indochina, as do those of his cartoonist creator. The *métis,* as artist and fictional character possessing a double perspective, is uniquely positioned to interrogate, inflect and cross the colonial affrontier.

As is also the case in the "Victor Levallois" comics and in *Les oubliés d'Annam,* which I analyze below, the reconstruction of French colonialism in Indochina is based here on a reworking of the figures of the adventurer and the reporter. In *Le dragon de bambou* we find young André Malraux, introduced as an adventurer dabbling in anti-colonial journalism in Indochina: "Le jeune aventurier André et sa femme Clara faisaient partie du comité de rédaction" [The young adventurer André and his wife Clara were members of the editorial committee] (1991: 7). However, his motivations for criticizing the excesses of French colonialism in Indochina are not as disinterested as one might anticipate. His defense of the colonized is rather ineffectual, and he appears more intent on drawing attention to himself—by dueling a rival newspaper editor, for example—than in helping the colonized. His wife remarks that "[l]'important pour André n'est pas la réalité, mais la légende" [what's important for André is not reality, but legend] (22)—his own legend, that is. Clearly, the cartoonists are suggesting that Malraux's self-aggrandizing tendency was a significant motivation behind his Indochinese adventure. The mix of myth and history is also at the center of the "Victor Levallois" comics series, to which I now turn.

"KO Kao Bang": The romantic epic of French loss[40]

Trafic en Indochine (1990) and its sequel, *La route de Cao Bang* (1992)—by Stanislas and Rullier—provide an example of the way in which recent comics have reworked France's withdrawal from Indochina as the romantic epic of a failed relationship between a French man and a Vietnamese woman. They also weave together many of the images of French Indochina scattered throughout several other French and Belgian comics. The two books represent the collapse of colonialism as primarily a personal loss for the protagonist, because his contact with French Indochina brought excitement to his life. It takes him from his position as an accountant's assistant in an import-export firm based in Paris to Indochina, whose imperialist allure is described to him by a colonial returnee in the epigraph to this chapter. The comic's nostalgic tone is produced in part by the narrative framing device. In the frame narrative, Victor Levallois recounts his Indochinese adventure to a younger Frenchman, who has just purchased, in Cholon, a lost photo-album containing pictures of Victor and his friends. This trope recurs in French-language comics about colonialism, dating back at least to Hergé's story (1942–43) about the colonialist ancestor of his Captain Haddock in the Tintin series (Hergé 2006–7).[41]

Both Victor and his photographer friend are journalists who are leaving Saïgon in 1968, at the height of the imperialist war fought by the United States in Southeast Asia. Throughout most of the two books the memory of the earlier French war in Indochina displaces the ongoing American one—which Fromental had enjoined French cartoonists to do—but in an ironic mode. Victor is a lackluster comic-book anti-hero, a French everyman who only momentarily appears to master the course of events, before his world falls apart: the back of each book in the series proclaims this principle— "Poursuivi par l'aventure, il rencontre l'histoire" [Pursued by adventure, he encounters history].[42] Because Victor is "pursued by adventure" instead of seeking it, the book may fall short of incarnating the ideal of romantic adventure proclaimed by Fromental. However, Victor's failings are compensated for by his protector: the dashing, clear-sighted but doomed Lieutenant Arnaud de Cottigny, who is clearly modeled at least partially on Lieutenant Bernard de Lattre de Tassigny (cf. Lattre 1952). The latter was the only son of Maréchal Jean de Lattre de Tassigny, a general who commanded French forces (1950–52) during the Indochinese War, before succumbing to cancer. Historian Guy Pervillé (1993: 127) suggests that the general's own death was hastened by that of his son Bernard, in 1951, in a skirmish at Ninh Binh. In *La route de Cao Bang,* Arnaud de Cottigny is killed by the Vietnamese nationalist forces during the French retreat from Cao Bang, along the Route Coloniale (RC) 4 (Stanislas and Rullier 1992: 44; 1994: 12–14). Through Arnaud de Cottigny, the comic book uncritically resurrects Bernard de Lattre as a heroic figure from French colonial history.

Just as problematic are the other historical types that the comic book reworks, also in a semi-ironic mode of colonialist nostalgia. One mem-

ber of the household represents French Marxist sympathizers of Vietnamese nationalists: "Ça, c'est le grand Max. Un marxiste-léniniste qui a égaré
sa dialectique dans les méandres de la philosophie zen et les brumes de
l'opium" [That's Big Max. A Marxist-Leninist who has lost his dialectic
in the meanders of zen philosophy and in opium fogs] (35). Max's political engagement is limited to his readings of revolutionary materials and to
occasional sententious pronouncements. In fact, a Groupe culturel marxiste
did bring together some French Communists sympathetic to the Vietnamese cause.[43] After it was outlawed in 1949 by the French government, one
of the Communists, Georges Boudarel, joined the Viet Minh in 1950 and
was eventually assigned to reeducate French prisoners in a Viet Minh camp,
October 1952–August 1954 (Ruscio 1992: 167–73). After an amnesty law
was voted on 18 June 1966, Boudarel and similar French participants in the
war were able to return to France. By 1991, Boudarel had been working in
Paris for many years as a professor of history, specializing in Vietnam, when
he was recognized by a former French prisoner of war, and what became
known as the "Affaire Boudarel" broke out. A group of French veterans
of the Indochinese war who had survived the Viet Minh prison camps formally brought suit against Boudarel on April 3 for crimes against humanity,
but the courts eventually ruled that he could not be tried for two reasons:
his actions in the prison camps did not fit the French definition of crimes
against humanity, and the amnesty law of 1966 applied to his case.[44] In *Les
soldats blancs de Ho Chi Minh*, published long before the Boudarel scandal
erupted, Jacques Doyon recounts the story of Boudarel, under the pseudonym of Boris.[45] Doyon (1973: 317–18) describes the young Boudarel,
before his defection, as a bookish figure with romantic aspirations and a
penchant for smoking opium, forming a portrait that recalls the comic-
book figure Max. It is not clear whether or not Stanislas and Rullier based
their character on Doyon's portrait of Boris/Boudarel, although other cartoonists did so at around the same time (see below). What is certain is that
Max is far less firmly committed to his ideals than Boudarel was: his only
comrades appear to be his motley group of French housemates and, like
them, he mostly benefits without thinking from the labor of the Vietnamese
woman refugees and their children living with them (1990: 39). The group
is a far cry from Boudarel's group of Communist activists, who congregated
in a similar colonial villa in a comfortable suburb of Saïgon (Doyon 1973:
308). Other members of Victor's household include a lesbian or bisexual
journalist and a bank employee. The fictional housemates are generally presented as sympathetic but rather eccentric and even marginal members of
French colonial society. Their main group activities are attending parties
and lounging about.

However, Werner, the remaining member of Victor's housemates, is a former Nazi whose past is too unpalatable even for the French Foreign Legion (Stanislas and Rullier 1990: 35), a French colonial force, although it later turns out that he works as a paid assassin killing Vietnamese nationalists, probably for the French secret police [Sûreté] (Stanislas and Rullier 1992: 17–18, 29). This too appears to be loosely based on historical facts: according to Jacques Doyon (1973: 33–36, 183–84, 258–59), the French Foreign Legion first accepted into its ranks a number of German anti-fascists fleeing Hitler, before it took on a more fascist coloring under Admiral Decoux, named Governor General of Indochina in July 1940. After the end of the Second World War some German fascist soldiers even joined the Legion (187). Werner meets a violent end, when he is assassinated by a Vietnamese boy designated by nationalists to execute a death sentence (Stanislas and Rullier 1992: 29). However, he saves Victor's life earlier by killing a French sailor who is threatening him (Stanislas and Rullier 1990: 49–50), and is happily tolerated by Victor and his other housemates despite his Nazi past and present colonial activities.

Another unsavory character whom the cartoonists resurrect from the graveyard of colonial history is a French soldier, Roger Vandenberghe. According to Doyon (1973: 177–78, 192, 208–14), he was turned into a colonial legend by the French media and army propagandists at the time. Long after the war one could find websites that celebrate the figure.[46] At least two other comic books rework him, whether in a celebratory mode (Bucquoy and Sels 1990) or a sharply critical one (Lax and Giroud 1990, 1991, 2000). Doyon (209) describes the origin of the Vandenberghe legend:

> Commandos were in fashion in Indochina. De Lattre said: "I must have commandos!" Vandenberghe—who in the meantime had become a sergeant-major, a kind of angelic, blue eyed killer—created a light unit composed of former Viet Minh combatants, the "black commando," which would become famous within the ranks of the French fighting force.

However, the Viet Minh infiltrated Vandenberghe's commando and assassinated him on 6 January 1952, while he was in bed with his Chinese mistress. In *La route de Cao Bang* (Stanislas and Rullier 1992: 31–37), Vandenberghe appears as the Capitaine Van Blick, who leads a commando of former Viet Minh.[47] The colonial troops fighting for France wear the black uniforms of the nationalist army, but as a disguise. There is no mention in the comic book of the atrocities that Doyon describes as the principal reward that Van Blick offered the Viet Minh prisoners of war whom he recruited: "He could only offer his men massacres, money, theft, the booty of vengeance" (1973: 211; cf. 212). Instead, in *La route de Cao Bang,* Van Blick is simply a courageous French soldier who saves Victor Levallois from the approaching Viet Minh and helps him continue his search for Tuyet, his Vietnamese mistress, by getting him plane rides that take him to Cao Bang.

The cartoonists also rework the colonial cliché of the wealthy Corsican businessman engaged in currency trafficking and speculation ("le roi des Corses, l'empereur de la piastre" [the king of Corsicans, the emperor of the piastre]; Stanislas and Rullier [1992: 3]). His name in the comic (M. Fenucci), his ethnicity (alluded to by a black bust of Napoleon Bonaparte, who was from Corsica, in his office [14]), his wealth and his reputation for currency trafficking and speculation point clearly towards the historical figure after whom he is modeled: Mathieu Franchini, a Corsican who ran the Continental Palace Hotel in Saigon, one of the most important *lieux de mémoire* in comics about French Indochina (cf. Charpier 1984: 24–25; Franchini 1993: 18–20).[48] Fenucci's money from an illegal currency transfer gone awry is recuperated by Victor, allowing him to participate in the same illicit activity until Fenucci realizes what happened and demands reimbursement, forcing Victor to flee Saïgon. Fenucci fades from the plot when he is no longer needed to make things difficult for Victor (Stanislas and Rullier 1992: 27).

The historical events of the war that the cartoonists weave into their narrative play a similar function. These include the activities of Vandenberghe, assassinations organized by the Sûreté, Vietnamese nationalist assassinations of Europeans in Saïgon, a street demonstration by Vietnamese nationalists, and especially the disastrous French withdrawal from Cao Bang and the decimation of the Lepage column. Those events, as well as the comic book characters based on historical figures—Arnaud de Cottigny, Max, Werner, Van Blick and Fenucci—serve a function remarkably similar to that of the events of colonial history in the film *Indochine,* analyzed by Norindr (1996: 137): "What is disturbing, however, is the manner in which 'historical events' are used and framed simply to advance the plot and to play up and render more harrowing the predicament of our 'heroines,' rather than to question French colonial practices." The result is that the comic book uncritically recalls and rehearses colonial icons and ideology, thereby perpetuating them, but without any substantive or sustained critique. History therefore plays the role here of *"effet d'histoire"* [history effect] analyzed by Pierre Fresnault-Deruelle (1979).

It is perhaps through their feminization of Indochina that the cartoonists follow colonial ideology most closely. This is especially evident in the use of prostitutes and other Indochinese women to represent the French defeat as a romantic epic. In the two volumes, the first suggestion of the trope occurs when Arnaud de Cottigny sights Indochina upon his return from France and exults: "Adieu, vieux monde décati! J'abandonne tes femelles austères qui ne boivent ni ne fument! A moi, les petits seins d'encens d'Indochine! Bienvenue au Viêt-Nam!" [Adieu, feeble old world! I abandon your austere females who neither drink nor smoke! To me, the small breasts of incense of Indochina! Welcome to Vietnam!] (30). This echoes the distinction between Odette, the French girlfriend whom Victor abandons, described as average (1990: 9), and Tuyet, the pretty and exotic Vietnamese woman with whom he becomes romantically involved after his arrival in Saïgon (1992: 5, 10). In an *élan* of drunken generosity Victor hires Tuyet, a homeless refugee, although he protests that she will be his maid [domestique], not his con-cubine, when his business partner teasingly suggests that he is purchasing [s'offre] a *congaï* [concubine] (5). When Tuyet begins to recount her story, Victor's impulsive gesture appears even more humanitarian: Tuyet's father was killed by the Communists and her mother subsequently worked her-self to death in a convent, where she had taken refuge. After her mother passed away, the nuns handed her over to the French settlers, the "Letour-nelle, de méchants planteurs" [Letournelles, mean planters], from whom she then fled to Saïgon (5–7). Through Tuyet's narrative, the cartoonists suggest that two pillars of French colonialism, the settler-planters and the religious orders, were abusive to the Vietnamese. By contrast, Victor treats Tuyet much better: he requires very little cleaning work, pays her adequately, and even gives her spending money to gamble at a casino-brothel in Cholon. The jackpot that she wins the first time that she plays provides an auspi-cious sign for their romantic relationship, which they inaugurate the very same evening (6–11). In many ways, the liaison between the two is con-structed as an ideal colonial relationship, as opposed to the bad one that plagued her before. Victor treats Tuyet with apparently benign paternalism, even defending her honor when his business partner suggests that her sexual favors should be available to Victor and his friends (10). Moreover, Tuyet's experiences with both Communists and Catholic nuns have taught her to keep her distance from the rival camps struggling to control the hearts and minds of the Vietnamese. On the other hand, her youthful experiences have provided her with an elegant French appearance: she speaks French fluently and makes herself a beautiful evening gown based on pictures in French magazines that Victor brings home to her. At this point, Tuyet seems to be more than a *congaï*, in the traditional French colonial sense (Cooper 2001: 154–59): she represents a sexualized ideal of secular association between France and Indochina.

Yet Tuyet quickly acquires a penchant for gambling, which makes things go awry—she dilapidates part of the fortune that Victor was amassing through illicit currency speculation and exchange ("le trafic des piastres" [piastre trafficking]). This makes it impossible for Victor to adequately reimburse Fenucci, who unwittingly provided his seed money. From his vantage point twenty years later, Victor wonders about Tuyet's compulsive activity: "Je me demande ce que nous serions devenus si elle n'avait pas pris goût au jeu. . . . Peut-être étais-je trop présent dans son existence. Je décidais de tout, . . . sauf des caprices de la roulette" [I wonder what we would have become if she hadn't taken a liking to gambling. . . . Perhaps I was too present in her life. I decided everything, . . . except for the whims of the roulette] (1992: 11). This is the speculation of colonialist nostalgia: what might have happened to the French-Indochinese relationship if only it had been a bit less constraining for the colonized partner? The cartoonists closely tie the French loss of Indochina to Victor's loss of Tuyet: first she rejects him for the Chinese owner of the casino-brothel and then disappears after Victor's rival is murdered by Vietnamese nationalists (20, 28). Her downward slide is revealed to Victor when he discovers a battle-weary French soldier kissing an autographed picture of Tuyet: "Mais c'est pas eux [les Viets] qui m'empêcheront de te baiser, ma poulette. . . . Tiens, mate ça! Le plus joli cul du Tonkin! . . . Tu la connais, Tuyet? La pute la plus classe de Cao Bang!" [But they (the Viet forces) won't keep me from fucking you, babe. . . . Here, feast your eyes on that! The prettiest ass in Tonkin! . . . Do you know Tuyet? The classiest whore of Cao Bang!] (1992: 35). When Victor finds Tuyet again, she lies mentally deranged and dying (probably of venereal disease) in a brothel in Cao Bang, where the French are besieged by the Viet Minh (38–39). The only people tending to her are an old Vietnamese woman and the soldier Arnaud de Cottigny, who drug her with opium to relieve her pain. Her death coincides with the withdrawal of the French army (40), whose retreating columns are ambushed and defeated by the Viet Minh (41–46).[49] Arnaud disappears in the fighting, but Victor and the other survivors from the French army columns are captured by the Viet Minh and interned (44–45). However, Victor and two colonized soldiers (Moktar, a North African, and Salif, a black African) manage to flee into the jungle and are rescued by a French unit (46–47).[50] From the hospital where he is recuperating, Victor watches American-supplied tanks roll in, as the war effort continues (48). Here as throughout the volume, the cartoonists redraw factual elements in telling ways. For example, the reference to a genuine continuity between French and United States imperialism at the end of the work recalls Fromental's comparison of the two and call for a focus on French colonial history. And the association of Victor and colonized soldiers implicitly looks forward to the ethnic composition of postcolonial France.

The cartoonists suggest that France's love affair with Indochina was foolish and misguided: Victor's voyage to Indochina is a youthful mistake initially motivated by the prospect of easy gains (1990: 13–19); his infatuation with Tuyet leaves him vulnerable to deceiptful manipulation (1992: 25); and his name is an ironic reference to French defeat. The last page of *La route de Cao Bang* comments ironically on the inability of Victor Levallois to recognize history in the making. When he and his photographer friend (the narratee located in the frame narrative) finally manage to fly out of Saigon and arrive in San Francisco in March 1968, they meet a group of peace activists demonstrating against the imperialist American war in Southeast Asia. Victor dismisses the anti-war effervescence on college campuses: "Ça n'arrêtera pas cette guerre, en tout cas . . . " [It won't stop this war, in any case . . .] (1992: 48). Despite this final, knowing wink at the reader, the defeat inflicted on the French outpost in Cao Bang—"KO Kao Bang" [knock-out Cao Bang], to borrow the title of a 1983 song by Indochine—and the illness and death of Tuyet produce no genuine reflection on the systemic injustices and exploitation of French colonialism. Although this is not the place to analyze it, the third volume of the trilogy, *Le manchot de la butte rouge* [The Amputee of the Red Butte] (1994), reworks the early events of the Cold War in France in a similarly uncritical and nostalgic manner.

Remembering anti-colonial struggle in *Les oubliés d'Annam*

C'est que . . . dans nos livres d'histoire, il manque parfois certaines pages!

[It's that . . . in our history books, sometimes certain pages are missing!]
(*Les oubliés d'Annam*, Lax and Giroud 2000: 51)

There is a stark contrast between the comics by Stanislas and Rullier and the two-volume *Les oubliés d'Annam*, by Frank Giroud and Lax (1990, 1991; combined in 2000), whose divergences are all the more striking because the two series, published close together, rework some of the same historical figures and character types from France's war in Indochina. *Les oubliés d'Annam* recounts the search for the hidden history of the conflict as a quest to discover the identity and whereabouts of a French soldier who defected to the Viet Minh. The character who embodies the hermeutical principle of investigating disturbing aspects of colonial history is a left-leaning television reporter named Nicolas Valone (2000: 9, 19). He embarks on his quest after having watched a television news report about the return to France in October 1986 of the remains of French soldiers killed in the war (13–16). He wishes to rehabilitate the memory of some of these soldiers in order to bring history alive. In the end, he produces a television documentary entitled *Les oubliés d'Annam,* just like the comic book that recounts the making of the film. The book is important because it successfully reworks a key trope of anti-colonialist memory also found in another seminal text from popular culture, Didier Daeninckx's *Meurtres pour mémoire* (1994; first published in 1984), a detective novel translated as *Murder in Memoriam* (1991b): the search for the truth about a mysterious colonial past that violently intrudes upon the present. The comic book does so in a way that encourages the reader to reevaluate the stock of colonialist images and narratives about French Indochina found uncritically rehearsed in other French comics about the war. In order to achieve this, the cartoonists borrowed freely and openly from the history of anti-colonial struggle in Indochina as recounted by Doyon (1973) in *Les soldats blancs de Ho Chi Minh* (see above, Figure 1.5). The result is a comic book that—like *Murder in Memoriam*—suggests that the French nation-state bears responsibility for atrocities committed during a colonial war and for subsequently denying them and otherwise blocking or failing to facilitate access to knowledge of the facts.[51] There is a parallel worth making here, between the "counter-*fait divers*" [counter-news item] in nineteenth-century working class newspapers analyzed by Foucault in *Discipline and Punish* (1979: 285–92) and recent works of popular fiction such as *Murder in Memoriam* and *Les oubliés d'Annam:* they are counter-narratives that contest depoliticizing criminalization by the state of acts of resistance by the oppressed, as well as dominant interpretations of history and society (Figure 3.3).

As in Daeninckx's novel, which may well have served as a model for Lax and Giroud, *Les oubliés d'Annam* begins by suggesting a mysterious connection between the memory of past colonial violence and a death in the present. Both works harness the detective novel's hermeneutic for uncovering evidence of a crime to the search for historical truth about colonial torture and murder—and the genocidal killing of Jews, in the novel—for which the French nation-state bears responsibility. A key difference between the two fictions is that whereas Daeninckx has a police inspector conduct much of the investigation, Lax and Giroud use a reporter, which has certain implications for the methods of inquiry, handling of evidence, and end result of the search for facts. For example, whereas Daeninckx's police Inspector Cadin is a narrator who can glean and reveal information provided to him by members of the state's espionnage apparatus (here, the Renseignements Généraux [1994: 72]), the latter is solely a repressive, censurious force in the comic book. There a top member of the Direction Générale de la

Figure 3.3: Visual evidence from a counter-history of anti-colonial commitment: a photograph of a French soldier who rallied to the Viet Minh shows him as a romantic revolutionary. From Lax (art) and Frank Giroud (script), *Les oubliés d'Annam* [The Forgotten Ones from Annam], vol. 2 (Marcinelle: Dupuis, 1991), p. 52. © Lax and Frank Giroud.

Sécurité Extérieure (DGSE), the French equivalent of the CIA, orders wire-tapping of Valone, the murder of his potential informants, the beating of the reporter and the spread of misinformation—all to cover up the role of the official in a war crime that he committed in Indochina.[52] Key pieces of evidence are provided to Valone by a fellow reporter, which helps to under-line the fact that the independence of the news media from abusive state control is necessary to help open up the colonial record. A lack of inde-pendent media sources helps those in power to cover up the sordid history of colonialist and imperialist violence. Refusal of state officials to openly address these issues—whether in the media or in the educational system—lends even greater importance to popular fictions, such as the detective novel and comics, that open up colonial and imperialist history to pub-lic scrutiny and debate. Moreover, the ability to publish or import comics that contest French colonial and imperialist power is relatively recent, for two reasons. First, self-censorship and government censorship in all media forms existed during the colonial period, especially wartime (Stora 1992: 25–73; Stora 1997: 111–25). Second, government censorship of publications for young readers was formally instituted by the law of 16 July 1949 (Crépin and Groensteen 1999; *Neuvième Art* 1999).[53] Although the law is still in effect and the surveillance commission that it created still functions, direct governmental censorship for political reasons has been greatly relaxed over the last several decades.

Les oubliés d'Annam represents historical knowledge about the violent colonial history of the French nation-state as a threat to it today. Ernest Renan describes this danger in well-known passage of his classic discourse on nationalism (Renan 1993: 11; cf. 1947: 891):

> Forgetting, I would even go so far as to say historical error, is a crucial factor in the creation of a nation, which is why progress in historical studies often constitutes a danger for nationality. Indeed, historical enquiry brings to light deeds of violence which took place at the origin of all political formations, even of those whose consequences have been altogether beneficial. Unity is always effected by means of brutality. . . .

Renan's insistence that brutality is essential to the formation of the nation, as well as his mention of supposedly beneficial consequences, suggest that he viewed that originary violence as a necessary evil.[54] However, its victims might not desire to either forget it or view it in this manner (cf. Anderson 1991: 199–206). Many historians have argued that colonial expansion played a key role in the development of modern French nationalism. Important specific examples of this include the substitution or compensation provided by colonial conquests for the lost provinces of Alsace and Lorraine to Germany in 1870 (Pervillé 1993: 45–46; Girardet 1995: 51–75; Ahounou 2001: 149), and French reliance on colonial empire during the two world wars (Girardet 1995: 175–78, 278–88). On the other hand, one finds another originary, national violence in the liberation of French colonies through armed struggle. However, these two forms of violence cannot be equated in a simple manner, because anti-colonial violence is often a desperate response to an initial violence, that of colonization, as Frantz Fanon (1968, 2002) argued in *Les damnés de la terre* [*The Wretched of the Earth*] (cf. Benot 2001: 36–48).

Still, "the progress in historical studies" referred to by Renan can pose a threat to national cohesion in both the country that wins formal independence and the former colonial power, especially insofar as: (1) the struggle or participants in it violated the nation's own foundational principles or values (such as those embodied in the French "Déclaration des droits de l'homme et du citoyen" [Declaration of the rights of man and the citizen], or in its national motto—"liberté, égalité, fraternité" [liberty, equality, fraternity]); (2) there was strong internal resistance to the war, whose most radical expression would be treason, or regarded as such by national and military authorities (examples for France would be Boudarel and similar figures, in the Indochinese War; or the participants in the network of Francis Jeansòn, during the Algerian War); (3) the creation of national unity for the war effort victimized members of the nation; (4) war crimes or crimes against humanity were committed; and (5) evidence of the latter is suppressed by the state. *Les oubliés d'Annam* suggests that all of these were true in the case of France's attempt to retain control of Indochina.[55] Long after the war, the graphic narrative represents the suppression of internal dissent that colonialism required for preserving national unity, by representing a journalist's attempt to uncover and interpret forgotten and hidden historical facts. We can interpret the state television network's refusal to air Valone's documentary at the end of the book to indicate the cartoonists' belief that the state, or powerful agents within it, still considers the widespread knowledge or discussion of French actions during the war to constitute a threat.

In addition, the historian's work (Doyon's book) contributes two other things to the graphic novel: (1) crucial information that the reporter Valone requires to unravel the enigma through which the cartoonists elicit and maintain the interest of the reader; and (2) legitimacy needed by a popular form of fiction, whose status is relatively low in mainstream culture, in order to credibly contradict dominant narratives about colonialism. Lax and Giroud openly acknowledge that the colonial army's efforts to silence anti-colonial resistance within its own ranks have already been challenged by French historians, including Doyon, whose *Les soldats blancs de Ho Chi Minh* is explicitly discussed by characters in *Les oubliés d'Annam* (Lax and Giroud 1990: 37).[56] The cartoonists thereby foreground their efforts to spread anti-imperialist history of the conflict in popular culture. They also encourage their readers to prolong their own investigation of colonial history by reading Doyon's work after having finished the comic book. Moreover, *Les oubliés d'Annam* anticipated wider debate in France about the historical record of the Indochinese war, because the first volume was originally published in October 1990, about six months before the Boudarel Affair made headlines in France. The publisher drew attention to this sequence of events by giving a promotional flyer the bold title "Quand la BD précède l'histoire . . . " [When comics precede history . . .] (Dupuis n.d.).

The specific ways in which Lax and Giroud reworked colonial history and mythology provide a revealing contrast to the treatment of similar material in the graphic narrative by Stanislas and Rullier. Three figures are key to the transformation of colonial material in *Les oubliés d'Annam:* the adventurer, the reporter, and the *métisse*. Here again, we encounter Roger Vandenberghe, the French soldier elevated to the status of legend who is the model for a friendly military adventurer, Van Blick, in *La route de Cao Bang*. However, in *Les oubliés d'Annam* Vandenberghe is transformed into a rather different kind of character, named Roger Corbin. Whereas Vandenberghe was assassinated by the Viet Minh, Corbin survives the war and becomes the high-ranking officer in the DGSE who will stop at nothing to prevent Valone from learning the truth about the past. Corbin tries to hide the fact that he killed several captured Vietnamese soldiers in cold blood and, before that, tortured to death Henri Joubert (nicknamed Riton), an army deserter who had joined the Viet Minh. Although he has strong leftist sympathies, Joubert is significantly different from "le grand Max" [Big Max], the Communist character imagined by Stanislas and Rullier. Joubert becomes simultaneously attracted to Vietnamese culture, embodied especially by a Vietnamese woman named Tú-Anh, and appalled by French military violence against Vietnamese civilians (Figure 3.4). This leads him to switch sides.

In "Quand la réalité dépasse la fiction" [When Reality Surpasses Fiction], Giroud's preface to the second edition of *Les oubliés d'Annam,* he states (2000: 11) that Joubert was partly modeled on the story of Boris, a.k.a. Boudarel, as recounted in *Les soldats blancs de Ho Chi Minh* (Giroud learned that Boudarel was behind the pseudonym only after the Boudarel Affair broke). However, the fictional character Joubert owes at least as much to a French deserter named Chabert in Doyon's history (1973: 173–214). Chabert was apparently vilified by the French army as an archetypal deserter and juxtaposed to the courageous Vandenberghe, who earned nine combat medals. Chabert became known for a series of surprise attacks, in which he was said to pose as a French officer leading a group of colonial soldiers. In fact, although Chabert did indeed participate in at least one such attack, the French army attributed subsequent ones to him, even though he was not involved. The intended effect was to discredit Chabert as the incarnation of treason (Doyon 1973: 191):

> This time, it involved a Frenchman, a real "traitor," who could not be pardoned. Chabert took the form of a state criminal; he became the mythic head of a "band" of deserters that continued to run rampant in the delta according to mess-hall gossip, until 1952 . . . —when he was credited with

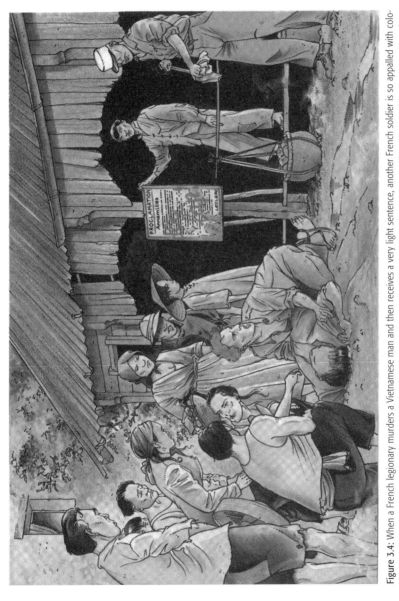

Figure 3.4: When a French legionary murders a Vietnamese man and then receives a very light sentence, another French soldier is so appalled with colonial violence and double standards that he joins the Viet Minh. From Lax (art) and Frank Giroud (script), *Les oubliés d'Annam* [The Forgotten Ones from Annam], vol. 1 (Marcinelle: Dupuis, 1990), p. 47. © Lax and Frank Giroud.

another "strike" in Nam Dinh, whereas he was resting in a camp of Viêt Bac—in the Tonkinese highlands.

The final exploit was the assassination of Vandenberghe at Nam Dinh, allegedly by Chabert, although Chabert later proclaimed his innocence to Doyon (208–14). Blaming Chabert for Vandenberghe's death was a logical conclusion to the official French construction of the two figures as a binary pair, representing evil and good, cowardice and courage, treason and patriotism, although ironically both were credited with similarly deceptive methods of disguise (209):

> The Chabert-Vanden struggle reached its peak in 1951. The two men were talked about in French newspapers. Vanden the hero, the Flemish Asian who, with former "Viets," sowed terror among the "Viets." Chabert, the troubling "deserter," commando leader, "traitor," who closes himself off in the dialectic of the anti-France. . . . These two opposite destinies were seized upon.

Other real-life models for the Henri ("Riton") Joubert character include "Riton" (another of Doyon's research subjects, 153–72), and Erwin Borchers, a German who fled Nazi Germany, joined the French Foreign Legion to avoid being deported back to Germany, but then became the first European to desert the French army and join the Viet Minh, in 1945 (59).

There are several interesting aspects to Lax and Giroud's use of these historical figures (Figure 3.5), both Vandenberghe and the deserters from the French army—called "ralliés" [rallied] by Doyon, because they rallied to the cause of Vietnamese liberation. The first is the extent to which they rewrite colonial mythology. Whereas in reality Vandenberghe died in Vietnam, and Boudarel and Chabert lived to return home to France, the cartoonists instead have Corbin return to France after torturing Joubert to death (Figure 3.6), executing the Viet Minh soldiers accompanying the French *rallié,* and then covering up the crime. In fact, it is questionable whether the French army would have considered this death a crime, given the status of the victims. But what Lax and Giroud have done is to invert a colonial myth in which Vandenberghe is a French patriot and the victim of Chabert, a renegade formerly under Vandenberghe's command. Instead, it is Joubert who maintains the revolutionary ideals of fraternity and freedom from oppression, which he had fought for in the French Resistance as a member of the Communist-affiliated FTP (Francs Tireurs et Partisans [Irregular Soldiers and Partisans]), before deserting the French army to help liberate the Vietnamese. Conversely, in the graphic novel Corbin is a war

Figure 3.5: Two legendary figures from the Indo-chinese War confront each other: when Joubert/Chabert confronts Corbin/Vandenberghe, the latter declares that the former, as a traitor, is no longer French. From Lax (art) and Frank Giroud (script), *Les oubliés d'Annam* [The Forgotten Ones from Annam], vol. 2 (Marcinelle: Dupuis, 1991), p. 18. © Lax and Frank Giroud.

criminal, now comfortably lodged in a state spy apparatus. Their graphic novel redefines the French-Vietnamese affrontier as it was drawn by French officialdom and the mainstream media during the French war in Vietnam.

That the violence of the colonial war continues to wreak havoc on the present is suggested by Corbin's decision to order the murder of the surviving French war veterans who participate in torturing and killing Joubert and

Figure 3.6: A French officer tortures to death a French soldier who deserted to join the Viet Minh, before killing the deserter's Vietnamese comrades and hiding the bodies. From Lax (art) and Frank Giroud (script), *Les oubliés d'Annam* [The Forgotten Ones from Annam], vol. 2 (Marcinelle: Dupuis, 1991), p. 48. © Lax and Frank Giroud.

the Vietnamese soldiers. He endeavors to eliminate them in order to prevent Valone from discovering the damning truth about his past: the pages missing from the history books, to which Valone refers in my epigraph, above. It is an established fact that torture by the French army was widespread during the war in Indochina, despite official denials (Benot 2001: 165–69, 180), and that the French colonial empire, including Indochina, was founded on massacres (Benot 2001: specifically 97–103 for Indochina). Nonetheless, according to historian Yves Benot, even well-reputed French historians of colonialism have tried to ignore or cast doubt on this fact. This is part of a revisionist approach to colonial history, or more accurately, a negationist one, whose proponents try to downplay or even deny the systemic violence of colonization (Benot 2001: ii–iv, xv–xvi, 82, 173–77) and make a rear-guard defense of empire (Flood and Frey 2002). The debate that was reopened in France in 2000, over the use of torture during the Algerian War, needs to be extended to the Indochinese War and beyond, to colonialism and imperialism in general, which are not at all relics of the past (Benot 2001: 178–81). The decision by Lax and Giroud to have Joubert die at the hands of Corbin, instead of the other way around, as colonial mythologists would have had it, serves to foreground the use of torture during the French war in Indochina. The investigative framework of their graphic novel allows them to draw attention to ongoing denial of the initial and persistent violence of French colonialism. The (failed) attempt to bring Boudarel to trial for crimes against humanity in 1991 is but one clear example of the refusal to acknowledge that violence. It also illustrates the fact that the French-Indochinese colonial affrontier, although much weaker than the French-Algerian one, has extended long beyond the end of the war (1954).

Along with its sharp critique of French colonialism, *Les oubliés d'Annam* also contains some elements that surprisingly echo what we have already seen in the Victor Levallois series, by Stanislas and Ruller. For example, the two graphic novels share various narrative devices for evoking the end of the direct colonial relationship: an unexpected viewing of images provokes a traumatic reliving of events from the war; a voyage by a reporter (Victor; Nicolas) to Vietnam at a later period, after the French withdrawal, enables reconnection with a severed past; and the interrogation of direct participants in the events to reconstruct them and try to make sense of the past. There is also a romantic aura of adventure surrounding Henri Joubert, symbolized by his physical appearance: he is red-headed (like Nicolas Valone) and wears a blood-red headband, representing his revolutionary activity and martyrdom (Lax and Giroud 2000: 79–82, 109–11). It is perhaps a perverse comparison to make, but one cannot help but note one similarity between him and Arnaud de Cottigny, despite the fact that they represent antagonistic points of view: both characters embody a robust French masculinity destroyed during the war. The two men are also closely associated with Vietnamese women: in *La route de Cao Bang*, when Victor finally discovers Tuyet, Arnaud is taking care of her; and Joubert falls in love with and marries Tú Anh, a Vietnamese woman (74, 82). The death of both women is associated with war: Tuyet's life ends just as the French are about to retreat hastily from Cao Bang (40), and Tú Anh perishes in 1975, during the last fighting against the United States troops (73). However, Tuyet is a prostitute who leaves no descendants, whereas the nationalist fighter Tú Anh gives birth to Kim-Chi, a *métisse,* whom Valone virtually adopts as his own daughter by the end of novel. This lends a physical continuity to the connection that Lax and Giroud try to establish between French Indochina and present-day France. Valone ends up bringing Kim-Chi to France to unite her with Joubert's mother (her French grandmother; 98–99). The authors make the link in other ways too. For example they proclaim that despite having been renamed Ho Chi Minh City, "dans le coeur de chacun, l'ancienne capitale reste toujours SAIGON" [in each person's heart, the former capital forever remains SAIGON]. Moreover, the first Vietnamese person that Valone meets in Vietnam is a product of the French school system (65–66).

All of the elements just mentioned have clear roots in the colonial era. The francophone status of Vietnam remains a factor in the relationship between the two countries. The romantic aura of adventure surrounding Joubert was borrowed from descriptions by Doyon of part of what attracted French *ralliés* to the cause of the Viet Minh. The feminized representation of Indochina was a cliché of the colonial era. Moreover, the *métis/ se* was a key, pivotal figure in French Indochina (Gantès 2006), leaving an imprint on colonial fiction (Ruscio 1996), and even on Doyon's history of the *ralliés*—here, for example, is how he describes a daughter of Chabert: "Sa fille aînée, une jolie Eurasienne de seize ans, aux longs cheveux qui lui descendent jusqu'aux reins, le regard effronté, vient se blottir comme une chatte auprès de lui" [His oldest daughter, a pretty Eurasian of sixteen, with long hair that falls down the length of her back, with a brazen look, comes and cuddles up like a cat next to him] (206). In *Les oubliés d'Annam,* the cartoonists redeploy these elements within an anti-colonialist framework that inflects their meaning away from the colonial values formerly attributed to them. Turning now to a graphic novel about the beginnings of the twentieth-century nationalist movement in Vietnam, we find a *métis* figure who embodies even more strongly the ambivalence of a critique of colonialism mixed with an attraction for a lost colonial milieu of cultural mixing.

Visiting Hanoi and leaving Saïgon

Clément Baloup has drawn or scripted some of the most fascinating French
comics about Vietnam and the Vietnamese, in stories set in the 1920s up
through the present. In significant ways, his work represents a continuation
of the stories about Vietnamese resistance to French domination drawn by
Truong, who has since left cartooning and now works as a book illustrator.
There are also important similarities between *Les oubliés d'Annam,* by Lax
and Giroud, and comics by Baloup and Mathieu Jiro, his co-author on several works: for example, their critiques of French and American imperialism
in Vietnam do not prevent them from criticizing the rigidity and the repression of the post-colonial, Communist regime. In *Le chemin de Tuan* [Tuan's
Way] (2005), set in Marseille and Paris during the 1920s, Baloup and Jiro
depict colonial subjects engaged in anti-colonial activities within the colonial metropolis.[57] The artists went on to publish a sequel, *Le choix de Hai*
[Hai's Choice] (2007), where we find Hai, one of the protagonists of *Le
chemin de Tuan,* who has returned from Paris to the south of Vietnam. The
story begins in 1945, at the outset of the Indochinese War. We learn that
between the two episodes Hai spent time in the Soviet Union, where disillusionment with Stalinist methods led him to abandon its version of Com-
munism and join the Trotskyists (58). The political orientation of Hai and
the focus on this period of history allow the cartoonists to show the struggle between different political parties and tendencies within the Vietnamese
nationalist struggle against the French, during the transition from Japanese defeat to French reconquest, via the proclamation by Ho Chi Minh of
Vietnam's independence. *Le choix de Hai* might remind us of *La condition
humaine* [Man's Fate] (Malraux 1982), first published in 1933 and set in
China (but with references to French Indochina), which recounts a similar
struggle for power between non-Communist nationalists, Communists and
(especially French) imperialists at a historically significant moment.

As in Malraux's novel, *Le choix de Hai* examines the place of women
in a revolutionary struggle. Thi Mung is a young Vietnamese woman
who leaves the Trotskyists when Hai treats her contemptuously and she is
accused of spying on them (32–34). She temporarily joins Ho Chi Minh's
party and tries to assassinate Hai when the Communists ask her to do so
to prove her loyalty (36–39). After failing to kill her former leader, she
ends up helping him to remain hidden from both the Communists and the
French, and even has sex with him. However, to help Hai, Thi temporarily
abandons an elderly family member whom she was taking care of, and he
dies (69–71). The changing allegiances of Thi, her courage and determination to survive, and the cowardice of Hai—who stays in hiding while his

followers are decimated by the Communists, determined to take control of the nationalist movement in southern Vietnam—illustrate the fluidity of identities during this period of national crisis, which destabilizes traditional social structures and gender roles. At the end of the book, Hai chooses to escape from Saigon with Thi, but dies before he can leave, the victim of a blast from a booby-trapped cadaver (Figure 3.7), which he had thought was perhaps Diem (88–92), a former Trotskyist leader who had betrayed his comrades and joined the Viet Minh (56). The story ends when Thi and Moteki—a shell-shocked Japanese soldier who wanders through the narrative like a zombie, witnessing the madness and destruction of the war, and even attempting to protect others, including Thi and Hai, from the cadaver-bombs—are led away by a French unit of Vietnamese soldiers.

Here, as in *Le chemin de Tuan,* the cartoonists use some striking, nontraditional cartooning techniques to show and tell their story. In both books the artists dispense almost entirely with *récitatifs* [textual narration] on their drawn and painted pages, by inserting a short explanatory text at the beginning of each chapter, which provides background information on characters and situates the action with respect to historical events. The artists also use symbolism to denote the hallucinatory, predatory nature of the war: Moteki watches a tiger walk out of an alleyway in war-torn Saigon to catch a fleeing rat and then disappear again (47–48; cf. 15–17). The tiger in *Le choix de Hai* may remind us of the wild cats in the wartime-era comics "Bernard Chamblet: En mission au pays jaune" (two tigers) and "Parachutés au Laos" (Kao, the panther).[58] However, the animal can symbolize the wartime violence of French forces as much as that of the Japanese occupiers and Vietnamese nationalists, because the animal appears just as the French begin to retake the city (Figure 3.8), indiscriminately rounding up and beating civilians who proclaim their innocence. In similar ways Baloup and Jiro create viewpoints at once subjective and historical: for example, a mute, nine-frame sequence composed with black, white and red paint evokes the assassinations of rival nationalists by the Viet Minh—the framing of the sequence suggests that Hai is imagining it (28–29). Later, drunk and prey to intense feelings of anxiety and guilt, Hai sees dragons and soldiers wearing masks, which seem to emerge from the decor of the temple where he is hiding (60–61). Subsequently, when Thi appears to see a beheaded statue, a dragon shape and then a crow (75; cf. 67, 69), we cannot help but wonder whether these are hallucinations too. In any case they symbolize the death and destruction afoot in the city. Another sequence uses framing to represent the erasure of personal identity within the Communist party. On a nine-panel page, where Communists decide to test Thi's commitment to them by asking her to kill her former leader, Hai, the only face that we see in its

Figure 3.7: Thi Mung and Moteki look on in horror as Hai, a former Trotskyist leader, turns over a booby-trapped body in Saigon, which French colonial forces are retaking after the Japanese defeat in the Second World War. From Clément Baloup (script) and Mathieu Jiro (art), *Chinh Tri*, vol. 2: *Le choix de Hai* [Politics: Hai's Choice] (Paris: Le Seuil, 2007), p. 91. © Clément Baloup, Mathieu Jiro and Le Seuil.

Figure 3.8: Communist and nationalist Vietnamese guerillas fight French forces retaking control of Saigon in September 1945 and brutalizing civilians as they do so. From Clément Baloup (script) and Mathieu Jiro (art), *Chinh Tri*, vol. 2: *Le choix de Hai* [Politics: Hai's Choice] (Paris: Le Seuil, 2007), p. 50. © Clément Baloup, Mathieu Jiro and Le Seuil.

entirety is Thi's. All the others are amputated at the top or framed from an angle that prevents us from seeing them, suggesting a reified violence (36). The willingness of the Communists to dehumanize and crush their nationalist rivals, even when they share similar goals and beliefs (the Vietnamese Trotskyists), is symbolized on the page by a man's foot crushing an insect at the same time that a Communist leader asks Thi to find and help destroy Hai, as "un agent du fascisme" [an agent of fascism]—the language suggests the ideologically motivated squashing of Hai's political identity.

In *La concubine rouge* (2012), Baloup and Jiro return to the Indochinese War, this time reworking various figures seen in earlier works too, including the French Communist who sympathizes with the Vietnamese independence cause (15–17, 61–64, 78–83), the Vietnamese-French *métis* as a liminal figure relegated to a subaltern position by the French (21, 34, 103–4), and the eponymous Communist "red concubine" who seduces a French officer in an isolated and besieged military outpost (cf. Bucquoy and Sels 1990). In this work the mixed couple composed of a Vietnamese Communist woman and a French soldier who sympathizes with the Vietnamese independence movement is of short duration and produces no children. Their separation foreshadows the French withdrawal from Vietnam. The physical and moral disfiguration of a ruthless *métis* soldier in the French army represents the colonial influence as a perverse one. By contrast, as we have seen in *Les oubliés d'Annam*, but also in *Dans la nuit la liberté nous écoute* (Le Roy 2011), the mixed couple composed of a French *rallié* and a Vietnamese woman produces a daughter who moves to France, symbolizing a positive post-colonial connection.

In other works, Baloup too investigates post-colonial connections between France and Vietnam. In his *Un automne à Hànôi* [An Autumn in Hanoi] (2004), about his internship at the fine arts school of Hanoi, and *Quitter Saigon: Mémoires de Viet Kieu* [Leaving Saigon: Memories of Viet Kieu] (2006, 2010), where he retells the stories of Vietnamese exiles and expatriates in France (including his own father), he applies similar colors and composition techniques. He uses color expressively: for example, dramatic reds—in single, final panels that follow a series of panels in drab colors—accentuate the violence of a young girl killing a helpless chick (Baloup 2004: 11), or of Americans leaving behind their panic-stricken Vietnamese employees and advisees in April 1975, despite having promised to bring them along upon withdrawal from the country (Baloup 2006: 23; 2010: 26). These comics, as was the case in *Le chemin de Tuan* and *Le choix de Hai*, give us the perspective of Vietnamese or French-Vietnamese protagonists, including Baloup himself, through subjective elements such as ocularization, where the reader is put in the viewing position of a character (cf.

Miller 2007: 91–94). For example, when an American soldier pledges to remain faithful to his protégés, Baloup presents him looking straight at the reader-viewer, and zooms in on his face from one frame to the next—this places us in the position of the South Vietnamese to whom he makes the promise, soon to be broken (Figure 3.9). Even if one allows for a difference in cartooning techniques due to genre and generation, this represents a radical change from colonial-era comics about French Indochina, which consistently gave the perspective of French colonizers.[59]

Métissage, whether political or ethno-cultural, is a recurring theme in the comics of Baloup, both his single-authored works and those made with Jiro. Although in *Le chemin de Tuan* Hai is alienated by condescending and racist treatment that he receives in France, in *Le choix de Hai* he insists on the French origins of some of his ideas of liberation, when Thi dismisses all French as cruel (Baloup and Jiro 2007: 58). In the first story of *Quitter Saigon: Mémoires de Viet Kieus* we see "Marseille" emblazoned on the bright yellow tee shirt of Baloup (Baloup 2006: 14–15; 2010: 18–19). This is an hommage to the multicultural city (France's third largest) that the artist has adopted as his home, and which the opening passages of *Le chemin de Tuan* depict in the 1920s, as a colonial port where Vietnamese students arrive in France (Baloup and Jiro 2005: 14–27; see also McKinney 2011b: 104). In the first story of *Quitter Saigon: Mémoires de Viet Kieus,* yellow is a dominant color in the preparation of a Vietnamese dish, "crevettes au carry" [shrimp curry], that Baloup's father teaches his son to make in the frame narrative, just as his own father had taught him in Japanese-occupied Vietnam, in the embedded story.

Yellow gains another layer of symbolic significance in the third story, about André, a Vietnamese man now living near Paris: "Enfant, j'étais blond avec les yeux verts-bleus. Mes parents sont vietnamiens, bruns aux yeux noirs, mais comme j'ai un grand-père français, les gènes ont dû ressortir" [As a child, I was blond with blue-green eyes. My parents are Vietnamese, dark haired with black eyes, but because I have a French grandfather, the genes must have come out again] (Baloup 2006: 42; 2010: 44). Yellow is the color that Baloup paints André's childhood hair, where it is the only hue other than the blue-greys and blacks of the embedded narrative—here it moves from being a marker of Asian identity to serving as a symbol of an atavistic French identity with an ambivalent status. André explains that his mother refused to cut his long blond hair, even though he asked her to do so because other children taunted him (they called him a girl). Other Vietnamese women admired it too: "Les voisines s'extasient sur moi, ressembler à un occidental est visiblement à la mode" [The neighbor women admire me. Looking like a westerner is clearly in fashion]. This acceptance and even

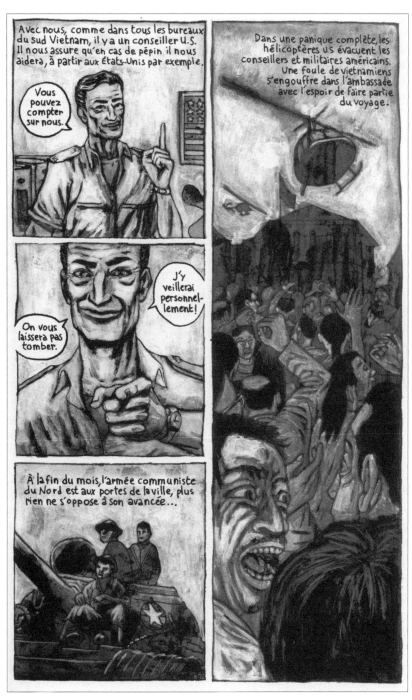

Figure 3.9: A Vietnamese man or Viet Kieu now living in France recounts the taking of Saigon by Communist forces in April 1975: Baloup juxtaposes the promise of an American advisor not to let down his advisees and, on the right, the anguish of Vietnamese abandoned by the American advisors and soldiers leaving the city in a panic in helicopters. From Clément Baloup, *Quitter Saigon: Mémoires de Viet Kieus* [Leaving Saigon: Memories of Viet Kieus] (Antony: La Boîte à Bulles, 2006), p. 23. © Clément Baloup and La Boîte à Bulles.

admiration of physical *métissage* by a Vietnamese family and friends is a far cry from the dystopian image of colonial-era literature, but fits with the evidence of how ethnically mixed children were actually treated by Vietnamese society (Franchini 1993; Gantès 2006; Saada 2007). By contrast, during the Second World War, Japanese soldiers occupying Saigon twice attempt to catch the boy to imprison him, because his blond hair makes them think that he is not Vietnamese, but white (46–51). Ironically, he must wear a colonial pith helmet to hide his hair color (Figure 3.10), during his trip out of occupied Saigon, to safety with relatives in the countryside (52–56). This provides the cover image of the book. However, it is André's second departure from Saigon, in 1961 when he is a twenty-one year old university student, that leads to a less superficial form of *métissage*. His parents send him away to France to escape the repression of the Diem government (59–62). Although he does not realize it at the time, this becomes a permanent move, in part because of the regime change in 1975 (69–70).

The use of color by Baloup, and by Jiro too, is related to aesthetic considerations, ethnic ones (such as *métissage*) and narrative ones. The cartoonists (2007: 40) cite specific painters in their presentation of Donald, a failed British painter who is a friend of Hai and resides in France: "L'inspiration n'étant pas au rendez-vous et la guerre s'approchant à grands pas, Donald décide d'aller chercher la lumière de la Provence à l'instar de Van Gogh, Gauguin ou encore Braque qui y ont trouvé l'épanouissement plastique que l'on sait" [Since inspiration did not come knocking and the war is approaching with great strides, Donald decides to go look for the light of Provence, like Van Gogh, Gauguin or Braque, who blossomed there in artistic terms, as we know]. The vibrant hues in the books analyzed here evoke impressionist and fauvist paintings. Baloup's beautiful images of flowers and gardens in Provence form the backdrop—tending towards abstract patterns—for the frame narrative of a story about a political refugee in *Quitter Saigon* (2006: 20–21, 37–38; 2010: 23–24, 40–41). They suggest an influence from the European painters cited above (one thinks too of Matisse), but also recall the tropical luxuriance of Vietnam: Baloup makes a transition from inner to frame narrative via bright red and yellow drawings of orchids against the otherwise drably colored Communist past recounted by Baloup's interviewee. In *Le choix de Hai,* Baloup and Jiro indirectly point to another source of artistic inspiration for their work when they refer to the color schemes of traditional Vietnamese art and the failure of the French school system to recognize its value (76):

La lumière que cherche Donald pour réveiller son talent est peut-être celle du sud-est asiatique. Les couleurs saturées et criardes y forment parado-

Figure 3.10: A Vietnamese boy with a French grandfather must hide his blond hair under a colonial helmet as he leaves Saigon, accompanied by his cousin, to avoid capture and imprisonment by the occupying Japanese army during the Second World War. Here they walk past the French-built city hall. From Clément Baloup, *Quitter Saigon: Mémoires de Viet Kieus* [Leaving Saigon: Memories of Viet Kieus] (Antony: La Boîte à Bulles, 2006), p. 53. © Clément Baloup and La Boîte à Bulles.

xalement une harmonie délicate. L'art traditionnel vietnamien l'a déjà compris depuis longtemps et tandis que les peintures à la laque brillent de couleurs incandescentes, les peintures sur soie dégagent une enveloppante douceur nacrée. Ce qui n'empêche pas l'administration scolaire française d'écraser l'art traditionnel pour inculquer les standards académiques européens aux Indochinois.

[Perhaps the light that Donald is looking for, to awaken his talent, is that of Southeast Asia. Saturated and shrill colors paradoxically form a delicate harmony there. Traditional Vietnamese art understood that long ago, and while lacquer paintings shine with incandescent colors, paintings on silk give off an enveloping, pearly softness. That does not prevent the French school administration from crushing traditional art in order to inculcate European academic standards in the Indochinese.]

In "Xin Chào" and "L'école, rue Yê't Kiêu," the first two stories in *Un automne à Hànôi*, Baloup shows himself perfecting his artistic techniques at the fine arts school of Hanoi. His first work there is a tongue-in-cheek version of French-Vietnamese art—"'la condition du touriste' ou comment faire du joli avec du vomi" ["the tourist condition" or how to make something pretty with vomit] (4–5): the striking image shows him spewing out a firey red and bright yellow stream, after having fallen ill upon arriving in the city. The multi-armed goddess on his head and the dragon on his stomach give a Vietnamese touch to the drawing. In the second story, he has trouble learning how to efficiently apply the final layer of lacquer to his painting, in the traditional Vietnamese way. These elements all point towards an important truism: that cultural identity and artistic production are not inherited traits, but instead are learned. It appears that the bright colors used by both Baloup and Jiro are indebted to this double source of inspiration, from France and Vietnam. Among European cartoonists, the Italian artist Lorenzo Mattotti springs to mind as a possible influence on the cartoonists, for their use of color.

Baloup has also incorporated elements from mangas into his comics: for example, in one frame he blocks out his eyes with a black cloud to indicate that he is angry or dismayed (2004: 23.6). In another, he represents a murderer as a demon (31.7).[60] Michel Laronde (1993: 183–85) labels the adoption of North African or Arab cultural or artistic practices by French of North African background as "neo-orientalism." The drawback of this usage of the term is that it carries strong negative connotations of othering and cultural alienation (cf. Said 1994a), despite Laronde's insistence on more or less freely chosen cultural hybridity by descendants of groups that have been "orientalized" in the past, leading me to reject it here (I use it in a different way, above, pp. 75–77, 138). On the other hand, the mixing of artistic influences from East and West certainly has a long lineage in Europe (MacKenzie 1995). France has historically benefitted from the influx of foreign artists from many countries (e.g., Kaspi and Marès 1989). The comics of Baloup and Jiro, Truong and Séra are in some ways a continuation of that mixed artistic heritage. What is new in the comics of French artists of Southeast Asian background, and their artistic collaborators (here, Jiro), is both their remixing of specific cultural influences, and their choice to use their art to reread the history of colonialism and imperialism in the region, and its impact on France (through immigrants and exiles), in ways far different from the traditional French presentation of *l'Indochine française* in comics. This represents a radical break from the past.

Conclusion

We have seen that colonial-era French comics about the Indochinese War are characterized by their French partisanship: they condemn and caricature the Communist nationalists among the indigenous peoples of French Indochina and are unremittingly on the side of France's army and its colonial project. Their colonial manicheism is evident in the racist imagery, slurs and ideology about Asians that they spread, even in the case of "Parachutés au Laos," which presents Méos and other ethnic minorities positively, but not other Asian groups. As Guillemin (2006: 177) notes, the Japanese are unremittingly cruel and ugly in the story (cf. Baloup 2006: 44–54; 2010: 47–56), and I have shown how Kao, the panther, expresses an indiscriminate aggression against the Vietnamese. There is a clear break between those comics and several of the post-colonial ones that we have seen. Some cartoonists today stand colonial representation on its head: for example, Grégory Jarry and Otto T., in their mordantly satirical, multi-volume *Petite histoire des colonies françaises* [A Short History of the French Colonies] (2006–11), whose title is borrowed from a 1941 volume by French colonial authority and administrator Robert Delavignette.[61] There, French colonialism is no longer the vaunted civilizing mission, but a long history of rape, massacre and economic exploitation. In their recounting of the French defeat at Dien Bien Phu (Figure 3.11), they lampoon the colonial comics image of the French soldier as hero (Jarry and Otto T. 2009: n.p.). In works as different as *Le dragon de bambou* (Truong and Leroi 1991), *Les oubliés d'Annam* (Lax and Giroud 1990, 1991), *Le choix de Hai* (Baloup and Jiro 2007), and *Quitter Saigon: Mémoires de Viet Kieu* (Baloup 2006, 2010),

Figure 3.11: A satirical take on the French soldier as colonial hero: during the French defeat at Dien Bien Phu in Vietnam, parachutist Marcel Bigeard captures a medal, airdropped by the French, from Vietnamese soldiers hoping to find cans of *cassoulet* [beans and meat] or bottles of wine. His bravery is duly rewarded. From Grégory Jarry and Otto T., *Petite histoire des colonies françaises*, vol. 3: *La décolonisation* [A Short History of the French Colonies: Decolonization], colors by Lucie Castel and Guillaume Heurtault (Poitiers: FLBLB, 2009), n.p. © Grégory Jarry, Otto T. and Editions FLBLB.

we find robust critiques of various foreign imperialisms in Southeast Asia (French, Japanese and American) that do not always spare anti-colonial figures either, whether French (e.g., the Malraux couple) or Southeast Asian (e.g., the character Hai and rival Vietnamese nationalists). These activists are sometimes depicted as ineffectual in their anti-colonial activities and prone to human failings and contradictions. Some comics, drawn by authors from France and elsewhere, and published in France, focus on American imperialist intervention in Southeast Asia, for example, Dutch cartoonist Jack Staller published *Après la guerre* [After the War] (1993), which features Viet Minh agents, American soldiers and intelligence officers, and a disabused French officer, and ends with the French bombing of Haïphong in 1946 (cf. Benot 2001: 97–113). Spanish cartoonist Manfred Sommer drew *Viet-Song* (1989), featuring an American reporter who witnesses the crimes of both American and Viet Minh soldiers. And "Le meurtrier de Hùng" ["The Murderer of Hung"] a comic scripted by Dominique Grange (1985, 1991), drawn by Jacques Tardi and first published in 1982 in a special issue of *L'écho des savanes* [The Echo of the Savannahs] on New York, recounts the aftermath of the Vietnam War as a post-war search by a Vietnamese woman immigrant in New York for the American soldier who raped her and killed Hùng, her infant son. Comics in French sometimes also incorporate critiques of the post-imperialist regimes in Vietnam and Cambodia, including regime-mandated artistic models and policies (Baloup 2004: 6). The multi-volume depiction by Séra (1995, 2003, 2005, 2007, 2011) of the Khmer Rouge genocide, its prelude and aftermath, constitutes one of the most extensive and artistically accomplished of these representations (other work by him also evokes the genocide and Western imperialism in Cambodia, through violence and the uncanny; e.g., Séra and Saimbert [2001–3]). *Le dragon vert* [The Green Dragon] (Wasterlain 1987), serialized in 1982, contains one of the earliest critical depictions of Pol Pot, renamed Pô Potte, and his criminal regime (cf. Douvry 1991: 72–73).

The interest in autochtonous ethnic minorities found in "Parachutés au Laos" (Verdon and Perrin-Houdon 1951–52) recurs in comics produced decades after the French defeat: *Le dragon de bambou* (Truong and Leroi 1991), *L'ombre du triangle* (Christin and Aymond 1999), *Piège en forêt Moï* [Trap in the Moï Forest] (Bartoll and Coyère 2007) and *Le temple de l'épouvante* (Chapelle, Marniquet and Chanoinat 2009). These groups continue to serve in French comics as a source of cultural marginality, exotic local color and connection with nature, but also as potential allies of outsiders. Baloup provides a fascinating, critical twist on this motif in *Un automne à Hànôi* (2004: 30–35), by representing the government requirement for Vietnamese art students to visit ethnic minorities once a year, "pour mettre en valeur la campagne et la diversité culturelle du pays" [to give importance to the countryside and the cultural diversity of the country] (30), as producing a nightmarish trip for Hoa, a Vietnamese art student. She comes face to face in the highland forest with a local sexual predator and murderer, who is also the local official of the Communist party. By contrast, in *Little Saigon: Mémoires de Viet Kieu* (Baloup 2012: 161–63), the hatred of a Moï man for the Communist regime leads him to help two women escape from a prison camp and back to Saigon.

Colonial-era eroticism is another type of fascination with French Indochina that links present-day comics and the colonial era. However, this time the connection is not so much with *comics* from the past, which were aimed at young readers and—we have seen—sometimes published by the Catholic church, but instead with other aspects of colonial culture, including songs (Ruscio 2001; Liauzu and Liauzu 2002), prose fiction (cf. Ruscio 1996: 9–38; 431–592) and caricature (Joyeux 1912; Vann and Montague 2008; Vann 2009). With the post-1968 relaxing of censorship on comics, and the creation of a market for comics with adult themes—even when they are read by adolescents—there has been an importing of colonial-era eroticism into comics about French Indochina. This means that the theme of the Indochinese mistress or *congaï* of Frenchmen has made a strong comeback, but now in *comics* about French Indochina. Others depict amorous or sexual relations between, on the one hand, Southeast Asian or *métis* men and, on the other hand, French women: for example, Marcel Clément-Rivière and Yvonne Beauprée in *Le dragon de bambou;* or, in *Le chemin de Tuan* (2005), Hai and a French woman whom he meets in a jazz club called La Boîte Nègre [The Negro Club] in Paris (62–73), and Tuan with a French prostitute in Marseille (22–26).

Curiously, the parents of French-Vietnamese offspring are glaringly absent from most of the comics by Truong and Baloup, despite the presence of *métis* offspring of mixed couples—for example, Baloup (2006: 16; 2010: 20) ends the first story of *Quitter Saigon: Mémoires de Viet Kieus* with the following words, spoken by his father: "Une fois guéri je suis parti chercher du travail à Paris. Et j'y ai rencontré ta mère. . . . Enfin ça, c'est une autre histoire" [When I was well again I went to find work in Paris. And there I met your mother. . . . Well, that's another story]. It is as though the mixed couple, still so much part of the exotic décor of comics about France's relation to Indochina, were too private a matter to be shared with outsiders, when it directly concerns the authors of semi-autobiographical comics. This may constitute a form of resistance to the exoticizing, orientalizing gaze that still exists in French culture and comics, and to the language of empire that often figured the relationship of the French *métropole* [metropolis] to its colonies in terms of couples (Ross 1996: 123–26).

A sub-genre of contemporary comics about post-independence Vietnam and Cambodia mixes tourist travel narrative and reportage, often expressed in exotic, erotic and feminized terms, with references to the French colonial past, sometimes in ironic terms: *Livre vert: Vietnam* [Green Book: Vietnam], by Swiss cartoonist Wazem (1997), *Les fantômes de Hanoï* [The Phantoms of Hanoi] (Gorridge 2006), by a Frenchman who teaches cartooning in Angoulême, and *Yêu Yêu Saigon,* by Belgian cartoonist Eco (2009).[62] The eroticism, exoticism, colonial nostalgia and post-colonial irony of some of these works are also found in many French comics about Algeria, but a significant difference between the two groups is that French comics on Algeria are usually set in colonial times. The rare exceptions recounting a post-colonial trip to Algeria are not usually by cartoonists as ordinary tourists, as one can find for Southeast Asia, but instead by those of *Pied-Noir*[63] or Algerian heritage making a kind of pilgrimage or return, in the sense that Fernando Ainsa (1982) describes for the offspring of immigrants: for example, in *Gags à l'harissa* [Hot Sauce Jokes] (Boudjellal 1989), *Les Slimani* [The Slimani] (Boudjellal 2003), *Retours à Alger* [Returns to Algiers] (Ferrandez 2006) and *D'Algérie* [About/From Algeria] (Morvandiau 2007). As I noted in the introduction to this chapter, French cartoonists of Southeast Asian heritage—including Séra, Baloup and Tian—have made similar returns.

In the introduction to this chapter I mentioned the absence of a large settler community forced to move from Southeast Asia to France at the end of the colonial period, compared to the *Pieds-Noirs* for Algeria, and the consequent absence of cartoonists from French settler families in Indochina. As a result the French-Indochinese colonial affrontier in and around comics is generally less hardened, conflictual (fewer *affrontements* [confrontations]) and polarized than the French-Algerian one is in terms of nationalist and ethnic positions, for example between an unapologetically pro-French-Algeria stance right after the war (Coral 1962, 1964) or much more recently (Joyaux-Brédy and Joux, ca. 1993–98) and, on the other hand, a resolutely pro-independence and anti-French one, as in comics about the Algerian War published by Algerian cartoonists in the 1970s and 1980s (cf. McKinney 2007a, 2008c). Nor are there works about Indochina by cartoonists of colonial settler heritage who might both recognize the legitimacy of the anti-colonial struggle for independence and try to negotiate between settler and indigenous positions along the colonial affrontier, as do Ferrandez, Mérezette, Sibran, Sfar and Morvandiau for the French-Algerian encounter. The affrontier is therefore generally less complex for Indochina than for Algeria in terms of ethnic texture and the range of positions on colonial society taken by artists. Some French cartoonists continue to exploit and recirculate colonial clichés about *l'Indochine*. However, an increasing number of books, especially those (co-)authored by cartoonists of Southeast Asian heritage, but also some by ethnic mainstream French cartoonists, provide a rich and fascinating reevaluation of that historical and cultural heritage.

4
THE ALGERIAN WAR AND ITS AFTERMATH

RAS[1]:
The slow arrival of the Algerian War on the French comics scene

> It is notable that it will have taken 28 years (!) to read a comic book that deals directly with the Algerian War. Is this an isolated work, or are we going to witness a blossoming of the subject? Personally, I would lean toward the first proposition. (Douvry 1983: 36)

> We are still waiting, and we can wait a long time, for a significant French output of comics on the Algerian War. (Basfao 1990: 28)

As one of the most violent and protracted decolonization conflicts, the Algerian War would seem to offer a rich subject matter for comic books. However, writing in 1990, Kacem Basfao observes that the preceding colonial period—stretching from France's initial invasion of Algeria in 1830 until the outbreak of the war on 1 November 1954—is a theme of predilection for French cartoonists, whereas the war (1954–62) is much more of a theme in Algerian comics (cf. Douvry 1983). He credits this remarkable dichotomy to the blinding effects of opposing nationalist biases in Algerian and French historical viewpoints. On the Algerian side one finds, first, the central role that heroic discourses about the Algerian War have played in politics and society, especially through the Front de Libération Nationale

[National Liberation Front] (FLN), the revolutionary group that initiated the insurrection, won the war and ruled the country for approximately three decades after independence. There is also a concurrent downplaying of the importance of French rule and the colonial period as a basis for the Algerian nation or an important source of its distinct cultural and national character today (cf. Douglas and Malti-Douglas 1994: 182–84).

Inversely, the French have long tended to discount or ignore the Algerian War and their loss. During the war, some editorial cartoonists denounced it in political cartoons that were at times censored, no doubt especially those of far-left and far-right cartoonists critical of the government's conduct of the war (Siné 1965, 1992; Gervereau 1992: 182–89). And with a few significant exceptions, from the outbreak of the Algerian War until 1979, it was almost non-existent as a theme in French comics, usually appearing only briefly and often in veiled terms, sometimes anachronistically. For example, Douvry (1983) mentions *La francisque et le cimeterre* [The Hatchet and the Scimitar] (Sirius and Snoeck 1987; serialized 1959–60), which recounts a conflict between Europeans and Sarrasins in a medieval past, and *Matricule 45000* [Roll Number 45000], a science-fiction story about a war set in a North African landscape sometime in the future (Andrevon and Veronik 1982; cf. Andrevon and Veronik 1985).[2] In French society more generally, the Algerian War was for a long time a "war without a name," referred to mainly through euphemisms—as "pacification," "troubles," "événements" [events]—that masked its violence and nationalist character.[3] By contrast, French cartoonists often emphasized the preceding period of colonial rule as a time of exotic adventure. This dichotomy divides the comics produced in the two countries along a French-Algerian affrontier.

However, there are French comics today, years after the observations by Douvry and Basfao, that represent a wide array of perspectives on the war. Several factors have contributed to this change. First, a significant amount of time has now passed since the war, allowing people slowly to come to terms with its meaning for them as individuals but also as members of ethnic and political groups positioned differently with respect to the conflict. As state surveillance and censorship of comics have progressively diminished, comics have increasingly thematized the war. In addition to wartime censorship that operated across French media—film, books, newspapers, etc. (Stora 1992: 25–73; Liauzu and Liauzu 2003)—censorship of sensitive current events in comics long existed via the 1949 law on youth publications (Crépin and Groensteen 1999). However, the influence in France of the U.S. underground comics movement (Robert Crumb, Spain, Art Spiegelman, etc.) helped create a field of adult comics, whose existence Douvry (1983:

35) specifically mentions as a condition allowing the publication of the first mainstream comic about the war.

The appearance in France of cartoonists from minorities whose members played a key role in imperialism, colonialism and decolonization has also helped bring these themes forward in recent decades. Such groups include the *Pied-Noir* settler minority, which was produced by the mixing of many different national, religious and ethnic groups in colonial Algeria. The second major one, people of Algerian Arab or Berber descent, is often described only in terms of immigration, as though its settlement in France were not directly linked to colonial history. In fact, Algerians have lived and worked in France in significant numbers since the First World War, although one may then distinguish between two sub-groups with distinctly different connections to the Algerian War. The *Harkis*[4] fought with or otherwise assisted the French during the Algerian War. Limited numbers of them managed to move with their families to France to avoid being massacred in Algeria (Stora 1992: 200–202, 206–8; Jordi and Hamoumou 1999). The other, much larger group of Algerians (and other North Africans) in France consists of working-class families who settled there as part of a flow of labor migration to France long encouraged by the French government and industry. Another segment of the population in France, not an ethnic minority but nonetheless with close personal connections to the Algerian War, consists of French soldiers (and their families), among which one can distinguish a larger group of conscripts and a smaller one of enlistees. Additionally, some metropolitan French cut their political teeth on war-related activism: these range from pro-colonial activists on the right to anti-colonial activists on the left. These categories can certainly overlap: for example, some *Pieds-Noirs* and French soldiers joined the Organisation Armée Secrète (OAS) [Secret Armed Organization], a French terrorist group created in February 1961 to fight a desperate and losing battle against the FLN and, even more so, against the Gaullist government, in order to keep Algeria French (Horne 1978: 441; Stora 1992: 87–91). Other members of both of these groups chose instead to assist the FLN, to fight for Algerian independence from France.

The history of the Algerian War is then in many ways a family story (cf. Balibar 1998: 73–88, esp. 82–83). Most of the recent comics about the Algerian War were created by artists with a family connection—through parents, grandparents, aunts or uncles—to the colonization of Algeria and the Algerian War. Many such cartoonists inject personal or family experiences into their representations of the Algerian War and its aftermath. They thereby fit personal and family history into the larger historical events that affect the ethnic, social and national groups to which they and their read-ers are connected, producing genealogies that implicitly or explicitly trace out the reasons for current situations of exile, marginality and victimhood, but also for promoting cultural identity and *métissage*,[5] national contri-butions of minorities, and full citizenship rights for them. Taken together the comics implicitly also suggest some limits to the French acceptance of responsibility for colonial injustice. For example, it is telling that the only demands for concrete reparations considered to be legitimate in public debate in France, and to receive actual compensation from the French gov-ernment for losses created by the processes of de/colonization in Algeria, have been made by former colonial settlers and their allies, not by the for-merly colonized. Groups such as the Cercle Algérianiste have been involved in making such demands. The issue of reparations for colonial injustice, including state crimes, in comics by cartoonists has not been expressed in terms of monetary compensation, but rather is usually articulated through a desire for relief from guilt, a thirst for violent revenge, and attempts to cor-rect the public record through the airing of counter-histories and minority memories, often painful counter-memories: for example, the depiction of shootings of unarmed *Pied-Noir* or Algerian civilians. This resembles what Raphaëlle Branche and Jim House (2010: 131) describe as a demand for "symbolic reparations" from the French state.

Several comics specifically thematize—through preface, story or after-word—the difficult recontruction of historical memory about the war and its (non-)transmission from one generation to the next.[6] In some sense all comic books about the Algerian War "participate in the construction of the representations and of the memory of the Algerian War" (Stora, in Lax and Giroud 1998: 3). However, this memory is not always the singular, national French one that historian Benjamin Stora appears to call for, but often rather the isolated, parallel or even conflicting memories of specific minority groups (Stora 2012). French comics often figure relations between groups related to the war through mixed couples and *métis* offspring. Cartoonists also repre-sent inter-group relations as dishonest seduction, prostitution, miscegenation and rape. However, one should remember that whereas mixed, French-Algerian couples were historically rare outside of brothels, rape was a wide-spread crime during the war (e.g., Ighilahriz 2001; cf. Branche and House 2010: 122). In a landmark decision on 22 November, 2001, Mohamed Garne, conceived through the rape of his Algerian mother by a French soldier in 1959, was declared by the Cour régionale des pensions de Paris [Regional Court of Pensions of Paris] to be a victim of the Algerian War.

Among French historians, Stora especially has argued that the masking of the Algerian War—including war crimes—and its effects has been responsible for the non-resolution of the war and the prolongation of its conflicts in French society (and in Algeria too). Specifically he (1999: 89–93) and others (Giudice 1992, 1993) have alleged that the failure to fully account for war crimes, especially police attacks on Algerian immigrants on and around 17 October 1961, has facilitated post-war attacks on Algerians in France. Stora (1993) has also argued that the offspring of Algerian immigrants have had trouble integrating into French society in part because they cannot easily situate themselves within partial and conflicting official and unofficial histories of the Algerian War. Mainstream politicians (François Mitterrand, Jacques Chirac, Nicolas Sarkozy, etc.) bear considerable responsibility for the lack of official historical clarity, because they have repeatedly avoided acknowledging the true nature of French colonialism, including the Algerian War. This is related to the fact that all French presidents from De Gaulle through Chirac played a direct role of some sort in the Algerian War. Perhaps more importantly, their reticence is also linked to electoral concerns: for example, on 24 November 1982, apparently as part of a prior vote-getting agreement designed to defeat Valéry Giscard d'Estaing in 1981, Mitterrand's Socialist government amnestied and rehabilitated members of the administration, police and army sanctioned for their participation in the putsch of April 1961 and OAS operations (Stora 1992: 282–83). This rehabilitation—satirized by Grégory Jarry and Otto T. in their series on *Petite histoire des colonies françaises* [A Short History of the French Colonies] (2009: n.p.; Figure 4.1)—has allowed politicians, including far-right ones such as Jean-Marie and Marine Le Pen, to capitalize on (neo-)colonial racism and turn it to their electoral advantage. Moreover, for a long time France's national educational system mainly avoided teaching young people about the colonial past. On the other hand, the Algerian War has been a theme in film and prose since the time of the conflict. In comics too, in the late 1970s and early 1980s there began an interest in reexamining the Algerian War. The theme became increasingly important from the 1990s, as taboos on colonial history were gradually lifted (Branche and House 2010).

There are now French comic books representing the war and its aftermath from the viewpoint of one or more of most of the major wartime protagonists. This means that it has now become much easier to analyze, in the field of French comics, some of the issues raised by Ella Shohat (1992: 103) about the term "post-colonial":

> Does the "post" indicate the perspective and location of the ex-colonized (Algerian), the ex-colonizer (French), the ex-colonial-settler (Pied Noir), or the displaced hybrid in First World metropolitans (Algerian in France)? Since the experience of colonialism and imperialism is shared, albeit asym-

Figure 4.1: A comic-strip satire of the official French rehabilitation of former members of the OAS after the Algerian War. A vision of tranquil domesticity is disturbed by framed OAS posters promoting violence. From Grégory Jarry and Otto T., *Petite histoire des colonies françaises*, vol. 3: *La décolonisation* [A Short History of the French Colonies: Decolonization], colors by Lucie Castel and Guillaume Heurtault (Poitiers: FLBLB, 2009), n.p. © Grégory Jarry, Otto T. and Editions FLBLB.

metrically, by (ex)colonizer and (ex)colonized, it becomes an easy move to apply the "post" also to First World European countries. Since most of the world is now living after the period of colonialism, the "post-colonial" can easily become a universalizing category which neutralizes significant geopolitical differences between France and Algeria. . . .

One of my primary goals in this book is to delineate as precisely as possible the political, ethnic and historical positions on colonialism and empire that cartoonists have staked out in French comics. One of the most effective ways of doing this is by carefully examining their choice and interpretation of colonial events. By charting the positions that French cartoonists take on the Algerian War we can understand how and how much they have decolonized or recolonized the field of comics, how they have redrawn French empire. Throughout this chapter I continue to focus primarily on comics and graphic novels created by French cartoonists mainly for the French-speaking European comics market. My analysis is also informed by readings of French-language Algerian comics about the war, although I do not focus on them here.[7]

In the rest of the chapter I analyze several comics published from 1962 to the present that depict the war. I single out ones that inaugurate new or convincing ways of looking at it, or represent an important political, ethnic or artistic perspective on it. I spend the most space analyzing the more ideologically complex works, which engage most fully with the difficulties, ironies and paradoxes of a protracted colonial war, and the most artistically accomplished ones, which exemplify the representational capabilities of the medium. I am especially interested in polyphonic works that redraw empire critically and dialogically, from various, conflicting historical perspectives. This is not the liberal fallacy that multiple perspectives should meet as though they were somehow morally or historically equivalent. Most French comics about the war represent the well-known negative effects of the unequal relations of colonialism, including economic exploitation, alienation, racializing and physical violence. With significant exceptions, the cartoonists who have most extensively represented the Algerian War are from the generations born or raised during it or after, which sometimes witnessed the conflict and are now trying to make sense of it. The exceptions to that general rule include cartoonists who were also combatants, which I analyze in the next section, below. I then go on to examine comics representing the perspective of the other major groups involved in or affected by the conflict, including *Pieds-Noirs*, *Harkis*, the Algerian-French immigrant community, and the non-combatant metropolitan French. My categories respond to the challenge by Shohat (above) and reflect the fact that several cartoonists who depict the war do so principally from the perspective of the wartime groups with which they are personally connected. However, these categories are even more complex than Shohat's statement suggests: for example, there are multiple viewpoints and approaches among cartoonists of *Pied-Noir* heritage, even though they share a history (cf. Woodhull 1993: e.g., 222).

In fact, the comics studied here largely exceed these categories. First, no cartoonist depicts only one group associated with the war: it involved various groups allied with, or fighting, each other. Any comic about the war must engage with that fact, and several artists convincingly represent the perspectives of other groups too. A striking example of this concerns the *Harkis*: not only do most stories include them as characters, but several French cartoonists with family ties not to *Harkis* but to other groups (e.g., *Pieds-Noirs*, Algerian immigrants) feature them as protagonists. The comics I study here also explore issues and articulate viewpoints that transcend the specific interests or perspectives of the groups on which they focus. For example, they often highlight shared cultural traits or histories, compare the pain, victimhood and responsibility of warring groups, critique extralegal means of warfare (e.g., torture and terrorism), and share memorial frameworks and places of memory (cf. Rigney 2005: 21–24). To some extent there has been an evolution and even a partial convergence of post-colonial perspectives in recent years in comics about the Algerian War. The post-colonial therefore serves as a complex and productive category, helping us understand shared ways of redrawing empire that cross the colonial affrontier, sometimes despite the cartoonist's avowed goals, as well as conflictual approaches to redrawing empire that reinforce the affrontier.

French (post-)combatant comics

Cartoonists personally connected to groups involved in or directly affected by the war have created both simplistic, manichean works, and some of the most complex and dialogical representations. During the conflict and in its immediate aftermath this included cartoonists who had themselves participated in war-related political and military activities, which strongly colored their representations. The far-right cartoonist Coral depicted an OAS perspective, and on the opposing side there are Siné's pro-FLN, anti-governmental and anti-OAS cartoons, to which the French terrorist organization responded by sending him a threatening letter (Siné 2002: 18). Siné, born in 1928, had already spent nine months in prison in the army in 1950 (Siné 2004: n.p.). During the war he even produced false documents for the FLN (Siné 2004: n.p.). His anti-Gaullist and pro-independence cartoons on the

Algerian War were collected and republished after the war (e.g., Siné 1965, 1992, 2002, 2004). The key theme of the French-Algerian mixed couple already appears in Siné's work, but in a satirical vein: for example, a French soldier dances with a veiled Algerian woman (Siné 1992: 26). According to historian Claude Liauzu (1993: 270), during the war "[t]he antimilitaristic vein, revived by Algeria, seems to limit its target to the lost soldier, the mercenary, the paratrooper, and it skirts around the participation of draftees in military operations." He also observes that "Siné massacres the centurions with vitriol, Bosc shows the inhumanity of the military order, Cabu attacks the flock, but mostly expresses his distress."

Siné and Cabu, ten years younger, eventually became colleagues at *Charlie Hebdo* [Weekly Charlie], a satirical, left-wing magazine, but their earlier, wartime experiences were different. During the final eight months of his twenty-three month conscript service in wartime Algeria, Cabu used his drawing ability to produce propaganda for the army (Cabu 2004: 41). Nonetheless, his earlier, traumatic experiences as an average soldier contributed greatly to his politicization and motivated his very critical perspective on the wartime conduct of the French army in subsequent comics and cartoons (Cabu 2001: 12–22): he has described his shock at French torture and summary murder of Algerian prisoners (euphemistically described as "corvées de bois" [wood-gathering duties]), the death of other French conscripts, as well as the brutishness and inequality of treatment in French army life (e.g., conscripts being abused by career military men).[8] His well-known French "beauf" [redneck] character was directly inspired by this: "one can say that it's the former [combatant] of Algeria in his most negative guise" (2004: 42).

Other cartoonists, including Georges Wolinski (2001, 2004), Jacques Lob (lived 1932–1990) and Gérard Lauzier (2004) have recounted their experience as French soldiers in Algeria during the war. Lob's description to cartoonist David B. of his departure for Algeria is sinister (in David B. 1998: 29–31; 2006: 30–32). Wolinski and Lauzier, on the other hand, describe their time there as relatively painless and trouble-free on a personal level. Wolinski was assigned to the Centre saharien d'expérimentation militaire [Saharan Center for Military Experimentation] (CSEM), the French nuclear testing site at Reggane, in the Sahara desert, where he had a relatively easy life and spent much of his time reading, drawing and generally enjoying himself, eating and drinking with his wartime friends, who lived and worked in air-conditioned buildings. Wolinksi, who was born in Tunis and lived there until the age of twelve (Gaumer and Moliterni 1994: 671), felt more at ease with Arabs than with *Pieds-Noirs* but did not see many members of either group in or around the isolated base. In *Ma vie historique:*

Je montre tout! [My Historical Life: I Reveal Everything!] (2001: 12–13), Wolinski shows himself going to have sex with Aïcha, the only Algerian prostitute in Reggane, and then returning to his drawing table at the base, where he is mainly concerned about his future, post-military career.[9] Lauzier (2004) portrays his time in Algeria as almost idyllic: "I went all over the place, and I can say that it was one of the best times of my life." However, he admits that his encounter with torture during the month that he was posted to "a [French military] center that was in a way the 'gestapo' of Constantine" was "extremely disagreeable." He describes torture that often included rape: "They tortured there all sorts of people and even young girls. I saw eighteen-year-old girls being forcibly interrogated." On the other hand, he justifies the use of torture against terrorists, including during the Algerian War. For his part, cartoonist Guy Vidal (1987: 87–88), a conscript during the war, admits with brutal honesty, "And in which events does one not share some responsibility? I remember one night in Algeria when some of my friends went and raped a young Arab girl or woman who had been picked up. I didn't go, but there was nonetheless a part of me that wanted to rape the young Arab too. . . . " The colonial violence plainly described here by two cartoonists is still denied or minimized by others in France today (e.g., Kappel 2003: 37; cf. Arzalier 2006).

There is no direct or easy equivalence between the prior political orientation of these three cartoonists and their wartime experiences: before enlistment, both Cabu and Wolinski were politically neutral, according to their accounts. By contrast, Lauzier (2004: 108–9) says that prior to conscription he was a leftist who hated the army, but describes most of the career soldiers whom he met there as wonderful people: "For me, the paratroopers were brutes, SS, and like any good leftist, I thought I was going to be able to revolt. I landed in the most sympathetic unit that I had ever encountered! . . . Moreover, I only met charming people in the army." However, there is a striking dissonance between this language and his description of the Constantine "gestapo," where professional soldiers and police tortured Algerians, but even conscripts "participated sometimes, voluntarily and for pleasure" (Lauzier 2004: 109; cf. Cabu 2004: 40). It appears that Lauzier is defending the army professionals ("l'armée"; as opposed to the conscripts, "le contingent"), whom he sees as simply doing the dirty job that politicians asked of them (Lauzier 2004: 110).

The earliest French comic books about the Algerian War were drawn by Frenchmen who played a more or less direct role in the conflict. They are (semi-)autobiographical and focus on the role of French combatants. Jacques de Larocque-Latour, under the pseudonym of Coral (a partial palindrome of his family name: Laroc/Coral), drew what are to my knowledge the first comic books recounting the Algerian War and its sequels: *Journal d'un embastillé* [Journal of a Prisoner of the Bastille] (1962; Figure 4.2) and *Journal d'un suspect* [Journal of a Suspect] (1964). Marginal in audience size and extreme in political orientation, they are probably the first published comic books about the Algerian War, and one of the first openly autobiographical comic books in France in the twentieth century. In any case, he published them several years before American autobiographical comics from the underground tradition appeared, led by Justin Green's *Binky Brown Meets The Holy Virgin Mary* (1972; cf. Mercier 1999). Coral's two books, which I analyze at length elsewhere (McKinney 2011c), were political interventions for the OAS and against the Gaullist government. Coral presents *Journal d'un embastillé* as a work that he drew while confined to the Santé prison in Paris for his OAS activities. Coral depicts his arrest and incarceration, as well as the jailhouse resistance of himself and other incarcerated members of the OAS, and key episodes of the Algerian War, including the departure into exile of the *Pieds-Noirs*. Coral devotes a considerable amount of space to satirizing President De Gaulle, other government officials, and the police, which apparently triggered legal proceedings by the government against the artist and his publisher, leading to censorship, seizure of published copies and a fine. Both of Coral's comics were published by the Editions Saint-Just, directed by Dominique Venner—a prominent far-right activist and author who now directs the *Nouvelle revue d'histoire* [New Review of History], which specializes in colonial negationism, among other things—and financed by OAS members or sympathizers. *Journal d'un embastillé* is a colonial combatant comic: it is a form of manichean, pro-colonial propaganda that intervenes directly in the war as it is ending. It is therefore on the cusp of the movement to the neo-colonial period. The transition is even more visible in *Journal d'un suspect*, which begins to recount the post-war period from a resolutely colonialist perspective that is nonetheless informed by the formal independence of most French colonies. *Journal d'un embastillé* and *Journal d'un suspect*, which express the views of a political fringe group (in mainland France), appeared so far outside of mainstream comics that they have gone largely unnoticed.

Douvry (1983: 35)—who, like Basfao, appears to be unaware of Coral's books[10]—argues that the initial significant appearance of the war in French comics was through Pierre Christin and Annie Goetzinger's *La demoiselle de la Légion d'honneur* [The Young Lady of the Legion of Honor] (1990; serialized in 1979 in *Pilote*,[11] then directed by Vidal; initial book publication in 1980). However, it was not until 1982, twenty years after the war's conclusion, that the first book-length, uncensored and open treatment of the Algerian War appeared in mainstream French comics, in *Une éducation*

Figure 4.2: The first, autobiographical comic book about the Algerian War recounts the imprisonment in the Santé prison in Paris of the artist and others for unspecified activities in favor of the OAS, a European terrorist organization. From Coral, *Journal d'un embastillé* [Journal of a Prisoner of the Bastille] (Paris: Éditions Saint-Just, 1962), front cover.

algérienne [An Algerian Education], scripted by Vidal (1939–2002), drawn by Alain Bignon (1947–2003), and published by Dargaud (France). Until then, such themes had been unthinkable there, according to Vidal (2004: 161), when asked in 1983 why he waited twenty years to produce the book: "I had the idea in mind for a long time, but its time hadn't come yet. Even though I've been working in comics for more than fifteen years, it would have been unthinkable to depict the Algerian War in comics, because at the time only certain topics could be represented through this mode of expression." The book, scripted by a former soldier, is a combatant's text in outlook: it focuses on the last throes of French empire and their impact on French conscripts. On the other hand, whereas *Journal d'un embastillé* is a combatant and combative comic, *Une éducation algérienne* is a post-combatant one, insofar as it was published twenty years after the war's conclusion. It incorporates that historical perspective even in its form, which owes much to the photo album, journal and scrap book: at the book's opening (Vidal and Bignon 1982: 4–6), the protagonist writes down his observations about the war in a spiral notebook, underneath his photographs from Algeria, and the motif returns at the conclusion (55–56), thereby framing the story.[12] Just as the artist's sketchbook is the primary symbol of the work of the orientalist painter as reportage (Porterfield 1998: 121–35), so also the amateur photograph and personal diary or journal symbolize the French colonial conscript's role as an amateur front-line reporter, documenting his wartime experience. The cartoonists present this vision as more authentic than colonial propaganda, for example, but it is nonetheless framed by representational conventions, either directly or in reaction to them (cf. Mauss-Copeaux 2004). By extension, they present the comic book itself as a journal, an annotated scrapbook or photo album salvaged from history, much as Ferrandez does with Constant's sketchbooks.[13] We have already seen a similar device in Coral's comic books about the war, and Vidal and Bignon may have borrowed it from *La demoiselle de la Légion d'honneur* (Christin and Goetzinger 1990; serialized 1979).[14] This chronotope is a memorial device shared by many comics about the colonial era, despite their different perspectives on that past. Formal similarities between comics and these other text-image media help make this chronotope ubiquitous, but just as importantly the device suggests a personal vision and voice that bear witness today to a vanished past. It also convincingly resembles real-life travelogues and sketchbooks, such as those of Delacroix copied by Ferrandez, or ones by genuine French conscripts in the Algerian War (see below). The chronotope can suggest both the individual perspective of a participant in, or observer of, world-historical events, and a shared family, ethnic, national or artistic history.[15]

Through this and other devices, Vidal and Bignon create an archival, visual-textual memorial of the war, in ways that later works do too. For example, they incorporate into their narrative much emblematic visual and oral material, such as: popular songs (9), including the French-Arab song "Mustapha," by Bob Azzam (11);[16] photographs (20; cf. Vidal 2004: 162); a direct reproduction of an army brochure for new recruits sent to Algeria (Vidal and Bignon 1982: end pages); a scene of jubilant Algerians in a demonstration for independence, no doubt that of 11 December 1960 (Vidal and Bignon 1982: 6);[17] OAS and *Pied-Noir* posters and slogans (26–27);[18] images of *Pieds-Noirs* burning their possessions before going into exile (40); an advertisement that may allude to torture;[19] a photo of French colonial statues awaiting repatriation (52);[20] and frames showing *Pieds-Noirs* waiting on the quay and then sailing away towards the French mainland (53–54).[21] Significantly, Vidal wanted to be a journalist, and saw his comics as journalistic (Vidal 2004: 162): his semi-autobiographical protagonist too dreams of becoming a journalist (Vidal and Bignon 1982: 9). This documentary effort, typical of the most complex and well-researched comics analyzed here, exemplifies the importance of the reality effect in historical comics, theorized as an "effet d'histoire" [history effect] by Pierre Fresnault-Deruelle (1979; cf. Barthes 1985).[22] It also reworks the role of colonial reportage in comics, which Ann Miller (2004; 2007: 57–59) analyzes. The recycled visual material retains a high use value for cartoonists because it condenses important ideas and references, and conveys them in a striking and convincing manner. This is important in graphic narratives, as image-text creations produced under tight space constraints—for decades, the standard length of French and Belgian comic books has been approximately forty-four pages. The imagery helps to reactivate and recreate or perpetuate powerful memories and views about the war. The cartoonists use this imagery and text in complex ways that to some extent critically dialogize government propaganda and French military ideology.[23]

Une éducation algérienne opens in the spring of 1962, at the end of the war, and focuses on Albert, a French conscript who has almost completed his tour of duty in Algeria. Douvry (1983) argues that *Une éducation algérienne* is a "récit-témoignage" [story-testimony] by Vidal, who expresses his viewpoint through Albert, the disabused French conscript protagonist of the story. Vidal himself has stated that most of the characters and events depicted in the book are based on real-life models and experiences from the war (Vidal 2004; cf. 1987: 86–88). The book's opening, splash page shows a French unit marching back into its compound in Algeria and singing a blustering cavalry song about adventure in Algeria, but the effect is grotesque, because the occupying army did not manage to keep Algeria French (cf. McKinney 2009: 78). The principal cast of characters found in subsequent comic-book treatments of the war already appears here: Algerian civilians, French conscripts and professional soldiers, Algerian colonial soldiers (*tirailleurs*, *Harkis*, etc.), *Pied-Noir* settlers, and OAS terrorists. The book represents Algerians in various roles: women and children demonstrating for independence (Vidal and Bignon 1982: 6), men and women who have been rounded up by the army in one of its "rafles" [raids] (14), suspects being tortured by the French (11–12), and an Algerian mother inquiring about her detained son (19). However, FLN soldiers are strikingly absent as characters. An authentic OAS poster that the cartoonists reproduce on one page (26) suggests the reason for this. Its caption—"Aux armes, citoyens" [To arms, citizens]—is borrowed from the national anthem, the Marseillaise, and the imagery is modeled after Delacroix's allegorical painting, *La liberté guidant le peuple* [Liberty Leading the People] (1830), about the revolution of 1830 ("les Trois glorieuses" [the three glorious days]). It suggests that the comic depicts the Algerian War not so much as a struggle between the French and the Algerians, but rather as principally a French revolution: a fratricidal struggle between different French factions (cf. Gervereau 1991: 133; 1992: 182).

The fighting between the OAS and the French state (represented here by *barbouzes*[24] and the French army) provides the primary dilemma for Albert. The protagonist is torn between his knowledge that the OAS is fighting a losing battle and his admiration for his superior officer, Commandant Blois, who supports the desperate cause of the OAS, made up of *Pied-Noir* civilians and renegade French army personnel (including elite paratroopers and legionaries) determined to keep Algeria French. Here, as often in contemporary comics about France's lost empire, political conflicts are represented in sexual terms. After Albert has sex with the wife of his officer, the latter suicidally walks into a French army ambush with an unloaded gun, crying "Vive les cocus!" [Long live the cuckolds!] (Vidal and Bignon 1982: 51). Douvry (1983: 35) correctly observes that this has a political connotation, referring to the OAS's political impasse. However, it also ironically decries De Gaulle's betrayal of the army's imperialist project, as Blois's wife explains to Albert:

> Mon mari a suivi De Lattre en Indochine. A la fin après la mort du roi Jean
> il était à Dien Bien Phu. Après, il est venu ici. Il est tombé amoureux de ce
> pays. Le 13 mai 1958, il a vraiment cru que l'Algérie française était née.
> (Vidal and Bignon 1982: 29)

[My husband followed De Lattre to Indochina. At the end, after the death of king Jean (i.e., the Maréchal Jean de Lattre de Tassigny) he was in Dien Bien Phu. Afterward, he came here. He fell in love with this country. On 13 May 1958, he really believed that French Algeria had been born.]

Just as many on the right saw the Fourth Republic as having sold out Indochina after the French army's ignominious defeat at the battle of Dien Bien Phu, so also French colonists and many army professionals saw De Gaulle, brought to power by the army putsch of 13 May 1958, as later reneging on his commitment to keep Algeria French. Douvry concludes (1983: 35) that the lesson Albert takes away from his Algerian education is that Blois is the only true hero around. Perhaps, but Blois is a cuckold, his death is a futile suicide, and before dying he carries out an OAS order to purge his closest civilian collaborator, shooting him in the back and then hypocritically attempting to comfort the wife of the slain man (Vidal and Bignon 1982: 39, 47–48).

The political is articulated with homosexuality too, associated here with boredom, especially as the war winds down, and with the promiscuousness of barracks life, but also with the decadence of declining empires, Roman and French (11). This satirizes the old imperialist theme that France was destined to inherit the mantle of Roman empire in North Africa (Guilhaume 1992: 94, 199), similar to the colonialist claim that it was also the legitimate heir of the Khmer kingdom in Indochina (Norindr 1996: 26–27). However, when Albert mocks his barrack-mates for their homoerotic activity (including a unisex dance), he is ridiculed for his hypocrisy: "Vaut mieux bien bander que gamberger à moitié, eh patate!" [Better to get a good hard-on than to stall halfway, huh knucklehead!]. The soldier refers here to an earlier dance session, when Albert had an erection while dancing with a gay soldier (see McKinney 2009: 87). Albert later has sex with his girlfriend (Vidal and Bignon 1982: 24), the young daughter of a rich *Pied-Noir*. Together they incarnate a rare variation of the mixed couple: *Pied-Noir* and metropolitan French. Albert then has his fling with Blois's middle-aged wife (31–33). Yet these two heterosexual encounters only appear to compound his alienation and lack of purpose, so it is hard to read them as an expression of self-confidence.

Fundamentally, Albert's sexual ambivalence is the expression of a political one, which becomes a crisis in the crucible of the war. Like many conscripts, Albert finds himself pulled in several opposing directions at once, unable or unwilling to take an strong stand on the war, a political ambivalence that appears to be characteristic of its author too (Douvry 1983; Vidal 1987). Speaking with Blois, Albert criticizes the army for torturing Algerian captives (Vidal and Bignon 1982: 12), but then (somewhat unwittingly) helps him plant an OAS bomb to blow up the Gaullist *barbouzes* (35–36). He bitterly criticizes the rich father of his *Pied-Noir* girlfriend, causing her to immediately dump Albert and tell him that the metropolitan French have no legitimate grounds for judging the conduct of the *Pieds-Noirs* (37–38). He betrays the confidence of Blois by having sex with his wife, but then warns his commanding officer that he has been denounced to the police (49). Only at the very end of the book does Albert take a political stand, expressed once again in sexual terms. He uses a homophobic slur to express his revolt at the imperialist debacle, in a passage whose political ambivalence is perceptively analyzed by Douvry (1983: 35). When Albert lashes out verbally at a superior, calling the French army officers "tantes" [faggots] for having lost so much in Indochina and Algeria (Vidal and Bignon 1982: 56), we may interpret this as implying that the French imperial project has failed because it lacks leaders such as Blois, with a genuinely virile commitment to their ideals, which have been betrayed by others. Yet although Albert's revolt obliges him to finish his military service in prison, his is only a feeble, verbal and ineffectual act, fortified by drunkenness.

The French army's crisis is also a crisis of the imperialist tradition in comics, insofar as they have traditionally been used to promote imperialist masculine role models for metropolitan boy readers. Blois strongly suggests this, just before he rides off to certain death: "Je crois que tu as eu tort de ne pas apprécier cette guerre, Albert. Tu aimes Napoléon, les westerns, la chevalerie, l'histoire! . . . Eh bien, ne loupe pas la coche! Tu es en train d'en vivre une belle tranche! La prochaine génération finira par t'envier! . . . " [I think you were wrong not to appreciate this war, Albert. You love Napoleon, Westerns, knighthood, history! . . . Well don't miss the boat! You're living a nice slice right now! The next generation will end up envying you! . . .] (49). The irony is that in some sense the cartoonists do celebrate the Algerian War as epic history—France's Western adventure in Africa—weaving it together with fictional elements to create a narrative meant to be thrillingly authentic. For example, the bulk of the political-military plot here is based on a notorious sequence of inter-group blood-letting by the OAS, Gaullist *barbouzes* and *Pied-Noir* bystanders that occurred in Algiers from November 1961 through January 1962.[25]

I now move from comics by wartime combatants (Coral and Vidal) to ones featuring French combatants, but which were drawn long after the war by cartoonists of subsequent generations, and generally aim to reduce tensions on the French-Algerian colonial affrontier, by more directly confronting the origins of the conflict. These are therefore post-combatant in multiple ways. Among these comics, Lax and Frank Giroud's *Azrayen'* (1998, 1999)

stands as one of the most complex, in-depth treatments of the Algerian War
in comics to date, so it is therefore unsurprising that Stora agreed to preface
it, as he did earlier for Ferrandez's *Le centenaire* [The Centenial/Centenar-
ian] (1994d). When it was first published, the two-volume, 112-page story
was the longest graphic novel about the war issued by a mainstream publisher, although Ferrandez's five volumes on the war now surpass *Azrayen'*
in total length. Giroud, who scripted the two-volume *Azrayen'* (Lax and
Giroud 1998, 1999), is the son of a French conscript soldier who fought
in Algeria and to whom Giroud dedicated his story. Lax, who drew it, was
eight years old in 1957, when his father was a French soldier in the Kabylia
region. Giroud's discovery of his father's scrapbook about the war helped
spark his interest in depicting it in comics. The paternal document supplied
characters, images and events for *Azrayen'*. Moreover, in the second volume (1999) Giroud also included a short foreword with contextual material
about the war and a lengthy afterword about making the story, including
photos of both cartoonists' fathers as soldiers in Algeria,[26] selections from
the handwritten post-war journal by Giroud's father about the war, prepa-
ratory sketches by Lax, other photographs and visual documents from the
war and after, and a select bibliography of some of the historical works that
the artists consulted about Algeria and the war (Figure 4.3).

The combined effect impressively suggests the extent of the cartoonists' efforts to do justice to the complexities of the situation, especially
when compared to the sparer stories of the industry's standard book length.
Moreover, although the narrative mainly focuses on the perceptions and
experiences of French conscripts, the authors made a concerted effort to
inform themselves about a variety of Algerian and French perspectives on
the conflict by reading historical and fictional accounts of the war (including novels and war comics by Algerian artists), but also by talking with
many individuals from different groups that participated in or witnessed the
conflict: *Pieds-Noirs*, conscripts, professional soldiers, and others. In order
to round out his documentation, Giroud made a trip to Algeria in 1993 to
speak with FLN veterans and visit sites where the war was fought. By that
time civil war had broken out in Algeria and hundreds of people were being
massacred. Nonetheless, the trip took place and became a real return to a
colonial place of memory, because Giroud's father, whose war-time experiences were a major source of inspiration for the comic, accepted his son's
invitation to accompany him. Giroud's afterword, which recounts the trip,
provides a second-generation perspective on the events: his desire to gain a
better understanding of his father's war-time experience, but no doubt also
a need to see his father, a former conscript, as an involuntary victimizer, and
therefore mostly relieved of personal responsibility for the war's horrible

Une épopée algérienne
par Frank Giroud

D'abord, il y a eu la photo. Quatre soldats dans la neige, sanglés dans un uniforme inquiétant, casque lourd sur la tête, chargeur enclenché dans la mitraillette… À la gauche de l'homme au regard mauvais, un militaire aux yeux songeurs. Mon père.

Et puis ce texte, en dessous, à la calligraphie sage et appliquée.

Halte dans la neige

Le plus petit des gars au centre est ▓▓▓▓▓▓ pied-noir. Son père fut tué au début de la rébellion par un de ses employés arabes. La violence engen-drant la violence, ▓▓▓▓▓▓ devint le patron des interrogatoires. Ces interrogatoires qu'en d'autres temps on aurait appelés tortures. Mais les temps de guerre n'autorisent-ils pas tous les subterfuges? Et puis le cœur d'un fils dont le père vient d'être assassiné ne se pétrifit-il pas?

Figure 4.3: In his afterword, "Une épopée algérienne" [An Algerian Epic], Frank Giroud recounts the artists' inspiration for the comic book: their fathers were both French soldiers conscripted to fight in the Algerian War. Here, Giroud includes two of his father's photographs, as well as excerpts from his handwritten account of his wartime experience. From Lax (art) and Frank Giroud (script), *Azrayen'*, vol. 2 (Marcinelle: Dupuis, 1999), p. 59. © Lax and Frank Giroud.

violence. This appears to be at issue when Giroud describes the first encounter between his father and a former FLN combatant, Ahmed, in a bar in
Bejaïa, formerly Bougie (unpaginated; pp. 10–11 of the afterword):

> He asks him the fatal question. My father, for whom bitterness is a for-
> eign feeling, answers him without beating around the bush. Yes, during the
> same period he too was fighting on Algerian soil . . . on the other side. The
> fact that he had been an ordinary conscript reassures the former djounoud
> [soldier], but he can't hide his bitterness, especially when he describes the
> torture camps, the summary executions, and the graves dug by their own
> occupants. A moment of unease. During our stay, it will be the only one:
> astonishing though it may seem, we won't find that morosity again, in any
> other guerilla fighter.

In their fiction the authors take care to represent Algerian perspectives
marked by morosity and bitterness against the French during the war.
Indeed, they do their best to create a polyphonic account of the war that
confronts markedly different and opposing perspectives, influenced by ethnicity, colonial and personal history, and gender. However, they try to balance the inevitability of Algerian independence from the French against
moments where the perspectives of settlers, soldiers and Algerians meet.
Like Ferrandez, they are concerned with demonstrating that chances for
mutual respect and understanding existed, but that these were unseen or
squandered. The authors explore France's so-called civilizing mission in
Algeria, which they articulate through the relationships of two couples,
one endogamous (Algerian-Algerian) and the other exogamous (Algerian-
French), which are implicitly contrasted, allowing the reader to draw les-
sons about the brutality unleashed by the war, but also about the cultural
values of both sides. The narrative is structured by a hermeneutic already
used by Lax and Giroud in *Les oubliés d'Annam* [The Forgotten Ones of
Annam] (see above, Chapter 3): the search for information about the disappearance of a French soldier, whose adherence to the goals of French
colonialism and to his military mission has been shaken. Here too, the
investigation unearths events that led the soldier to strongly react to, or even
rebel against, the brutality of the colonial war. Moreover, in both series, this
process is closely intertwined with a soldier's amorous relationship with a
colonized woman, suggesting the degree to which French cartoonists still
very often view relations between colonizers and colonized as intimate,
erotic, exotic and gendered (Figure 4.4). However, there are also significant
differences. For example, this time the search for the soldier, Francis Messonier, is undertaken by other French soldiers during the war, rather than by

Figure 4.4: A mixed couple, composed of a French conscript soldier and an Algerian schoolteacher, figures the possibilities and limits of the colonial-era relationship between France and Algeria. From Lax (art) and Frank Giroud (script), *Azrayen'*, vol. 1, preface by Benjamin Stora, translations into Kabyle by Saïd "Amnukel" Mella (Marcinelle: Dupuis, 1998), p. 34. © Lax and Frank Giroud.

an independent, socially conscious reporter who digs up clues many years after its end. The soldiers comb the mountains of Kabylia for Messonier, the leader of a special SAS (Section Administrative Spécialisée [Specialized Administrative Section]) unit composed of *Harkis* (Horne 1978: 254–55). Lax and Giroud's decision to focus on this type of unit echoes, in Ferrandez's *L'année de feu* [The Year of Fire] (1994b) and *Les fils du sud* [Sons of the South] (1994c), the positive depiction of the motivations and actions of an officer in the French army's Bureaux Arabes [Arab Offices], in the nineteenth and early twentieth centuries, who learns Arabic, is friends with francophile Kabyle leaders, and ends up digging artesian wells for the desert population in the south.[27]

In *Azrayen'*, Messonier becomes increasingly distant from his Algerian girlfriend, Takhlit Allilat, a Kabyle woman who teaches in a French school in Bougie (1998: 14). In a series of flashbacks, Allilat remembers the beginning of their love affair (17–21, 33–34), but refuses to divulge any information about Messonnier to the French soldiers, who force her to accompany them in their search for the missing man. However, after she has been slapped by a soldier and has witnessed similar treatment of villagers interrogated by the unit, she finally tells what she knows about Messonnier's mental state, as a way of reflecting back the true nature of the French army's activities. She describes how Messonnier carried out criminal orders from his superior that led to the deaths of unarmed, impoverished Algerian men working for exploitative settlers running a French winery (Figure 4.5). The cartoonists carefully model this episode on a horrifying series of real events first revealed during the war (Vidal-Naquet 2001 [1975]: 100–106; Horne 1978: 201–2; Stora 1992: 33; Branche 2001: 157–60; Righi 2003: 97–103). Messonnier responded by filing a report against his superior officer, which had little effect, aside from getting him transferred to a SAS section, as a way of shunting him aside (51–58). However, the murder of the Algerians clearly destroyed his self-respect and sapped his will to live, including his desire to continue seeing Allilat, who now believes that her lover is dead. Like Ferrandez's Bureaux Arabes officer, Messonnier becomes completely disillusioned with the French army.

The first volume of *Azrayen'* ends with two images of Algerians turned against the French by the soldiers' brutal conduct: Allilat, who symbolically exchanges her European clothing for Algerian dress and chooses to abandon her career as a French schoolteacher in order to marry an Algerian, a village cobbler; and two children, one of whom is molested by a brutal, racist French sergeant, as a way of trying to force villagers to cooperate with the investigation. There is no equivalent in *Azrayen'* to the *métisse* of *Les oubliés d'Annam* (1990–91), who symbolizes within the present the legacy of an anti-colonialist link between a dissident colonizer and colonized insurgents.[28] Consequently within the story there is no clear, present-day solidarity between the two groups that such a living link would represent. Instead of a post-colonial *métisse* (in *Les oubliés d'Annam*), in *Azrayen'* a colonized Algerian woman (Allilat) accompanies and assists Frenchmen trying to solve the riddle of a soldier's disappearance. This hermeneutic, which drives the narrative forward and unleashes further colonial violence in both series, is clearly cyclical in *Azrayen'* and illustrates two principal facts: (1) what were labeled "pacification" measures by the French army were actually brutal acts of war; and (2) the French army's violence was self-defeating, because it only succeeded in making enemies of Algerians, who otherwise might have been favorably disposed towards the French, and in damaging the humanity of French soldiers. The second volume of *Azrayen'* (1999) further illustrates the cyclical and counter-productive nature of the violence, as the increasingly frustrated soldiers, having just been ambushed by an Algerian insurgent group (17–23), go on to torture and kill innocent civilians (44–45), before blowing up a village and taking away all of its men for further interrogation (46–47). After one of the French conscripts

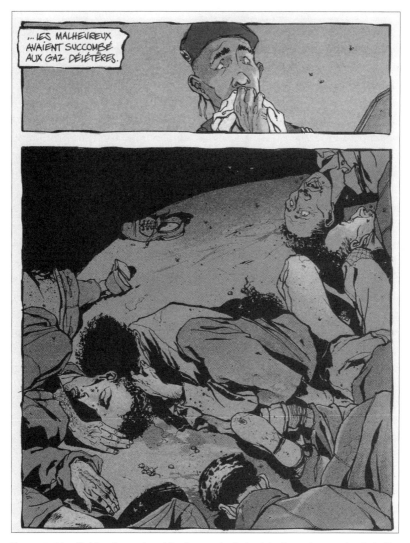

Figure 4.5: A horrified French conscript soldier discovers that he has helped commit a war crime by locking up Algerian prisoners overnight in empty wine fermentation vats, where they die of poisoning. From Lax (art) and Frank Giroud (script), *Azrayen'*, vol. 1, preface by Benjamin Stora, translation into Kabyle by Saïd "Amnukel" Mella (Marcinelle: Dupuis, 1998), p. 56. © Lax and Frank Giroud.

unexpectedly discovers that Messonnier and his men were killed by flood waters during a thunderstorm (48–54), he announces that, like Messonnier, he too wishes to join the SAS (55).

Lax and Giroud also represent brutality on the Algerian side, but—curiously—approach the issue first through a subplot revolving around the subordinate place of women in Kabyle society. Including this perspective in a story mainly focused on the blind spots of French colonialism raises prickly questions. For instance, given the authors' impressive preparations through extensive background reading, they must have known that, to argue for the superiority of French mores and thereby justify colonialism, French colonizers often raised the theme of liberating Algerian women (Woodhull 1993: 16–24). This historical context makes one wonder why the authors included the following phrase and its accompanying visual illustration of a Kabyle soldier killing his adulterous wife: "En Kabylie, un adultère simple peut déjà finir dans le sang . . . / . . . mais lorsqu'il est perpétré en l'absence d'un mari parti en guerre sainte, tout espoir de clémence s'évanouit" [In Kabylia, a simple adultery can already end in bloodshed . . . / . . . but when it is perpetrated in the absence of a husband away in a holy war, all hope of clemency vanishes] (45). My point is not that enraged husbands have not murdered their wives in Kabylia (and in France and the United States) but rather that the manner of presentation is problematic in this context. Regardless of the cartoonists' intentions, the text quoted above sounds very much like an axiomatic, ahistorical observation about Kabyle society borrowed from colonial ethnology.[29] Indeed, the view that the authors put into the mouth of Mohan, a westernized Algerian character, could easily be interpreted by readers as fitting the common eurocentric view that relegates non-western societies to an earlier, more savage period of European history: "A quoi bon un pays débarrassé de l'occupant s'il y règne encore la tyrannie des coutumes et des barbaries d'un autre âge!?" [What's the good of a land freed from its occupier if the tyranny of customs and barbaric acts from another age still reigns there!?] (46). Moreover, the narrative seems to suggest a corollary: that the peaceful and civilized person who accepts what is presented here as a general truth about Kabyle culture would quite naturally reject the latter in favor of French society. Mohan, the sister of Hassibah (the murdered woman), is depicted as a liberated engineering student who respects his sister's autonomy (44–45). He leaves his studies in the capital city of Algiers to join the independence fighters near his home in Kabylia, but then switches sides and joins the French army after having witnessed the horrible murder of his sister and her lover (46–47).

Therefore, the cultural itineraries and choices of Mohan and Takhlit mirror each other: Mohan is revolted by Algerian blood vengeance and joins the French, whereas Takhlit's disgust at the savagery of French soldiers leads her to return to her village and marry the Algerian suitor chosen by her family. Yet despite the similarities between the two situations, they differ radically: organized mass terror by a colonial army is not the same thing as the admittedly horrible murder of an individual. In fact, it may make more sense to read this juxtaposition of characters, barbaric acts and itineraries within a *post*-independence context. It is quite possible that, as they were creating their story, Lax and Giroud had in mind the brutalities of the Algerian civil war, then unfolding. Coordinated murderous attacks against women were indeed carried out during the civil conflict, which was waged by Islamists as a holy war. It is also true that Algerian women's hopes of equal rights were dashed soon after independence.

This contemporary, post-colonial context may also help us interpret another juxtaposition that the authors make, between the perspectives of two soldiers on opposing sides: a settler man and an Algerian woman. When Cosme Tirard and Taous Yacine meet, the Algerian woman has been wounded during a massacre that she and other members of the FLN have just carried out in a village that supports the MNA (cf. Horne 1978: 221–23, 258; Ruedy 1992: 164; Buch 2005: 130; Le Sueur 2005: 185–204). Amid the dead and dying children, women and old people, the French soldiers discover Yacine, a childhood friend of Tirard. We learn now why she earlier prevented her unit from ambushing the French soldiers (1998: 29–32): it was in memory of Tirard's grandmother, who saved Algerians during a flu epidemic in the 1930s by vaccinating them, when French doctors chose to save only French settlers (1999: 27–28). Yacine then asks Tirard why he helps kill people like her, with whom he played as a child. However, Tirard's response—an account of how his parents were killed by FLN guerillas in Philippeville two years previously, along with 71 other European settlers and about a hundred Algerians friendly to the French (29; Figure 4.6)—calls forth Yacine's counter-memory of the exponentially larger, retributory massacre, by settlers and the French army, of masses of Algerian civilians after the Philippeville massacres by the FLN. Against this, Tirard then sets the massacre of unarmed Algerian civilians in which Yacine has just participated.

The explicit confrontation that Lax and Giroud make here, between two versions of collective, historical memory—of the *Pieds-Noirs* and the FLN—that support radically opposed perspectives, does much more to illuminate the nature of the colonial situation before and during the war than does the earlier, implicit juxtaposition between Takhlit and Mohan. This subplot illustrates important facets of the war: the French divide-and-conquer strategy toward the Algerian insurrection, which reinforced the already existing rivalry between the MNA and the FLN; the FLN's ruthless response to this, mentioned by Stora in his preface (in Lax and Giroud 1998: 3), which entailed waging a merciless war against the MNA, in both Algeria and France; and the calculated decision by some FLN leaders to widen the rebellion into a full-scale revolution, through the Philippeville massacre

Figure 4.6: A *Pied-Noir* intepreter for the French army describes to his former childhood friend, an Algerian woman who is now a FLN soldier, the murder of his parents in the Philippeville massacre on 20 August 1955. From Lax (art) and Frank Giroud (script), *Azrayen'*, vol. 2 (Marcinelle: Dupuis, 1999), p. 29. © Lax and Frank Giroud.

of 20 August 1955, which triggered disproportionate French massacres in response and thereby drove a permanent wedge between French settlers and the Algerian people (Ruedy 1992: 162–63). Forced to compare his position with Yacine's, Tirard the *Pied-Noir* appears to finally realize the shared human cost of the war, and not just its effects on him and his own ethnic group. To the credit of the artists, their graphic novel confronts these two radically opposed perspectives in a direct and open manner (Figure 4.7). This is especially important because *Pied-Noir* resentment at having lost what many members of that community considered, or even hold today, to

Figure 4.7: A *Pied-Noir* demands that his former friend, now a soldier on the opposing side, reveal who informed her that a French military unit would pass through the area and could be ambushed there. From Lax (art) and Frank Giroud (script), *Azrayen'*, vol. 2 (Marcinelle: Dupuis, 1999), p. 31. © Lax and Frank Giroud.

be their legitimate homeland continues to fuel anti-Maghrebi sentiment in France. On the other hand, the comic book's images of defenseless Algerians massacred by armed bands of fellow Algerians is also likely to echo eerily for many readers with the massacres carried out during the Algerian civil war of the 1990s.

The futility and injustice of France's war against the Algerians is underscored by the story's conclusion, which, however, hesitates revealingly between a mythical and an historical explanation for the French defeat. On the one hand, the discovery that Messonnier and his men were victims of a flash flood and a resulting mud slide is the occasion for comments about Allah's will and the inevitability of Messonnier's fate, because an old Kabyle woman had nicknamed him "Azrayen'" ("Angel of the shadows"), an ethnographic reference to a Kabyle belief about the association between death and the butterflies that Messonnier collected (1998: 5–7, 34; 1999: 52–54). The narrator also suggests that it was the land itself that killed

Messonnier: "Pourtant le convoi s'éloigna rapidement de cette montagne si prompte à chasser de ses flancs les corps étrangers, et à les digérer dans ses entrailles . . . " [Nonetheless the convoy rapidly moved away from that mountain so quick to chase foreign bodies from its flanks, and to digest them in its entrails . . .] (1999: 56; cf. Lax in Buch, Vernet and Ratier 2010: 39–40). Providing this solution to the enigma of Messonnier's death curiously rewrites images of the colonized country as an edenic paradise for settlers, whose relationship to the land is often expressed in erotic terms.[30] In fact, there is just such an eroticized image of an Algerian seascape earlier in the story, although it is offset by foreshadowing about the tragedy in store for Messonnier and Allilat (1998: 33–34). In his preface, Stora links the artists' choice of the mountainous locale to the history of Kabyle resistance to invaders since Antiquity. He also observes that Lax's expressionistic drawing style helps turn the natural setting into a threatening presence.[31] One gets the absurd impression that the land itself has rejected the French occupiers. On the other hand, the cartoonists also supply a plausible, human cause for the inevitability of the French defeat. The final images of the fiction in the second volume recall and reinforce those of the first. Here again we see Algerian children who have witnessed French military brutality and will—the soldiers realize—surely reject France, even if its military offensive succeeds.

Pied-Noir perspectives on the war

Nostalgic longing for a lost country and community, now dispersed and much assimilated in mainland France, predominates in comics by cartoonists of Pied-Noir heritage. In this section I analyze commonalities and differences in their approaches to redrawing empire. I have found only one that resolutely articulates an unapologetic colonialist perspective: it was scripted by Evelyne Joyaux-Brédy, who founded the Cercle Algérianiste [Algerianist Circle] of Aix-en-Provence, for which she was inducted into the Légion d'honneur (Le Monde 1998). She also served on the Haut Conseil des Rapatriés [High Council of the Repatriated, i.e., Settlers], an advisory board to the French government. By contrast, all of the other comics about the Algerian War by authors of Pied-Noir heritage that I analyze here critique various forms of French colonial violence. This is a very positive development, which gives hope for the long-term reconciliation of former antagonists from the war, and the eventual erasure of the French-Algerian colonial affrontier. Here again, I proceed more or less chronologically, from the earliest work, published in the mid-1980s, through the 2000s, when most of the comics appeared, although some continue series that began in the 1990s. I also analyze conflicting positions on the war in different works, ranging from trenchant critique of racism within the *Pied-Noir* community to a colonialist, blanket defense of *Pieds-Noirs*. I spend considerable time on the comics of Ferrandez, who has produced the longest depiction of the war, and one of the most complex and interesting ones, in both ideological and artistic terms.

Here, as with (post-)combatant comics, the journal, photographic album or artistic sketchbook serves as a chronotope for representing an intimate, familial and ethnic connection to the colonial past "là-bas" [down there]. Denis Mérezette, a friend of Algerian-French cartoonist Farid Boudjellal and one of the authors of *Algérie française!* [French Algeria!] (Mérezette and Dumenil 1985), dedicates his book to "mes chers parents et aux heureux jours de mon enfance, là-bas . . . " [my dear parents and to the happy days of my childhood, down there . . .] in Algeria. He reproduces family photographs, which he labels "Souvenirs de Ghardaïa (1961)" [Memories of Ghardaïa (1961)] on the *pages de garde* [endpapers] of *Algérie française!* and uses some of them as models for decors and secondary characters (Mérezette and Dumenil 1985: e.g., 19, 28–30, 43–44). The fiction reworks the myth of the Western in Algeria, through a glorification of the romantic outsider.[32] The vision of Algeria as an equivalent of the American west or south is an old trope, dating back to the Algerian War and earlier (Stora 1999). In *A Savage War of Peace* Alistair Horne (1978: 154) reports that Governor-General Robert Lacoste used a trans-Atlantic comparison to deflect American criticism during the Algerian War: "To American journalists critical of conditions in Algeria he would hit back reflexively with acrid comments about Indians and Negroes," as though one vicious colonial policy justified or exonerated another one. Horne (472) later implies that during negotiations with the FLN over the status of the Sahara and its oil reserves, French officials again evoked the model of the American West as a justification for its position: "In simplest terms, the French view was that the Algerians had no more right to the vast desert under-belly than the Indians had to Texas." The story by Mérezette and Dumenil moves from Algiers to Ghardaïa, in a southward trajectory common in French fictions about the Maghreb (Vatin 1985), which we already saw in "Carnets d'Orient" [Oriental Sketchbooks] (see Chapter 2, above).

The book opens with a description of Algiers as a western frontier town: "Ces hommes à l'ombre des terrasses et ces jeunes cailles de Bab-El-Oued à l'ombre des militaires qui tournaient autour. . . . Ces *beaux cowboys cradingues* comme pour rappeler qu'en ce printemps 57 c'était la guerre dans la cité. . . . " [These men in the shade of the terraces and these young chicks from Bab-El-Oued in the shade of the soldiers who gravitated around them. . . . These *handsome grungy cowboys* as though to remind one that in this springtime of 57 there was war in the city. . . .] (3; my emphasis). This description of French soldiers as symbols of male virility (cf. Horne 1978: 203; Aussaresses 2003: 118; Kauffer 2004: 462), the reference to a popular, working-class *Pied-Noir* neighborhood of Algiers, and the emphatic, provocative title of the book, *Algérie française!*, together suggest a defiant colonialist perspective.[33] However, Mérezette and Dumenil take a dissident position on the war, producing instead a disaffiliation from clearly defined anti-colonialist and colonialist positions. The French-Algerian couple in this gritty, black and white comic is composed of Ahmed, an Algerian man, and Nadine, a *Pied-Noir* woman, living together in the casbah of Algiers. Ahmed is hiding out because the French caught him and some friends, who had been helping the FLN by planting bombs, and then released the men on condition that they inform on the banned organization (14). Although the men's sympathies remain with the Algerian nationalist cause, both the French army and the FLN now suspect the group of working for the opposing side (cf. Aussaresses 2003: 147). To avoid capture and torture, Ahmed must now flee Algiers, to which end Nadine seduces and helps trap Jean Kerbronec, a Breton on visit in Algeria, who owns a car (Figure 4.8): this creates another mixed-couple—a variation on the *Pied-Noir* and metropolitan French one we saw in *Une éducation algérienne*. Providentially assisted by a bomb explosion just as they are being detained at a French army checkpoint (21–22), Jean and Ahmed succeed in escaping to Ghardaïa in southern Algeria (the city of Mérezette's dedication), but not without Ahmed killing a FLN soldier who commandeers their car (23–27). However, when Ahmed kills a French colonial profiteer (38), he is captured by the French army and tortured until rescued by Jean (42). The final, incredible escape of the trio (Ahmed, Jean and Nadine) from their pursuers is facilitated by the providential defection of Marcel, a soldier in a French army helicopter that had been pursuing them. He forces the pilot to land, pick up the fleeing threesome and fly them all to safety across the border in Tunisia.

The politically ambiguous connotations of the conclusion are fascinating. On the one hand, Ahmed's alienation from both the FLN and the French army suggests an anarchistic rebellion against all forms of authority (13–14). This seems confirmed by the conclusion, where Marcel's decision to highjack the army helicopter to fly them to safety in Tunisia replicates his grandfather's mutinous conduct during the First World War, for which he had been executed (5, 46). However, in partial contradiction to this anarchistic viewpoint, there is an anti-colonial undercurrent, which brings

NADINE HABITAIT LA CASBAH ET MÊME SI À CETTE HEURE LE SOLEIL BRIL-LAIT ENCORE HAUT DANS LE CIEL ... IL FAISAIT BIEN SOMBRE DANS LA CITADELLE ...

6

Figure 4.8: A *Pied-Noir* woman leads a Breton man to her apartment in the casbah of Algiers to seduce him so that he will save her Algerian lover: an anarchistic perspective on the war is articulated through mixed French and Algerian couples. From Denis Mérezette and Dumenil, *Algérie française!* [French Algeria!] (Brussels: Michel Deligne, 1985), p. 8. © Denis Mérezette, Dumenil and Editions Michel Deligne.

together representative members of ethnic or national groups affected by internal and external French colonialization, and even Spanish colonialism: by the end, Ahmed, the Algerian, has joined forces with Jean Kerbronec, the Breton, and Marcel, from the Pyrénées (5). As the lover of all three men, Nadine unites them, making possible their collective escape from the war-torn country. Nadine, as a working-class *Pied-Noir* woman (6), might not be expected to play such a role, but the book explains this by references to mistreatment of her by French interrogators (18), the loss of her father, and her consequent need to worship Ahmed as a romantic hero (Figure 4.9), at least until she meets Jean and realizes that the war has made her fragile and that she is tired of Ahmed's erratic behavior (35).

Although as readers we may find Nadine's grab-bag of motivations an implausible male fantasy, and wonder at the curious willingness of Marcel and Jean to compromise their own future by helping Ahmed and Nadine escape (true, Marcel is described as being war-weary, 6), the fact that the cartoonists have these characters make common cause together is interesting. The implied equivalence between the colonial situations of the three men could certainly spring from a broadly anti-colonial, Third-Worldist vision, and fits with connections being made around the same time by Claude Auclair, whose comics about black-white relations in Martinique (*Le sang du flamboyant* [The Blood of the Flame Tree] [Auclair and Migeat 1985]) and the domination of Britanny (*Bran Ruz* [Auclair and Deschamps 1981]) were innovative and influential treatments of colonialism and cultural difference. However, Mérezette's and Dumenil's somewhat negative treatment of the FLN would seem to jar with this perspective. On the other hand, *Le chemin de l'Amérique* [*Road to America*] (Baru, Thévenet and Ledran 1990) also shows FLN coercion of recalcitrant Algerians in a negative light, and elsewhere Baru (e.g., 2003) depicts in-fighting between Algerians during the war, as does *Azrayen'* (see above). This critical perspective on the FLN may be due in part to post-independence disillusionment with authoritarian Algerian national leadership, although it also reflects harsh realities of the war. The negative treatment of the FLN and colonial society in *Algérie française!* also opens up a space for reconciling dissident *Pieds-Noirs* (Nadine) and Algerians (Ahmed), and for recuperating Algeria as a minoritarian meeting ground, though at the price of an anarchistic departure from the FLN as the vehicle of anti-colonial struggle (acting on his own, Ahmed kills the colonial profiteer, though with FLN explosives he discovers). One wonders too whether there is not some *Pied-Noir* and mainstream French colonial nostalgia in this configuration of characters and allegiances, as is apparent in the focus on settler *lieux de mémoire* [places of memory], such as the casbah of Algiers and the desert in the

Figure 4.9: Ahmed, once a member of the FLN, goes outside at night to look for explosives to kill a racist Frenchman: here the cartoonists represent him as a romantic figure standing against the skyline of Ghardaïa on the northern border of the Sahara desert. From Denis Mérezette and Dumenil, *Algérie française!* [French Algeria!] (Brussels: Michel Deligne, 1985), p. 37. © Denis Mérezette, Dumenil and Editions Michel Deligne.

south, both of which figure prominently in the work of Ferrandez, as we saw in Chapter 2, above.

The comics of Ferrandez currently comprise the most extensive treatment of the Algerian War in the medium. At various points in the first five volumes in his "Carnets d'Orient" series he foreshadows the war of independence and *Pied-Noir* exile, for example through the haunting disappearance of Djemilah and through Joseph Constant's longing for her and Algeria at the end of *Carnets d'Orient* (1994a), and in the kidnapping of a settler's wife and the burning of his crop in the conclusion to *L'année de feu* (1994b). The conclusion of *Le cimetière des princesses* [The Cemetery of Princesses] (1995) contains even more pronounced allusions, especially the loss of Constant's sketchbooks, and then a catastrophic earthquake in Orléansville (Horne 1978: 87; Fletcher 2006), which provokes coïtus interruptus between Sauveur and Marianne in the symbolically named Hôtel de France,[34] and also destroys Marianne's family home and Constant's painting of Djemilah (cf. Chapter 2, above). For several years after publication of the latter volume, Ferrandez produced a series of illustrated, non-fictional travelogues in his "Carnets d'Orient" series, depicting his visits to various locations in the Arabo-Islamic world, including Algiers (Ferrandez 1999, 2000, 2001, 2005b, 2006; Ferrandez and Dugrand 2001; cf. Ferrandez in Buch 2005: 93–106). These are again inspired by orientalism, including orientalist painting. However, in other publications he began to edge toward a direct representation of the Algerian War (Ferrandez 1998; Vittori and Ferrandez 2001). Still, it was not until seven years after his first Algerian comic-book cycle ended that he launched a new cycle of five books recounting the war, beginning with *La guerre fantôme* [The Phantom War] (Ferrandez 2002). I analyze here two principal features of Ferrandez's wartime volumes: the ongoing importance of orientalist exoticism, again articulated via an Algerian-French couple, and a continuing "ideological balance effect" (Halen 1993b) between colonial and counter-colonial violence, in favor of an illusory third position of French-Algerian harmony (cf. Ferrandez in Buch 2005: 130–32). I also suggest the ways that Ferrandez uses the medium to depict historical events and to intervene in debates about them.

The five new volumes, which finally represent the war itself, again bear the series title "Carnets d'Orient" and continue his earlier project in important ways: several main characters return; the preoccupation with orientalist art continues—e.g., an Algerian goat-herd boy miraculously recovers Constant's sketchbooks (Ferrandez 2002: 6–7), which are eventually returned to *Pieds-Noirs* (2002: 57, 60; 2009a: 57); and Ferrandez continues to memorialize key places (the casbah of Algiers; the Algerian south) and historical figures (especially Camus) of *l'Algérie française*. Moreover, as he did in *Carnets d'Orient*, the first volume of the series, Ferrandez once again chooses to figure the union of France and Algeria as a love affair between a Frenchman (Octave Alban, a French paratrooper captain) and an Algerian woman (Samia, a young doctor in residency). He thereby once again creates an exceptional French figure, who surprisingly manages to partially escape the prejudices of his milieu (Figure 4.10). Paratrooper Octave Alban joins

Figure 4.10: An improbable mixed couple, composed of a *Pied-Noir* officer in the French army and an Algerian woman who assists the FLN, on the opposing side, is taunted by another French soldier. From Jacques Ferrandez, *Carnets d'Orient*, vol. 6: *La guerre fantôme* [Oriental Sketchbooks: The Phantom War], preface by Gilles Kepel (Tournai: Casterman, 2002), p. 63. © Casterman. Reproduced with the kind permission of Jacques Ferrandez and Editions Casterman.

the cartoonist's collection of fictional and real-life, humane French coloniz-ers,[35] who are genuinely interested in Algerians, their history and culture: for example, he reads a biography of Algerian nationalist leader Abdelkader and begins his affair with Samia despite her criticism of the army's oppres-sion of the Algerians (2002: 60) and his own participation in the war against the FLN. For historian and comics critic Pascal Ory (2002–3), Octave is "one of the most developed characters . . . , a *Pied-Noir* officer just back from Indochina, troubled by the absurdity and the injustice of the combat that is his mission."[36] In partial opposition to Octave, stands his superior, Commandant Loizeau, a crude, ruthless, racist officer determined to recon-quer Algeria by any means necessary.[37]

Similarly, Samia, who joins the FLN, is flanked by other Algerian charac-ters ready to use all available means to win the war (2004: 15–16, 49–50). The artist's decision to frame the colonial period with mixed couples (Joseph and Djamila during the conquest; Octave Alban and Samia during the war of independence), but mainly eschew their use in the intervening years (cf. Calargé 2010: 114), symptomatically suggests the extent to which French-Algerian fraternization is a foundational myth necessary to justify the French presence in Algeria in times of crisis, but is antithetical to the normal functioning of a colonial society founded on systemic French exploitation of Algeria and Algerians (cf. Tribak-Geoffroy 1997: 128–29).[38] Just as signifi-cantly, in both cases the Frenchman is associated with the French army and the Algerian woman apparently acts under constraint: in *Carnets d'Orient* (1994a) Djemilah is confined to a harem and then tricked into an arranged marriage; and in *La guerre fantôme* (2002) Samia ostensibly begins her affair with Octave Alban to protect her cousin Ali and Mourad (a.k.a. Bouzid), a wounded FLN fighter (62). Less plausible is Ferrandez's decision to make Samia and Octave have sex on the first date, and then suggest that she has already fallen in love with him—she sheds a tear while reading his letter of adieu, as he sails away on the ill-fated French expedition to the Suez Canal (64). The closing words of the letter, inserted as a collage against the book's closing image, of Octave sailing away, are ambiguous, and could be either hers or his: "Je t'aime, Octave" [I love you, Octave]. However, in the following volume, *Rue de la bombe* [Bomb Street] (2004: 23), a remark by Marianne suggests that the relationship between the French officer and the Algerian doctor may not be fully consensual or egalitarian: "C'est le foulard de Samia. . . . Tu l'as gardé, ou bien elle te l'a donné?" [That's Samia's scarf. . . . Did you keep it, or did she give it to you?]. This reminds the reader that Octave Alban apparently took the scarf without Samia's permission. His act evokes the fundamental issue of the legitimacy of France's presence in Algeria. Here, as in so many French comic books, colonization is depicted as an ill-fated historical romance between a masculinized France and a feminized Algeria (see Basfao 1990; Calargé 2010; and above). Once more, love may or may not conquer all, but certainly cannot retrospectively allow the French to stay in Algeria, the true lost love of Ferrandez and the *Pied-Noir* community, whose story he recreates. The next three "Carnets d'Orient" after *Rue de la bombe* (2004)—*La fille du Djebel Amour* [The Girl of Djebel Amour] (2005a), *Dernière demeure* [Final Dwelling] (2007) and *Terre fatale* [Fatal Land] (2009a)—continue to figure the theme of the shrinking middle ground through the French-Algerian mixed couple. First Octave-Alban rescues Samia and her cousin Ali from the clutches of Bouzid (a.k.a. Mourad), a fanatical and paranoid nationalist, who tortures Samia to make her confess to being a double-agent working for the French (cf. Calargé 2010: 116–17). This is not true, but he succeeds in learning that she had an affair with the French officer. *La fille du Djebel Amour* (2005a: 9) opens with images of her, naked and trussed up on a bed that Ferrandez later connects explicitly to the conventions of orientalist painting (22) and which recall the association between torture and eroticism in *Une éducation algérienne* (see above). He thereby continues his heavy investment in orientalist eroticism and exoticism, which characterizes his work on Algeria from the beginning (Ferrandez 1994a). The rescue of the beautiful and beleaguered Algerian woman is also part of an attempt by the French army to defeat the FLN, through sabotaged rifles that Octave and his soldiers deliver to Samia's captors and falsified FLN documents that they use to hide their identity. In this sense, saving Algeria—as incarnated by Samia—means liberating it/her from the paranoid, less assimilated and educated, nationalist Algerian men (such as Bouzid) who would impede cultural and sexual encounters between the French (men) and the Algerian (women).

This heterosexual French-Algerian erotics remains central to the project of Ferrandez, although he complicates things by showing that Octave is manipulated by his superior officer, who uses the lovers' relationship to further the official French agenda (Ferrandez 2005a: 26–27; 2009a: 7–9, 16–17). The cartoonist also has his parachutist captain protagonist distance himself progressively from a hard-line military solution, first by becoming a SAS officer (Ferrandez 2005a: 27–57), whose goal was to combat the Algerian insurgency through a variety of measures, including the creation of dispensaries and schools for Algeria's rural population,[39] and then by resigning from the army and taking Samia with him into exile in Québec, which serves here as an example of successful French deep settler colonization, unlike in Algeria, which the *Pieds-Noirs* were forced to leave (Ferrandez 2007: 13–17; cf. McClintock 1992: 88). However, by the end of *Dernière demeure* (2007), Ferrandez has brought Samia, with her hair dyed blond to hide her Algerian identity, and Octave back to Algeria, so the latter can pay his last respects to Casimir, the settler family patriarch, now dying. He then splits the couple apart again. After a FLN attack on the French farm, during which her torturer, Bouzid, reappears and calls her a sell-out to the French, Samia (her hair covered with a traditional turban) leaves, having first asked Octave to make love to her "comme si c'était la dernière fois" [as though it were the last time] (Ferrandez 2007: 57). Her departure and a subsequent radio announcement that Camus has died (59) signal the apparent disappearance of any middle ground between radical extremisms. At this time of crisis, Ferrandez uses Sauveur, a character partially modeled on his own father, to make an authorial pronouncement on the history of *l'Algérie française*, which sums up the main perspective of the entire series: "Malheureusement, cette histoire n'est qu'une succession d'occasions manquées . . . " [Sadly, this story/history is nothing but a series of lost opportunities . . .] (55; cf. Buch 2005: 87–88). The following volume, *Terre fatale* (Ferrandez 2009a), confirms this judgment and brings the war to a close. There, the mixed couple has a boy named Paul (28, 38), who will live in France with his parents in exile at the end of the war.

Like his model figure of Camus, Ferrandez tries to trace a middle path along the colonial affrontier, by criticizing the excesses of both the FLN and the French army. It is no surprise that he (2009b) adapted the short story "L'hôte" [The Host] from Camus's *L'exil et le royaume* [*Exile and the Kingdom*]: it shows a humanistic, idealistic French teacher caught between the colonial administration and Algerian nationalists, "trying to remain [a] 'foreigner' to the conflict" (Henry 1991: 306). His comic book story in the second cycle of "Carnets d'Orient" includes propaganda comic strips and cartoons created by French psychological warfare specialists[40] and lapidary written warnings affixed by Algerian nationalists and French soldiers to the dead bodies of enemies (Ferrandez 2002: 47, 58; cf. Horne 1978: 134–35, 172, 258).[41] The propaganda contains visual and textual material (a corpse and a hand-lettered sign) and is to that extent like a cartoon or a captioned photograph. The complex story into which Ferrandez inserts these mini-caricatures created by the opposing forces suggests that they are over-simplistic representations of a conflict for whose cruelty both sides are responsible. A crucial episode in Ferrandez's dual critique is located about three quarters into *La guerre fantôme* (Ferrandez 2002). The left side of a double-page (54–55) shows the aftermath of a FLN ambush on a French convoy of conscripts, whereas the right one depicts a French paratroop regiment that, having cornered the men of the FLN unit, is now burning them out and killing them. Ferrandez again makes his characteristic visual distinction between a watercolor sketchbook drawing, here as the background, and a sharper finished image, here filling the comic strip frames, which are arranged across or on top of the background, in the cartooning technique that Thierry Groensteen (1999: 100–106) calls "incrustation." The single panoramic background image unites both pages and acts as part of what Benoît Peeters (2002b: 23) calls the "péri-champ" [peri-field], that is the material that the comic-book reader sees around any particular frame (cf. Groensteen 1999: 44–48). Although the sketchbook image still derives from an orientalist aesthetic founded on Ferrandez's problematic reading of Delacroix's North African sketchbooks as more or less unmediated renderings of North African reality, here wartime violence intrudes into the painterly celebration of Algerian light and landscape. The middle frame on the left page functions as a lens to literally bring into focus the shocking violence in the otherwise beautiful, lushly rendered scenery, although the sexual mutilation of the dead French conscripts by their FLN attackers is both strongly suggested and carefully masked from the viewer. The correlation between background tableau and comic-strip frames functions like a cinematic jump cut, because not quite all of the black outlining on the inside of the frame matches up with the watercolor background around it, especially in the lower left-hand side of that frame. Like other related techniques that Ferrandez uses throughout his series,[42] this partial mismatch is visually unsettling and might lead an alert and reflective reader to question the status of the representation and her or his relationship to it.

Specifically, the visual mismatch may remind us that Ferrandez often bases his fictional events on historical material, but transforms the latter and calls attention to both the model and his redrawn displacement of it.[43] Two pages before the killing of the French conscripts, they are discussing the torture of Algerian suspects, including through the infamous *gégène*, or *groupe électrogène* [dynamo], attached to genitalia. They compare French army torture with a FLN killing of French conscripts, in which the genitalia of the latter were cut off and stuffed into their mouths. Although they do not mention the name of Palestro, the infamous incident at that location, widely publicized at the time, is clearly Ferrandez's model (Horne 1978: 152–54, 231, 252; Chominot 2004: 591–96; Branche 2010).[44] The artist may do this double-take to protect himself from accusations of historical inauthenticity, while nonetheless guaranteeing that his work will be taken as believable: it is grounded in history, but he is free to develop his own story line. It also allows him to intervene, through his fiction, in ongoing debates about the war. In this sense Ferrandez's use of history is different from the "history effect" described by Pierre Fresnault-Deruelle (1979): the cartoonist is not interested in producing the simple distractions grounded in history that Fresnault-Deruelle theorizes.[45]

The scene on the right-hand side of the double-page also cannot fail to remind the reader acquainted with Ferrandez's series of a related passage in *Carnets d'Orient*, during the French conquest of Algeria in the nineteenth century. The historical event depicted there is also recounted in *L'amour, la fantasia [Fantasia, an Algerian Cavalcade]*, by Algerian novelist Assia Djebar (1985: 77–93; 1993: 64–79), who builds on the research of a French colonial historian (Gautier 1920: 11–54; cf. Julien 1964: 320–21; Ruedy 1992: 64): how during the conquest of Algeria the French army massacred Algerian men, women and children, and their animals, who were hiding in caves, by inducing suffocation and smoke inhalation.[46] Ferrandez's fictionalized rendering of the infamous smoking-outs [enfumades] is strongly critical of conquest-era French military action. His decision to place a similar scene during the Algerian War suggests that excesses of the Algerian War are comparable to the violence of conquest. By contrast, just after this event Ferrandez endorses a more conciliatory approach, especially toward the civilian population, through his character Octave Alban (Ferrandez 2002: 57).

Ferrandez here reworks the colonial figure of the French soldier as heroic adventurer, from pre-1962 comics, by splitting him in two: one half is the ruthless commanding officer, Loizeau (homophonically "the bird" [l'oiseau]), with a falcon-like face, whereas Octave Alban is more handsome and humane. This is a manichean aspect of comics grammar, but also suggests something more troubling: an attempt to partially rehabilitate the French professional army, whose fierce determination to win the colonial war, after having lost in Indochina, was responsible for much bloodshed.

On the other hand, Ferrandez again bases his protagonist on recognizable historical models. A passage in the following volume, *Rue de la bombe* (Ferrandez 2004: 47), suggests that the General Jacques Pâris de Bollardière, who publicly condemned torture and was punished for that (cf. Horne 1978: 203, 233; Eveno and Planchais 1989: 124; Liauzu 2003: 5–8, 135), was a model for Ferrandez's paratrooper captain.

Terrorism and torture were prominent and controversial features of the Algerian War and remain so in debates surrounding the representation, memory and history of the conflict. Ferrandez explores the causes and effects of these forms of violence in his series. *Rue de la bombe* opens with a night-time bombing of the Algiers casbah by *Pieds-Noirs*, led by a French police commissioner (2004: 11–15). The presentation of this episode is clearly inspired by Italian film director Gillo Pontecorvo's classic film *The Battle of Algiers*,[47] which also transparently serves as the basis for an extended passage in *Pierrot de Bab El Oued* [Pierrot from Bab El Oued], an Algerian comic book about the war and its memory (Melouah: 2003: 9–14). Ferrandez's inclusion in *Rue de la bombe* of this damning sequence about French terrorist violence against sleeping Algerians, borrowed from a notoriously pro-FLN film, is remarkable for a cartoonist of *Pied-Noir* heritage, and suggests the degree to which he is ready to critique certain forms of French colonial violence.

In his narrative, this is followed by a debate between FLN members, including Samia, about carrying out terrorist bombing of civilians, including children. An Algerian leader argues (Ferrandez 2004: 15; cf. 2005a: 26):

C'est l'arme du pauvre et de l'opprimé! Quelle différence entre l'aviateur qui bombarde des mechtas, en tuant des femmes et des enfants innocents, et le patriote qui va mettre une bombe dans le quartier européen? . . . Juste une différence de moyens . . .

. . . Qu'on nous donne des avions et des armes lourdes, et nous leur laisserons des bombes dans les couffins! . . .

[It's the weapon of the poor and the oppressed! What difference is there between the aviator who bombards hamlets, killing innocent women and children, and the patriot who plants a bomb in a European neighborhood? . . . Just a difference of means . . .

. . . Give us airplanes and heavy weapons, and we'll let them have the bombs in the baby baskets! . . .]

This closely resembles what Larbi Ben M'Hidi says in *The Battle of Algiers* and also what historian Alistair Horne (1978: 186) attributes to FLN leader

Ramdane Abane. Bombardment of Algerian villages was indeed one of the ways that France maintained its colonial domination, which was massively supported by the French civilian population in Algeria and which left the FLN few options in the pursuit of its struggle for independence. Throughout his saga Ferrandez memorializes French Algeria, while still acknowledging the legitimacy of some charges by Algerian nationalists against French colonialism. However, this approach generates untenable contradictions, much like those that Albert Memmi (1985: 47–69; 1991: 19–44) describes in his portrait of "le colonisateur qui se refuse" [the colonizer in denial].

In contrast to Ferrandez's attempt at a balanced critique of the opposing sides, one finds an unapologetic and uncompromising colonialist approach to the history of the war in *Les rivages amers: L'Algérie—1920–62* [Bitter Shores: Algeria—1920–62], the conclusion to the *Pied-Noir* family saga by Joyaux-Brédy and Joux (n.d. [ca. 2003]).[48] Nowhere do they show or mention physical violence by *Pieds-Noirs* against unarmed Algerian civilians, as Ferrandez does (2004: 11–14, 26–28; 2009a: 23–24). Instead, they visually depict FLN violence: murders of a defenseless old Algerian man and veteran (59–60), peaceful *Pied-Noir* farmers plowing their fields (60), innocent French children (60), café-goers in Algiers (61) and *Pieds-Noirs* in Oran (79). However, their most extended visual treatment (76–78) of violence against French civilians is reserved for the firefight of the Rue d'Isly, when Algerian colonial troops in the French army (the 4th regiment of Tirailleurs algériens [Algerian riflemen]) wounded or killed almost three hundred *Pied-Noir* civilians. This occurred when a *Pied-Noir* crowd, participating in a banned demonstration organized on the instructions of the OAS, tried to break through French army lines around the Bab El Oued neighborhood, a stronghold of support for the OAS. The firefight that broke out may have been provoked by an OAS sniper on a building rooftop or balcony (Horne 1978: 526; Stora 1992: 107; cf. Ferrandez 2009a: 51–53), although *Pieds-Noirs* surmised FLN provocation and immediately lynched ten Algerians in the Belcourt neighborhood (Droz and Lever 1991: 334; Stora 1992: 107). It is revealing that Joyaux-Brédy and Joux do not mention this last fact.[49] Instead, they borrow the pietà theme to represent the tragic death of a French boy, the son of the *Pied-Noir* family whose saga the cartoonists tell throughout the five volumes. The cartoonists convey the message that not only were the *Pieds-Noirs* and friendly Algerians the innocent victims of a murderous FLN, but that they were also betrayed by the French government, led by De Gaulle.

The wounds of war and exile, the difficulties and burdens of remembering, and the risks of forgetting are also central to *Là-bas* [Down There] (2003), scripted by Sibran, of *Pied-Noir* heritage, but born and raised in

France, and drawn by Didier Tronchet, best-known for his comics set in northern France.[50] The cartoonists explicitly allude to Ferrandez in a frame toward the end of the volume, thereby acknowledging his influential model for creating comics about Algeria from a *Pied-Noir* perspective. The main focus of *Là-bas* is the transfer of colonial memory from the *Pieds-Noirs*, directly marked by the violence of war and exile, to their offspring, whose knowledge of Algeria and the war can only be second-hand and indirect. Wartime violence is symbolized through a massacre of innocent Algerians towards the end of the war, by OAS terrorists in the Lyre marketplace. The retrieved event (2–3) and its reworked memory (57–59) frame the graphic novel, as do splash pages first depicting Algiers (1) and then a fantastic, neo-orientalist merger of Paris with Algiers (60). The shift from terrorist attack to a transformed memory, and from an image of Algiers to one of Paris-Algiers (Palgiers/*Palger* or Algieris/*Algéris?*), coincides with the transfer of narrative authority from the *Pied-Noir* parental generation to its descendants. The graphic novel shows the French-Algerian *affrontière* [affrontier], apparently the result of an "affrontement d'hier" [confrontation of yesteryear], as a pressing issue for both generations. The narrator, Anne Sibran's double (Anne becomes Jeanne, or "Je-Anne" [I, Anne]; cf. Dana 2005: 224), soothes the tortured conscience of her *Pied-Noir* father by reassuring him that he could have done nothing to save the Algerian victims of the OAS attack, and by remembering and telling it to him differently, magically effacing the massacre. The erasure of *Pied-Noir* responsibility for, or implication in, the violence of the OAS is problematic, because at first most *Pieds-Noirs* generally strongly supported the European terrorist organization (Lever 1982). However, this historical fact is elided by the graphic novel. The other symptomatic erasure or omission by Sibran and Tronchet is any reference to the offspring of Algerian immigrants in France, despite the presence of a lone Algerian construction worker in a Parisian suburb (29–30).

My final example of a *Pied-Noir* comic about the Algerian War is the only clearly non-fictionalized one. The personal and family history that Morvandiau recounts in *D'Algérie* [About/From Algeria] (2007: n.p.) is oriented by the death of a family member assassinated in Algeria in 1994, during the civil war. His missionary uncle Jean was among the few *Pieds-Noirs* to stay on in Algeria after 1962, and so symbolized a real-life solidarity across the French-Algerian colonial affrontier after the end of the war. He did social work as a public writer [écrivain public] helping needy Algerians. Morvandiau articulates the story of his uncle with that of other *Pied-Noir* members of his family, including his parents, and an autobiographical account of a family trip to Algeria in 1988, when he was thirteen. He considers what probably led his ancestors to emigrate from France to Algeria

(Figure 4.11), the benefits they derived from that move, how they viewed Algeria and the Algerians, and why his uncle lived as a Catholic priest in Algeria during the post-independence years, until his assassination. He constantly intercuts his genealogical inquiry about his family history with the history of Algeria and its relations with France, from the conquest to the present.

At the end of *D'Algérie*, the cartoonist recalls Jean-Marie Le Pen's reported admission that he tortured Algerians during the war, and his defense of that, in a published interview in *Combat* in 1962 (Figure 4.12; see Morvandiau 2011: 115, 119). On the facing page he reflects on his last, disillusioned memories of his *Pied-Noir* grandfather who supported the Front National in his final years. This makes Morvandiau one of the rare *Pied-Noir* cartoonists to directly connect French colonial violence in Algeria to anti-Arab racism in France. He also mentions the neo-colonial relations between the French and Algerian regimes. His innovative drawing style in *D'Algérie* oscillates between more simply drawn figures, usually in the comic-strip sequences, and more finished drawings, often full-page tableaux. The cartoonist produced many of the latter by redrawing colonial-era engravings and photographs (see Morvandiau 2011: 105, 110, 118), which is common practice by French cartoonists who revisit colonial history, as we have seen. He also redrew photographs of family members in Algeria. And although he did not include a bibliography in his book, he provided documentation of many of his visual and historical sources on his weblog, about which periodically he informed his subscribers. In *D'Algérie*, Morvandiau traces a genealogy of his family, the *Pieds-Noirs* and France in a manner that critically interrogates their relation to the colonial past and the importance of that past to the present.

Taken together these *Pied-Noir* comics represent positions ranging from a defensive justification of the *Pied-Noir* community that presents them entirely as the victims of history (*Les rivages amers*) to a radical critique of French colonial injustices in Algeria that points to their consequences for the present in both France and Algeria (*D'Algérie*). "Carnets d'Orient" occupies a middle ground, trying to balance urban terrorism and other violent excesses (e.g., the Palestro killing and mutilations) by the FLN, terrorism by the European ultras and the OAS, lynchings of Algerians by *Pieds-Noirs*, as well as torture and other war crimes by the French army (cf. Halen 1993b). His series charts the logic of the war as an escalation of unjustified violence that gradually eliminates any possibility for people of good will on both sides to find common ground and preserve a French Algeria in which *Pieds-Noirs* and Algerians could live together harmoniously. Published in 1985, *Algérie française!* was a precursor, with subsequent *Pied-Noir* comics about

FIN D'ANNÉE RICHE EN ÉMOTIONS DONC POUR ANTOINETTE, MÈRE DE SUZANNE ET INSTITUTRICE LAÏQUE CONVAINCUE. CLÉMENT, LE PÈRE, VÉRIFICATEUR DES CULTURES À L'ADMINISTRATION DES TABACS, EST UN FRANC-MAÇON ÉRUDIT, RÉPUTÉ FRONDEUR ET FORT EN GUEULE. COMMENT ET POURQUOI CES DEUX-LÀ DÉCIDENT-ILS EN 1907 DE PARTIR POUR ALGER, JUSTE APRÈS LA NAISSANCE DE LEUR FILS JEAN ?

Figure 4.11: In an autobiographical comic book, the cartoonist narrator wonders what led his great-grandparents to move from France to Algiers in the early twentieth century. From Morvandiau, *D'Algérie* [About/From Algeria] (Rennes: L'oeil électrique/Maison Rouge, 2007), n.p. © Morvandiau and L'oeil électrique/Maison Rouge.

EN FRANCE, LES CONDAMNATIONS LIÉES À LA GUERRE D'INDÉPEN-
DANCE CONNAISSENT DES AMNISTIES SUCCESSIVES. EN 1999,
LA "GUERRE" EST OFFICIELLEMENT RECONNUE. AUSSARESSES
DÉBALLE EN SOURIANT SES HORREURS COMMISES. Le Monde
RÉVÈLE LE CARACTÈRE MASSIF DES VIOLS PERPÉTRÉS PAR
L'ARMÉE. EN FÉVRIER 2005, TANDIS QU'UNE LOI –ET SES AR-
TICLES RELATIFS AU "RÔLE POSITIF DE LA PRÉSENCE FRANÇAISE
OUTRE-MER" ET À L'INDEMNISATION DES ANCIENS CONDAMNÉS
DE L'OAS–EST VOTÉE, LES "MASSACRES DU 8 MAI 1945" SONT
QUALIFIÉES DE "TRAGÉDIE INEXCUSABLE" PAR L'AMBASSADEUR.

Je n'ai rien à cacher

J'ai torturé parce qu'il fallait le faire

Jean-Marie LePen interview à Combat 09 novembre 1962

Quand on vous amène quelqu'un qui vient de poser vingt bombes qui peuvent éclater d'un moment à l'autre et qu'il ne veut pas parler, il faut employer des moyens exceptionnels pour l'y contraindre

C'est celui qui s'y refuse qui est le criminel, car il a sur les mains le sang de dizaines de victimes dont la mort aurait pu être évitée

Figure 4.12: Morvandiau reminds his readers that Jean-Marie Le Pen, who founded the racist Front National in 1972, proudly declared during an interview in 1962 that he tortured prisoners during the Algerian War. In the textual recitative above the image, the cartoonist juxtaposes key post-war events, some of which reinforced a French colonial perspective on the war or helped obfuscate its nature, whereas others challenged that perspective or otherwise helped rectify the historical record. From Morvandiau, *D'Algérie* [About/From Algeria] (Rennes: L'oeil électrique/ Maison Rouge, 2007), n.p. © Morvandiau and L'oeil électrique/Maison Rouge.

the war created at least fifteen years later, from 2002. This suggests a growing willingness by cartoonists of *Pied-Noir* heritage who were mostly born
or raised in metropolitan France to revisit the war, usually to make peace
with the past in ways that reach out across the colonial affrontier to varying
degrees and in different manners.

Who speaks for the *Harkis?*

To my knowledge, no cartoonist with a family connection to the *Harkis* has
represented this group in comics, which has left the position open to artists
with other ethnic and social affiliations. And if cartoonists unrelated to the
Harkis have chosen to represent them, it is partly because *Harkis* are often
seen as both the worst traitors and the most victimized of wartime groups:
in both perspectives they are the ultimate outcasts. As a group, *Harkis* were
both perpetrators and victims of war crimes: Maurice Papon notoriously
recruited some to brutally police, torture and kill Algerian immigrants
in Paris (Péju 2000). In Algeria, *Harkis* have been viewed as traitors and
comparable to French collaborators of the Nazis (Stora 1992: 163, 264).
After the Evian Agreement and the ceasefire of 19 March 1962, they and
members of their families were massacred by the thousands in Algeria. The
French army, still in the country, had stern instructions (disobeyed by a few
officers) to neither transfer them to France, nor protect them in Algeria
(Horne 1978: 537–38; Stora 1992: 163–66, 200–2, 206–8; Jordi and Hamoumou 1999: 34–49). According to Stora, people on both the left and the
right of the political spectrum in France had reasons to abandon the *Harkis*
and remain silent about their fate, although Vidal-Naquet (in Péju 2000:
13) states that he spoke out in late 1962 against the massacres while they
were occurring. Among the small percentage who managed to flee to France
at the end of the war, often with the aid of French officers disobeying orders
to abandon them in Algeria, many ended up living in poverty for decades,
in make-shift camps (Stora 1992: 261–55; Hargreaves 1995: 78; Jordi and
Hamoumou 1999).

    Harkis appear mostly as secondary characters in graphic narratives
about the Algerian War, where they constitute a prototypical figure of
absence, abandon and betrayal. Depictions of *Harkis* in graphic narratives
point to France's broken promises, lost honor, and refusal to take responsibility for its colonial mess. The re-discovery of *Harkis* living in France,
and their descendants, as part of a project of recovering lost or suppressed
collective memory about the war, is a trope that recurs in various works
studied here. In the light-hearted *Les Beurs* [The Arabs] (Mechkour and

Boudjellal 1985, n.p.), republished in *Black Blanc Beur: Les folles années de l'intégration* [Black White Arab: The Crazy Years of Integration] (2004: 39), the contradictory status of *Harkis* as invisible victims of the French and as victimizers of Algerian nationalists is jokingly alluded to when a character, hiding in a bush to escape detection, requests that a movie be made about the plight of the *Harkis*. We have seen that in *Azrayen'* Lax and Giroud depict the frontier between *Harkis* and FLN combatants as relatively porous, as it also is in *Le chemin de l'Amérique* (Baru, Thévenet and Ledran 1990). Both works show Algerians first joining the French army and then deserting to the FLN, or vice versa. This illustrates the colonialist and nationalist struggle over the loyalty of Algerians: *Harkis* are exemplary figures of both indigenous fidelity and national treachery. They thereby help define the French-Algerian affrontier in comics.

The first published French graphic narrative depicting *Harkis* that I have found is a short story entitled "Un si joli sourire kabyle" [Such a Pretty Kabyle Smile], set in 1961, by Frank and Golo (1987: n.p.). There, *Harkis* put in a brief but threatening appearance in a working-class neighborhood of Paris. This was one of several short stories that they originally serialized between 1979 and 1981. The passing evocation is explained by the interest of the two artists—working in an underground or alternative comics vein—in a marginal, seamy Paris, populated by Third World immigrants, prostitutes and pimps, drug addicts and dealers, gamblers, criminals, and characters engaging in various forms of sexual transgression. Vidal and Bignon depict a *Harki* in a much more sympathetic manner in *Une éducation algérienne* (1982: 16, 18, 42): Ahmed goes AWOL at the end of the war, fearing that he will be abandoned by the French and executed by the FLN. At the story's conclusion the narrator wonders what became of his friend, but never learns, or tries to learn, the answer to his question (55; cf. Ferrandez 2009a: 56–57). This exemplifies the degree to which *Harkis* and questions surrounding their fate serve as an unsettling marker for hidden memories and missing information about the war and its aftermath.

Rivalry and alliances between national and ethnic perspectives, along with an ambivalence towards taking a position on the war, structure the French-Algerian couple in *O.A.S. Aïscha* (1990), by Belgian cartoonist Louis Joos and French author Yann. The title character is a *Harkie* who has joined the OAS. Aïscha's mission is to assassinate De Gaulle, but having been caught by a *barbouze*, she is secretly being smuggled back to France by boat for interrogation.[51] After the *barbouze* dies from an injury caused by shifting freight during a storm, Aïscha easily seduces the cowardly French captain and then teams up with a *Pied-Noir* officer of the ship. Here, as in *Algérie française!* (Mérezette and Dumenil 1985), minority ethnicities play a role in the allegiances of the characters: *Pied-Noir* and Corsican sailors, who are for *l'Algérie française*, band together against Gaullist Breton sailors. The ethnically and politically balkanized boat is an obvious metaphor for the doomed French colonial project in Algeria and, like Algiers on the evening towards the end of the war when the ship sets sail for Marseille (5 March 1962), it is rocked by an explosion from an OAS bomb in its hold (Joos and Yann 1990: 39). The French captain's attempt to save his Algerian lover, wounded and helpless in the sinking boat's hold, is thwarted by the ship's other officers, who put aside their quarrels to save their careers, and wish only to make all the evidence, including Aïscha, disappear into the maritime depths (43–44). The captain's infatuation with the attractive but dangerous Aïscha leads him to a take tepid, compromised and ultimately untenable third position, which is neither that of the *Pied-Noir* officer, representing a willingness to destroy Algeria if it will not remain French, nor the final Gaullist position, for Algeria's right to electoral self-determination and formal independence. The captain clearly represents metropolitan French fascination with Algeria and an inability to make a firm commitment during the conflict. At the end of the book everything falls into its proper place when the captain returns to his dull family life with wife and children, and Aïscha dissolves into a vague memory fleetingly brought back by a radio broadcast announcing Algerian independence (46).

One of the most interesting early examples of *Harki* characters who figure the violent return of painful memories of the war is in "Vengeance harkie" (1994), by Mérezette and Boudjellal. The story, originally titled "Bien mal harkis ne profite jamais" (a word play on the aphorism "bien mal acquis ne profite jamais" [ill-gotten gains are never good]) was commissioned in 1983 for a series of pocket comics targeted at an adult male readership. The publisher told the authors that the content must include "sexe et violence, [mais] pour le reste vous êtes libres" [sex and violence, but for the rest, you're free] (76). It was scripted and drawn, but never published in the original edition and did not appear in print until more than ten years later, in a shortened version. The combination of serious historical matter with sex and violence is a hallmark of the contemporary European cultural field, where the barriers between elite culture, the mass media and "art forms of popular culture" are disappearing, according to Marxist art historian O. K. Werckmeister (1991: 49). The title of "Vengeance harkie" refers to the wartime robbery, rape and murder of Algerian women by three *Harkis*, and the subsequent revenge taken by one of their victims for this wanton violence. The robbery and murder of the women characters are shown; however, the rape is not represented visually (Mérezette and Boudjellal 1994: 90).[52] In the story, set in 1983 and 1994, with flashbacks to the Algerian War, Driss, the adult orphan son of one of the murdered Algerian women, tracks down and summarily murders the *Harkis* one by one. Two try desperately to convince Driss that they are not guilty as he charges them, but to no avail: he cuts their throats. Throat-slitting by Algerians, dubbed "le sourire kabyle" by the French army during the war (Horne 1978: 112), is linked to the colonial stereotype of the knife-wielding North African, analyzed by Frantz Fanon (2002: 286) in *Les damnés de la terre* [*The Wretched of the Earth*] as the war was unfolding.[53] This image recurs occasionally in French comics about the war or North African immigrant communities in France, including "Un si joli sourire kabyle,"[54] discussed above.

"Vengeance harkie" represents unresolved war-time violence lingering on in France, years after the war. It is figured as a blood feud, transmitted as a poisonous inheritance from one generation of males to the next: Driss shows a photo of his father, significantly not his raped and murdered mother, to his first *Harki* victim before killing him (90); and the youngest son of his final victim seizes Driss's gun and kills him, to avenge the murder of his father (106). This might be read as an implicit critique of male responsibility for both the war-time violence and its post-independence perpetuation, through murderous revenge, but the final image leaves the reader wondering whether the feud will end. The comic represents another form of colonialist violence perpetrated against North Africans in mainland France after the end of the war. In "Vengeance harkie," Driss tracks down the second *Harki* in a shack located in an isolated camp in southern France. The young daughter of the *Harki* whom Driss has located is bed-ridden with bronchitis, which her father blames on the humidity in their miserable dwelling. The father's complaint highlights the unjust way that the French treated the *Harkis* in France and suggests that the cycle of violence should end: "Moi . . . c'est peut-être normal que je paye . . . mais elle!!!" [Me . . . it may be normal for me to pay . . . but her!!!] (85–86). Flagrant and sustained governmental disregard for Algerian immigrant and *Harki* communities, and the colonialist racism that continues to victimize both groups, have helped break down historical, nationalist barriers separating them. One also finds this theme in Maghrebi-French prose fiction, especially *Le harki de Meriem* [The *Harki* of Meriem], by Mehdi Charef (1989).

Yvan Alagbé's *Nègres jaunes* [Yellow Negroes] (1995), drawn in an experimental style, remains of the most convincing explorations of the *Harki* as both forgotten war victim and victimizer (cf. Frey 2008). The story returns to the Parisian streets and marginal underworld explored earlier by Frank and Golo, in "Un si joli sourire kabyle," of immigration, racism, prostitution and policing. However, it is set decades after the end of the war, and Alagbé's ex-*Harki* character is isolated and desperately lonely in contemporary France—a misfit who speaks nostalgically of De Gaulle's colonial campaigns in Africa. *Nègres jaunes* thematizes memory and nostalgia relating to the colonial period, and was issued by one of the most important alternative comics publishers in France: Amok, then run by Alagbé and Olivier Marboeuf, and now merged with Belgian publisher Fréon, as Frémok. Alagbé insistently raises ethical questions, visually and linguistically, about the reader/viewer's relationship to the subjects of his work, including the *Harki*, depicted as a social leper, and the most vulnerable of West African immigrants—illegal aliens.

By contrast, *On les appelait les . . . harkis. . et pourtant, . . . ils étaient soldats de France.!!* [They Were Called . . . Harkis. . . . and Yet, . . . They Were Soldiers of France!!] (1997) by Gilbert Carreras, no doubt an amateur cartoonist with little artistic experience (the drawings are naïvely done), uncritically champions *Harkis* as faithful soldiers of France during the war and neglected victims since then, but does not acknowledge the war crimes that some—like other French and Algerian soldiers—committed during the war. The proximity of this vision to French propaganda is underlined by the fact that the French Secrétariat d'état aux anciens combattants [Secretariat of State to Veterans] partially funded the publication. Although in artistic terms Ferrandez's work is light years away from Carreras' book, the former's principal *Harki* character is remarkably similar in substance to those of Carreras. Ahmed is the faithful sidekick of Octave Alban, but is even more intransigent than his French officer, in his views of the history and illegitimacy of Algerian nationalism (Ferrandez 2002: 42). He represents an unbroken line of fidelity to France and of resistance to Algerian nationalists, from Abdelkader, during the conquest, up to and including the FLN, during the Algerian War. One finds similar characters in the other main *Pied-Noir* comics series about colonized Algeria, by Joyaux-Brédy and Joux. They prop up their claim on colonial Algeria by constructing Algerian authenticity as consisting of strong devotion to French rule.

One of the most recent, compelling and complex comics about *Harkis* in my corpus is *Le cousin harki* [The *Harki* Cousin], again by Boudjellal (2012). It weaves together several stories of victimhood and betrayal. This includes the French abandonment of most of the *Harkis* in Algeria at the end of the Algerian War, their consequent massacre (Figure 4.13), and the prison-camp conditions to which those *Harkis* and their families who escaped to France were confined by authorities for years after the war. Boudjellal connects this with the genocidal killing of Jews in France during the Second World War, without effacing the specificities of the two histories. He critiques excessive violence by both the FLN (the emasculation also depicted in *La guerre fantôme*) and the French army (torture of both

French and Algerians), as well as anti-Algerian violence and homophobia in France during the 1970s. Moreover, this is the first of Boudjellal's comics since "Amour d'Alger" [Love in Algiers] (Boudjellal 1984; see below) to evoke the losses suffered by *Pieds-Noirs*: he represents them in an empathetic manner as they leave Algeria for exile in France at the end of the war. Space prevents me from analyzing in detail this nuanced story of reconciliation, which is masterfully drawn and told by Boudjellal.

We have seen *Harkis* depicted by cartoonists of varied backgrounds: former French soldier (Vidal) or descendants of one (Lax and Giroud), *Pied-Noir* (Ferrandez, Joyaux-Brédy, Mérezette), Algerian (Boudjellal) or other African immigrant heritage (Alagbé) and metropolitan French (Golo and Frank). They often represent *Harkis* as victimized through French abandonment (*Une éducation algérienne*, "Carnets d'Orient," *Les rivages amers*), as menacing ("Un si joli sourire kabyle"), or as both ("Vengeance harkie," *Nègres jaunes*). *Harkis* symbolize the extreme violence and flagrant injustices of the war, whether through a recalling of *Harki* torture of Algerian immigrants in Paris, or much more often, the abandonment and massacre of *Harkis* in Algeria, and the long mistreatment of those who managed to escape to France.

Algerian-French perspectives on (post-)colonial conflict

In "Amour d'Alger," one of the earliest post-independence French graphic narratives about the war, Boudjellal (1984) uses the obstacles to a friendship between a boy and a girl to symbolize the immense pressure to take sides during the Algerian War and the rupture in French and Algerian relations. Ramdane, a young Algerian water-vendor in Algiers, is a friend of Mireille, a French girl. Although the two would like to remain together, they are surrounded by forces that conspire to separate them. Each mother forbids her child to spend time with the other, because each family has experienced a war loss inflicted by the other side: Mireille's father was killed by Algerians, and Ramdane's brother is in prison as a suspected *fellagha*.[55] The separation of the two children foreshadows France's impending loss of Algeria. Although the story is set in Algeria, it suggests that from early in his career Boudjellal knew how important the memory of the war was to the Algerian immigrant community in France, which is the focus of most of his comics.

Many comics about the colonization of North Africa[56] and, we have seen, the Algerian War share references to the American Western. A comic by Boudjellal provides one of the most innovative reworkings of this theme in

Figure 4.13: Two former soldiers, a *Harki* and a French recruit, recall how the French army abandoned the *Harkis* during the withdrawal from Algeria at the end of the war. From Farid Boudjellal, *Le cousin harki* [The *Harki* Cousin] (Paris: Futuropolis, 2012), p. 53. © Farid Boudjellal.

the context of the Algerian War and immigration. In the first three volumes of his "Petit Polio" [Little Polio] series,[57] set during the Algerian War in the French port city of Toulon, where Boudjellal was born to Algerian parents in 1953, the cartoonist returns to the problem of how to represent the genesis and resolution of French-Algerian antagonisms that came to a head during the Algerian War.[58] The election in 1995 of a Front National mayor of Toulon, Jean-Marie Le Chevallier (Stora 1999: 93), probably helped motivate Boudjellal to create the series. He incorporates personal and family experiences into the three volumes as a way of drawing himself and the French-Algerian community into, and as part of, French society. He uses family photos taken during the Algerian War in 1950s Toulon for some of his visual documentation. The war first intrudes visibly into the life of Mahmoud Slimani—a six year-old Maghrebi-French boy disabled by polio (like Boudjellal himself)—when he and his friends see policemen beating up an "Arab" whom the officers caught riding a streetcar without a ticket (Boudjellal 2006a: 46–47). Unthinkingly, one of the boy's friends says that the man resembles Mahmoud's father, which renders the spectacle even more traumatic for him. Mahmoud returns home immediately and takes refuge in a comic book story about "Blek le Roc" [Blek the Rock] and his friends, a brave and hardy band of French Canadian trappers, whom he imagines coming to his rescue and going off to liberate the Algerians (48–49; Figures 4.14, 4.15). By redrawing another, older colonial story, the cartoonist literally draws Mahmoud into it: the boy temporarily enters it to join his heroes from the American frontier. Redrawing empire is here a very complex process. Mahmoud's imaginative reading of "Blek le roc" raises fascinating questions about how ethnic minority readers consume mainstream comic books with a colonial theme and perspective. According to Boudjellal and Slim, Algeria's best-known comics artist, "Blek le roc" was much appreciated by Algerians on both sides of the Mediterranean, partly because it was an inexpensive publication aimed at working class children, but also thanks to its story line about French settlers on the American continent who were struggling to maintain their independence from the colonizing English, into which they paradoxically read their own struggle against the colonizing French (cf. Labter 2009: 46–47, 53–55, 80). Further complicating matters, "Blek le roc" was drawn and scripted by a trio of Italian cartoonists, under the collective pseudonym Essegesse.[59] Originally issued in French translation as installments in a small-format magazine printed on pulp paper, the "Blek le roc" series was later republished in a multi-volume anthology by Mourad Boudjellal, Farid's brother (e.g., Essegesse 1995).[60]

The episode in "Petit Polio" raises interesting issues about empathy, group formation and reading culture (see Miller 2007: 171–75; 2009: 186–87). The failure of Mahmoud's friend to imagine himself in the Algerian

Figure 4.14: An Algerian-French boy, having just witnessed the beating of a North African man in Toulon during the Algerian War, seeks solace in his favorite food and his preferred comic, about French trappers at war with the British in colonial Québec. From Farid Boudjellal, *Petit Polio* [Little Polio], vol. 1 (Toulon: Soleil Productions, 1998), p. 48. © Farid Boudjellal.

Figure 4.15: The Algerian War for independence is echoed in the much earlier colonial struggle of French-Canadians, as Mahmoud tries to come to terms with his national identity. From Farid Boudjellal, *Petit Polio* [Little Polio], vol. 1 (Toulon: Soleil Productions, 1998), p. 49. © Farid Boudjellal.

boy's place leads the Euro-French boy to inadvertently insert Mahmoud, via his father, in the same category as the victimized Algerian man. This in turn leads Mahmoud and his friends to realize that he is indeed Algerian in some sense, even though the boys share a proficiency in the local Toulon culture, references to which Boudjellal delights in sprinkling throughout the series: for example, a tongue-in-cheek lexicon of regional expressions concludes the first volume. They help anchor his work somewhat in the way that lexical terms from Lyon do in Azouz Begag's first novel, *Le gone du Chaâba* [*The Shantytown Kid*] (2006), which also includes a French-Algerian glossary at the end of the book (cf. Hargreaves 1997: 39, 120–21).

The representational conventions of the North American frontier structure another confrontation in "Petit Polio" (cf. Woodhull 1997). In the first book (1998, republished in 2006a), Boudjellal reworks conventions of spaghetti Western showdowns between cowboys, such as one would find in the comics that Mahmoud reads or in films produced beginning in the early 1960s, just after the period when Boudjellal's three volumes are set (July 1958–April 1960). The showdown involves two men, Abdel Slimani, the father of Mahmoud, and César, a former friend and colleague (in the first volume they are fellow city employees), who is conscripted by the French army and sent to Algeria (Boudjellal 2006a: 19). There, César's best friend, another French soldier, is killed in an ambush by the FLN (69–71), leaving him embittered and hating all North Africans, including Abdel (73–80, 93–94). Their encounter occurs after Abdel is released from prison, where he was tortured by French police for his financial contributions to the FLN from his meager salary (72–73, 86–93). Just before the showdown we see them unknowingly walking towards each other in two juxtaposed panels (94). This, and the fact that César earlier threatened to kill Abdel, tell the reader that a confrontation is impending. On the following pages (95–96), the cartoonist represents the showdown through visual shots like those in a spaghetti Western: a four-frame sequence shows Abdel approaching César, daring the soldier to kill him. Three subsequent close-ups focus tightly on César's angry face, while Abdel taunts him. However, the final panel is a reverse shot that ironically shows not the visual spectacle of the fight itself, but instead a collective, textual (verbal) version of it, provided by a crowd of French onlookers after it has ended. Boudjellal uses a similar technique in the earlier police beating of the North African caught on the streetcar. By doing so, he accomplishes several things: he provides us with a child's perspective, whether or not there is a young spectator; he avoids sensationalizing anti-Arab violence; and he uses French onlookers dialogically, as a chorus that debates the nature of the spectacle that has been (partially) obscured for us. Here the spectators tell us that César easily beat Abdel, already weakened by the police mistreatment, but that now César is crying in Abdel's arms.

As Miller (2007: 175) has persuasively argued, the artist draws a parallel between, on the one hand, the murderous toll of the Algerian War and, on the other, the illness and death, from leukemia, of Viviane, the mother of Rémy, a young friend of Mahmoud (cf. Douglas and Malti-Douglas 2008). Images of the bed-ridden Viviane describing the need to tell children about death are intercut with the confrontation between César and Abdel. She tells her son the truth—that she is dying—at precisely the moment when the two men are fighting. We understand that Rémy and César must be crying at the same time. The following pages narrate the reconciliation of the two men, as they peacefully discuss the war in Abdel's apartment, surrounded by their wives and children. Victor Hugo's poem, "Demain, dès l'aube" [Tomorrow, at Dawn]—inspired by the death of his daughter Léopoldine—is a leitmotif throughout the first two volumes of "Petit Polio" (1998, 1999; cf. 2006a), serving as a litany not so much for the demise of l'Algérie française (Viviane and her husband, Armand Cosmetti, are not Pieds-Noirs), but generally, for the death and destruction caused by the war (cf. Douglas and Malti-Douglas 2008; Miller 2009). At one point Abdel calls it a "saleté de guerre" [filthy war] (Boudjellal 2006a: 57), while speaking with Rita, the pregnant wife of César, who is fighting in Algeria, but the irony is that Abdel too is aiding the war effort through his small monetary contribution to the FLN. The artist thereby implies that the "dirty war" produces paradoxes and contradictions, pitting Algerian and French friends against each other, despite their best intentions.

As we have seen, early in his career, in "Amour d'Alger" (1984), Boudjellal uses the mixed, French-Algerian couple to represent the tearing apart of French and Algerian communities in Algeria. More recently, in Les contes du djinn Hadj Moussa: La rupture [Tales of the Genie Hadj Moussa: The Rupture] (Boudjellal and Leïz 2008), he depicts a mixed couple similarly in a story set in Algeria during the run up to the First World War. By contrast, in several of his other comics he represents the Algerian War in ways that violently tear apart characters but then reconcile them again in (post-)colonial France: Jambon-Beur: Les couples mixtes [Ham-Butter/Arab: Mixed Couples] (1995), "Petit Polio" (1998, 1999; 2006a) and Le cousin harki (2012). His contrasting treatment of the French-Algerian affrontier in Algeria during the colonial period and in (post-)colonial France redraws empire in a nuanced manner that recognizes the legitimacy of nationalist demands for Algerian independence from French colonial rule, while also favoring the integration of post-colonial minorities within France today and the reconciling of key wartime antagonists.

Metropolitan memories and mediations

The Algerian War deeply affected metropolitan France at the time and has an ongoing impact on French society. This helps explain why one finds comics about the war, including its effects in mainland France, by cartoonists who were not French conscripts (or their descendants), nor belong to post-colonial ethnic minority groups. The cartoonists whose work I analyze in this section again inflect post-colonialism in France by redrawing empire, often to recover alternate histories of anti-colonial activism and to expose colonial injustices at the heart of French empire, still repeatedly neglected, distorted and even denied. By redrawing empire they help rework the colonial heritage of French comics, produce collective memory about the colonial past, and thereby shift public discourse about it. The war can appear in the background, as for example in some of Jacques Tardi's adaptations of Léo Malet's *romans policiers* [detective novels], where it appears mainly as an unexplained and unsettling visual-textual presence, through graffiti and posters on Parisian walls and fences.[61] Other cartoonists foreground the event in their narrative.

Christin's negative representation of the French army in Algeria and of the OAS, in his ground-breaking *La demoiselle de la Légion d'honneur* (Christin and Goetzinger 1990; serialized 1979; cf. Douvry 1983: 35), is rooted in his political activism of the time: "I came to political maturity during the period of decolonization. I went to my first demonstration against the Algerian War, and [Pierre] Mendès-France was my first hero" (Christin and Goetzinger 1996). The book's protagonist is a naive French woman. She marries a fascistic army officer who soon joins the OAS. Gradually gaining autonomy, the protagonist moves across a series of historical backdrops, from colonialism to the events of May 1968, and then the feminist movement. Midway through this trajectory of self-discovery, the story carries the reader from the death throes of French Algeria to neo-colonialism in francophone black Africa and draws a contrast between typical French military men of the two periods: the protagonist's husband is an idealistic, aristocratic cavalryman whereas her lover is a cynical military advisor who delights in torturing captured Africans. In the conclusion the death of the protagonist's husband from a wound received in a neo-colonial war in Africa provides her with a sizeable inheritance, allowing her to choose her own future. It was the first in their series of historical romances about de-/colonization, aimed at young female readers.

Several other cartoonists were too young to fight in the war, but were personally affected by it either in France or Algeria and have depicted various aspects of it. The best example is Baru (Hervé Barulea), who witnessed war-related attacks in the working-class housing projects where he grew up, in the Lorraine region (Baru 2011). In three comic books he represents internecine Algerian violence, including the harsh punishment (even executions) meted out by the FLN in France against Algerian emigrants who refused to pay a war tax: *Vive la classe!* [Long Live the Draftees!] (1987), *Le chemin de l'Amérique* (Baru, Thévenet and Ledran 1998, 2002), which won the Angoulême festival prize for *meilleur album* [best comic book] in 1991, and *Boncornards têtes-de-lard!* [Stubborn-Headed Cuckolds!] (Baru 2003). It has been argued that the spectacle of fratricidal, wartime Algerian violence made a strong and lasting impression on working-class French in metropolitan France (Alidières 2006). In these three comics the violence often surges up unexpectedly and hauntingly to disrupt the lives of Baru's characters: for example, it returns as a frightening spectacle, recalled after the war, of a dead Algerian lying in the street in *Vive la classe!* (Baru 1987: 17–18). During the war it bursts through the doors of Saïd Boudiaf's boxing gym, as pro-FLN demonstrators pour inside to flee the massive French police repression in Paris on 17 October 1961 in *Le chemin de l'Amérique* (Baru, Thévenet and Ledran 1998: 42–43). In *Boncornards têtes-de-lard!* (Baru 2003: 32–35) it strikes at night, when Algerians rake the house of young Leïla Bouhibi with gunfire, forcing her family to flee. Her Italian-French boyfriend Igor D'Alvise desperately searches for her the next morning, and then tries to kill himself when he realizes that she appears to be gone forever.

In *Fais péter les basses Bruno!* [Blow Out the Bass Speakers, Bruno!] (2010: 110–11) the memory of the Algerian War again explodes into the narrative, in the post-colonial present, when drunken French military veterans at a reunion mistake some Maghrebi-French gangsters for their enemies of yesteryear and begin shooting at them, as though reliving the conflict through a flashback caused by post-traumatic stress disorder (Figure 4.16; cf. Baru 2011: 232–34). In another comic by Baru (2007: 134), about the end of military conscription in France, which went into effect on 27 June 2001, a single frame powerfully recalls the extra-judicial execution of Algerian prisoners by the French army, who threw prisoners out of helicopters to kill them and dispose of their bodies—the victims who were thrown into the ocean, were sometimes called "crevettes Bigeard" [Bigeard shrimp], after a prominent French military officer who was among the colonial paratroopers in the Battle of Algiers (cf. Horne 1978: 167–68, 190).[62] In several of Baru's other comics the war lurks behind the scenes, unstated but clearly shaping the racist attitudes, insults and physical violence of Franco-French charac-

Figure 4.16: The memory of the Algerian War explodes into a comic-book narrative set decades later, when drunken French military veterans at a reunion mistake some Maghrebi-French gangsters for their former enemies. From Baru, *Fais péter les basses Bruno!* [Blow Out the Bass Speakers, Bruno!] (Paris: Futuropolis, 2010), p. 110. © Baru.

ters who attack young Maghrebi-French men. Baru also takes great care in many of his comics to show French-Algerian solidarity, especially but not only among young people (cf. Baru 2008: 246–51; 2011: 226–32).

In the first volume of one of the most acclaimed graphic narratives of recent years, the multi-volume, autobiographical series *L'ascension du haut mal* [*Epileptic*] (1998; 2006: 1–52), David B. deconstructs the formation of anti-immigrant hatred among French youths. His boy protagonists, living in Orléans in 1964, two years after the end of the Algerian War, encounter Mohamed, an immigrant construction worker (1998: 2, 12–15; 2006: 3, 13–16). Some of them, who have heard stories about knife-wielding Arabs from a father who fought in Algeria, fear Mohamed and call him racist names. By contrast, the two main protagonists, whose parents have told them no such stories, are unafraid of asking to share the lunch of the workman, who kindly complies. Although short, the episode suggests that North African immigrants and French children too could be victims of resentment left over from the recently ended war and of colonial racism produced over the 132 years of French colonial occupation of Algeria. To illustrate the conception of the war held by the main protagonist, Pierre-François—the narrator's younger self and a budding cartoonist—David B. inserts into his realist, but highly imaginative, narrative a short, five-frame sequence representing the war as an epic confrontation between scimitar-wielding, camel-riding, turban-clad Bedouins, who rid their country of French Foreign Legionaries (Figure 4.17). Although David B. presents the Algerian "events" here in a child's simplified, imagined version, he places

Figure 4.17: A French child's perspective on the Algerian War, as a war between Bedouins and French Legionaries. From David B., *L'ascension du haut mal* [*Epileptic*], vol. 1, preface by Florence (Paris: L'Association, 1998), p. 14. © David B., L'Association, 1996.

them alongside other great mythical and historical wars that fascinate the boy (e.g., Biblical conflicts, the conquest of the Aztecs by Cortez, the First and Second World Wars).

The way that David B. shows his protagonist gradually learning about the war's true nature—not through books, but instead via personal anecdotes gleaned from participants—appears to support the argument by Stora (1992: 238–48), that the enormous number of publications about the war did not indicate or produce a cohesive national memory of it, especially in the absence of serious attention paid to the war by the national school system or other public institutions. (By contrast, the books that he reads about the two World Wars help him contextualize the wartime experiences of his grandfathers [David B. 1998: 21, 28; 2006: 22, 29].) The young protagonist of *L'ascension du haut mal* overhears adult conversations between his parents and family friends about sadistic French conscripts who tortured Algerian prisoners, which destroy his hieratic, juvenile image of the war (Figure 4.18): "Je saisis des conversations qui anéantissent la belle image d'Epinal que je me suis dessinée" [I overhear conversations that destroy the beautiful cartoonish image that I drew for myself] (1998: 29; 2006: 30). The narrator also describes a strange experience that he had later, as an adult: twice, a man who fought on the French side during the war told him a personal anecdote about it, and each time the man died of cancer soon after, before Pierre-François saw him again (1998: 31; 2006: 32). Although the narrator does not say that the participants' wartime experiences eventually led to their early death from illness, the artistic presentation strongly suggests that

Figure 4.18: A French boy overhears adult conversations about conscripted French soldiers torturing Algerians during the war. From David B., *L'ascension du haut mal* [*Epileptic*], vol. 1, preface by Florence (Paris: L'Association, 1998), p. 29. © David B., L'Association, 1996.

connection: the narrative sequentiality—two juxtaposed segments indicate an impending death after the retelling of wartime experiences; the narrator's comments on the uncanny similarity of the two sequences; and the visual treatment of the witnesses—the shading of their faces to black just after or during the telling of their war stories.[63] The two men—the first of whom is the French cartoonist Lob—may be compared with Vidal's semi-autobiographical character Albert, in *Une éducation algérienne*. Both the experience of the "dirty war," with its torture and killing, and the bottling up of that experience inside the minds of those who lived it, imported colonial violence into the metaphorical body of mainstream French society. The way David B. links the Algerian War with terminal cancer is similar to how Stora (1992) uses the metaphor of gangrene to describe the effects on French society of the failure to adequately deal with the painful and conflicting memories of the war.[64]

Today the event most emblematic of the official denial of colonial violence in France during the Algerian War is the horrific police repression—what has been described a massacre (cf. Branche and House 2010: 117)—of Algerian men, women and children peacefully demonstrating in Paris on

17 October 1961, for which the French government long acknowledged 11,538 people arrested but only 64 wounded and 3 dead (including one Frenchman), whereas a FLN official later estimated 2,300 wounded and 200 killed (Péju 2000 [first ed., 1961]; Levine 1985; Einaudi 1991; Tristan 1991; House and Macmaster 2006). *Le chemin de l'Amérique*, first published in 1990, was to my knowledge the first comic book to depict the event (see McKinney 2008b). Since then, several cartoonists have represented or alluded to it in their comics, including *Nègres jaunes* (Alagbé 1995: n.p.; cf. Frey 2008: 120–21) and *Le feuilleton du siècle* [The Soap Opera of the Century] (Willem 2000: 127–28). At least four such works were timed to coincide with symbolic anniversaries: *17 octobre—17 illustrateurs* [17 October—17 Illustrators] (Baudoin et al. 2001) was published forty years on, *17 Octobre 1961, 17 bulles: Tragédie-sur-Seine* [17 October 1961, 17 Bubbles: Tragedy-on-the-Seine] (Kebir 2011) and *Octobre noir* [Black October] (Daeninckx and Mako 2011) on the fiftieth anniversary of the event, and *Demain, demain: Nanterre, bidonville de la Folie, 1962–66* [Tomorrow, Tomorrow: Nanterre, Shantytown of la Folie, 1962–66] (Maffre 2012) was published on the fiftieth anniversary of Algerian independence. *Octobre noir* was scripted by Didier Daeninckx, whose prose detective novel *Meurtres pour mémoire* [*Murder in Memoriam*] (1994; first edition, 1984) was instrumental in raising awareness about this event in French popular culture and was read by Baru before he drew *Le chemin de l'Amérique* (cf. McKinney 2008b).[65] Along with the latter, *Octobre noir* is the most extended comic-book representation of the event, showing the anti-colonial protest in the capital's streets, followed by the hiding and recovery of knowledge about the French repression. In these works, cartoonists effectively use comics to recall a protest march by the colonized in Paris and the suppressed history of its horrible repression by the colonizers. In *Le chemin de l'Amérique* and *Octobre noir,* respectively, the Algerian(-French) protagonists even fight back or speak out against the repression. Each also explores metropolitan French attitudes toward Algerians, including both racist reactions and rare but important examples of solidarity with the colonized.

Conclusion: Beyond the affrontier?

We have seen that the post-colonial perspectives of French comics on the Algerian War are informed to a significant degree by cartoonists' personal connections to the war, whether through ethnicity (the Algerian-French and *Pied-Noir* communities), participation in the conflict (or descent from a participant) or personal observation of its unfolding in France. Although the post-colonial paradigm cannot of course explain the entire field of French and Belgian comics, it is necessary for investigating key dimensions of it, including a large and growing number of works. It allows us to plot different positions on a map of possible perspectives on the colonial past and, by extrapolation, helps us understand how French artists and the groups whose views they articulate envision their present and future in light of that history. Most important is the encouraging evidence that some artists are able to create a dialogical, polyphonic and critical vision of the colonial past. Several redraw the colonized as agents of history who liberate themselves, sometimes assisted by French anti-colonialists. Many works analyzed here also show the horror of French torture and the reality of French state violence against unarmed non-combatants—this was covered up and denied during the war and dismissed afterwards by a blanket amnesty that stifled debate and discussion (Stora 1992: 211–16). To ignore or downplay the fundamental, systemic nature of French colonialism as various forms of war and brutal, criminal subjugation (e.g., terrorizing and economically exploiting the colonized) is to leave the field open to all kinds of negationist approaches to colonial history.[66]

Moreover, many of these comics make important connections between different colonial wars, evoking the importance of the Indochinese experience as a preparation for the Algerian War, both as a training ground for French war techniques (e.g., Lax and Giroud 1999: 6) and as a war that many French soldiers believed should have been won, which increased their determination to keep Algeria French.[67] On the other hand, Boudjellal (among others) demonstrates an awareness of the need to set up a dialogue between different kinds of memory about the Algerian war as a way of moving beyond bitter, revengeful positions. The perspective in his comics has evolved considerably. In the early works "Vengeance harkie" (first drawn in 1983) and "Amour d'Alger" (1984), he respectively emphasized the colonial affrontier between *Harkis* and their Algerian victims, and between *Pieds-Noirs* and Algerians. By contrast, in *Jambon-Beur* (1995a) and the "Petit Polio" series, including *Le cousin harki* (2012), he focuses on healing wounds and reconciling communities divided by colonial history: Algerian immigrants, French conscripts, *Harkis* and even— *Le cousin harki* suggests—*Pieds-Noirs*. On the other hand, he has not yet represented an encounter between *Pieds-Noirs* and the Algerian community in post-colonial France. Inversely, with the exception of one early short story printed in a fanzine, "Le pain des Français" [The Bread of the French] (1979), Ferrandez has never depicted either the immigrant Algerian community in France or its historical visions of the war. He has focused on Algeria (not metropolitan France) and there almost exclusively on the period before Algerian independence and the loss of *l'Algérie française*. The separate perspectives of cartoonists of *Pied-Noir* and Algerian immigrant background on the Algerian War is therefore palpable in a dearth of characters from the other—still apparently opposing—side in their publications. This suggests that the French-Algerian affrontier continues to divide and separate the Algerian and *Pied-Noir* communities in France (cf. McKinney 2007a, 2008c, 2011a). Nonetheless, in Ferrandez's "Carnets d'Orient," as in *Jambon-Beur*, the Algerian civil war that began in the 1990s triggered a return to the preceding Algerian war, of decolonization, and once again threw open to question the multiple, often familial, ties that bind France and Algeria (cf. Balibar 1998). This process has encouraged both cartoonists to deal with difficult issues raised by the war.

Because they have no family connections to either the *Pieds-Noirs* or the Algerians, it may be easier for Giroud and Lax to confront the two ethnic or national(ist) positions, confronting an Algerian guerilla soldier's memories with those of a French soldier of settler extraction (see above). The agonized dialogue by the two characters over the historical record—as well as the conclusion to the comic—shows the readers that, although atrocities were indeed committed by both sides, the disproportionate, retaliatory massacres by the French were a logical outgrowth of extensive colonial violence that permeated French Algeria. French massacres showed the civilizing mission to be a lie and assured the ultimate success of the radical Algerian nationalists. By contrast, it is much more difficult to decipher the logic behind the war violence in Ferrandez's Algerian War series: its spiraling escalation appears above all to be unwarranted and absurd. This historical vision reflects a liberal, humanist, and utopian *Pied-Noir* belief that if the violence had been avoided—if the Algerians and French could somehow have gotten along—then it would have been possible to create a vibrant, rich and ethnically diverse society.

Cartoonists participated in the fifty-year commemoration of the events in the Algerian War by publishing several comics: *Leçons coloniales* [Colonial Lessons] (Begag and Defali 2012) for the May 1945 uprising and repression, *Octobre noir* (Daeninckx and Mako 2011) for the French police repression of the Algerian immigrant demonstration of 17 October 1961 (see above), *Dans l'ombre de Charonne* [In the Shadow of Charonne] (Frappier and Frappier 2012) for that of the anti-OAS demonstration of 8 February 1962, "France, Algérie: Je n'oublie pas" [France, Algeria: I Don't Forget] (Morvandiau 2012) for the signature of the Evian Agreement (19 March 1962), as well as *Le cousin harki* (Boudjellal 2012), *Demain, Demain: Nanterre, bidonville de la Folie, 1962–1966* (Maffre 2012) and *Retour à Saint-Laurent-des-Arabes* [Return to Saint-Laurent-of-the-Arabs]

(Blancou 2012) for the war and its sequels. Many of these works focus on historical events previously absent from, or little explored in, French comics, through both innovative and more traditional cartooning techniques. Cartoonists therefore continue to redraw French empire and its aftermath in ways that often cross and help to dismantle the colonial affrontier.

5
THE VOYAGE OUT AND THE VOYAGE IN

New perspectives and new ethnic minorities

What is "the meaning of the colonial voyage" (Memmi 1985: 33) today? The "voyage out"—to colonize, survey or draw empire, for example—is a corollary to what Edward Said (1994b) calls the "voyage in."[1] I use these two tropes here to summarize some of the most important transformations in comics about French colonialism and imperialism. One of the meanings that Said gives to the voyage in is the arrival of exiles and immigrants in (former) colonial and imperialist countries and cities. It seems clear that Said saw himself as having made a voyage in, from Mandate Palestine to New York, where he was a University Professor of English and Comparative Literature at Columbia University. In many ways French cartoonists from regions and countries formerly, or still, colonized by France have made a voyage in, to France as a (former) colonial and imperialist center. This is even true for cartoonists born and raised in France who are members of an ethnic minority group originating in a (former) colony, because they are citizens of a nation that has not yet accepted full responsibility for its colonial history and the far-reaching consequences of its imperialist actions in the past and present. For cartoonists this means—among other things—finding a place for their work within a comics literature still full of alienating stereotypes about the (formerly) colonized (McKinney 2011b). Today there are French cartoonists with family connections to a range of (former) French colonies, including Algeria (Farid Boudjellal, Larbi Mech-kour, Kamel Khélif, Leïla Leïz), Benin (Yvan Alagbé), Cambodia (Séra, Tian), Ivory Coast (Marguerite Abouet), Guadeloupe (Roland Monpierre), Syria (Riad Sattouf) and Vietnam (Clément Baloup, Marcelino Truong). There has now even been a major comics publisher—Mourad Boudjellal, of Soleil Productions, based in Toulon—who has made a similar voyage in.[2] Several of these cartoonists come from ethnically mixed families: Alagbé, Baloup, Sattouf, Séra and Truong all have a French mother of European extraction; and one of the grandmothers of Farid and Mourad Boudjel-lal was Armenian. Some have represented *métis/se* [ethnically or culturally mixed] characters in their fictional or autobiographical comics (Alagbé, Baloup, Farid Boudjellal, Sattouf and Truong). Some have ethnically mixed children from their relationships with members of the ethnic majority group in France. Whether or not they, their forebears or their progeny are ethni-cally mixed, all of these cartoonists have a mixed cultural heritage, which has informed their work. In this volume I have focused on the history of colonialism and imperialism, which several of the cartoonists just men-tioned have thematized in their comics. Many of them have also represented contemporary, multicultural France in their comics, which is the main focus of my next book. On the other hand, some of these cartoonists have also published comics on themes that have no clear connection with colonial-ism, imperialism, exile, immigration or postcolonial ethnic minorities in France. There is of course no deterministic correlation between their ethnic and cultural background and their art. Nonetheless, several of these artists have created some of the most compelling, critical and nuanced accounts of colonial history and its aftermath. These cartoonists may act as "entre-preneurs de mémoire" [memory entrepreneurs], much as Sylvie Durmelat (2000) finds film director Yamina Benguigui doing in and around *Mémoires d'immigrés: L'héritage maghrébin* [Memories of Immigrants: The Maghrebi Heritage] (1998). By reconstructing aspects of French colonial history, they help to create a collective, cultural memory for immigrant ethnic minori-ties, but also for the French in general, who share that past in important ways (cf. Rigney 2005). Some in France resent and denounce this process because it can open up old wounds and may be or appear accusatory. They may also fear a cultural and social disintegration of France or an exacerba-tion of ethnic cleavages. However, creating comics with an ethnic minority perspective—whether Algerian, Vietnamese, West African or Caribbean—on colonial history can be part of a voyage in as a positive and necessary part of integration into French society and history. Certainly this activity can potentially lead to excesses, including what Said (1994b) decried as a "rhetoric of blame" for past colonial misdeeds. Nonetheless, one should remember that French government administrations on the right and left have already recognized and repaired what have been presented as colonial injustices against people of European ancestry: for example, several laws have provided restitution for *Pieds-Noirs*[3] and even for former members of the OAS, although the latter was an illegal terrorist organization that attacked the French state and repeatedly attempted to assassinate President Charles De Gaulle. Given that, it is unfair to blame members of (other) post-colonial ethnic minority groups in France, including cartoonists, for pointing to the damage that French colonialism and imperialism inflicted or still inflict on their communities, both in their ancestral homelands and in the metropolitan center, or even for demanding reparations. It is perhaps surprising, then, that French cartoonists from formerly colonized groups such as the Algerians or the Vietnamese have not expressed demands for monetary reparations in their comics or in interviews. Instead, by depicting the negative effects on colonized victims they have represented the need for righting the historical record of colonialism. They have worked to decolonize comic-book representations, including by deconstructing colonial figures, such as the colonial adventurer. Of course this memorial and historical activity could certainly prepare the ground for demands for monetary reparations: public recognition that historical wrongs have been committed is a pre-condition for restitution and reparations.

Members of other ethnic groups, including the European majority, can assist ethnic minority cartoonists, say by helping them to redraw empire in ways that revisit colonial history and reconstruct memory to undermine the colonial affrontier separating (ex-)colonizer from (ex-)colonized: for example, Mathieu Jiro drew the two *Chính Trị* books scripted by Baloup (2005, 2007), on interwar anticolonial activism and the Vietnamese nationalist movement, and Martine Lagardette produced a dossier about *métissage*, published in *Jambon-Beur: Les couples mixtes* [Ham-Butter/Arab: Mixed Couples] (Boudjellal 1995a), and another about Boudjellal's mixed, Algerian and Armenian heritage, and the Armenian genocide by the Turks, for the second edition of *Mémé d'Arménie* [Grandma from Armenia] (Boudjellal 2006b). Other publications by ethnic majority cartoonists may play a similar role: for example, *Les oubliés d'Annam* [The Forgotten Ones of Annam] (1990–91) and *Azrayen'* (1998–99), by Lax and Frank Giroud, focus on the history and memory of the two longest French wars of decolonization, and present favorably several Vietnamese, Algerian and French characters who criticize colonial violence (see Chapters 3 and 4, above). In the remainder of this concluding chapter I continue my examination of the voyage out and the voyage in. Here as throughout this study, my focus is on comics (re)published since 1962, although I occasionally refer to earlier works that have not been reissued.

The voyage out, the voyage home and the voyage back

In the pre-1962 French comics and cartoons studied here, one finds a variety of characters who made the voyage out to the colonies: administrators, adventurers, doctors, foreign criminals or provocateurs, missionaries, reporters, sailors and soldiers. For most, the voyage out consists of attempts to undertake what was seen as France's civilizing mission, in its secular and religious dimensions. Conquest and related military violence are generally presented as a duty to pacify and a right to self-defense (against indigenous outlaws[4] and foreign provocateurs[5]), and colonization as an obligation to civilize peoples and to fructify [mettre en valeur] otherwise untended natural resources. Characters who make the voyage out sometimes remain abroad more or less indefinitely: an extreme case would be the martyred missionaries in "Parachutés au Laos" [Parachuted into Laos] (Verdon and Perrin-Houdon 1951–52) and in *Charles de Foucauld* (Jijé 1994, serialized 1959), but there are also settlers depicted as living in French colonies,[6] even when challenged or besieged by local nationalists, in various French comics from the period.[7] Those who return to France may pine for the colony that they left behind, as the retired father does at the beginning of "Parachutés au Laos" (Verdon and Perrin-Houdon, no. 215 [14 January 1951]). Representations of colonial exploration and discovery in such comics are generally designed to cultivate support for colonialism among young French readers while amusing them. It informs them about supposedly primitive and exotic peoples, and about ancient civilizations now replaced by European empires, including the French one. Art historian David Kunzle (1990: 298–307; 2007) has analyzed how nineteenth-century European cartoonists sometimes took a critical look at the imperialism of their own governments. He attributes this to the class positions of cartoonists and their readers: members of the middle and working classes were less likely to benefit directly and significantly from imperialism than the ruling class did, and they often paid a higher price for it, including through military service. However, in the twentieth- and twenty-first-century French comics that are my primary focus here, there is little critique of French colonialism, or a disengagement from its values, until after 1962.[8] Mainstream comics publishers, cartoonists and their readers generally supported French colonialism during approximately the first half of the twentieth century. Some Pieds nickelés [Leadfoot Gang] episodes are among the rare exceptions, but they too remain suffused with colonial racism: in black Africa, the French protagonists simply replace the local French colonial authorities in order to extract the very same benefits (labor and profit) from the colonized for as long as they are able—until Louis Forton sends his characters elsewhere (McKinney 2011b). The vein of related European French-language picaresque comics and cartoons featuring civilian tourists and travelers (i.e., not on a colonial mission per se) extends forward from early in the second wave of French colonialism and from the beginnings of the comic art form (cf. Groensteen 1998): e.g., Rodolphe Töpffer's *Histoire de Monsieur Cryptogame* [*Story of Mr. Cryptogame*] (first sketched in 1830),[9] Cham's *Les voyages d'agrément* [Pleasure Travels] (1849), Christophe's travels of the Famille Fenouillard (from 1893),[10] and the adventures of "Zig et Puce" (serialized beginning in 1925; cf. Groensteen 1998: 16–19; McKinney 2011b). Although the voyage out in those tales is often perilous—and their European protagonists are usually relieved to return home, if they are able to—the stories mostly do not critically investigate or undermine the colonial project. On the contrary, the voyage out in them is enabled by, and an occasion for, colonial occupation and domination. And the mild mockery of the foibles of metropolitan French tourists to Algeria in *Gringalou en Algérie* [Gringalou in Algeria] (Pinchon and Noé n.d.; serialized 1947) does not question French colonial ideology in the least: if the gullible tourists are distracted and easily fleeced (thereby generating humor), it is by pernicious Algerian thieves and highway bandits, whose criminal activities in the comic implicitly help justify the French colonial presence.

The voyage out to French (ex-)colonies, as depicted in comics created since 1962, is a more complex affair. Cartoonists often draw upon the same colonial-era set of outward-bound characters, especially in comics set in the colonial past. Though with significant differences from colonial times, the French voyage out remains marked by the humanitarian paradigm analyzed by Pierre Halen (1993a, 1993b) in Belgian colonial-era and post-independence comics about the Congo. Exoticism and colonial nostalgia are also important motivators of the voyage out. However, today's cartoonists often point to a disjuncture between professed humanitarian ideals or an ideology of (neo)colonialism and, on the other hand, reality in the (neo)colony. This debunking can be disinterested, cynical or in the service of another ideal, such as anti-colonialism. In recent works the French slave trader or slave owner[11] sometimes replaces the European liberator of slaves, such as David Livingstone[12] or Savorgnan de Brazza, who were celebrated in earlier comics.[13] Although colonial soldiers and administrators often professed an ideal of service to the colonized, the violence and repression for which they were responsible can make it difficult to take seriously their humanitarian claims. The voyage out by the French soldier has therefore dramatically changed in some recent comics. In *Déogratias* Stassen (2000) represents a French soldier first enforcing ethnic discrimination before the genocide in Rwanda and and later helping bands of Hutu killers to escape during the French military Opération Turquoise, which Stassen represents as neo-colonial support of the defeated Habyarimana regime. The soldier's transformation into a sexual tourist in Rwanda after the genocide completes Stassen's satire of French military neo-colonialism. In *D'Algérie* [About/From Algeria], Morvandiau also draws a clear line from colonial violence abroad to racism in France today, via the actions and words of Jean-Marie Le Pen, who volunteered as a soldier in both Indochina and Algeria (see above, Chapter 4).

By contrast with colonial administrators and soldiers, missionaries may been seen as more noble, for example in *Le dragon de bambou* [The Bamboo Dragon] (Truong and Leroi 1991), and even saintly, as in the hagiographic *Théophane Vénard: Dans les griffes du tigre* [Théophane Vénard: In the Tiger's Claws] (Brunor, Bar and Gilles 2007), about a Catholic priest martyred in Vietnam in 1861—its defense of illegal French Christian proselytizing in Vietnam does not differ from pre-1962 works, except perhaps through some criticism of French military and political leadership for ineffective support of missionaries. However, the role of missionaries is sometimes different in recent comics (cf. Delisle 2007, 2008, 2010). Christian missionaries are featured in comics about post-independence Vietnam (*L'ombre du triangle* [The Shadow of the Triangle] [Christin and Aymond 1999]), Rwanda (*Déogratias* [Stassen 2000]) and Algeria (*D'Algérie* [Morvandiau 2007]). *L'ombre du triangle* updates the humanitarian paradigm (Halen 1993b) by depicting Father Kevin Morissette, a French-speaking Canadian who teaches at a Catholic missionary school and was formerly a chaplain in a military commando, as now helping to fight international drug trafficking. In *Déogratias* and *D'Algérie,* the cartoonists date the implantation of missionaries back to colonial times, but their roles in the two books are radically different, even opposed. In Stassen's fiction a cynical and predatory Belgian missionary flees in 1994 to save his own skin, leaving behind most of his African parishioners to be slaughtered in the genocide. In his family history in comics, Morvandiau presents his *Pied-Noir* missionary uncle, a *Père blanc* [White Father] in the Berber city of Tizi-Ouzou, as intensely dedicated to the Algerians (Figure 5.1), to the point of remaining with them during the bloody civil war, leading to his assassination in 1994—supposedly by an Islamist GIA group, but which had perhaps been infiltrated and directed by the Algerian army (cf. Miller

SES CONFRÈRES ET LUI ONT CRÉÉ
UN SECRÉTARIAT SOCIAL ET
POPULAIRE. ONCLE JEAN EST TENACE
DANS LES DOSSIERS QU'IL DÉFEND.

IL EST SÉRIEUX AUSSI - PRÉOCCU-
PÉ? - ATTENTIF SANS DOUTE À
NE PAS ÊTRE PROVOCANT: LA
CUISINIÈRE, KABYLE, NOUS GUIDE

POUR UNE PROMENADE EN VILLE.
JE SOURIS QUAND MON ONCLE ME
CONFIE LA RESPONSABILITÉ DE
MES SOEURS AÎNÉES. PAS LUI.

LA KABYLIE EST POURTANT, PARAÎT-
IL, ASSEZ LIBÉRALE ET REBELLE.
LONGUE HISTOIRE BERBÉRO-ARABE.

Figure 5.1: Morvandiau (born in 1974) depicts his Uncle Jean, a *Pied-Noir* Catholic missionary, during a post-colonial trip that the cartoonist's family made to visit him in Algeria when Morvandiau was thirteen. His uncle and fellow missionaries were later assassinated in 1994, during the Algerian civil war. From Morvandiau, *D'Algérie* [About/From Algeria] (Rennes: L'oeil électrique/Maison Rouge, 2007), n.p. © Morvandiau and L'oeil électrique/Maison Rouge.

2009). Although this part of Morvandiau's semi-autobiographical comic book may remind us of the dedication and martyrdom of Charles de Foucauld in Jijé's hagiography—serialized in 1959, during the Algerian War—Morvandiau's book is a far cry from Jijé's swan song for French colonialism in North Africa (cf. Douvry 1983: 31; Delisle 2007: 140–41; 2010: 132–34; McKinney 2009: 82–83). Morvandiau (2007) tells the history of Algerian nationalism and anticolonialism as a legitimate and necessary historical development. He also recounts the anti-colonial activism of some members of the French Catholic clergy in Algeria during the Algerian War, and mentions accusations of post-1962, neo-colonial links between France and Algeria, the manipulation of which may have led to the death of his uncle. In works set in the present, members of humanitarian NGOs, French cooperation officials, and UN employees often replace, or work alongside, Christian missionaries. This is the case in three books that Stassen set in Rwanda: *Déogratias* (2000), *Pawa: Chroniques des Monts de la lune* [Pawa: Chronicle of the Mountains of the Moon] (2002) and *Les enfants* [The Children] (2004)—all provide a withering critique of the motivations and effectiveness of these secular western voyagers who travel out to former European colonies.

Some comics depict rivalry between colonialist powers, for example to show colonialism as a European power struggle, or that some colonial projects were better or more interesting than others. Comparisons between French colonizers and American imperialists in Vietnam, or between the Algerian settler colony and the United States, can be self-justifying.[14] For similar reasons, *Pied-Noir* cartoonists representing colonial Algeria often represent the voyage out as mostly the lot of poor and persecuted Europeans, who were tricked, manipulated or had few other choices. Once they arrive in the colony, comic-book voyagers may be endowed, whether credibly or not, with a realization that they have joined the side of the oppressors, but may nonetheless remain in place (e.g., in Ferrandez 1994b; Tronchet and Sibran 2003; see McKinney 2011a). The principal blame for the ills of colonization can then be laid at the feet of mainland politicians or French soldiers, who have no understanding of local conditions and needs. Some *Pied-Noir* cartoonists also blame rich colonizers, who reap significant financial benefits from colonization (e.g., Tronchet and Sibran 2003: 21; McKinney 2011a). The voyage out can also be the occasion for a return to, and reevaluation of, past struggles and ideals—including anticolonial and Third World activism—related to today's debates in France about postcolonial ethnic minorities or the meaning of world-transforming events such as the Cold War. All of these come together in the representation of the Indochinese and Algerian Wars, which is part of why they remain intriguing periods, when so-called adventure existed in various forms that have disappeared since then.

Voyagers travelling outward include figures, whether fictional or real, who return to colonial places of memory and are associated in some way with the colonizers. Their voyage out may be a pilgrimage, and is sometimes a return to a lost home (Ainsa 1982). This is already the case with the sons of the retired colonialist in "Parachutés au Laos" (Verdon and Perrin-Houdon 1951–52), who return from France to Indochina, where they were raised. Cartoonists who are the sons and daughters of *Pieds-Noirs* also make the voyage out, both in person and in their published work: Jacques Ferrandez and Morvandiau have depicted, in their comics and other works, the trips that they made to Algeria, and the people whom they met there.[15] The same can be true for the offspring of former French conscripts from colonial wars: Giroud made the voyage out by travelling to Algeria with his father, for whom the trip was a voyage back in time and memory. The journey enabled both father and son to come to terms with the conflict, in part by meeting and speaking with Algerians, including men who had fought on the opposing side. The wartime voyage out of French conscript soldiers that is depicted in *Azrayen'* (Lax and Giroud 1998–99, 2004) owes much to the father-and-son trip to Algeria, made years after the war.

Outbound voyagers may therefore be colonial returnees, travelling back to a *lieu de mémoire* [place of memory] that they once inhabited, or else members of a new generation, usually born and raised in France. In the latter case, the voyage out may be to a family home or homeland that, until then, only existed in the voyager's mind and through stories and photographs passed on from one generation to the next (cf. Ainsa 1982). The voyage out may be essentially imagined, because the second generation can only return to the colonial past via fiction or a reconstructed history, whether familial, ethnic or national—this is strikingly true in *Là-bas* [Down There] (2003), by Didier Tronchet and Anne Sibran, the daughter of *Pieds-Noirs*.[16] The prevalence of certain kinds of materials used to reconstruct and authenticate colonies as *lieux de mémoire* paradoxically points to the inaccessibility and intangibility of the latter: found notebooks, colonial postcards, old maps, creased photographs in sepia tones or shades of grey, and black-and-white television and film images. Many characters and voyages out self-reflexively foreground the colonial order. In Hergé's *Tintin au Congo* [*Tintin in the Congo*] (1973, first ed., 1930–31), Tintin the reporter helped maintain a still existing colonial order (Halen 1993a: 147–85). Investigative reporters in fiction now may serve as surrogates of cartoonists and readers interested in disinterring the colonial past to perpetuate or to demystify the so-called colonial adventure (cf. Miller 2004).[17] The painter,[18] photographer[19] or cartoonist [20] character in comics often alludes to the conditions of production of (post-)colonial representation, including through references to the colonial imagery on which authors base their work. In *L'ombre du triangle* (Christin and Aymond 1999), set in contemporary Vietnam, an anthropologist, a figure dating back to colonial times and specializing in representing the (formerly) colonized, makes the voyage out and appears in a modern guise: she provides cover for European drug smugglers, and may also point to ethnographic sources consulted by the cartoonists. In some instances the voyage out is not to far-off colonies, but to exoticized places within the metropolitan center itself—this is one way in which the voyage out meets the voyage in. French visiters to the 1931 Paris Colonial Exposition travelled outward in their minds by going to see colonized subjects who had made the voyage in, from their homelands to the colonial center (McKinney 2011b). Readers of the colonial exhibition episode in the "Zig et Puce" comics series also travelled outwards virtually, by reading about Alain Saint-Ogan's imagined African cannibals working at the Paris exhibition (Saint-Ogan 1995). Versions of this type of voyage continue in the present, for example in comic-book trips to the multi-ethnic Barbès and Belleville neighborhoods of Paris.

The voyage in, the voyage home and the voyage back

In colonial-era comics, participants in colonial exhibitions, colonized soldiers, indigenous rulers visiting France, servants of the French, or other immigrant workers are among those who make the voyage in. The voyage out and the voyage in are often closely connected there, but are generally not the occasion for a critique of colonial hierarchy or ideology. There is sometimes a permanent voyage back, suggesting that characters belong in colonized space and not in mainland France—this is true in *Sam et Sap* [Sam and Sap] (Candide and Le Cordier 1908), an early French comic featuring an African boy brought back to France, along with a monkey (cf. Patinax 1985; Pigeon 1996: 142–44). In other cases, they remain abroad, far from their colonized homeland, generally as secondary or minor characters, for example: the African cannibals turned servants in Saint-Ogan's "Zig et Puce" (see McKinney 2011b), and the Southeast Asian servant at the outset of "Parachutés au Laos" (Verdon and Perrin-Houdon 1951–52). In post-1962 comics, those who make the voyage in are often the same character types as in earlier works, but others help throw into question the positive, colonial-era comic-strip depiction of the colonial era; for example, colonized students, anticolonial activists, slaves of the French, and *métis/se* characters. Today the voyage in is often the occasion for a critique of colonial ideology, through the discovery of racism in France, which is not the paradise that had been described in the colony.[21] The (formerly) colonized are often the main protagonists of these fictions, in which there may not be a definitive voyage back, especially when immigrants and their offspring are portrayed—which is far more common today than before the late 1970s—although there may be brief trips to an ancestral homeland.[22] The voyage in of fictional characters can serve to work out the complexities of integration by the post-colonial minority group to which the artist belongs. For example, whereas the rare occurrences of the mixed couple in pre-1962 comics were usually examples of the colonial grotesque and evoked in passing (McKinney 2011b),[23] recent comics give more prominence and a wider range of meanings to the mixed couple and their *métis/e* offspring, as characters that make the voyage in.[24] Today they are sometimes strongly eroticized, especially in adult and alternative comics, but this is not always so. In *Les oubliés d'Annam* (Lax and Giroud 1990–91), a French reporter's attachment to a *métisse* helps anchor him in the colonial past (a pursuit of truth about the Indochinese War) while also connecting him to the post-colonial present (postcolonial exiles and emigrants to France), but in an ambivalent way. Kim-Chi, the Vietnamese-French *métisse* character, makes the voyage in to France thanks to the reporter protagonist (Figure 5.2).[25] In essence, he sacrifices his paternal relationship to his own daughter for a new connection to the daughter of a French soldier, because of his commitment to the political struggles of a past era that extend beyond France, to Vietnam. By contrast, his biological daughter is more interested in contesting new restrictions on access to French universities, a struggle that mainly concerns contemporary France, not a far-off former colony. The France that concerns her is nonetheless a multicultural, post-colonial one, as readers are reminded by the cartoonists' pointed reference to Malik Oussekine, killed in the police repression of student protests in Paris in 1986.

The voyage out and the voyage in, as they exist in and around comics, rework links between France and its (former) colonies, thereby crossing and inflecting the colonial affrontier. These connections may be clearly neocolonial, as in comics scripted by Serge Saint-Michel about French colonial army units and African dictators who have closely collaborated with France to the detriment of people of their countries, but also contravening democracy and citizenship in France.[26] However, there are also attempts in other comics to foster decolonized and otherwise non-exploitative relationships between, on the one hand, France and the French, and, on the other, (former) French colonies and their peoples. In such cases, redrawing empire involves undermining the colonial affrontier. The voyages to

Figure 5.2: Kim-Chi, a *métisse* character, travels from Vietnam to France, where she meets her French grandmother for the first time. From Lax (art) and Frank Giroud (script), *Les oubliés d'Annam* [The Forgotten Ones from Annam], vol. 2 (Marcinelle: Dupuis, 1991), p. 37. © Lax and Frank Giroud.

former French colonies taken by authors from ethnic minorities (e.g., Baloup, Boudjellal, Séra, Tian) and sometimes even by offspring of colonial settlers (e.g., Ferrandez, Morvandiau) or of colonial soldiers (e.g., Giroud, Lax), and the books that these cartoonists set there, whether autobiographical or fictional, may be conceived in this spirit.[27] Sometimes the works inspired by, or researched during, these trips include a critique of post-independence regimes and of neo-colonial relationships with France. However, the financing of such trips by French governmental agencies raises questions about the independence of the artists' work, and especially how it may fit into larger national and governmental strategies for maintaining French cultural and economic hegemony or influence in former colonies.[28]

In this book I have focused primarily on colonial-era conflicts and ideologies. I have therefore only briefly touched on the many new types of characters, settings and narratives that will be the focus of my next book: postcolonial immigrant families and communities, including Maghrebi-French and DOM-TOMiens;[29] and French racists, from far-right skinheads to politicians, in post-1962 France. We saw some of these types of characters, for example, in "Petit Polio," Boudjellal's series whose first three volumes (1998–2002) are set in colonial-era Toulon, about his fictional Slimani family (see above, Chapter 4), and in *Quitter Saigon: Mémoires de Viet Kieu* [Leaving Saigon: Memories of Viet Kieu] (2006, 2010), containing Baloup's short biographical stories of Vietnamese childhood, exile and emigration (see above, Chapter 3). Comic-book stories set in the post-1962 era have been produced simultaneously with, or even prior to, many of the contemporary comics about colonialism studied here, and often by the same authors. Although I am well aware of the important connections between these two groups of texts—contemporary narratives about the second period of French colonialism (roughly 1830–1962), which has been my primary focus here and in my previous book (McKinney 2011b), and about the post- or neo-colonial era—I have chosen to mostly separate them, for analytical and practical reasons. Assessing the ways that cartoonists have redrawn French empire and reworked the colonial affrontier is necessary for determining the space that they have created for representing new ethnic minorities within France.

NOTES

Chapter 1

1. "Beur" is French backslang for "Arab," and the homophonic "beurre" means "butter." A ham-and-butter sandwich is typical French lunch fare, but eating ham is, of course, forbidden by Islam.

2. In *Petit Polio* [Little Polio], vol. 2 (Boudjellal 1999: 43–53), whose story chronologically precedes *Jambon-Beur* (Boudjellal 1995) but was drawn and published after it, Abdelsalem Slimani (the paternal grandfather of Charlotte-Badia) is arrested in 1959 in Toulon on suspicion of belonging to the FLN and is beaten by the French police. This could be viewed as the source of his war-related scars in *Jambon-Beur* (14). The same volume of *Petit Polio* (front cover, 24–25) also depicts the death of a French soldier as the motivation for a split between Abdelsalem and his French workmate, César, who is conscripted to fight in Algeria, where a comrade soldier is killed in an ambush. Boudjellal first configured wartime divisions in a related fashion in "Amour d'Alger." On the war in these stories, see below, pp. 195, 197–201.

3. My analysis of this page in *Jambon-Beur* is indebted to my discussions of it with Michel Pactat and Valérie Dhalenne, to whom I am grateful.

4. This image is reproduced on the website of Morvandiau, whose experimental comic book *D'Algérie* [About/From Algeria] (2007) challenges the French-Algerian affrontier; cf. http://dalgerie.over-blog.com/article-14179863.html (accessed 9 December 2012).

5. See below, pp. 197–201.

6. Smith (1993); Merchet (1996).

7. A daughter, Marine Le Pen, replaced him as president of the party.

8. Bourgeon (1980–1994d).

9. Ferrandez (1994a, 1994b).

10. Bardet and Jusseaume (1985–89).

11. See, for example, Dine (1994), on the myths of the French paratrooper, colonial settler and conscripted soldier in and around the Algerian War.

12. The European colonial settlers of Algeria, who mostly moved to France in 1962, at the end of the Algerian War of Independence. "Pied-Noir" literally means "Black-Foot."

13. At one point Begag (Begag and Defali 2012: 64) represents his father taking part in the nationalist uprising.

14. See below, pp. 69–72, 76, 230n38.

15. In my study I refer to it in this manner, or as the French war in Indochina, in part to distinguish it from the Vietnam War fought by the United States. However, there is an irony in this terminology, which Alain Ruscio (1992: 16) states: "Un des paradoxes de la terminologie historique est que la guerre dite d'Indochine (phase française: 1945–54) ne se déroula presque que sur le territoire du Viet Nam, alors que la guerre dite du Viet Nam (phase américaine: 1954/62–75) ravagea l'ensemble de la région, laboura les terres de toute l'ancienne Indochine" [One of the paradoxes of the historical terminology is that the so-called Indochinese War (French phase: 1945–54) unfolded almost solely on the territory of Vietnam, whereas the so-called Vietnam War (American phase: 1954/62–75) ravaged the entire region, plowed the fields of the entire former Indochina].

16. Cf. Balibar (1998: 82): "Plus encore que la langue, la question des structures familiales et des généalogies est fondamentale" [More than language, the question of family structures and of genealogies is fundamental]. See also Miller (2007: 151–59).

17. If it is true, as Hergé's biographers have suggested, that he wondered whether Belgium's King Léopold II was his paternal grandfather (Assouline 1998: 27; Peeters 2002a: 22), then Haddock's search for his colonial inheritance in *Le secret de la Licorne* [*The Secret of the Unicorn*] and *Le trésor de Rackham le rouge* [*Red Rackham's Treasure*] (Hergé 2006, 2007), and Tintin's defense of the colonial riches of the Belgian Congo against American criminals in *Tintin au Congo* [*Tintin in the Congo*], could have had a personal grounding for the cartoonist. See also McKinney (2011b: 3–8).

18. The search for the founding mothers of French comics has barely begun.

19. On the place of the Algerian War in French and Algerian schools, see, for example, Laamirie, et al. (1993).

20. Abdelwahab Meddeb, quoted in Balibar (1998: 82).

21. E.g., *Les soldats blancs de Ho Chi Minh* [The White Soldiers of Ho Chi Minh], in *Les oubliés d'Annam* [The Forgotten Ones of Annam] (Lax and Giroud 1990).

22. E.g., *Azrayen'* (Lax and Giroud 1999), and *La guerre fantôme* [The Phantom War] (Ferrandez 2002). On this strategy, see Ferrandez in Buch (2005: 54) and Lax in Buch, Vernet and Ratier (2010: 18, 39).

23. Morvandiau, for his *D'Algérie*, on http://dalgerie.over-blog.com/ (accessed 9 December 2012).

24. Cf. http://bd.casterman.com/zine/articles/5/31/?id=446 (accessed 7 January 2004).

25. I define this broadly: the category of historian includes here those with university training as historians and who may teach (whether in school or university) or research history (e.g., the CNRS), but also those without formal historical training, but who nonetheless publish historical works (cf. Vidal-Naquet 2001: vii).

26. By Eliette Abécassis, Fellag and Georges Moustaki; the last two volumes are prefaced by friends of the author who are associated with cartooning and comics, but without a clear connection to North Africa (Jean Giraud [Moebius]; Philippe Val).

27. For a summary of de Chezal's account, see Ruscio (2002: 200), also cited by Guillemin (2006).

28. I am grateful to Paul Gravett for having kindly given me a copy of the English version of the catalog, which he translated from French.

29. Accessible at www.lire.fr.

30. Serge de Beketch, another far-right activist (on Radio Courtoisie [*sic*], for example) and also a cartoonist, published similar reviews of the series (Beketch 1995, 1997).

31. See pp. 154–56, below, and McKinney (2011c).

32. Hunt (2002) makes a fascinating reading of the colonial archive of comics in and around the Belgian Congo.

33. See Groensteen (1988: 65–66) on the difference between a non-narrative series and the sequential narrative arrangement of comic-strip panels.

34. On ocularization in comics, see Miller (2007: 91–94, 106, 110–19). For further exploration of the relationship between comics and film, see, for example, Ciment (1990), Peeters (2002b: 19–24), Miller (2007: 106–8) and Grove (2010: 35–36, 52–54, 108–10).

35. On Algerian comics, see Douglas and Malti-Douglas (1994) and Labter (2009), and on comics in former French colonies in Southeast Asia, see Lent (2011).

Chapter 2

1. E.g., Apter (1995: 170). This omission is all the more surprising because Nora (1961) himself published a book on the *Pieds-Noirs*. Another, related lacuna, to which Gérard Noiriel (1988: 18–19) drew attention was the absence of immigration as a topic in the same set of volumes. Noiriel's sharp criticism was apparently effective, because Nora invited him to contribute an essay to a later volume in the series.

2. For example, Algeria was declared a French territory and administratively transformed into French *départements* by the Second Republic (Ruedy 1992: 74; cf. Dine 1994: 9), and all residents of Algeria were made citizens of France by the organic law of 20 September 1947 (Ruedy 1992: 150–53).

3. See below, p. 226n12.

4. I am well aware that modernizing and secularizing are not necessarily synonyms: for example, religious revival has often been central to modernity and modernizing.

5. Cf. Bernasconi (1970: 33–37, 68–72), Porterfield (1998: 135–41) and Sessions (2011: 50–51). Porterfield (1998: 211) brought Bernasconi's thesis to my attention.

6. The use of the definite article in "Le sérail" suggests that the seraglio belongs to the most important man of the city. In her novel *L'amour, la fantasia,* Algerian novelist Assia Djebar (1993: 6–8) represented a similar scene, in a passage that may have been inspired by the French caricature.

7. Cf. Julien (1964: e.g., 67–68, 83, 89–94, 128, 132, 153, 192, 201–2, 227–29, and esp. 314–23).

8. Exceptions include Bernasconi (1970), Kunzle (1990), Porterfield (1994, 1998) and Childs (2004). The literature on both orientalist painting and colonial postcards especially is extensive (see below).

9. E.g., Gaumer and Moliterni (1994: 629), Töpffer (1994) and Kunzle (2007). Cf. Miller (1999); McKinney (2008c).

10. Cf. Kunzle (1990: 64–68), Groensteen in Töpffer (1996: 12–13) and Kunzle (2007: 95–108).

11. On Daumier and the harem, see Childs (2004: 170–72).

12. See also the lions and French tourists in North Africa, in Cham's *Les voyages d'agrément* (1849: 14.2; 15.3).

13. On the themes of the voyages out and in, see especially Chapter 5, below.

14. "By the 1850s, the Zouaves were a corps of native French men serving in the French infantry, while the Turcos were indigenous Algerians, recruited by France as skirmishers to serve in separate regiments of the infantry. The Zouave, whose appearance had been familiar to Parisians since the July Monarchy, was now supplanted by the Turco as the most exotic type of French soldier" (Childs 2004: 82); cf. Julien (1964: 273–97), cited by Childs (2004: 96).

15. Cf. Porterfield (1998: 133–34, 207–8) and Alaoui (1999: 22, 96, 105, 114–25).

16. Cham's reference (1849: 14.1) to the length of Ramadan is equally fanciful.

17. See below, pp. 55, 72–78.

18. In the few copies of *Wrill* held by the Cité internationale de la bande dessinée et de l'image (by no means a complete run of the publication), I found "Gringalou en Algérie" serialized in no. 107 (17 July 1947). Serial publication was over by no. 185 (13 January 1949). It was also published as a book, in both French and Flemish, no doubt after serial publication (Tilkin 1987: 53; Evrard and Roland 1992: 108, 111). Noé's name is given as "Jean Noé" on the comic book's cover and as "Noë[,] Jean" in Evrard and Roland (1992: 108). According to a website of the Association Jeune Pied Noir, which republished the work in 2011, it is set during the Centenaire de l'Algérie française [Centennial of French Algeria], in 1930 (http://jeunepiednoir.pagesperso-orange.fr/jpn.wst/Expositions.htm; http://jeunepiednoir.pagesperso-orange.fr/jpn.wst/Histoire%20&%20Memoire.htm; consulted 10 December 2012). I have found no clear support for this reading, either in the book or in the publication history of the work as I have been able to determine it. The one page in the work that refers to a celebration (p. 25), does not clearly indicate that it is the Centennial. This apparent misreading by Jeune Pied Noir, as well as the republication and celebration of the comic book, suggest that both the work and the Centenial are *lieux de mémoire* for *Pied-Noir* activists determined to return to an *Algérie heureuse* [happy Algeria] (Siblot 1985), that is, to reproduce a colonial, nostalgic vision of Algeria that effaces all traces of French colonial violence, the contradictions that produced the Franco-Algerian affrontier, and decolonization (see above, Chapter 1). For an in-depth analysis of comics related to the Centennial and to other French colonial exhibitions, see McKinney (2011b).

19. For an analysis of similar imagery, see Benjamin (2003b: 102–5) and Prochaska (2003: 133). This is an iconic character for Ferrandez (1994d: 21; cf. Azoulay 1980: 42, 150–51), who inserted an Algerian shoeshine boy into a scene modeled after a couple of famous Tintin episodes (Hergé 1979: 238; and especially Tintin's defense of Zorrino in *Le temple du soleil* [*Prisoners of the Sun*]).

20. See also the racist portrait of an Algerian thief in the casbah (Pinchon and Noé n.d.: 6); and a possible caricature of a Jewish cloth seller (26).

21. The visit seems a bit strange, given the fact that Algeria was then part of France itself, so was administered through the Ministry of the Interior, not the Ministry of Colonies. I analyze the visit of the Pieds Nickelés to Africa in McKinney (2011b: 132–39).

22. MacKenzie (1995: 14) takes Said to task for his lack of interest in popular culture (cf. Said 1992: 246, cited by MacKenzie) and a resulting elitist approach in his analyses of orientalism and imperialism, which is certainly a valid criticism. A telling example of this is Said's (1994a: 330) decision to single out comic books as an example of cultural impoverishment in Japan, despite the long and rich history of comics in Japan (cf. Schodt 1986)—certainly an example of blinding elitism. However, most of MacKenzie's (1995) own subsequent analysis of orientalism remains dedicated to an analysis of arts not usually thought of as popular—such as architecture (though with some examination of orientalist cinema façades and interiors), painting, opera and design. Elsewhere, however, MacKenzie (1986) has significantly increased our understanding of the relationship between imperialism and popular culture. My own study focuses on an art form widely considered to be popular, which on occasion nevertheless "aspire[s] to high art" (MacKenzie 1995: 47) and engages in a conflictual dialogue with its better-connected artistic kin, especially painting (Beaty 2007).

23. Ferrandez (1994–2009). Throughout my study, "Carnets d'Orient" refers to the multi-volume series, which bears this supertitle, whereas *Carnets d'Orient* (Ferrandez 1994a) designates the first volume in the series. Ferrandez began publishing his Algerian comic book saga in 1986.

24. Other models proposed include Regnault, Jean-Joseph Bellel and Benjamin Constant, though the latter was not born until 1845 (all these possibilities are mentioned by Topin [1987]). Ferrandez (1988) also named Pierre Loti. As I show below, a primary model that Ferrandez used for Constant is "Léon Roches, a one-time convert to Islam, and former secretary to the Emir Abd-El-Kader" (Lazreg 1994: 26). Constant studies the Koran (Ferrandez 1994a: 41) and, in order to search for Djemilah, decides to pass himself off as a convert (Ferrandez 1994a: 45) and serve as interpreter to Abdelkader (Ferrandez 1994a: 43, 51, 67), just as Roches claimed to have done. On Roches, see Roches (1904) and French historians Liauzu (2000: 34–35) and Julien (1964: 176, 180, 182, 184, 200).

25. For example, Ferrandez (1994a: 18) based two Jewish women on colonial postcards reproduced in *La nostalgérie française* [French Nostalgeria] (Azoulay 1980: 100–101; cards entitled "Jeune fille juive" [Young Jewish Girl] and "Algérie—Jeune juive de Constantine" [Algeria—Young Jewess from Constantine]), and on the account of Gautier (1973: 186–89).

26. In *Carnets d'Orient* (Ferrandez 1994a), on p. 11, two lower frames; p. 13, center frame; p. 18, lower-right frame; p. 26, top frame; and in *Le centenaire* (Ferrandez 1994d), the same building is shown on the book's back cover and on pages 55–56.

27. In Djebar (1984), on pages 28–29; 30–31; 32–33; and 50–51, respectively.

28. The reader will no doubt also recognize Ferrandez's allusion to Mario Puzo, the Italian-American author of *The Godfather*. Ferrandez (1996) explained that in the comic-book character he was also playfully representing a personal friend. On French imperialism and battlefield paintings, see Porterfield (1998: 43–79).

29. A websearch for this image, using its caption, on 27 January 2007, via Google Images, produced a symptomatic pair of websites (the only ones) with it: the Ligue des droits de l'homme de Toulon [Human Rights League of Toulon] (http://www.ldh-toulon.net/spip.php?article489) and a *Pied-Noir* site (http://aj.garcia.free.fr/site_hist_colo/livre2/L2p257.htm).

30. Julien's *Histoire de l'Algérie contemporaine: La conquête et les débuts de la colonisation (1827–1871)* [History of Contemporary Algeria: The Conquest and the Beginnings of Colonization, 1827–71] is Ferrandez's source for a great quantity of facts, text and images in *Carnets d'Orient*. There is some overlap between Esquer (1929), Julien (1964) and Djebar (1984), in terms of nineteenth-century imagery, so it is not always clear from which work Ferrandez borrowed certain images.

31. Also sometimes given as "Kulughlis," but spelled "Couloughs" in Ferrandez. They are described in the graphic novel as tyrants who preceded the French in the domination of Algeria (1994a: 42–43). This ethnically mixed group, descended from Turkish soldiers and Algerian women, was one of the pillars of Ottoman authority in Algeria. See Ruedy (1992: 22, 35, 43, 53, 58–59) and Abun-Nasr (1987: 159, 167–68, 255). For another Coulougli character in a comic about Algeria, see Bardet and Jusseaume's *Les portes d'Alger* [The Doors of Algiers] (1989: 12, 46).

32. Adrien Marnier (Ferrandez 1995: 41), the orientalist painter who utters these words, is himself "boursouflé" and represents (Ferrandez 1995: 14) the kind of untalented painting that he criticizes (cf. Tribak-Geoffroy 1997: 125–26).

33. The two paintings by Dinet from which Ferrandez copies in this frame are *Le petit fellah* [The Young Peasant] (also known as *L'enfant à la citrouille* [The Child with the Pumpkin]) and *Fillettes revenant du jardin* [Young Girls Returning from the Garden], both painted during the period 1904–13 (Brahimi and Benchikou 1991: 94–95, 177, 210).

34. In fact, Ferrandez (1994a: 67–70) provides one of the few accounts in fiction of one of the French army's horrendous massacres of Algerians who had taken refuge in caves. In *L'amour, la fantasia*, Assia Djebar (1985: 77–93) reconstructs the same events. Cf. Gautier (1920: 11–54); Julien (1964: 201–2). A more recent French comic-book biography of *Abd*

el-Kader (Corteggiani and Dupuis 2009: 70) also represents the massacres. See also below, p. 183, on a similar scene in a later book in Ferrandez's series.

35. The notebooks from Delacroix's visit to North Africa are clearly the model and inspiration for the title ("Carnets d'Orient") and the sketchbook format of Ferrandez's series.

36. Cf. reproductions of Dinet's work in Brahimi and Benchikou (1991) and Pouillon (1997). Nochlin (1989) and Goldberg (1999: 15) describe the tendency toward kitsch in orientalist painting.

37. Ferrandez (1996) acknowledged that Dinet's painted Orient might be just as contrived as the other orientalist works that the cartoonist dismissed as artificial within his series:

> FERRANDEZ: The good [in orientalist painting] would be Dinet, but Dinet is later in fact [than Delacroix], so he too may have had the chance to digest all that, and plus since he really then lived in Algeria and converted to Islam, he came to appreciate. . . . Having said that, in discussing with a true specialist of Dinet, he told me that [the work of] Dinet was just as fantasized as the rest: the young girl who bathed in streams, even. . . in Bou Saâda, wasn't as common as all that. There too is a version. . . .
> MCKINNEY: A bit fictionalized?
> FERRANDEZ: Yes, a bit fictionalized.

38. Biblical imagery and references appear periodically throughout the series: for example, (1) Joseph Constant could be seen as the Old Testament Joseph, sold into exile in Egypt and working for the Pharaoh (Abdelkader?), or as a New Testament Joseph, the human father of Jesus, which raises interesting questions about filiation; (2) edenic colonial imagery of a pioneer couple bathing (Ferrandez 1994b: 76); (3) two later characters (first in Ferrandez 1995) are Sauveur [Savior], a medical student, and Marianne, whose name is an obvious allusion to the figure symbolizing the French Republic, but also perhaps to the biblical Mary (and her mother, Anne), the mother of Jesus, or to Mary Magdelene—Marianne's virginity is questioned, because she does nude modeling in order to pay her way through art school. Cf. the biblical allusion in Cham's *Les voyages d'agrément* (n.p.).

39. See also Rosenthal's (1982: 137–41) discussion of a related painting by Lewis, *The Hhareem*, probably shown at the 1855 Exposition Universelle in Paris.

40. The painting is bequeathed by Victor Barthélémy—who returned to France to buy it when Amélie died (Ferrandez 1994c: 74)—to his daughter, Olympe, the wife of the stationmaster and Paul's mother (Ferrandez 1994c: 72–74; 1994d: 52–53).

41. Khamès (1995: 71). Other possible models are Albert Londres (mentioned in Ferrandez 1994d: 38) and Tintin, Hergé's comic-book character. Ferrandez (in Poncet and Morin 1996: 77) speaks of the remarkable similarities between Camus's description of childhood in *Le premier homme* [*The First Man*] and the childhood of Ferrandez's own father, who was a few years younger than the celebrated author, lived in a house opposite Camus's childhood home in the Belcourt quarter of Algiers, and attended the same lycée as Camus.

42. I.e., the oldest section of the city, which became the Algerian quarter when the French arrived and began building housing for themselves.

43. It does, however, echo the cover of an earlier comic book set in Morocco in the same time period (Loustal and Paringaux 1985, 1991). The visual composition and the tensions represented on the cover are similar in the two books. It has also been plausibly suggested to me that Ferrandez's (1994d) cover and the tensions it reflects were inspired by Julien Duvivier's film *Pépé le Moko* (1937).

44. Alloula (1981: 56, 71; 1986: 83, 110); the same women appear in other postcards reproduced in Alloula (1981: 25, 40, 77, back cover; 1986: 30, 56, 121).

45. Lazreg (1994: 190–91) argues that Alloula did the same thing through the publication of his book (specifically, she discusses the English translation published in the United States). She makes important points: for example, the fact that the publication of Alloula's book makes these images available to "contemporary 'orientalists'" (Lazreg 1994: 191) as well as to American college students interested in it mainly for "its 'pornographic' import."

46. Alloula (1981: 56, 77, back cover, 78–79; 1986: 83, 121, 123–24). Ferrandez's watercolors are reproduced in Ferrandez (Buch 2005: 75) and Poncet and Morin (1996: 70–71); information on the exhibition is from the latter (p. 83).

47. The book by Mimouni and Ferrandez (1993) is unpaginated. The images to which I refer here are the 23rd and 24th.

48. Cf. other related passages in Flaubert (1996: 129–30, 157–59, 200, 220).

49. E.g. Azoulay (1980), Alloula (1981, 1986, 2001), Zimmerman (1986), Hebrard and Hebrard (1990), as well as Ferrandez and Joann Sfar.

50. For a perceptive critique of the colonialist ideology of Algerian postcards, see Prochaska (1990a), and on their problematic role in post-colonial French books, especially those by *Pieds-Noirs,* see Siblot (1985: 156–57).

51. "There's a treatment of the Orient [in orientalist painting] that is really on the order of fantasy, and moreover that one finds—I have a compelling book on it, on *The Colonial Harem.* The photographers acted in the same manner, by having the girls pose in a completely unrealistic manner."

52. Although I focus my analysis on the way that Ferrandez uses colonial-era postcards as sources of representations of Algerian women, there is another important related area on which I have not commented here: his use of these postcards as sources for various other North African ethnic types, including blacks, Jews and Italians. Ferrandez's reproduction of these types in his comics raises questions about the extent to which he succeeds in escaping the erroneous and degrading colonial ethnographic assumptions of which the postcards and their ideology of the picturesque are one expression (cf. Nochlin 1989: 50–52).

53. Cf. Laronde (1993: 183–85), and below, pp. 138–39.

54. Inaccurately associated with the second of the five French volumes (instead of the first) in the copyright listings within the published version in English translation. The inclusion of Vidal-Bué in the copyright line of some subsequent French and English editions of "The Rabbi's Cat" raises the question of whether his wholesale borrowing of images from Vidal-Bué's book (see also below) without acknowledgment of his source constituted copyright infringement. Sfar also thanked the painters of Algiers in subsequent editions of his comic book: e.g., in the collected edition (*L'intégrale*) "Cet album est un hommage de l'auteur à tous les peintres d'Alger au XXe siècle. Il tient en particulier à citer l'ouvrage de Marion Vidal-Bué, *Alger et ses peintres, 1830–1960,* publié aux Editions Paris Méditerranée" [This album is an homage by the author to all the painters of Algiers in the 20th century. He especially wishes to cite the work by Marion Vidal-Bué, *Algiers and Its Painters, 1830–1960,* published by Editions Paris Méditerranée] (Sfar 2010: 6).

55. Another one is Leroy (2011), who makes a brilliant analysis of the roles of Chagall and painting in the fifth volume of "Le chat du rabbin."

56. On Masmoudi, see *Festival international de la bande dessinée et de la caricature. Bordj-el-Kiffan du 30 juin au 5 juillet 1987* [International Festival of Comics and Caricature. Bordj-el-Kiffan, 30 June to 5 July 1987] (1987: n.p.) and Labter (2009: 213, 244).

57. I recognize that the ideological and historical position that Masmoudi and his coauthors present in their comic book was central, not marginal, in Algeria when they published their comic book, and to a considerable extent still is (see Khelladi 1995; McKinney 2007a, 2008c; Labter 2009). Its marginality is therefore retrospective (i.e., within the context of colonial Algeria) and to some extent external (say, in France today).

58. For example, Bessaih, Bakhti and Masmoudi (1986: 14) and Ferrandez (1994a: 14.1) both redrew *Pavillon de la Casbah* [Pavillion of the Casbah], a famous engraving by W. Wyld, which depicts the place of the fly-whisk incident, purported to have sparked the French attack on Algiers in 1830. The cartoonists no doubt copied it from a work edited by Assia Djebar (1984: 51; for a photograph of it, see Adès and Zaragozi [1999: 30]). Whereas Ferrandez leaves the famous building in Algiers where it belongs, the Algerian cartoonists move it to Oran and modify its features (e.g., adding bars over windows and a crenelated wall on top), turning it into a French military fortress. In his unpublished comic book "Le coup de l'éventail" (n.d.), Algerian cartoonist Slim inserts excerpts from, or copies, this and many other engravings that are no doubt from Djebar's volume. Space unfortunately prohibits me from analyzing that fascinating work here.

59. For example, Sfar borrows from a work that was also earlier a source for Ferrandez: Azoulay's *La nostalgérie française* (1980). Already in the first volume of "Carnets d'Orient," Ferrandez copies a postcard depicting a Jewish Algerian man (Azoulay 1980: 20; Ferrandez 1994a: 47.5) and two North African Jewish women (see above). Later borrowings include a racist postcard depiction of a black man (Azoulay 1980: 25; Ferrandez 1994c: 44.6). These examples do not exhaust the list of the cartoonist's borrowings from Azoulay—on them, see also above, pp. 228n19, 229n25, and McKinney (2001). The most striking and absolutely unmistakable of Sfar's borrowings from Azoulay is an image of a brass stand or pot (a fire urn?) and a kettle, originally on a postcard representing a Jewish artisan at work in front of his shop (Azoulay 1980: 153), which Sfar (2003a: 31) copies into his nostalgic nightmare sequence of the Rabbi's world turned upside down (drinking wine from a hookah, his cat turned into a non-kosher, bottom-feeding catfish, etc.). Other, possible borrowings include architectural features of homes (Azoulay 1980: 64, 138–39), again in the Rabbi's nightmare (Sfar 2003a: 30), and the same postcard depictions of Jewish women used by Ferrandez (see above), here for the clothing of Zlabya, the Rabbi's daughter (Azoulay 1980: 100–101; Sfar 2003a: 4–5, 21, etc.). By inserting images from *La nostalgérie française* into the nostalgic nightmare sequence, Sfar figures precisely the sense of loss that Azoulay's book appeals to and is a product of, as well as (inadvertently?) the problematic nature of the ethnographic and historical iconography on the colonial postcards.

Another, less troubling use of imagery that Sfar may have borrowed from a colonial postcard occurs in *Le malka des lions* [*Malka of the Lions*] (Sfar 2003b: 13–18). The Rabbi's French dictation clearly represents the cultural colonization by French mainland Jews of Algerian Jews after the Crémieux decree imparted French citizenship to the latter (Eisenstein 2008: 169–70; Harris 2008: 184). The dictation unfolds in a French school outside of which looms a statue that, although unnamed, is recognizably that of Jean Pierre Hippolyte Blandan (1819–1842), a French sergeant from Lyon who died while fighting to colonize Algeria (cf. Eisenstein 2008: 169–70, 180n32). The statue, originally erected in colonial-era Boufarik (Algeria), was repatriated to Nancy (France) at the end of the Algerian War (Amato 1979: 136–42; cf. Bourdieu, Schultheis and Frisinghelli 2003: 48; Sessions 2011: 169). In *Le malka des lions* it threateningly connects France's linguistic imperialism with its military conquest and domination of Algeria. Another statue of the same soldier plays a similar role in *Le gone du Chaâba* [*The Shantytown Kid*], by Algerian-French novelist Azouz Begag (2006: e.g., 195).

60. This is the case already for the volume by Bessaih, Bakhti and Masmoudi (1986): Boualem Bessaih based his comic strip script on his earlier film script for a historical film on Cheikh Bouamama. Bessaih was a professor of letters and holds a doctorate in Letters and Human Sciences. He held a high position in the FLN during the Algerian War and subsequently occupied many high positions in the Algerian government. He has published several

historical and literary studies. See www.conseil-constitutionnel.dz/cv_bessaih.htm (accessed 9 December 2012).

61. For example, Masmoudi's work was based on a movie about Bouamama, and the comic book borrows from the conventions of the film western, which suggests that the movie may well have done so too.

62. Ferrandez partially serialized the first volume in his "Carnets d'Orient" series in 1986, and it was first issued as a book in 1987. However, I have not detected any references to or borrowings from Dinet in this first volume (I explore Masmoudi's debt to Dinet below); instead, his influence appears later in the series.

63. Sfar's borrowings from Delacroix include: Zlabya's clothes and the domestic setting—door, wall hangings, tapestries, and cushions—(Sfar 2003a: 9.2) from *Homme et femme dans un intérieur—chez les Bouzaglo* [Man and Woman In An Interior—In the Home of the Bouzaglo] (Alaoui 1999: 74), *La femme et la fille d'Abraham Ben-Chimol* [The Wife and Daughter of Abraham Ben-Chimol] (album of the comte de Mornay; Alaoui 1999: 179), *Etudes de femmes juives* [Studies of Jewish Women] (sketchbook; Alaoui 1999: 64) and *Une cour à Tanger* [A Courtyard in Tangiers] (1832; Sérullaz 1951: 17; Alaoui 1999: 170–71), reworked in *Noce juive au Maroc* [Jewish Wedding In Morocco] (1837–41; Alaoui 1999: 68–69). However, Sfar does not explicitly refer to Moroccan Jews until volume two, *Le Malka des lions* (2003b: 27).

64. Sfar also goes through Algerian Arabs and their music to re-/produce the ethnic identity of Algerian Jews in Paris in the 1930s (see Benhaïm [2007] and McKinney [2009] on this topic).

65. Other borrowings from famous orientalist paintings include Zlabya's posture (Sfar 2003a: 36.4) from Henri Matisse's *Odalisque à la culotte rouge* (1923; Benjamin 2003b: 15); cf. Renoir's *Femme d'Alger* (1870; Benjamin 2003b: 18).

66. The extensive borrowings by Sfar (2003a) [S] from Vidal-Bué (2000) [VB] include: the rabbi's clothes and white beard (S, e.g. 2.3) from Alphonse Lévy, *Rabbin enseignant un enfant* (VB 167); the clothes of Zlabya (e.g., S front cover, 4–6.3, etc.) from numerous possible sources, including Alexandre Lunois, *Femmes juives écoutant la lecture des textes sacrés* (VB 168), François Lauret *La danse de la jeune mariée* (VB 169) and especially Eugène Delacroix, *Femmes d'Alger dans leur appartement* (1834; VB 218; cf. *Etudes de femmes juives*, in Alaoui [1999: 64])—Zlabya's pose in a later image (S 8.1) is modeled after that of the seated woman on the right of Delacroix's *Femmes d'Alger;* profiles of Zlabya (S 4.1–4) from Baya, *L'oiseau de paradis* (VB 236); a panorama shot of the old neighborhood of Algiers (S 16.6) from Louis Bénisti, *Terrasses du quartier de la marine,* and Simon Mondzain, *La casbah vue d'une terrasse* (VB 188–89); an image of a cemetery, with mosque in the background (S 20.2) from Abdelhalim Hemche, *Djamâa Sidi Abder Rahmane* (1937; VB 161); an image of the port of Algiers (S 20.3) from William Wyld, *Bureaux et magasins de la Marine* (1833; VB 91, also reproduced in Djebar [1984: 33], another probable source of Sfar; for an almost identical image, see Ferrandez [1994a: 1]); another port scene (S 20.4) from René Levrel, *Les voûtes de l'Amirauté* (VB 94); yet another one (S 20.6) from Maurice Bouviolle, *La Pêcherie* (VB 97); a fisherman at the port (S 21.2) from Marius de Buzon, *La kémia, port d'Alger* (VB 109); fisherman in the port (S 21.3) from Benjamin Sarraillon, *Le départ des pêcheurs* (VB 96); the port and its balcony (S 21.4) from Jean Bouchaud, *Le balcon du port* (1928; VB 105); an interior courtyard with columns and balcony (S 27.1) from Hippolyte Dubois, *Femme dans la galerie d'une villa algéroise* (VB 229); a column in the Rabbi's nightmare (S 29) from Jean-Abel Lordon, *Café maure à Alger* (1834; VB 122); a courtyard (S 30.5) from Gustave-Clarence Boulanger, *Le harem, Alger* (VB 201); a stand with cups and pitchers (S 31.6) from Eugène Girardet, *Café arabe* (VB 123); a street in the casbah (S 32.2) from Numa Marzocchi de Bellucci, *Une rue de la Casbah* (VB 125);

an outdoors garden, patio and arcades (S 37.1–3) from Eugène Deshayes, *Jardin d'Alger*, David E. de Noter, *Villa Mahieddine, Alger* and Georges-Antoine Rochegrosse, *L'allée de la noria, Djenan Meryem* (VB 206); two French women at/and the Place du Gouvernement (S 39.1–5) from Jean-Désiré Bascoulès, *Les élégantes, place du Gouvernement, Alger* (VB 136; cf. 137–39, 148–49); a high shot of the Place du Gouvernement (S 39.6) from André Hambourg, *Place du Gouvernement* (around 1941; VB 137); a café terrace with sailors drinking (S 42.1) from Etienne Bouchaud, *Café rue Bab-el-Oued* (VB 152; cf. other props in S 42.1 taken from other paintings on VB 152–53—oranges and possibly clothing and characters); a synagogue (S 42.4) from Charles Brouty, *La synagogue de la place Randon* (VB 159); and prostitutes and their neighborhood (S 44–46) from Eugène Corneau, *Les dames de la Casbah* (VB 128; cf. esp. S 44.1), Jean Launois, *Femmes algériennes au rideau rose* (around 1924; VB 129; cf. esp. S 44.3)—cf. Armand Assus, *Les tirailleurs sénégalais* (VB 130) for the warm colors in these pages of Sfar's *La bar mitsva*. There may be other correspondences between Sfar and Vidal-Bué that I have missed.

67. Goldberg (1999: 15); cf. Liauzu (2000: 41). Benjamin (2003a: 92) states that "many critics of his [Dinet's] day were unhappy about its literality [i.e., that of Dinet's art], brazen color, and frequent mawkishness." Cf. Benjamin (2003a: 103, 238).

68. Masmoudi borrows from other paintings by Dinet: e.g., elders in the southern Algerian village brutally attacked by the French army (Bessaih, Bakhti and Masmoudi 1986: 41.1) from Dinet's *La procession* (Brahimi and Benchikou 1991: 99). Masmoudi also (Bessaih, Bakhti and Masmoudi 1986: 14.2) redraws the "Pavillon du coup d'éventail" [Pavillon of the Fly Whisk Blow], moving it from Algiers to Oran. Ferrandez (1994a: 26.1) too redraws this building. The source of both artists is probably Djebar (1984: 51); cf. Julien (1964: plate 1); Adès and Zaragozi (1999: 30).

Chapter 3

1. On the French government's censorship of the book in 1950, see Crépin and Groensteen (1999: 122).

2. Because the comics of Séra and Tian set in Southeast Asia focus primarily not on French Indochina and the Indochinese War, but instead on the Khmer Rouge and the horrific carnage under their regime, I analyze them elsewhere. Of course the rise of the Khmer Rouge was linked to the history of French colonialism and American imperialism in the region.

3. Cf. http://electricblogbaloup.over-blog.com/; www.krinein.com/bd/automne-hanoi-4799.html (accessed 9 December 2012).

4. See pp. 8–19, 56, 78, 173, 185–87, above and below.

5. Chancel went on to host "Radioscopie," one of France's longest-running radio shows.

6. E.g., Jack Yeager (1987), Panivong Norindr (1996), Dina Sherzer (1998), Nicola Cooper (2001), Leakthina Chau-Pech Ollier (Winston and Ollier 2001) and Jane Winston (2001).

7. Cf. Stora (1997: 33–34, 247); Norindr (1996: 137).

8. See Stora (1997: 214–19) on the French distribution and reception of U.S. films on the Vietnam War; a review article by Jean-Luc Macia (1992) "Dien Bien Phu, notre 'Apocalypse Now,'" *La Croix L'Evénement*, March 6, p. 2—of Pierre Schoendoerffer's war movie, *Dien Bien Phu* (1992)—quoted in Norindr (1996: 179).

9. Pp. 6, 78–83, above.

10. E.g., of civilians in Haiphong, in November 1946 (Ruscio 1992: 77–81; Benot 2001: 97–113).

11. On French torture during France's war in Vietnam, see Ruscio (1992: 161–64), Benot (2001: 165–69), Vidal-Naquet (2001: 15–20).

12. Cf. www.primalinea.com/slocombe (accessed 9 December 2012). The eroticization of tortured bodies of the colonized also appears in comics about the Algerian War (e.g., Ferrandez 2005a: 9, 21–22); on this, see Chapter 4, below.

13. According to Guillemin (2006: 174), "Commandant Perrin-Houdon . . . served in 'Indochina.'" Elsewhere (185) he refers to "the *Captain* Perrin-Houdon" (my emphasis).

14. He goes on to say that "The other two books were about the adventures of Buck Danny by the Belgian authors Jean-Michel Charlier and Victor Hubinon: *Ciel de Corée* [Korean Sky] and *Avion sans pilote* [Plane without a Pilot]. They related the fight of American pilots against the Communist Korean Army." Crépin cites as his source the minutes of the Commission's second meeting of 31 March 1950.

15. My analysis is based on thirteen parts of the serialized version, nos. 191–203 (24 February–19 May 1949), at the Cité internationale de la bande dessinée et de l'image, Angoulême (accessed summer 2006) and on Le Rallic (1976). According to Evrard and Roland (1992: 122), the episode ran in issues 178–202. The last issue of the magazine was no. 204 (26 May 1949; cf. Béra, Denni and Mellot 1996: 583; Evrard and Rolland 1992).

16. Guillemin (2006: 187–88) concludes that, although propagandistic, the message of "Parachutés au Laos" is primarily religious, not military: "It makes audible the voice of the Catholic church, and also gives the aspergillum preeminence over the saber, that nonetheless attends to the salvation of the Empire. . . . One completely imagines the two brothers, Henri and Xavier, having returned to Viêt-Nam, trying to build, with Hmongs and Annamites of good will, a harmonious society, nourished with Christian values and respect for the other." Although I agree with much of his analysis of the comic, this conclusion is inaccurate. One can certainly imagine that this undepicted ending is what the future would ideally hold, according to the logic of the Christian comic and publisher, but the overwhelming focus of the comic is precisely on the French war to retake Indochina: although Henri and Xavier are shown praying and seeking out Christian friends, they are soldiers first and foremost, and Henri's prayer is for success in his military mission (no. 215, 14 January 1951). Even when French missionaries are depicted, their association with, and assistance of, French soldiers is foregrounded (no. 222 [4 March 1951]; no. 243 [29 July 1951]; no. 244 [5 August 1951]). It is therefore inaccurate to argue, as Guillemin (2006: 180) does, that in "Parachutés au Laos": "What brings together the members of this coalition, of French and indigenous allies, against the 'Viets,' the 'rebels,' is less the defense of French colonization than that of the Christian West."

17. No. 246 (19 August 1951).

18. No. 259 (18 November 1951).

19. No. 268 (20 January 1952). For a more detailed summary of this military itinerary in the comic, see Guillemin (2006: 175).

20. Henri Joubert, in *Les oubliés d'Annam* (Lax and Giroud 1990, 1991), analyzed below.

21. E.g., in *L'année de feu* [The Year of Fire] (Ferrandez 1994b) and *Le centenaire* [The Centenial/Centenarian] (Ferrandez 1994d); see Chapter 2, above.

22. E.g., Cosme Tirard in *Azrayen'* (Lax and Giroud 1998, 1999, 2004); and Octave Alban in the "Carnets d'Orient" series, beginning in *La guerre fantôme* [The Phantom War] (Ferrandez 2002). See below, Chapter 4.

23. Guillemin (2006: 176) attributes the declaration of loyalty, just quoted, to Hao Ming. However, it is a different character who speaks: this one has no earrings, whereas Hao Ming wears a large hoop in each ear.

24. No. 247 (26 August 1951); no. 248 (1 September 1951). Guillemin mistakenly states that Mr. Hoan, the family friend, also goes to the cathedral with Xavier.

25. E.g., the Kha group in "Parachutés au Laos" (nos. 230, 29 April 1951; 231, 6 May 1951); the montagnards Moï in *Paul* (Raives and Varnauts 1986: 20), *Little Saigon: Mémoires de Viet Kieu* (Baloup 2012: 161–63) and *Le dragon de bambou* (Truong and Leroi 1991: 36–39); the montagnards Muong, in *L'ombre du triangle* (Christin and Aymond 1999: 20–23; cf. 14); possible images of montagnards, but not named, in *Soldats de la liberté* [Soldiers of Liberty] (Saint-Michel and Le Honzec 1994: 18, 20). Cf. *La voie royale* [*The Royal Way*] (Malraux 1962: e.g., 101–2, 110–12); "Rue Catinat, Saïgon" (Charpier 1984: 24); Pervillé (1993: 128); Norindr (1996: 8, 88, 170–71).

26. No. 250, 16 September 1951. Cf. a later installment where another French soldier tries to save a young Cambodian child from a python (no. 270 [3 February 1952]). Xavier informs him that it is a tame one, kept to eat rats.

27. By contrast, a group of elephants calmly obeys its pro-French Vietnamese masters in an earlier episode (nos. 228 [15 April 1951]; 229 [22 April 1951]). Through his uncanny mastery over wild animals, Xavier ressembles Tarzan, which is ironic, given the claim by the magazine that the French series is different from the American one. Cf. Guillemin (2006: 177), who also makes a connection between exotic jungle stories, including Tarzan, and the taming of the panther by Xavier.

28. No. 257 (4 November 1951); no. 258 (11 November 1951); no. 259 (18 November 1951).

29. Female French soldiers appear in "Parachutés au Laos," but only in minor roles, as "Marinettes" [ship's nurses] (e.g., no. 259 [18 November 1951]; 260 [25 November 1951]; no. 261 [2 December 1951]). The doctor figure, Dr. Vital, is male.

30. Norindr (1996: 132).

31. In *Paul* (Raives and Varnauts 1986: 26–9), *Le carrefour de Nâm-Pha* (Maltaite and Lapiere 1987: 42–44), *Le rendez-vous d'Angkor* (Renard and Fromental 1987: 31–34), *Le dragon de bambou* (Truong and Leroi 1991: 15–17), *Opium* (Dimberton and Hé 1991: 32–38) and *La route de Cao Bang* (Stanislas and Rullier 1992: 19, 38–40).

32. Gaumer and Moliterni (1994: 78, 654–55). By 1994, some 30 million copies of more than 160 Bob Morane novels had been sold, mostly by Marabout (Gaumer and Moliterni 1994: 78). Another very well known adventurer in comics about imperialism is Corto Maltese, who is the protagonist of a series, by Italian author Hugo Pratt, that has been translated into French and extremely well received in France. Jacques Ferrandez serialized some of his series of comics about the French colonization of Algeria in the French version of a magazine entitled *Corto Maltese*.

33. E.g., Estray, in Ruscio (1996: 435–44).

34. E.g., "La mort du dragon" (Mallet and Truong 1984), *Le carrefour de Nâm-Pha* (Maltaite and Lapiere 1987), *Le rendez-vous d'Angkor* (Renard and Fromental 1987) and *Opium* (Dimberton and Hay 1991).

35. E.g., *L'ombre du triangle* (Christin and Aymond 1999), *La colonne* (Martin and Simon 2001).

36. On the other hand, both André Malraux's *La voie royale* (1962) and—even more so—*Nos vingt ans* [Our Twenties] (1986), Clara Malraux's memoirs of the period, must have helped inspire *Le dragon de bambou*. For example, all include dangerous visits to Moï villages (Malraux 1962: 101–2, 110–45; Malraux 1986: 242–43, 249–50; Truong and Leroi 1991: 36–39). However, the relationship between outside visitors and ethnic minority groups is otherwise almost completely opposite in *Le dragon de bambou* (Truong and Leroi 1991) and *La voie royale* (Malraux 1962).

37. Cf. Norindr (1996: 26–27). In *Le centenaire* (Ferrandez 1994d: 33) the protagonist vomits during a guided visit in 1930 to the Roman ruins in Tipasa, Algeria. The cartoonist thereby provides a critique of a similar French colonial thesis, that France had inherited the mantle of Roman imperialism in North Africa.

38. One exception is Cooper (2001: 219).

39. Cf. Lebovics (1992: 114–15), Norindr (1996: 46, 72–106, 163), Lebovics (1997) and Cooper (2001: 21, 70, 124–25). As I mentioned above, in *Le dragon de bambou* Leroi and Truong (1991) borrow much from *Nos vingt ans* (1986), Clara Malraux's memoir of the time that she and André Malraux spent in French Indochina. The borrowings that I have found—of characters, places, plot developments, and even direct quotes from the memoirs in *Le dragon de bambou*—are too numerous to mention here, so I give just a few examples: (1) characters: André and Clara Malraux, of course, but also (among others) *métis* figures, including the main protagonist (Maurice Sainte-Rose, in *Nos vingt ans* [201, 238–41, 250–51, 278–79, 310], who is a model for Marcel Clément-Rivière, the main protagonist in *Le dragon de bambou*; and Dejean de la Batie, in *Nos vingt ans* [217–18, 284] and in *Le dragon de bambou* [13, 29]); (2) direct quotations: "Maintenant il ne me reste plus d'autre solution que d'écrire" (*Nos vingt ans* [323]; *Le dragon de bambou* [35]); "La vie est une fête désespérée" (*Nos vingt ans* [56]; *Le dragon de bambou* [39]); (3) plot developments: e.g., the trip through Moï territory, cited above.

40. From "Kao Bang," by the French rock group Indochine, released on *Le péril jaune* [The Yellow Peril] (1983). Although the song's title refers to the French defeat in Cao Bang in 1950, the lyrics appear to be about an Asian woman character, Changhaï Li (unnamed in the song), who fights imperialist occupiers of China in Hugo Pratt's comic *Corto Maltese en Sibérie* [*Corto Maltese in Siberia*] (1979). Other references in the song, shared by the book, include dragons, Manchuria and stolen gold. On the epic, romance, the novel and imperialism, cf. Bakhtin (1990), Brennan (1993), Sommer (1993) and Norindr (1996).

41. See also pp. 25–26, 71–72, 178, and McKinney (2011b: 4–7).

42. On the role of anti-hero in French films about the Algerian War, see Stora (1997: 184–86).

43. In *La nuit de Saigon* (Slocombe 1986), the character Marc Raffaëlli is based on these historical figures. He appears there as a doomed romantic figure, who is executed at the end of the story by the Vietnamese Communists whose cause he had served.

44. Cf. Castex (1993), *Le Monde* (1993), Brocheux (2004) and Boudarel (1991).

45. Doyon (1973: 27, 305–34, 479–82) and Lax and Giroud (2000: 11).

46. E.g. www.fncv.com/biblio/grand_combattant/vandenberghe_r.html, www.farac.org/php/article.php3?id_article=203 and http://www.ensoa.terre.defense.gouv.fr/PJ/documents/VotreEspace/histtrad/027.pdf (accessed 9 December 2012).

47. In *Une épopée française: Indochine* (Bucquoy and Sels 1990: 13), the "Caporal Vercrysse, un flamand grand et costaud" [Corporal Vercrysse, a big, strong Flemish man] is no doubt partly based on Vandenberghe.

48. In his autobiographical work *Métis*, Philippe Franchini (1993: 110–14), a Eurasian son of Mathieu Franchini, criticizes the stereotype of the violent Corsican mafioso or policeman in Vietnam (in Wargnier's film *Indochine*) and France. Philippe Franchini ran the Continental from 1965 to 1975, having taken over from his father, according to the back cover of *Métis*.

49. On this French defeat, see Ruscio (1992: 146–50) and Pervillé (1993: 127).

50. On colonized soldiers in the Indochinese War, see Ruscio (1992: 156).

51. On this aspect of Daeninckx's novel, see Kristin Ross (1992: 61).

52. In *Murder in Memoriam* (Daeninckx 1991b) one finds a similar police official, who is no doubt modeled on Maurice Papon, convicted for crimes against humanity for his role in the deportation of Jews from Vichy-era Bordeaux and also responsible for the police massacre of Algerian demonstrators on 17 October 1961.

53. For mention of the invocation of this same 1949 law to justify the censorship of films touching on colonialism, see Stora (1997: 114). For specific examples of censorship

and self-censorship of comics for reasons related to French colonialism, see Douvry (1991, esp. pp. 11, 54, 71) and Crépin and Groensteen (1999: 122).

54. *Meurtres pour mémoire* recalls several violent episodes from French history that are connected to the nation-state: the defeat of Vercingetorix at Alesia by Julius Cesear (Daeninckx 1994: 168, 175); the St. Bartholomew's Day massacre of the Huguenots by Roman Catholic mobs (168); the conflict between Thiers and the Communards (132); the Vichy government's death sentence against De Gaulle (42) and its contribution to the genocide of Jews; anti-colonialist resistance to the Indochinese War (158); and the conflict between the French government, the FLN and the OAS during the Algerian War (e.g., 74–75, 148, 153–55, 166).

55. As I show below, the comic book addresses the issue of the suppression of history by the post-independence Vietnamese government through the denial of colonial *métissage,* that is, the erasure of French influence.

56. There are significant differences between how the comic book and the detective novel treat the figure of the historian. In *Murder in Memoriam,* a father and a son, both historians, are characters who are murdered to cover up a heinous crime: the deportation of Jews, including many children, from Vichy France, to the Nazi death camps. They had been writing the history of the father's hometown, Drancy, which contained a French prison camp through which the condemned had been shipped, and had stumbled upon key evidence about the crime in the municipal archives of Toulouse.

57. I analyze this work elsewhere (McKinney 2011b).

58. Wild and exotic animals, ranging from elephants, crocodiles and tigers to giant snakes, continue to play an important role in comics about Southeast Asia, including *La colonne* (Martin and Simon 2001), *Théophane Vénard: Dans les griffes du tigre* [Théophane Vénard: In the Tiger's Claws] (Brunor, Bar and Gilles 2007), *Piège en forêt Moï* (Bartoll and Coyère 2007), *Le temple de l'épouvante* (Chapelle, Marniquet and Chanoinat 2009); cf. Douvry (1991: 68–73).

59. E.g., in "Parachutés au Laos," the French unit saves a downed American pilot (no. 236 [10 June 1951] through no. 240 [8 July 1951]). On U.S. aid to the French for the Indochinese War, and the transition from French colonialism to American imperialism at the end of the war, see Ruscio (1992: 130, 144–53, 186–89, 200–4, 216–18, 225–34).

60. Cf. "Parachutés au Laos" (no. 259 [18 November 1951]), where Verdon and Perrin-Houdon represent Kao as an orientalized demon in a thought balloon: "Effrayés par cet ennemi qui leur paraît un démon, les rebelles s'enfuient" [Frightened by this enemy that looks like a demon to them, the rebels flee].

61. In *The Colonial Heritage of French Comics* (2011b: 118–20), I analyze how Jarry and Otto T. parody the 1931 Paris Colonial Exposition, and also the counter-exhibition jointly organized by Communists and the Surrealists.

62. There is some overlap between these books by cartoonists and illustrated travel books, such as *Mon oncle de Hanoï* [My Uncle from Hanoi] (Lê Van 2003) and *Cambodge* [Cambodia] (Chavanat 2003).

63. See above, p. 226n12.

Chapter 4

1. RAS is the acronym for "rien à signaler" [nothing to report], a military phrase that took on new meaning during the war that France did not declare but nonetheless fought in Algeria. It is also the title of a film about the Algerian War (Yves Boisset 1973; cf. Hennebelle, Berrah and Stora 1997: 201)

2. Andrevon did his military service in Algeria at the end of the war; http://jp.andrevon. com/bio.htm (accessed 9 December 2012).

3. Cf. Barthes (1987: 137–44). This only later changed in official French documents; cf. Garcia (1999).

4. See above, p. 32.

5. See above, pp. 7, 63.

6. Especially these: *Le chemin de l'Amérique* (Baru 1990), "L'Algérie" (Ferrandez 1994e), "Vengeance harkie" (Merezette and Boudjellal 1994), *Jambon-Beur: Les couples mixtes* (Boudjellal 1995), "Le deuil" (Alagbé and Stein 1997), *Algérie: La douleur et le mal* [Algeria: The Pain and the Evil/Illness] (Baudoin et al. 1998), vol. 2 of *Azrayen'* (Lax and Giroud 1999), *Là-bas* (Tronchet and Sibran 2003), *D'Algérie* (Morvandiau 2007), and *Tahya El-Djazaïr* [Long Live Algeria] (Galandon, Dan and Ralenti 2009, 2010).

7. Cf. Douglas and Malti-Douglas (1994); McKinney (2007a, 2008c). I thank Frank Giroud for having generously loaned me two Algerian graphic narratives about the Algerian War (Tenani 1985; Bouslah 1989). Other Algerian comic books about the war that I have consulted include Slim (1968), Tenani (1981), Amouri (1983), Masmoudi (1983) and Guerroui (1986).

8. Cabu (2004); on Cabu and the war, see also Stora (1992: 265) and Douvry (1983: 33). Cf. *Corvée de bois* [Wood Chore] (Daeninckx and Tignous 2002), and *Tahya El-Djazaïr* (Galandon, Dan and Ralenti 2010: 32–33).

9. I am grateful to Farid Boudjellal for having kindly provided this document to me.

10. Todd Shepard (2006: 91, 185) refers to Coral's *Journal d'un embastillé*.

11. Cf. www.bdoubliees.com/journalpilote/annees/1979.htm (accessed 9 December 2012).

12. The book also includes a critique of a *Pied-Noir* photo album (28): "Il n'y a pas d'Arabes sur ces photos—ou bien, ce sont des figurants silencieux . . . " [There are no Arabs in these photos—or else they are silent extras . . .]; cf. McKinney (2011b: 160–64) for an analysis of the critique of a colonial photo album in another post-colonial comic book.

13. See pp. 25–26, 71–72, 178.

14. For other examples, see pp. 111, 173, 239n12.

15. See Rigney (2005: 22–23) on the role of the historical novel.

16. Cf. Rioux (1992: 261), Ruscio (2001: 274), Liauzu and Liauzu (2002: 154–55, 174) and McKinney (2009: 87–88).

17. Cf. Horne (1978: 430–32), *Le chemin de l'Amérique* (Baru, Thévenet and Ledran 1998: 45) and the conclusion to Pontecorvo's film *The Battle of Algiers* (1966).

18. Cf. Gervereau (1991: 133), Hureau (1992: 284).

19. An advertisement for DOP soap (25), also mentioned by the Maghrebi-French singer and author Mounsi in Yamina Benguigui's film *Mémoires d'immigrés: L'héritage maghrébin* [Memories of Immigrants: The Maghrebi Heritage] (1997), where he relates his memories about Algerian immigrants in France in the 1960s. However, DOP was also an acronym for "détachement opérationnel de protection," a French army structure that helped turn torture into a general practice of the French army in Algeria (Branche 2001: 255–63). The cartoonists (Vidal and Bignon 1982: 5) refer precisely to this type of unit when an Algerian is arrested, perhaps one of those who is later tortured (8, 11–12).

20. Cf. Amato (1979: front cover, 151) and Gervereau, Rioux and Stora (1992: 168–69). On colonial statues in North Africa, see also Memmi (1985: 84, 123). On their repatriation to France, see also Kidd (2002: 185, 192), who cites Amato, and Aldrich (2005: 168–72, 187–88).

21. Cf. Rey-Goldzeiguer (2002: 62). This is a recurring image in *nostalgérique* [nostal-

geric] *Pied-Noir* comics about the end of the war, for example, *Les rivages amers* (Joyaux-Brédy and Joux n.d.: front cover, 80) and *Là-bas* (Tronchet and Sibran 2003: 13–14).

22. There may also perhaps be an attempt here by Vidal and Bignon to dominate the cultural field through an encyclopedic completeness. In an interview, Jean Debernard (2003), a now deceased bookseller and author, accused Vidal of blocking the publication of other comics or graphic novels on the Algerian War: "Par ailleurs, Guy Vidal, directeur chez Dargaud (et mort il y a quelques mois) qui avait lui-même réalisé des scénarios sur la guerre d'Algérie, nous avait promis de nous recevoir. Là il nous a dit, en gros: 'vos histoires m'ont passionné, mais je ne les prends pas et je vais tout faire pour les empêcher de paraître car la guerre d'Algérie je la garde pour moi.' C'était pour lui une sorte de chasse gardée, ce sujet" [Moreover, Guy Vidal, director at Dargaud (and deceased a few months ago), who had himself created scripts about the Algerian War, promised to meet with us. There he told us, more or less: "Your stories really moved me, but I won't take them and I'll do everything to keep them from appearing, because I'm keeping the Algerian War for myself." The subject was a kind of private hunting ground for him]. Debernard also states that Casterman refused to publish his graphic narrative because the Belgian publisher considered it too leftist.

23. Cf. Smolderen (2009: e.g., 59) on polyphony and polygraphy in nineteenth-century comics, and see Miller (2004: 312) on dialogism in recent works.

24. "Barbouze" [a fake beard] is a synechdochic term for a spy or secret agent. It refers to French counter-terrorist agents that De Gaulle's government used against the OAS during the Algerian War.

25. Horne (1978: 434–35, 492–95), Douvry (1983: 35) and Gauchon and Buisson (1984: 100–101). For Dine (1994: 143), the comic book includes "rather less persuasive anti-OAS action." Coral (1962) depicts some of the same events.

26. On photos taken by conscripts in the war, see Blondet-Bisch (1992).

27. Cf. Buch (2005: 64). Slama refers to the Bureaux arabes as "les ancêtres des officiers SAS" [the ancestors of the SAS officers] (2001: 17).

28. See pp. 128, 221–22.

29. This impression is reinforced by a footnote on the following page, which explains to the non-Kabyle French reader that an activity referred to in the text is a "rite nuptial kabyle" [Kabyle nuptial rite] (1998: 46). Related information is provided about arranged marriages and the repudiation of women accused of sterility (44).

30. E.g., in *L'année de feu* (Ferrandez 1994b: 76). See Said (1994b: 176–78) on this trope in Camus's short story "La femme adultère" [The Adulterous Woman].

31. In "Une épopée algérienne" [An Algerian Epic] (n.p.), the postface to vol. 2 of *Azrayen'* (Lax and Giroud 1999), Giroud describes the new drawing style that Lax created for their Algerian diptych.

32. Ferrandez's *L'année de feu* (1994b) has also been described as a Western (Buch 2005: 62). On the Western in French comics magazine *Pilote*, see Michallat (2007: 286–88).

33. Perhaps for this reason it was listed on the websites of ADIMAD, a pro-OAS association, http://ma.page.free.fr/adimad/livre-enfant-AFR.jpg, www.adimad.fr/archives.html (accessed 4 July 2008).

34. This was apparently a common name for a hotel in colonial Algeria; see, for example, Adès and Zaragozi (1999: 47).

35. E.g., Joseph Constant, Mario Puzzo, Isabelle Eberhardt (Ferrandez 1987, 1994c: 33–37, 46–47), Paul (Octave Alban's father) and Albert Camus (see above, Chapter 2).

36. In *Lire*; http://www.lexpress.fr/culture/livre/la-guerre-fantome_807135.html (accessed 9 December 2012).

37. His name recalls that of a well-known pair of comic-book villains, "les frères Loiseau," in Hergé's *Le secret de la Licorne* [*The Secret of the Unicorn*] (Hergé 2006). This is one of several borrowings by Ferrandez from Hergé.

38. Aside from the socially devalorized form of *métissage* [ethnic or cultural mixing], through visits to prostitutes, evoked in *Les fils du sud* (Ferrandez 1994c) and *Le centenaire* (Ferrandez 1994d); see Tribak-Geoffroy (1997: 128). Algerian historian Marnia Lazreg (1994: 41) argues that "intermarriages [between Algerians and French] existed but were extremely rare."

39. See Horne (1978: 108–9, 165–66, 173, 220, 251–52); and above, pp. 165–67.

40. This propaganda is mentioned, reproduced or analyzed in Ferrandez (2004: 6), Lever (1991: 196), Bancel and Blanchard (1997: 29) and Milleron (2003).

41. At least two other comic books represent the bodies of Algerians displayed by the French army: *Algérie française!* (Mérezette and Dumenil 1985: 7) and *Tahya El-Djazaïr* (Galandon, Dan and Ralenti 2010: 6).

42. E.g., the tilting of the last frame on page 50 of *Carnets d'Orient*; the reworked repetition of similar visual material in two sequences of *L'année de feu* (35–36, 40); and the inclusion of a subjective frame in a revealing way in *Les fils du sud* (23–24). For analysis of these issues, see Chapter 2, above.

43. See above, pp. 64–72.

44. It is also referred to in another comic about the war, *Tahya El-Djazaïr* (Galandon, Dan and Ralenti 2010: 10, 29).

45. On the "history effect," see above, pp. 20, 56–57. For a different approach to myth, fiction and colonial history, which privileges the mythical and fictional as "distractions from history," see Macdonald (2008).

46. See also above, p. 229n34.

47. The bombing happened on 10 August 1957 (Horne 1978: 184). Later, Ferrandez shows a firefight in the casbah between French soldiers and FLN militants, again inspired by the film (48–49).

48. On the first volume in the series, see Martini (1997: 213–14).

49. Nor does Ferrandez, although he depicts an earlier *Pied-Noir* lynching of Algerians (2004: 26–28).

50. For a more extensive analysis of this graphic novel see McKinney (2011a). The following paragraph summarizes a few of my main points from there. Sibran originally wrote this story as a prose novel (1999).

51. The book is not the best conceived and executed of the lot: its title character, Aïscha, is called Djemila on the back cover; and the Algerian FLN (Front de Libération Nationale) is incorrectly called the FNL throughout the novel.

52. *Tahya El-Djazaïr* (Galandon, Dan and Ralenti 2010: 40–41) is another French comic that openly refers to the rape of Algerian women and girls by French soldiers during the war. A few others suggest the possible rape of: Aïscha by French sailors (Joos and Yann 1990: 20); Allilat (whose lover Messonier has disappeared) by French soldiers (Lax and Giroud 1998: 36); and Nadine (the lover of Ahmed) by French soldiers (Mérezette and Dumenil 1985: 18).

53. Cf. Vaugeois (2003: 27) on the FLN as composed of "ennemis formés dans la culture islamique de la cruauté" [enemies formed in the Muslim culture of cruelty], a thesis of cultural essentialism illustrated two pages later by a photograph of a dead man with his throat slit, captioned: "Tout au long du conflit, les Musulmans seront les premières victimes du FLN. C'est par les égorgements et la terreur qu'il étend son emprise" [All throughout the conflict, the Muslims will be the first victims of the FLN. It is by throat-slitting and terror that it spreads its control].

54. Also in "Ote tes mains d'mon patrimoine" [Take Your Hands off My Inheritance] in the same book, *Rampeau 2 (Same Player Shoots Again)* (Frank and Golo 1987), first serialized 1979–81; *Le singe et la sirène* [The Monkey and the Siren], by Dumontheuil and Angéli (2001: 37). For a recent far-right reiteration of this theme (with an horrific photo), see Vaugeois (2003: 29).

55. I.e., "coupeur de route" [road cutter], or highway bandit, a derogatory term the French applied to Algerian independence fighters.

56. E.g., Ferrandez (1994b), Bucquoy and Hulet (1990).

57. Boudjellal (1998, 1999, 2002; republished in 2006a, 2006b).

58. On Boudjellal's treatment of the Algerian War and its sequels in *Jambon-Beur: Les couples mixtes* (1995), see above, pp. 1–5.

59. Esse G. Esse, or SGS, i.e., Giovanni Sinchetto, Dario Guzzon and Pietro Sartoris; cf. Gaumer and Moliterni (1994: 232–33).

60. Mourad Boudjellal's investment in the cowboy and Indian theme is evident in his decision to name one part of his publishing operations "Géronimo" (cf. Boudjellal, in Belle-froid 2005: 96).

61. E.g., Malet and Tardi (1982: 22, 60, 65), Tardi (1990: 20–21, 31, 46–47, 69, 90–91). I thank Paul Cohen for reminding me about this.

62. For a similar image, see Daeninckx and Tignous (2002: 41); see also p. 153, above, on "corvées de bois."

63. A similar connection is suggested by Didier Daeninckx (1994: 157, 195–97), in *Meurtres pour mémoire*, where Pierre Cazes, a former secret agent of the French government during the war, is dying from cancer. On this novel, see Ross (1992) and Dine (1994: 212).

64. Stora appears to have borrowed this metaphor from statements made while the war was in progress. See Vidal-Naquet (4 May 1961), republished in Eveno and Planchais (1989: 308); and Stora (1992: 68).

65. One edition of the novel is illustrated by cartoonist Jeanne Puchol (Daeninckx 1991a).

66. E.g., the special dossier "La guerre d'Algérie, est-elle terminée?" in *La nouvelle revue d'histoire* 8 (September–October 2003). Historians such as Liauzu (2003) have contested the negation of colonial violence.

67. In *Une éducation algérienne* (Vidal and Bignon 1982: 10, 29, 56); *La guerre fantôme* (Ferrandez 2002: 33, 64); *Rue de la bombe* (Ferrandez 2004: 20–21, 47).

Chapter 5

1. On the "voyage out," see also McKinney (2011b).

2. Boudjellal sold the majority of his company shares in Soleil Productions to Editions Delcourt in 2011 to focus his energy on directing the Toulon Rugby Club.

3. See above, p. 226n12.

4. E.g., in Breysse (1995: 15–17), serialized 1948–49.

5. E.g., in Jijé (1994: 142), serialized 1959.

6. See above, pp. 48, 50–53, 94, 99–101.

7. E.g., in *Gringalou en Algérie* (Pinchon and Noé n.d.; serialized 1947) and "Parachu-tés au Laos" (no. 247 [26 August 1951], by Verdon and Perrin-Houdon).

8. Pigeon (1996: 144) mentions an ambiguous sentence from the conclusion of *Sam et Sap* (Candide and Le Cordier 1908) as a possible critique of "the cost of colonization."

9. Töpffer (1996, 2007).

10. Christophe (1981, 2004).

11. French slave traders and owners are depicted in the voyeuristic "Les passagers du vent" (Bourgeon 1980–1994d). On this, see Pierre (1988: 118; 2000: 44–45). This aspect of French history is also represented in *Les Antilles sous Bonaparte: Delgrès* (Puisy and Chamoiseau 1981), *Le sang du flamboyant* (Auclair and Migeat 1985: 25, 28) and the mordant *Petite histoire des colonies françaises,* vol. 1: *L'Amérique française* (Jarry and T. 2006).

12. E.g., in *Stanley* (Hubinon and Joly 1994: 56; first ed., 1955).

13. E.g., in *L'oncle du Tchad* (Breysse 1998: 13; serialized 1949–50). On these representations, see, for example, Pierre (1988), Pigeon (1996), Delisle (2007, 2008) and Lefèvre (2008).

14. See above, pp. 89–90, 173.

15. Evoked by Ferrandez in Mimouni and Ferrandez (1993), Ferrandez (1995: 9), Poncet and Morin (1996: 76–77), Buch (2005: 90–92, 103) and Ferrandez (2006); and depicted by Morvandiau in *D'Algérie* (2007).

16. See above, pp. 185–86, and McKinney (2011a).

17. E.g., in "Ric Brio: L'oublié de la Croisière noire" (Armand and Bergouze 1985; on this, see McKinney 2011b: 142–48) and *Les oubliés d'Annam* (Lax and Giroud 1990–91).

18. E.g., in *Carnets d'Orient* (Ferrandez 1994a) and *Le cimetière des princesses* (Ferrandez 1995).

19. E.g., in *Coeurs de sable* (Loustal and Paringaux 1985) and *Le centenaire* (Ferrandez 1994d).

20. E.g., in *Nègres jaunes* (Alagbé 1995).

21. E.g., in *Le chemin de l'Amérique* (Baru, Thévenet and Ledran 1990) and *Le chemin de Tuan* (Baloup and Jiro 2005).

22. E.g., in *Gags à l'harissa* (Boudjellal 1989b) and *Un automne à Hànôi* (Baloup 2004).

23. E.g., Elvire and the Dey of Algiers in *Histoire de M. Cryptogame* (Töpffer 1996, 2007), *Bécassine nourrice* (Caumery and Pinchon 1951: 37; first ed., 1922)—cf. Couderc (2000: 226–27)—and *La vie est belle* (Forton 1949; first ed., 1933). For an atypical variation in the "Pieds-Nickelés" series, see Frémion (2007).

24. E.g., *Nègres jaunes* (Alagbé 1995c), *Jambon-Beur: Les couples mixtes* (Boudjellal 1995), "Le deuil" (Alagbé and Stein 1997) and *Kid Congo* (Loustal and Paringaux 1997).

25. See above, p. 128.

26. E.g., Saint-Michel and Fages (1976). For a critique of neo-colonial and neo-imperialist links between France and black Africa, see Verschave (2000, 2001).

27. See Pierre (2000: 45) and Arnaud (2000) on the comics of French cartoonist Jano as a possible example of a nonexploitative and funny relationship to Africans in comics.

28. See Chapter 4, above, p. 178, for questions raised by Ferrandez's acceptance of this type of sponsorship of his visits throughout the Arab and Muslim world. See also McKinney (2008a: 15–16).

29. People from French overseas departments [départements d'outre-mer] and territories [territoires d'outre-mer].

WORKS CITED

Abun-Nasr, Jamil M. 1990. *A History of the Maghrib in the Islamic Period*. Cambridge: Cambridge University Press.

Adès, Marie-Claire, and Pierre Zaragozi. 1999. *Photographes en Algérie au XIXe siècle*. Introductory essays by Mounir Bouchenaki and Itzhak Goldberg. Paris: Musée-Galerie de la Seita.

AFP [Agence France Presse]. 2005. "L'ambassadeur de France rend hommage aux victimes des massacres de Sétif." 27 February.

Ainsa, Fernando. 1982. "Utopia, Promised Lands, Immigration and Exile." *Diogenes* 119: 49–64.

Aït Hammoudi, Bachir. 1987. *Festival international de la bande dessinée et de la caricature. Bordj-el-Kiffan du 30 juin au 5 juillet 1987*. Exhibition catalog. Réghaïa: Entreprise nationale des arts graphiques.

Alagbé, Yvan. 1995. *Nègres jaunes*. Wissous [France]: Amok.

Alagbé, Yvan (art), and Eléonore Stein (script). 1997. "Le Deuil." *Le cheval sans tête*, vol. 4: *Un héritage* (November): 16–31.

Alaoui, Brahim, ed. 1999. *Delacroix: Le voyage au Maroc*. Paris: Institut du Monde Arabe; Flammarion.

Aldrich, Robert. 2005. *Vestiges of the Colonial Empire in France: Monuments, Museums and Colonial Memories*. New York: Palgrave Macmillan.

Alidières, Bernard. 2006. "La guerre d'Algérie en France métropolitaine: Souvenirs 'oubliés.'" *Hérodote* 120: 149–76.

Alloula, Malek. 1981. *Le harem colonial: Images d'un sous-érotisme*. Geneva: Slatkine.

———. 1986. *The Colonial Harem*. Translated by Myrna Godzich and Wlad Godzich and introduction by Barbara Harlow. Minneapolis: University of Minnesota Press.

———. 2001. *Le harem colonial: Images d'un sous-érotisme*. Paris: Séguier.

Amato, Alain. 1979. *Monuments en exil*. Paris: Editions de l'Atlanthrope.

Amouri, Manssour. 1983. *Sur les sentiers escarpés*. Algiers: Entreprise nationale du livre.

Anderson, Benedict. 1991. *Imagined Communities: Reflections on the Origin and Spread of Nationalism*. Revised Edition. New York: Verso.

Andrevon, Jean-Pierre (script), and Véronik (art). 1982. *Matricule 45000*. Grenoble: Glénat.

———. 1985. *Neurones Trafic*. Colors by Bill. Grenoble: Glénat.

Apter, Emily. 1992. "Female Trouble in the Colonial Harem." *Differences* 4 (1): 205–24.

———. 1995. "French Colonial Studies and Postcolonial Theory." In Lawrence D. Kritzman, ed., *France's Identity Crises*, special issue of *SubStance* 24 (1–2): 169–80.

Armande, Jacques [Martin, Jean-Jacques] (art), and Bergouze [Bernalin, Philippe] (script). 1985. "Ric Brio: L'oublié de la Croisière noire." *Métal aventure* 9: 39–46.

Arzalier, Francis. 2006. "Le négationnisme colonial de l'université à la littérature de gare." *Cahiers d'histoire: Revue d'histoire critique* 99: 37–48. http://chrhc.revues.org/1273 (accessed 1 November 2012).

Assouline, Pierre. 1998. *Hergé*. Paris: Gallimard [1996].

Assus, André, Jean-Pierre Badia, Jean Cuenat and Gabrielle Cuenat. 1999. *Salomon Assus: Illustrateur humoristique de l'Algérie, 1850–1919*. Nice: Jacques Gandini.

Auclair, [Claude], and François Migeat. 1985. *Le sang du flamboyant*. Tournai: Casterman.

Aussaresses, Paul. 2003. *Services spéciaux: Algérie 1955–57*. Paris: Perrin [2001].

Azoulay, Paul. 1980. *La nostalgérie française*. Paris: Eric Baschet Editions.

Baetens, Jan. 2004. "Autobiographies et bandes dessinées." In *L'étude de la bande dessinée*, special issue of *Belphégor* 4 (1). http://etc.dal.ca/belphegor/vol4_no1/articles/04_01_Baeten_autobd_fr.html (accessed 1 November 2012).

Bakhtin, M. M. 1990. *The Dialogic Imagination: Four Essays*. Edited by Michael Holquist and translated by Caryl Emerson and Michael Holquist. Austin: University of Texas Press.

Bal, Mieke. 1996. *Double Exposures: The Subject of Cultural Analysis*. London: Routledge.

Balibar, Etienne. 1998. *Droit de cité*. La Tour d'Aigues: Editions de l'Aube.

Balibar, Etienne, and Immanuel Wallerstein. 1991. *Race, Nation, Class: Ambiguous Identities*. Translated by Chris Turner. London: Verso.

Baloup, Clément. 2004. *Un automne à Hànôi*. Antony: La Boîte à Bulles.

———. 2006. *Quitter Saigon: Mémoires de Viet Kieus*. Antony: La Boîte à Bulles.

———. 2008. Telephone interview, 6 August.

———. 2010. *Quitter Saigon: Mémoires de Viet Kieu*, vol. 1. Antony: La Boîte à Bulles.

———. 2012. *Little Saigon: Mémoires de Viet Kieu*, vol. 2. Antony: La Boîte à Bulles.

Baloup, Clément (script), and Mathieu Jiro (art). 2005. *Chính Tri*, vol. 1: *Le chemin de Tuan*. Preface by Pascal Blanchard. Paris: Le Seuil.

———. 2007. *Chính Tri*, vol. 2: *Le choix de Hai*. Paris: Le Seuil.

———. 2012. *La concubine rouge*. Paris: Gallimard.

Bancel, Nicolas, and Pascal Blanchard. 1997. "De l'indigène à l'immigré: Images, messages et réalités." In *Imaginaire colonial, figures de l'immigré*, special issue of *Hommes et Migrations* 1207 (May–June): 6–29.

Bardet, Daniel (script), and Boutel. 2000. *Le Boche*, vol. 7: *La route Mandarine*. Colors by Jacky Robert. Grenoble: Glénat.

———. 2001. *Le Boche*, vol. 8: *La fée brune*. Colors by Jacky Robert. Grenoble: Glénat.

———. 2002. *Le Boche*, vol. 9: *L'affaire Sirben*. Colors by Jacky Robert. Grenoble: Glénat.

Bardet, Daniel (script), and Patrick Jusseaume (art). 1985. *Chronique de la maison Le Quéant*, vol. 1: *Le pain enragé*. Grenoble: Glénat [serialized in *Vécu* beginning in 1985; 7 vols. in total].

———. 1986. *Chronique de la maison Le Quéant*, vol. 2: *Les quarante-huitards*. Grenoble: Glénat.

———. 1987. *Chronique de la maison Le Quéant*, vol. 3: *Les fils du Chélif*. Colors by J. J. and Y. Chagnaud. Grenoble: Glénat.

————. 1988. *Chronique de la maison Le Quéant*, vol. 4: *Leïla*. Colors by J. J. and Y. Chagnaud. Grenoble: Glénat.

————. 1989. *Chronique de la maison Le Quéant*, vol. 5: *Les portes d'Alger*. Colors by J. J. and Y. Chagnaud. Grenoble: Glénat.

Bardet, Daniel (script), and Elie Klimos (art). 1997. *Le parfum des cèdres*, vol. 1: *Le sang d'Adonis*. Colors by Josette Massamiri. Grenoble: Glénat.

Bardet, Daniel (script), Eric Stalner (art) and Jean-Marc Stalner (art). 1995. *Le Boche*, vol. 6: *Nuit de Chine . . . .* Grenoble: Glénat.

Barthes, Roland. 1985. "L'effet de réel." In Roland Barthes et al., *Littérature et réalité*, 81–90. Paris: Le Seuil.

————. 1987. *Mythologies*. Paris: Le Seuil.

Bartoll, Jean-Claude (script), and Xavier Coyère (art). 2006. *Mékong*, vol. 1: *Or rouge*. Colors by Claire Champion. Paris: Dargaud.

————. 2007. *Mékong*, vol. 2: *Piège en forêt Moï*. Colors by Claire Champion. Paris: Dargaud.

Baru [Barulea, Hervé]. 1987. *Vive la classe!* Colors by Daniel Ledran. Paris: Futuropolis.

————. 1996. Personal interview. Nancy, 25 July.

————. 1999. *Les années Spoutnik*, vol. 1: *Le penalty*. Colors by Daniel Ledran. Tournai: Casterman.

————. 2000. *Les années Spoutnik*, vol. 2: *C'est moi le chef!* Colors by Daniel Ledran. Tournai: Casterman.

————. 2002. *Les années Spoutnik*, vol. 3: *Bip bip!* Colors by Daniel Ledran. Tournai: Casterman.

————. 2003. *Les années Spoutnik*, vol. 4: *Boncornards têtes-de-lard!* Colors by Daniel Ledran and Baru. Tournai: Casterman.

————. 2004. Conversation. Cincinnati, November 13.

————. 2007. "La fin du service national: 27 juin 2001." In David B. et al., *Le jour où . . . : 1987–2007 France Info 20 ans d'actualité*, 127–36. Paris: Futuropolis.

————. 2008. "The Working Class and Comics: a French Cartoonist's Perspective." In Mark McKinney, ed., *History and Politics in French-Language Comics*, 239–57. Jackson: University Press of Mississippi.

————. 2009. *Les années Spoutnik: Edition intégrale*. Colors by Daniel Ledran. Tournai: Casterman.

————. 2010. *Fais péter les basses Bruno!* Paris: Futuropolis.

————. 2011. "Interview with Baru: Part 1," with Mark McKinney. *European Comic Art* 4 (2): 213–37.

————. 2012. "Interview with Baru: Part 2," with Mark McKinney. *European Comic Art* 5 (2): 67–91.

Baru [Barulea, Hervé] (art and script), Jean-Marc Thévenet (script) and Daniel Ledran (colors). 1990. *Le chemin de l'Amérique*. Paris: Albin Michel.

————. 1998. *Le chemin de l'Amérique*. Tournai: Casterman.

————. 2002. *Road to America*. Translated by Helge Dascher. Montreal: Drawn and Quarterly.

Basfao, Kacem. 1990. "Arrêt sur images: Les rapports franco-maghrébins au miroir de la bande dessinée." *Annuaire de l'Afrique du Nord* 29: 225–35.

Baudoin, [Edmond], et al. 1987. *Le désert est plus beau que tout*. Paris: Comité français contre la faim; Souffles.

————. 1998. *Algérie, la douleur et le mal*. Blois: BD Boum.

————. 2001. *17 octobre—17 illustrateurs*. Introduction by Mehdi Lallaoui, Anne Tristan, and Benjamin Stora. Bezons: Au nom de la mémoire.

Beaty, Bart. 2007. *Unpopular Culture: Transforming the European Comic Book in the 1990s*. Toronto: University of Toronto Press.

———. 2008. "The Concept of '*Patrimoine*' in Contemporary Franco-Belgian Comics Production." In Mark McKinney, ed., *History and Politics in French-Language Comics and Graphic Novels*, 69–93. Jackson: University Press of Mississippi.

Begag, Azouz. 2006. *Le gone du Chaâba*. Paris: Le Seuil [1986].

Begag, Azouz (script), and Djillali Defali (art). 2012. *Leçons coloniales*. Paris: Delcourt.

Beketch, Serge de. 1995. "C'est à lire." *Le Libre Journal* 57 (20 January): 18–19.

———. 1997. "C'est à lire." *Le Libre Journal* 114 (2 January): 20–21.

Bellefroid, Thierry. 2005. *Les éditeurs de bande dessinée: Entretiens avec Thierry Bellefroid*. Brussels: Niffle.

Benguigui, Yamina. 1997. *Mémoires d'immigrés: L'héritage maghrébin*. Canal+ (film).

———. 1997. *Mémoires d'immigrés: L'héritage maghrébin*. Paris: Albin Michel.

Benhaïm, André. 2007. "La langue au chat (du rabbin): Itinéraires dans l'étrange bande dessinée de Joann Sfar." *Contemporary French and Francophone Studies* 11 (2): 241–52.

Benjamin, Roger. 2003a. *Orientalist Aesthetics: Art, Colonialism, and French North Africa, 1880–1930*. Berkeley: University of California Press.

———. 2003b. *Renoir and Algeria*. With an essay by David Prochaska. New Haven: Yale University Press.

Benot, Yves. 2001. *Massacres coloniaux, 1944–50: La IVe République et la mise au pas des colonies françaises*. Preface by François Maspero. 2nd ed. Paris: La Découverte.

Béra, Michel, Michel Denni and Philippe Melot. 1996. *Trésors de la bande dessinée: BDM*. Paris: Editions de l'Amateur.

Bernasconi, Dominique. 1970. "L'image de l'Algérie dans l'iconographie française, 1830–71." Mémoire, dir. Raoul Girardet. Institut d'Etudes Politiques de l'Université de Paris.

Bessaih, B. (script), B. Bakhti (script) and Benattou Masmoudi (art). 1986. *L'histoire de l'Algérie en bandes dessinées: L'épopée du Cheikh Bouamama*. Algiers: ENAL.

Biard, Jean-François (art), José-Louis Bocquet (script) and François Rivière (script). 1988. *38ème Parallèle*. Paris: L'Echo des Savanes; Albin Michel.

Biondi, Jean-Pierre, and Gilles Morin. 1993. *Les anticolonialistes (1881–1962)*. Paris: Hachette ("Pluriel" no. 8368).

Blanchard, Pascal, and Eric Deroo, eds. 2004. *Le Paris Asie: 150 ans de présence de la Chine, de l'Indochine, du Japon . . . dans la capitale*. Paris: La Découverte; ACHAC.

Blancou, Daniel. 2012. *Retour à Saint-Laurent-des-Arabes*. Paris: Delcourt.

Blatt, David. 1997. "Immigrant Politics in a Republican Nation." In Alec G. Hargreaves and Mark McKinney, eds., *Post-Colonial Cultures in France*, 40–55. New York: Routledge.

Blondet-Bisch, Thérèse. 1992. "La photo-déclic des appelés." In Laurent Gervereau, Jean-Pierre Rioux and Benjamin Stora, eds., *La France en guerre d'Algérie: Novembre 1954–Juillet 1962*, 232–36. Nanterre: BDIC.

Boëtsch, Gilles. 1993. "La Mauresque aux seins nus: L'imaginaire érotique colonial dans la carte postale." In Pascal Blanchard and Armelle Chatelier, eds., *Images et colonies: Nature, discours et influence de l'iconographie coloniale liée à la propagande coloniale et à la représentation des Africains et de l'Afrique en France, de 1920 aux indépendances*, 93–96. Paris: ACHAC; Syros.

Boltanski, Luc. 1975. "La constitution du champ de la bande dessinée." *Actes de la recherche en sciences sociales* 1: 37–59.

Boudarel, Georges. 1991. *Autobiographie*. Paris: Jacques Bertoin.

Boudjellal, Farid. 1984. "Amour d'Alger." *Révolution* 244 (November 2–8): 38–41.

———. 1989. *Gags à l'harissa*. Genève: Humanos, SA—Les Humanoïdes Associés.

———. 1995. *Jambon-Beur: Les couples mixtes*. Articles by Martine Lagardette. Colors by Sophie Balland. Toulon: Soleil Productions.

———. 1998. *Petit Polio*, vol. 1. Toulon: Soleil Productions.

———. 1999. *Petit Polio*, vol. 2. Toulon: Soleil Productions.

———. 2002. *Petit Polio*, vol. 3: *Mémé d'Arménie*. Toulon: Soleil Productions.

———. 2003. *Les Slimani*. Colors by Daniel C. Chambard, et al. Cachan: Tartamudo.

———. 2006a. *Petit Polio*, vols. 1–2. Paris: Futuropolis.

———. 2006b. *Mémé d'Arménie*. Postface by Martine Lagardette. Paris: Futuropolis.

———. 2012. *Le cousin harki*. Paris: Futuropolis.

Boudjellal, Farid (script), and Leïla Leïz (art). 2008. *Les contes du djinn Hadj Moussa*, vol. 2: *La rupture*. Toulon: Soleil Productions.

Bourdieu, Pierre, Franz Schultheis and Christine Frisinghelli. 2003. *Pierre Bourdieu: Images d'Algérie, une affinité élective*. Arles: Actes Sud; Camera Austria; Fondation Liber.

Bourgeon, François. 1980. *Les passagers du vent*, vol. 1: *La fille sous la dunette*. Grenoble: Glénat [serialized 1979–80].

———. 1994a. *Les passagers du vent*, vol. 2: *Le ponton*. Tournai: Casterman [1980].

———. 1994b. *Les passagers du vent*, vol. 3: *Le comptoir de Juda*. Tournai: Casterman [1981].

———. 1994c. *Les passagers du vent*, vol. 4: *L'heure du serpent*. Tournai: Casterman [1982].

———. 1994d. *Les passagers du vent*, vol. 5: *Le bois d'ébène*. Tournai: Casterman [1984].

Bournier, Isabelle, and Jacques Ferrandez. 2010. *Des hommes dans la guerre d'Algérie*. Preface by Jean-Jacques Jordi. Tournai: Casterman.

Bouslah, Mohamed. 1984. *La ballade du proscrit*. Algiers: ENAL.

———. 1989. *Pour que vive l'Algérie*. Algiers: Entreprise nationale du livre.

Brahimi, Denise, and Koudir Benchikou. 1991. *La vie et l'oeuvre de Etienne Dinet*. Courbevoie: ACR [1984].

Branche, Raphaëlle. 2001. *La torture et l'armée pendant la guerre d'Algérie, 1954–62*. Paris: Gallimard.

———. 2010. *L'embuscade de Palestro, Algérie 1956*. Paris: Armand Colin.

Branche, Raphaëlle, and Jim House. 2010. "Silences on State Violence during the Algerian War of Independence: France and Algeria, 1962–2007." In Efrat Ben-Ze'ev, Ruth Ginio and Jay Winter, eds., *Shadows of War: A Social History of Silence in the Twentieth Century*, 115–37. New York: Cambridge University Press.

Brennan, Timothy. 1993. "The National Longing for Form." In Homi K. Bhabha, ed., *Nation and Narration*, 4–70. New York: Routledge.

Breysse, Frédéric-Antonin. 1995. *Les aventures d'Oscar Hamel: L'idole aux yeux d'émeraude*. Paris: Editions du Triomphe. [1948–9]

———. 1998. *Les aventures d'Oscar Hamel et Isidore: L'oncle du Tchad*. Paris: Editions du Triomphe. [1949–50]

Brocheux, Pierre. 2004. "Le cas Boudarel." *Les collections de L'Histoire* 23 (April–June): 62–63.

Brunor (script), Dominique Bar (art) and Géraldine Gilles (color). 2007. *Théophane Vénard: Dans les griffes du tigre*. Tours: CLD Editions.

Buch, Serge. 2005. *Ferrandez: Une monographie*. Bibliography by Gilles Ratier. Saint-Egrève: Mosquito.

Buch, Serge, Jean-Michel Vernet and Gilles Ratier. 2010. *Lax: Une monographie*. Saint-Egrève: Mosquito.

Bucquoy, Jan, and Daniel Hulet. 1990. *Les chemins de la gloire*, vol. 3: *La kermesse ensablée*. Grenoble: Glénat.

Bucquoy, Jan, and Sels. 1990. *Une épopée française*, vol. 1: *Indochine*. Colors by Sonja L'Hoest and documentation by Léon Lekeu. Grenoble: Glénat.

Cabu [Cabut, Jean]. 2001. *Ma Ve république*. Preface by Pascal Ory. Paris: Hoëbeke.

———. 2004. "Cabu." Interview by Gérard Marinier. In *Ils ont fait la guerre d'Algérie: 40 personnalités racontent . . .*, vol. 1, 40–43. [Mâcon]: JPM Editions [1986].

Calargé, Carla. 2010. "Images de femmes: Une H/histoire de la France en Algérie à travers les *Carnets d'Orient* de Jacques Ferrandez." *Présence francophone* 74: 106–25.

Camus, Albert. 2003. *Chroniques algériennes, 1939–58: Actuelles III*. Paris: Gallimard [1958].

Candide, Rose (art), and Georges Le Cordier (script). 1908. *Sam et Sap: Aventures surprenantes d'un petit nègre et de son singe*. Paris: Delagrave.

Carreras, Gilbert. 1997. *On les appelait . . . les . . . harkis. . et pourtant, . . . ils étaient soldats de France!!* Paris: L'Harmattan.

Castex, Michel. 1993. "La Cour de cassation met fin à l'affaire Boudarel." *Agence France Presse*, 1 April.

Caumery [Languereau, Maurice] (script), and Joseph-Porphyre Pinchon (art). 1951. *Bécassine nourrice*. Paris: Gautier-Languereau. [1922]

Certeau, Michel de. 1994. *La prise de parole et autres écrits politiques*. Edited by Luce Giard. Paris: Le Seuil.

Cham [Noé, Charles Henri Amédée de]. Circa 1846. *A la guerre comme à la guerre*. Paris: Aubert et cie.

———. 1849. *Les voyages d'agrément*. Paris: Le Charivari.

———. n.d. *Chinoiseries, turqueries et autres maroquinades*. Paris: Arnauld de Vresse.

———. n.d. *Spahis et Turcos*. Paris: Maison Martinet.

Chapelle, Philippe (art), Frédéric Marniquet (script) and Philippe Chanoinat (script). 2009. *Le temple de l'épouvante*. Paris: Desinge and Hugo and Company.

Charef, Mehdi. 1989. *Le harki de Meriem*. Paris: Mercure de France.

Charpier, Frédéric. 1984. "Rue Catinat, Saïgon." *Métal Aventure* 8: 22–26.

Chavanat, Damien. 2003. *Cambodge*. Paris: Jalan.

Childs, Elizabeth C. 2004. *Daumier and Exoticism: Satirizing the French and the Foreign*. New York: Peter Lang.

Christin, Pierre (script), and Philippe Aymond (art). 1999. *Les 4 x 4*, vol. 3: *L'ombre du triangle*. Colors by Chagnaud. Paris: Dargaud.

Christin, Pierre (script), and Annie Goetzinger (art). 1990. *La demoiselle de la Légion d'honneur*. Geneva: Les Humanoïdes Associés—Humano, S. A. [1980].

———. 1996. Personal interview. Paris, 22 July.

Christophe [Colomb, Georges]. 1981. *Le baron de Cramoisy; La famille Fenouillard (inédits); Histoires en images; Ombres, jeux et découpages*. Edited by François Caradec. Paris: Pierre Horay.

———. 1989. *Les facéties du sapeur Camember*. Paris: Armand Colin [1896].

———. 2004. *La famille Fenouillard*. Paris: Armand Colin [1893].

Christophe, Bertrand, ed. 2012. *Algérie 1830–1962 avec Jacques Ferrandez*. Paris: Musée de l'Armée; Tournai: Casterman.

Ciment, Gilles, ed. 1990. *Cinéma et bande dessinée*, special issue of *CinémAction*, n.n., summer.

Conrad, Joseph [Korzeniowski, Józef Konrad]. 2006. *Coeur des ténèbres, précédé d'Un avant-poste du progrès*. Translated by G. Jean-Aubry and André Ruyters, with Dominique Goy-Blanquet, illustrated by Jean-Philippe Stassen and with commentaries by Jean-Philippe Stassen and Sylvain Venayre. Paris: Futuropolis-Gallimard.

Cooper, Nicola. 2001. *France in Indochina: Colonial Encounters.* Oxford: Berg.

Coral [Larocque-Latour, Jacques de]. 1962. *Journal d'un embastillé.* Paris: Editions Saint-Just.

———. 1964. *Journal d'un suspect.* Paris: Editions Saint-Just.

Corteggiani, François (script), and Tristan Dupuis. 2009. *Abd el-Kader.* Paris: Koutoubia.

Cottias, Myriam. 2006. "Et si l'esclavage colonial faisait histoire nationale?" In Claude Liauzu and Gilles Manceron, eds., *La colonisation, la loi et l'histoire,* preface by Henri Leclerc, 127–29. Paris: Syllepse.

Couderc, Marie-Anne. 2000. *Bécassine inconnue.* Preface by Jean Perrot. Paris: CNRS.

Couégnas, Daniel. 1992. *Introduction à la paralittérature.* Paris: Le Seuil.

Crépin, Thierry. 2003. "Deux regards sur la guerre d'Algérie en bande dessinée: *La guerre fantôme* de Jacques Ferrandez et *Azrayen'* de Frank Giroud et Christian Lax." *Vingtième siècle: Revue d'histoire* 78: 172–73.

Crépin, Thierry, and Thierry Groensteen, eds. 1999. *"On tue à chaque page!": La loi de 1949 sur les publications destinées à la jeunesse.* Paris: Editions du Temps.

Daeninckx, Didier. 1991a. *Meurtres pour mémoire.* Illustrated by Jeanne Puchol. Paris: Futuropolis; Gallimard.

———. 1991b. *Murder in Memoriam.* Translated by Liz Heron. London: Serpent's Tail.

———. 1994. *Meurtres pour mémoire.* Paris: Gallimard [1984].

Daeninckx, Didier (script), and Mako (art). 2011. *Octobre noir.* Preface by Benjamin Stora. Anthy-sur-Léman: Ad Libris.

Daeninckx, Didier (text) and Tignous (illustrations). 2002. *Corvée de bois.* Toulouse: Liber Niger; Montgiscard: Les 400 coups.

Dana, Catherine. 2005. "Sans retour: De Paris à Alger, *Bleu-figuier* d'Anne Sibran." In Lila Ibrahim-Lamrous and Catherine Milkovitch-Rioux, eds., *Regards croisés sur la guerre d'Algérie,* 221–31. Clermont-Ferrand: Presses universitaires Blaise Pascal.

David B. [Beauchard, Pierre-François]. 1998. *L'ascension du haut mal,* vol. 1. Preface by Florence. Paris: L'Association [1996].

———. 2006. *Epileptic.* Translated by Kim Thompson. New York: Pantheon Books.

Debernard, Jean. 2003. "Mémoire d'Algérie." Interview by Delphine Descaves. *L'oeil électrique* 28. http://oeil.electrique.free.fr/article.php?numero=28&articleid=494 (accessed 1 November 2012).

Delisle, Philippe. 2007. "Le missionnaire dans la bande dessinée franco-belge: Une figure imposée?" *Histoire et missions chrétiennes* 1: 131–47.

———. 2008. *Bande dessinée franco-belge et imaginaire colonial: Des années 1930 aux années 1980.* Paris: Karthala.

———. 2010. *Spirou, Tintin et Cie, une littérature catholique?: Années 1930 / Années 1980.* Paris: Karthala.

Dimberton, François (script), and Dominique Hé (art). 1989. *Mémoires d'un aventurier,* vol. 1: *Pierre de Saint-Fiacre.* Colors by Evelyne Hacquin-Dimberton. Grenoble: Glénat.

———. 1990. *Mémoires d'un aventurier,* vol. 2: *Ariane.* Colors by Evelyne Hacquin-Dimberton. Grenoble: Glénat.

———. 1991. *Mémoires d'un aventurier,* vol. 3: *Opium.* Colors by Hé and Dimberton. Grenoble: Glénat.

Dine, Philip. 1994. *Images of the Algerian War: French Fiction and Film, 1954–92.* Oxford: Clarendon Press.

Djebar, Assia. 1985. *L'amour, la fantasia.* Paris: Jean-Claude Lattès.

———. 1986. *Femmes d'Alger dans leur appartement.* Paris: des femmes [1980].

———. 1993. *Fantasia, An Algerian Cavalcade.* Portsmouth, NH: Heinemann.

Djebar, Assia, ed. 1984. *Villes d'Algérie au XIXe siècle: Estampes*, with Ahmed Kara-Ahmed. Translated by Larbi Yacoub. Paris: Centre Culturel Algérien; Algiers: Entreprise Algérienne de Presse.

Dorfman, Ariel. 1983. *The Empire's Old Clothes: What the Lone Ranger, Babar, and Other Innocent Heroes Do to Our Minds*. Translated by Clark Hansen. New York: Pantheon Books.

Dorfman, Ariel, and Armand Mattelart. 1984. *How to Read Donald Duck: Imperialist Ideology in the Disney Comic*. Translation and introduction by David Kunzle. New York: International General.

Douglas, Allen, and Fedwa Malti-Douglas. 1994. *Arab Comic Strips: Politics of an Emerging Mass Culture*. Bloomington: Indiana University Press.

———. 2008. "From the Algerian War to the Armenian Massacres: Memory, Trauma and Medicine in *Petit Polio* of Farid Boudjellal." *International Journal of Comic Art* 10 (2): 282–307.

Douvry, Jean-François. 1983. "La bande dessinée et la guerre d'Algérie." *Bulles-Dingues: Spécial nostalgie*, hors série no. 2, October, 31–36.

———. 1991. *Le grand atlas des pays imaginaires de la bande dessinée*. Illustrated by Claude Serrière and Marc Maldera. Grenoble: Phoenix.

Doyon, Jacques. 1973. *Les soldats blancs de Ho Chi Minh*. Paris: Arthème Fayard.

Droz, Bernard, and Evelyne Lever. 1991. *Histoire de la guerre d'Algérie (1954–62)*. Paris: Le Seuil.

Dumontheuil, Nicolas, and Eliane Angéli. 2001. *Le singe et la sirène*. Tournai: Casterman.

Duprat, François (art and script) and Denis Bernatets (colors). 2004. *Mon cousin dans la mort*. Darnétal: Petit à Petit.

Dupuis, N. D. "Quand la BD précède l'histoire . . . " Publisher's publicity flyer for *Les oubliés d'Annam*, by Lax and Giroud.

Durmelat, Sylvie. 2000. "Transmission and Mourning in *Mémoires d'immigrés: L'héritage maghrébin*: Yamina Benguigui as 'Memory Entrepreneuse.'" In Jane Freedman and Carrie Tarr, eds., *Women, Immigration and Identities in France*, 171–88. Oxford: Berg.

Eco. 2009. *Yêu Yêu Saigon*. Vallauris: Les Enfants Rouges.

Einaudi, Jean-Luc. 1991. *La bataille de Paris: 17 octobre 1961*. Paris: Le Seuil.

Eisenstein, Paul. 2008. "Imperfect Masters: Rabbinic Authority in Joann Sfar's *The Rabbi's Cat*." In Samantha Baskind and Ranen Omer-Sherman, eds., *The Jewish Graphic Novel: Critical Approaches*, 163–80. New Brunswick: Rutgers University Press.

Elbe, Eric d'. 1987. "Ferrandez: 'Carnets d'Orient': Un album qui insulte l'Algérie française." *Présent*, February 5.

Escanglon Morin, Valérie, François Nadiras and Sylvie Thénault. 2006. "Les origines et la genèse d'une loi scélérate." In Claude Liauzu and Gilles Manceron, eds., *La colonisation, la loi et l'histoire*, preface by Henri Leclerc, 23–58. Paris: Syllepse.

Esquer, Gabriel, ed. 1929. *Iconographie historique de l'Algérie, depuis le XVIe siècle jusqu'à 1871*. 3 vols. Paris: Plon.

Essegesse [Sinchetto, Giovanni, Dario Guzzon and Pietro Sartoris]. 1995. *Blek le roc: L'intégrale*, vol. 6. Lettering by Didier Fayolle. Toulon: Soleil Productions.

Eveno, Patrick, and Jean Planchais. 1989. *La guerre d'Algérie*. Paris: La Découverte; Le Monde.

Evrard, Dany, and Michel Roland. 1992. *Gordinne, éditeur liégeois: Pionnier de la bande dessinée*. N.p.: Deville Graphic.

Fanon, Frantz. 1968. *The Wretched of the Earth*. Preface by Jean-Paul Sartre and translated by Constance Farrington. New York: Grove Press.

———. 1986. *Peau noire masques blancs*. Paris: Le Seuil ("Points" no. 26) [1952].

———. 2002. *Les damnés de la terre*. Prefaces by Jean-Paul Sartre and Alice Cherki and Postface by Mohammed Harbi. Paris: La Découverte/Syros [1961].

Ferrandez, Jacques. 1987. Untitled comic about Isabelle Eberhardt. In Edmond Baudoin, et al., *Le désert est plus beau que tout*, 16–19. Paris: Comité Français Contre la Faim/Souffles.

———. 1988. "Une saga de l'histoire coloniale de l'Algérie en BD." Interview by Anne Roche. In *Impressions du sud* [Aix-en-Provence] 17 (first trimester): 23.

———. 1994a. *Carnets d'Orient*, vol. 1. Tournai: Casterman [partially serialized in *Corto* 8–10 (May–July 1986); first ed., 1987; also published as *Djemilah*].

———. 1994b. *Carnets d'Orient*, vol. 2: *L'année de feu*, Preface by Jean-Claude Carrière. Tournai: Casterman [serialized in *Corto* 19 (February 1989); first ed., 1989].

———. 1994c. *Carnets d'Orient*, vol. 3: *Les fils du sud*. Preface by Jules Roy. Tournai: Casterman [serialized in *A Suivre* 161–64 (June–September 1991); first ed., 1992].

———. 1994d. *Carnets d'Orient*, vol. 4: *Le centenaire*. Preface by Benjamin Stora. Tournai: Casterman [serialized in *A Suivre* 187–89 (August–October 1993); first ed., 1994].

———. 1994e. "L'Algérie." In Jean-Luc Fromental, ed., *Amnesty International: Au secours!*, 44–45. Paris: Albin Michel.

———. 1995. *Carnets d'Orient*, vol. 5: *Le cimetière des princesses*. Preface by Louis Gardel. Tournai: Casterman [serialized in *A Suivre* 201–4 (October 1994–January 1995); first ed., 1995].

———. 1996. Personal interview. La Colle sur Loup, 30 July.

———. 1998. Untitled. In Edmond Baudoin, et al., *Algérie, la douleur et le mal*. Blois: BD Boum.

———. 1999. *Carnets d'Orient: Voyage en Syrie*. Tournai: Casterman.

———. 2000. *Carnets d'Orient: Istanbul*. Tournai: Casterman.

———. 2001. *Carnets d'Orient: Liban*. Tournai: Casterman.

———. 2002. *Carnets d'Orient*, vol. 6: *La guerre fantôme*. Preface by Gilles Kepel. Tournai: Casterman.

———. 2004. *Carnets d'Orient*, vol. 7: *Rue de la bombe*. Preface by Bruno Etienne. Tournai: Casterman.

———. 2005a. *Carnets d'Orient*, vol. 8: *La fille du Djebel Amour*. Preface by Michel Pierre. Tournai: Casterman.

———. 2005b. *Les tramways de Sarajevo: Voyage en Bosnie-Herzégovine*. Tournai: Casterman.

———. 2006. *Retours à Alger*, with Rachid Mimouni. Tournai: Casterman.

———. 2007. *Carnets d'Orient*, vol. 9: *Dernière demeure*. Preface by [Mohand Saïd] Fellag. Tournai: Casterman.

———. 2009a. *Carnets d'Orient*, vol. 10: *Terre fatale*. Preface by Maïssa Bey. Tournai: Casterman.

———. 2009b. *L'hôte*. Preface by Boualem Sansal. Paris: Gallimard.

Ferrandez, Jacques (art and script), and Maurice Attia (text). 2012. *Alger la noire*. Tournai: Casterman.

Ferrandez, Jacques, and Alain Dugrand. 2001. *Carnets d'Orient: Irak: Dix ans d'embargo*. Tournai: Casterman.

Ferrié, Jean-Noël, and Gilles Boëtsch. 1995. "Contre Alloula: *Le harem colonial* revisité." In G. Beaugé and J. F. Clément, eds., *L'image dans le monde arabe*. 299–304. Paris: CNRS.

Flaubert, Gustave. 1991. *Voyage en Egypte*. Edited by Pierre-Marc de Biasi. Paris: Bernard Grasset.

———. 1996. *Flaubert in Egypt: A Sensibility on Tour*. Translated and edited by Francis Steegmuller. London: Penguin Books.

Fleury-Vilatte, Béatrice. 2000. *La mémoire télévisuelle de la guerre d'Algérie*, with Pierre Abramovici. Paris: Institut National de l'Audiovisuel; L'Harmattan.

Flood, Christopher, and Hugo Frey. 2002. "Defending the Empire in Retrospect: The Discourse of the Extreme Right." In Tony Chafer and Amanda Sackur, eds., *Promoting the Colonial Idea: Propaganda and Visions of Empire in France*, 195–210. New York: Palgrave.

Forton, Louis. 1949. *Les nouvelles aventures des Pieds-Nickelés*, vol. 10: *La vie est belle*. Paris: Société parisienne d'édition. [1933]

Foucault, Michel. 1979. *Discipline and Punish: The Birth of the Prison*. Translated by Alan Sheridan. New York: Vintage Books.

———. 1981. *Power/Knowledge: Selected Interviews and Other Writings, 1972–77*. Edited by Colin Gordon. Translated by Colin Gordon, Leo Marshall, John Mepham and Kate Soper. New York: Pantheon.

———. 1982. *The Archaeology of Knowledge and The Discourse on Language*. Translated by A. M. Sheridan Smith. New York: Pantheon Books.

Fournier (script), and Romain Slocombe (art). 1984. "L'Hôtel de l'Etoile." *Métal Aventure* 8 (October): 67–70.

Franchini, Philippe. 1993. *Métis*. Paris: Jacques Bertoin.

Frappier, Désirée (script), and Alain Frappier (art). 2012. *Dans l'ombre de Charonne*. Preface by Benjamin Stora. Paris: Mauconduit.

Frémion, Yves. 2007. "Manounou, le 4ème Pied-Nickelé." *Papiers nickelés* 14: 12–14.

Fresnault-Deruelle, Pierre. 1979. "L'effet d'histoire." In Jean-Claude Faur, ed., *Histoire et bande dessinée: Actes du deuxième Colloque international éducation et bande dessinée, La Roque d'Antheron, 16–17 février 1979*, 98–104. La Roque d'Antheron [France]: Objectif Promo-Durance; Colloque international Education et Bande dessinée.

Frey, Hugo. 2008. "'For All to See': Yvan Alagbé's *Nègres Jaunes* and the Representation of the Contemporary Social Crisis in the *Banlieue*." In Jan Baetens and Ari J. Blatt, eds., *Writing and the Image Today*, special issue of *Yale French Studies* 114: 116–29.

Fromental, Jean-Luc. 1984. Editorial introduction to *Indochine 54: L'empire français riz jaune . . .*, special issue of *Métal Aventure* 8 (October): 1.

Galandon, Laurent (script), A. Dan (art) and Albertine Ralenti (color). 2009. *Tahya El-Djazaïr*, vol. 1: *Du sang sur les mains*. Charnay-lès-Mâcon: Bamboo.

———. 2010. *Tahya El-Djazaïr*, vol. 2: *Du sable plein les yeux*. Charnay-lès-Mâcon: Bamboo.

Gantès, Gilles de. 2006. "Les métis franco-indochinois à l'époque coloniale: A l'interface des dominants et des dominés ou à leur marge?" In Françoise Douaire-Marsaudon, Bernard Sellato and Chantal Zheng, eds., *Dynamiques identitaires en Asie et dans le Pacifique*, vol. 2: *Pratiques symboliques en transition*, 149–71. Aix-en-Provence: Publications de l'Université de Provence.

Garanger, Marc. 1982. *Femmes algériennes 1960*. Paris: Contrejour.

———. 1984. *La guerre d'Algérie vue par un appelé du contingent*. Preface by Francis Jeanson. Paris: Le Seuil.

———. 1990. *Femmes des Hauts-Plateaux: Algérie 1960*. Preface by Leïla Sebbar. Paris: La Boîte à documents.

Garcia, Laure. 1999. "L'histoire comme désordre." Review of *Azrayen'*, vols. 1 and 2, by Lax and Giroud. *Le Nouvel Observateur*, 22–28 July, 73.

Gauchon, Pascal, and Patrick Buisson. 1984. *OAS: Histoire de la résistance française en Algérie*. Preface by Pierre Sergent. Bièvres: Jeune Pied-Noir.

Gaumer, Patrick, and Claude Moliterni. 1994. *Dictionnaire mondial de la bande dessinée*. Paris: Larousse.

Gauthier, Guy. 1993. "De l'imagerie d'une époque à sa représentation aujourd'hui." In Odette Mitterrand and Gilles Ciment, eds., *L'histoire . . . par la bande: Bande dessinée, histoire et pédagogie*, 55–61. Paris: Ministère de la jeunesse et des sports; Syros.

Gautier, Emile-Félix. 1920. *L'Algérie et la métropole*. Paris: Payot.

Gautier, Théophile. 1973. *Voyage pittoresque en Algérie (1845)*. Edited by Madeleine Cottin. Geneva: Librairie Droz.

Gervereau, Laurent. 1992. "Des bruits et des silences: Cartographie des représentations de la guerre d'Algérie." In Laurent Gervereau, Jean-Pierre Rioux and Benjamin Stora, eds., *La France en guerre d'Algérie: Novembre 1954–Juillet 1962*, 178–201. Nanterre: BDIC.

———. 1993. "L'exotisme." In Nicolas Bancel, Pascal Blanchard and Laurent Gervereau, eds., *Images et colonies: Iconographie et propagande coloniale sur l'Afrique française de 1880 à 1962*, 26–47. Nanterre: BDIC; Paris: ACHAC.

Gervereau, Laurent, Jean-Pierre Rioux and Benjamin Stora, eds. 1992. *La France en guerre d'Algérie: Novembre 1954–Juillet 1962*. Nanterre: BDIC.

Gilroy, Paul. 1993. *The Black Atlantic: Modernity and Double Consciousness*. Cambridge: Harvard University Press.

Girardet, Raoul. 1995. *L'idée coloniale en France de 1871 à 1962*. Paris: Hachette [1972].

Giudice, Fausto. 1992. *Arabicides: Une chronique française, 1970–91*. Paris: La Découverte.

———. 1993. "Arabicide in France: An Interview with Fausto Giudice," by Chris Woodall. *Race and Class* 35 (2): 21–33.

Glogowski, Philippe (art), and Marien Puisaye [Lehideux, Guy] (script). 2003. *La Légion: Histoire de la Légion étrangère, 1919–45*, vol. 2: *Bir-Hakeim*. Preface by Pierre Messmer. Paris: Editions du Triomphe.

Goldberg, Itzhak. 1999. "Clichés de clichés." In Marie-Claire Adès and Pierre Zaragozi, eds., *Photographes en Algérie au XIXe siècle*, 9–24. Paris: Musée-Galerie de la Seita.

Golo [Nadeau, Guy] (art), and Frank [Reichert] (script). 1987. *Rampeau 2 (Same Player Shoots Again)*. Paris: Futuropolis. [second ed.; serialized 1979–81; first ed., 1982, as *Same Player Shoots Again*].

Gorridge, Gérald. 2006. *Les fantômes de Hanoï*. Tournai: Casterman.

Graham-Brown, Sarah. 1988. *Images of Women: The Portrayal of Women in Photography of the Middle East, 1860–1950*. New York: Columbia University Press.

Grange, Dominique (script), and Jacques Tardi (art). 1985. "Le meurtrier de Hùng." In Dominique Grange, et al., *Grange bleue*. Paris: Futuropolis: N.p. [1982].

———. 1991. "The Murderer of Hung." In Bob Callahan, ed., *The New Comics Anthology*, 208–15. New York: Collier-Macmillan.

Groensteen, Thierry. 1996. "Hergé débiteur de Saint-Ogan." *9e art* 1: 9–17.

———. 1998. *La bande dessinée en France*. Paris: Ministère des affaires étrangères; Angoulême: CNBDI.

———. 1999. *Système de la bande dessinée*. Paris: Presses universitaires de France.

Grosrichard, Alain. 1979. *Structure du sérail: La fiction du despotisme asiatique dans l'Occident classique*. Paris: Le Seuil.

Grove, Laurence. 2010. *Comics in French: The European Bande Dessinée in Context*, New York: Berghahn Books.

Guerroui, Brahim. 1986. *Les enfants de la liberté*. Algiers: ENAL.

Guilhaume, Jean François. 1992. *Les mythes fondateurs de l'Algérie française*. Preface by Bruno Etienne. Paris: L'Harmattan.

Guillemin, Alain. 2006. "'Parachutés au Laos': La guerre du Viêt-Nam racontée aux enfants catholiques." In Françoise Douaire-Marsaudon, Bernard Sellato and Chantal Zheng, eds., *Dynamiques identitaires en Asie et dans le Pacifique*, vol. 2: *Pratiques symboliques en transition*, 173–89. Aix-en-Provence: Publications de l'Université de Provence.

Halbwachs, Maurice. 1994. *Les cadres sociaux de la mémoire*. Postface by Gérard Namer. Paris: Albin Michel.

Halen, Pierre. 1993a. *Le petit Belge avait vu grand: Une littérature coloniale*. Bruxelles: Labor.

———. 1993b. "Le Congo revisité: Une décennie de bandes dessinées 'belges' (1982–92)." *Textyles* 9: 365–82.

Hargreaves, Alec G. 1995. *Immigration, "Race" and Ethnicity in Contemporary France*. New York: Routledge.

———. 1997. *Immigration and Identity in Beur Fiction: Voices from the North African Immigrant Community in France*. 2nd ed. Oxford: Berg.

Hargreaves, Alec G., and Mark McKinney. 1997. "Introduction: The Post-Colonial Problematic in Contemporary France." In Alec G. Hargreaves and Mark McKinney, eds., *Post-Colonial Cultures in France*, 3–25. New York: Routledge.

Harris, Marla. 2008. "Borderlands: Places, Spaces and Jewish Identity in Joann Sfar's *The Rabbi's Cat* and *Klezmer*." In Samantha Baskind and Ranen Omer-Sherman, eds., *The Jewish Graphic Novel: Critical Approaches*, 181–97. New Brunswick: Rutgers University Press.

Hebrard, Jean-Louis, and Marie-Claude Hebrard. 1990. *L'Algérie autrefois*. Le Coteau: Horvath.

Hennebelle, Guy, Mouny Berrah and Benjamin Stora, eds. 1997. *La guerre d'Algérie à l'écran*, *CinémAction*, no. 85, 4th trimester.

Henry, Jean-Robert, ed. 1985. *Le Maghreb dans l'imaginaire français: La colonie, le désert, l'exil*, special issue of *Revue de l'Occident musulman et de la Méditerranée*, 37.

———. 1991. "Les 'frontaliers' de l'espace franco-maghrébin." *Annuaire de l'Afrique du Nord* 30: 301–11.

Hergé [Remi, Georges]. 1973. *Archives Hergé*, vol. 1: "Totor, c.p. des Hannetons," *Tintin au pays des Soviets* (1929), *Tintin au Congo* (1930), *Tintin en Amérique* (1931). Tournai: Casterman.

———. 1979. *Archives Hergé*, vol. 3: *Les cigares du pharaon* (1932), *Le lotus bleu* (1934), *L'oreille cassée* (1935). Tournai: Casterman.

———. 1980. *Archives Hergé*, vol. 4: *L'île noire* (1937), *Le sceptre d'Ottokar* (1938), *Le crabe aux pinces d'or* (1940). Tournai: Casterman.

———. 2006. *Les vrais secrets de la Licorne*. Edited by Daniel Couvreur, Frédéric Soumois and Philippe Goddin. Brussels: Moulinsart.

———. 2007. *A la recherche du trésor de Rackham le rouge*. Edited by Daniel Couvreur and Frédéric Soumois and preface by Dominique Maricq. Brussels: Moulinsart; Tournai: Casterman.

Hobsbawm, Eric, and Terence Ranger, eds. 1989. *The Invention of Tradition*. New York: Cambridge University Press.

Horne, Alistair. 1978. *A Savage War of Peace: Algeria, 1954–62*. New York: Viking Press.

House, Jim, and Neil Macmaster. 2006. *Paris 1961: Algerians, State Terror, and Memory*. Oxford: Oxford University Press.

Hubinon, Victor (art), and Octave Joly (script). 1994. *Stanley*. Marcinelle: Dupuis. [1955]

Hunt, Nancy Rose. 2002. "Tintin and the Interruptions of Congolese Comics." In Paul S. Landau and Deborah D. Kaspin, eds., *Images and Empires: Visuality in Colonial and Postcolonial Africa*, 90–123. Berkeley: University of California Press.

Hureau, Joëlle. 1992. "La mémoire rapatriée." In Laurent Gervereau, Jean-Pierre Rioux and Benjamin Stora, eds., *La France en guerre d'Algérie: Novembre 1954–Juillet 1962*, 284–88. Nanterre: BDIC.

Ighilahriz, Louisette. 2001. *Algérienne*, with Anne Nivat. Paris: Arthème Fayard; Calmann-Lévy.

Jarry, Grégory (script), and Otto T. (art). 2006. *Petite histoire des colonies françaises*, vol. 1: *L'Amérique française*. Colors by Guillaume Heurtault. Poitiers: FLBLB.

———. 2007. *Petite histoire des colonies françaises*, vol. 2: *L'empire*. Colors by Guillaume Heurtault and Thomas Tudoux. Poitiers: FLBLB.

———. 2009. *Petite histoire des colonies françaises*, vol. 3: *La décolonisation*. Colors by Lucie Castel and Guillaume Heurtault. Poitiers: FLBLB.

———. 2011. *Petite histoire des colonies françaises*, vol. 4: *La Françafrique*. Colors by Lucie Castel, Robin Cousin and Léo Louis-Honoré. Poitiers: FLBLB.

Jijé [Gillain, Joseph]. 1994. "Charles de Foucauld: Conquérant pacifique du Sahara." In *Tout Jijé, 1958–9*, 101–44. Marcinelle: Dupuis [serialized 9 April–10 September 1959, in *Spirou*].

Jobs, Richard I. 2003. "Tarzan under Attack: Youth, Comics and Cultural Reconstruction in Postwar France." *French Historical Studies* 26 (4): 687–725.

Joly, Eric, and Dominique Poncet, eds. 2006. *Séra en d'autres territoires*. Montrouge: P.L.G.

Joos, Louis, and Yann [Le Pennetier]. 1990. *O.A.S. Aïscha*. Grenoble: Glénat.

Joyaux-Brédy, Evelyne (script), and Pierre Joux (art). 1993. *Alger 1832: Le temps des rencontres*. Aix-en-Provence: Cercle Algérianiste d'Aix-en-Provence.

———. 1994. *Par l'épée et par la charrue: L'Algérie au temps du Général Bugeaud*. Aix-en-Provence: Cercle Algérianiste d'Aix-en-Provence.

———. 1996. *Naissance d'un pays: L'Algérie sous le Second Empire*. Aix-en-Provence: Cercle Algérianiste d'Aix-en-Provence.

———. 1998. *C'est nous les Africains . . . : L'Algérie de 1880 à 1920*. Aix-en-Provence: Cercle Algérianiste d'Aix-en-Provence.

———. n.d. *Les rivages amers: L'Algérie—1920–62*. Aix-en-Provence: Cercle Algérianiste d'Aix-en-Provence.

Joyeux, André. 1912. *La vie large des colonies*. Preface by Jean Ajalbert. Paris: Maurice Bauche.

Julien, Charles-André. 1964. *Histoire de l'Algérie contemporaine*, vol. 1: *La conquête et les débuts de la colonisation, 1827–71*. Paris: PUF.

Kappel, Jean. 2003. "La 'torture,' enjeu de mémoire." *La nouvelle revue d'histoire* 8 (September–October): 36–38.

Kaspi, André, and Antoine Marès, eds. 1989. *Le Paris des étrangers depuis un siècle*. Paris: Imprimerie nationale.

Kauffer, Rémi. 2004. "OAS: La guerre franco-française d'Algérie." In Mohammed Harbi and Benjamin Stora, eds., *La guerre d'Algérie: 1954–2004, la fin de l'amnésie*, 451–76. Paris: Robert Laffont.

Kebir, Benyoucef Abbas. 2011. *17 Octobre 1961, 17 bulles: Tragédie-sur-Seine*. Algiers: Editions Dalimen.

Khamès, Djamel. 1995. "L'Algérie fait des bulles." Review of Jacques Ferrandez, "Carnets d'Orient," vols. 1–4. *Arabies* 99: 70–71.

Khelladi, Aïssa. 1995. "Rire quand même: L'humour politique dans l'Algérie d'aujourd'hui." *Revue du monde musulman et de la Méditerranée* 77–78: 225–37.

Kunzle, David. 1990. *The History of the Comic Strip: The Nineteenth Century*. Berkeley: University of California Press.

———. 2007. *Father of the Comic Strip: Rodolphe Töpffer*. Jackson: University Press of Mississippi.

Laamirie, Abdeljalil, Jean-Michel Le Dain, Gilles Manceron, Gilles Morin and Hassan

Remaoun, eds. 1993. *La guerre d'Algérie dans l'enseignement en France et en Algérie.* Paris: Centre National de Documentation Pédagogique.

Labter, Lazhari. 2009. *Panorama de la bande dessinée algérienne 1969–2009.* Algiers: Lazhari Labter éditions.

Laronde, Michel. 1993. *Autour du roman beur: Immigration et identité.* Paris: L'Harmattan.

Lattre, Bernard de. 1952. *Un destin héroïque: Bernard de Lattre: Récits et lettres recueillis et présentés par Robert Garric.* Edited by Robert Garric. Paris: Plon.

Lauzier, Gérard. 2004. "Gérard Lauzier." Interview by Gérard Marinier. In *Ils ont fait la guerre d'Algérie: 40 personnalités racontent . . .* , vol. 1, 108–11. [Mâcon]: JPM Editions [1986].

Lax [Lacroix, Christian] (art), and [Frank] Giroud (script). 1990. *Les oubliés d'Annam,* vol. 1. Marcinelle: Dupuis.

———. 1991. *Les oubliés d'Annam,* vol. 2. Marcinelle: Dupuis.

———. 1998. *Azrayen',* vol. 1. Preface by Benjamin Stora and translations into Kabyle by Saïd "Amnukel" Mella. Marcinelle: Dupuis.

———. 1999. *Azrayen',* vol. 2. Marcinelle: Dupuis.

———. 2000. *Les oubliés d'Annam,* vols. 1–2 together. Marcinelle: Dupuis.

———. 2004. *Azrayen': L'intégrale.* Marcinelle: Dupuis.

Lazreg, Marnia. 1994. *The Eloquence of Silence: Algerian Women in Question.* London: Routledge.

Lebovics, Herman. 1992. *True France: The Wars over Cultural Identity, 1900–45.* Ithaca: Cornell University Press.

———. 1997. "Malraux's mission." *Wilson Quarterly* 21 (1): 78–87.

Lefèvre, Pascal. 2008. "The Congo drawn in Belgium." In Mark McKinney, ed., *History and Politics in French-Language Comics and Graphic Novels,* 166–85. Jackson: University Press of Mississippi.

Lejeune, Philippe. 1985. *Le pacte autobiographique.* Paris: Le Seuil.

Le Monde. 1998. "Légion d'honneur." 15 April.

Lent, John, ed. 2011. "Cambodian, Vietnamese Comic Art: A Symposium." *International Journal of Comic Art* 13 (1): 1–108.

Le Rallic, Etienne. 1949. "Bernard Chamblet: En mission au pays jaune." *Wrill* 191–203, 24 February–19 May.

———. 1976. *Bernard Chamblet et l'Indochine.* Brussels: Michel Deligne.

Leroy, Fabrice. 2011. "Joann Sfar Conjures Marc Chagall: The Politics of Visual Representation in *The Rabbi's Cat.*" *European Comic Art* 4 (1): 39–57.

Le Roy, Maximilien. 2011. *Dans la nuit la liberté nous écoute.* Brussels: Le Lombard.

Le Sueur, James D. 2005. *Uncivil War: Intellectuals and Identity Politics during the Decolonization of Algeria.* Foreword by Pierre Bourdieu. 2nd ed. Lincoln: University of Nebraska Press.

Lê Van, Catherine. 2003. *Mon oncle de Hanoi.* Preface by Tran Anh Hung. Paris: Les Editions du Pacifique.

Lever, Evelyne. 1982. "L'OAS et les Pieds-Noirs." *L'Histoire* 43: 10–23.

Levine, Michel. 1985. *Les ratonnades d'octobre: Un meurtre collectif à Paris en 1961.* Paris: Ramsay.

Liauzu, Claude. 1993. "L'iconographie anticolonialiste." In Nicolas Bancel, Pascal Blanchard and Laurent Gervereau, eds., *Images et colonies: Iconographie et propagande coloniale sur l'Afrique française de 1880 à 1962,* 266–71. Nanterre: BDIC; Paris: ACHAC.

———. 2000. *Passeurs de rives: Changements d'identité dans le Maghreb colonial.* Paris: L'Harmattan.

———. 2006. "L'histoire de la colonisation: Pour quoi?" In Claude Liauzu and Gilles Manceron, eds., *La colonisation, la loi et l'histoire*, preface by Henri Leclerc, 91–98. Paris: Syllepse.

Liauzu, Claude, ed. 2003. *Violence et colonisation: Pour en finir avec les guerres de mémoires*. Paris: Syllepse.

Liauzu, Claude, and Josette Liauzu. 2002. *Quand on chantait les colonies: Colonisation et culture populaire de 1830 à nos jours*. Paris: Syllepse.

———. 2003. "Violence coloniale et guerre d'Algérie." In Claude Liauzu, ed., *Violence et colonisation: Pour en finir avec les guerres de mémoires*, 119–48. Paris: Syllepse.

Liauzu, Claude, and Gilles Manceron, eds. 2006. *La colonisation, la loi et l'histoire*. Preface by Henri Leclerc. Paris: Syllepse.

Loustal, [Jacques de] (art), and Jean-Luc Coatalem (script). 2002. *Jolie mer de Chine*. Tournai: Casterman.

Loustal, [Jacques de] (art), and [Philippe] Paringaux (script). 1985. *Coeurs de sable*. Tournai: Casterman.

———. 1991. *Hearts of Sand*. Translated by Elizabeth Bell. New York: Catalan Communications.

———. 1997. *Kid Congo*. Tournai: Casterman.

Lowe, Lisa. 1991. *Critical Terrains: French and British Orientalisms*. Ithaca: Cornell University Press.

McClintock, Anne. 1992. "The Angel of Progress: Pitfalls of the Term 'Post-Colonialism.'" *Social Text* 31/32: 84–98.

———. 1993. "Family Feuds: Gender, Nationalism and the Family." In *Nationalisms and National Identities*, special issue of *Feminist Review* 44: 61–80.

Macdonald, Amanda. 2008. "Distractions from History: Redrawing Ethnic Trajectories in New Caledonia." In Mark McKinney, ed., *History and Politics in French-Language Comics and Graphic Novels*, 186–211. Jackson: University Press of Mississippi.

MacKenzie, John M. 1995. *Orientalism: History, Theory and the Arts*. Manchester: Manchester University Press.

MacKenzie, John M., ed. 1986. *Imperialism and Popular Culture*. Manchester: Manchester University Press.

McKinney, Mark. 1997a. "Haunting Figures in Contemporary Discourse and Popular Culture in France." *Sites* 1 (1): 51–76.

———. 1997b. "*Métissage* in Post-Colonial Comics." In Alec G. Hargreaves and Mark McKinney, eds., *Post-Colonial Cultures in France*, 169–88. New York: Routledge.

———. 1998. "Beur Comics." In Alex Hughes and Keith Reader, eds, *Encyclopedia of Contemporary French Culture*, 66. London: Routledge.

———. 2000. "The Representation of Ethnic Minority Women in Comic Books." In Jane Freedman and Carrie Tarr, eds., *Women, Immigration and Identities in France*, 85–102. New York: Berg.

———. 2001. "'Tout cela, je ne voulais pas le laisser perdre': colonial *lieux de mémoire* in the Comic Books of Jacques Ferrandez." *Modern and Contemporary France* 9 (1): 43–53.

———. 2004a. "Framing the *Banlieue*." In Roger Célestin, Eliane DalMolin and Alec G. Hargreaves, eds., *Banlieues, Part 2*, special issue of *Contemporary French and Francophone Studies* 8 (2): 113–26.

———. 2004b. "Histoire et critique sociale dans les bandes dessinées africaines-américaines et franco-africaines." In Alec G. Hargreaves, ed., *Minorités ethniques anglophones et francophones: Etudes culturelles comparatives*, 199–218. Paris: L'Harmattan.

———. 2007a. "La frontière et l'affrontière: La bande dessinée et le dessin algériens de langue française face à la nation." In Mireille Rosello, ed., *Images, imagination: Algérie*, special issue of *Expressions maghrébines* 6 (1): 113–33.

———. 2007b. "Georges Remi's Legacy: Between Half-Hidden History, Modern Myth and Mass Marketing." *International Journal of Comic Art* 9 (2): 68–80.

———. 2008a. "Representations of History and Politics in French-Language Comics and Graphic Novels: An Introduction." In Mark McKinney, ed., *History and Politics in French-Language Comics and Graphic Novels*, 3–24. Jackson: University Press of Mississippi.

———. 2008b. "The Algerian War in *Road to America* (Baru, Thévenet, Ledran)." In Mark McKinney, ed., *History and Politics in French-Language Comics and Graphic Novels*, 139–65. Jackson: University Press of Mississippi.

———. 2008c. "The Frontier and the Affrontier: French-Language Algerian Comics and Cartoons Confront the Nation." Translated by Ann Miller. *European Comic Art* 1 (2): 177–201.

———. 2009. "'On connaît la chanson . . . ': Le colonialisme français au Maghreb en chansons et en musique dans la bande dessinée." *Etudes Francophones* 24 (1–2): 70–95.

———. 2011a. "Redrawing the Franco-Algerian Affrontier in *Là-bas*." *International Journal of Comic Art* 13 (1): 127–52.

———. 2011b. *The Colonial Heritage of French Comics*. Liverpool: Liverpool University Press.

———. 2011c. "The Colonial Beginnings of Autobiography in French Comics." *International Journal of Comic Art* 13 (2): 344–68.

McKinney, Mark, ed. 2008. *History and Politics in French-Language Comics*. Jackson: University Press of Mississippi.

Maffre, Laurent. 2012. *Demain, Demain: Nanterre, bidonville de la Folie, 1962–66*. Postface by Monique Hervo. Arles: Actes Sud; Paris: Arte Editions.

Malet, Léo (script), and Jacques Tardi (art). 1982. *Brouillard au pont de Tolbiac*. Tournai: Casterman.

Malka, Richard (script), and Frédéric Volante (art). 2011. *Les Z*, vol. 1: *Sétif-Paris*. Colors Bruno Pradelle. Paris: 12bis.

Mallet (script), and Marcelino Truong (art). 1984. "La mort du dragon." *Métal Aventure* 8: 27–33.

Malraux, André. 1962. *La voie royale*. Paris: Livre de poche (no. 86) [1930].

———. 1982. *La condition humaine*. Paris: Gallimard ("Folio no. 1").

Malraux, Clara. 1986. *Nos vingt ans*. Paris: Bernard Grasset.

Maltaite, Eric, and Denis Lapiere. 1987. *Le carrefour de Nâm-Pha*. Paris: SEFAM.

Mardon, Grégory. 1999. *Vagues à l'âme*. Geneva: Les Humanoïdes Associés.

Marijac [Dumas, Jacques] (script), and [Noël] Gloesner (art). 1979. *Colonel X en Extrême-Orient*. Grenoble: Jacques Glénat [first serialized in *Coq hardi*, 1952–53].

Martini, Lucienne. 1997. *Racines de papier: Essai sur l'expression littéraire de l'identité pieds-noirs*. Preface by Jean-Robert Henry. Paris: Publisud.

Masmoudi, Benattou. 1983. *Le village oublié*. Algiers: ENAL.

Mauss-Copeaux, Claire. 2004. "Photographies d'appelés de la guerre d'Algérie." In Mohammed Harbi and Benjamin Stora, eds., *La guerre d'Algérie: 1954–2004, la fin de l'amnésie*, 557–74. Paris: Robert Laffont.

Mechkour, Larbi (art), and Farid Boudjellal (script). 1985. *Les Beurs*. Paris: L'Echo des Savanes; Albin Michel.

———. 2004. *Black Blanc Beur: Les folles années de l'intégration*. Songs by André Igwal. Cachan: Tartamudo.

Melouah, Sid Ali. 1983. *Cité interdite*, with Abahri. Algiers: ENAL.

———. 1988. *La secte des assassins*. N.p.: n.p.

———. 2003. *Pierrot de Bab el Oued*. Algiers: Limage.

Memmi, Albert. 1985. *Portrait du colonisé, précédé de Portrait du colonisateur*. Preface by Jean-Paul Sartre. Paris: Gallimard [1957].

———. 1991. *The Colonizer and the Colonized*. Introduction by Jean-Paul Sartre and afterword by Susan Gilson Miller. Boston: Beacon Press.

Merchet, Jean-Dominique. 1996. "Chirac ou la nostalgie des colonies." *Libération*, 12 November, 13.

Mercier, Jean-Pierre. 1999. "Autobiographie et bande dessinée." In Philippe Lejeune, ed., *Récits de vies et médias: Actes du colloque des 20 et 21 novembre 1998*, special issue of *Cahiers RITM* 20: 157–65.

Mérezette, Denis (art), and Farid Boudjellal (script). 1994. "Vengeance harkie." *El building* 2 (December): 76–106.

Mérezette, Denis, and Dumenil. 1985. *Algérie française!* Brussels: Michel Deligne.

Michallat, Wendy. 2007. "*Pilote* 'Hebdomadaire' and the Teenager *Bande Dessinée* of the 1950s and 1960s." *Modern and Contemporary France* 15 (3): 277–92.

Miller, Ann. 1999. "*Bande dessinée*: A Disputed Centenary." *French Cultural Studies* 10 (part 1), no. 28: 67–87.

———. 2004. "*Les héritiers d'Hergé*: The Figure of the Aventurier in a Postcolonial Context." In Yvette Rocheron and Christopher Rolfe, eds., *Shifting Frontiers of France and Francophonie*, 307–23. New York: Peter Lang.

———. 2007. *Reading Bande dessinée: Critical Approaches to French-Language Comic Strip*. Bristol: Intellect.

———. 2009. "Enfants de la bulle." In Driss El Yazami, Yvan Gastaut and Naïma Yahi, *Générations: Un siècle d'histoire culturelle des Maghrébins en France*, 183–88. Paris: Gallimard; Génériques; Cité nationale de l'histoire de l'immigration.

Milleron, Christine. 2003. "L'action psychologique et la déshumanisation de l'adversaire." In Claude Liauzu, ed., *Violence et colonisation: Pour en finir avec les guerres de mémoires*, 155–73. Paris: Syllepse.

Mimouni, Rachid (text), and Jacques Ferrandez (illustrations). 1993. *La colline visitée: La casbah d'Alger*. Paris: Editions D.S.

Le Monde. 1993. "Rejetant le pourvoi formé contre l'universitaire, la Cour de cassation met fin à l'"affaire Boudarel."' 3 April.

Mora, Victor (script), and Annie Goetzinger (art). 1986. *Felina: L'ogre du Djebel*. Paris: Dargaud.

Morvandiau [Cotinat, Luc]. 2007. *D'Algérie*. Rennes: L'oeil électrique.

———. 2011. "Comic Art and Commitment: An Interview with Morvandiau," by Ann Miller. *European Comic Art* 4 (1): 105–23.

———. 2012. "France, Algérie: Je n'oublie pas." *Libération*, 3 March.

Nader, Laura. 1989. "Orientalism, Occidentalism and the Control of Women." *Cultural Dynamics* 2 (3): 323–55.

Nederveen Pieterse, Jan. 1992. *White on Black: Images of Africa and Blacks in Western Popular Culture*. New Haven: Yale University Press.

9e art 1–15. 1996–2009.

Nochlin, Linda. 1989. "The Imaginary Orient." In *The Politics of Vision: Essays on Nineteenth-Century Art and Society*, 33–59. New York: Harper and Row.

Nora, Pierre. 1961. *Les Français d'Algérie*. Introduction by Charles-André Julien. Paris: René Julliard.

Nora, Pierre, ed. 1984–92. *Les lieux de mémoire*. Paris: Gallimard.

Norindr, Panivong. 1996. *Phantasmatic Indochina: French Colonial Ideology in Architecture, Film and Literature*. Durham: Duke University Press.

Pasamonik, Didier, and Eric Verhoest, eds. 2005. *White Man's Remorse*. Translated by Paul Gravett. Exhibition catalog. Charleroi: Christian Renard-Charleroi Images.

Peeters, Benoît. 2002a. *Hergé: Fils de Tintin*. Paris: Flammarion.

———. 2002b. *Lire la bande dessinée*. Paris: Flammarion ("Champs").

Péju, Paulette. 2000. *Ratonnades à Paris, précédé de Les harkis à Paris*. Preface by Pierre Vidal-Naquet, introduction by Marcel Péju, and postface by François Maspero. Paris: La Découverte [1961].

Pervillé, Guy. 1993. *De l'empire français à la décolonisation*. Paris: Hachette.

———. 2003. *Atlas de la guerre d'Algérie: De la conquête à l'indépendance*. Cartography by Cécile Marin. Paris: Autrement; Ministère de la défense; Secrétariat général pour l'administration; Direction de la mémoire, du patrimoine et des archives.

Petit, Léonce. ca. 1868. *Les mésaventures de M. Bêton*. Paris: Librairie internationale.

Pierre, Michel. 1988. "La B.D., terre des grands fantasmes." *Notre librairie* 91 (January–February): 116–19.

———. 1992. "Les mille et une bulles: L'orient imaginaire dans la bande dessinée." *A Suivre* 170 (March): 25–29.

———. 2000. "L'Afrique dans la bande dessinée européenne: Un continent décor!" Interview by Emmanuelle Mahoudeau, in a dossier on "BD d'Afrique." Edited by Sébastien Langevin. *Africultures* 32 (November): 43–47.

Pigeon, Gérard. 1996. "Black icons of colonialism: African characters in French children's comic strip literature." *Social Identities* 2 (1): 135–59.

Pinchon, Joseph-Porphyre (art), and Jean Noé (script). N.d. *Gringalou en Algérie*. Liège: Chagor [Editions Charles Gordinne et fils] [serialized 1947].

Poncet, Dominique, and Philippe Morin. 1996. "Dossier Ferrandez." *P.L.G. (Plein La Gueule)* 32 (Fall): 66–83.

Porterfield, Todd. 1994. "Western Views of Oriental Women in Modern Painting and Photography." In Salwa Mikdadi Nashashibi, et al., *Forces of Change: Artists of the Arab World*, 58–71. Lafayette, CA: The International Council for Women in the Arts; Washington, D.C.: The National Museum of Women in the Arts.

———. 1998. *The Allure of Empire: Art in the Service of French Imperialism, 1798–1836*. Princeton: Princeton University Press.

Pouillon, François. 1997. *Les deux vies d'Etienne Dinet, peintre en Islam*. Paris: Balland.

Prochaska, David. 1990a. "The Archive of *Algérie Imaginaire*." *History and Anthropology* 4 (part 2): 373–420.

———. 1990b. *Making Algeria French: Colonialism in Bône, 1870–1920*. New York: Cambridge University Press.

———. 2003. "The Other Algeria: Beyond Renoir's Algiers." In Roger Benjamin, *Renoir and Algeria*, 121–42. New Haven: Yale University Press.

Puisy, Georges (art), and Patrick Chamoiseau (script). 1981. *Les Antilles sous Bonaparte: Delgrès*. Fort-de-France: Emile Désormeaux.

Raives, S. [Servais, Guy] (art), and E. Varnauts [Warnauts, Eric] (script). 1985. *Paris Perdu*, vol. 1: *Marie-Lou*. Louvain-la-Neuve: Editions du Miroir.

———. 1986. *Paris Perdu*, vol. 2: *Paul*. Louvain-la-Neuve: Editions du Miroir.

Renan, Ernest. 1947. "Qu'est-ce qu'une nation?: Conférence faite en Sorbonne, le 11 mars 1882." In *Oeuvres complètes de Ernest Renan*, vol. 1, ed. Henriette Psichari, 887–906. Paris: Calmann-Lévy.

———. 1993. "What Is a Nation?" Translated and annotated by Martin Thom. In Homi K. Bhabha, ed., *Nation and Narration*, 8–22. New York: Routledge.

Renard, Claude (art), and Fromental, Jean-Luc (script). 1987. *Le rendez-vous d'Angkor: Une aventure d'Ivan Casablanca*. Paris: Les Humanoïdes Associés.

Rey-Goldzeiguer, Annie. 1993. "Réflexions sur l'image et la perception du Maghreb et des Maghrébins dans la France du dix-neuvième et du vingtième siècles." In Pascal Blanchard and Armelle Chatelier, eds., *Images et colonies: Nature, discours et influence de l'iconographie coloniale liée à la propagande coloniale et à la représentation des Africains et de l'Afrique en France, de 1920 aux indépendances*, 33–40. Paris: ACHAC; Syros.

———. 2002. "France-Algérie: 172 ans de drames et de passions." Interview by Christian Makarian and Dominique Simonnet. *L'Express international* 2645 (14–20 March): 48–63.

Rigby, Brian. 1991. *Popular Culture in Modern France: A Study of Cultural Discourse.* London: Routledge.

Rigney, Ann. 2005. "Plenitude, Scarcity and the Circulation of Cultural Memory." *Journal of European Studies* 35 (1): 11–28.

Rioux, Lucien. 1992. "De 'Bambino' à 'Mustapha': Le fonds sonore de la guerre." In Laurent Gervereau, Jean-Pierre Rioux and Benjamin Stora, eds., *La France en guerre d'Algérie: Novembre 1954–Juillet 1962*, 256–61. Nanterre: BDIC.

Roches, Léon. 1904. *Dix ans à travers l'Islam, 1834–44.* Paris: Perrin.

Rodinson, Maxime. 1989. *La fascination de l'Islam, suivi de, Le seigneur bourguignon et l'esclave sarrasin.* Paris: La Découverte.

Rosaldo, Renato. 1989. "Imperialist Nostalgia." In Natalie Zemon Davis and Randolph Starn, eds., *Memory and Counter-Memory*, special issue of *Representations* 26: 107–22.

Rosenthal, Donald A. 1982. *Orientalism: The Near East in French Painting, 1800–80.* Rochester: Memorial Art Gallery of the University of Rochester.

Ross, Kristin. 1992. "Watching the Detectives." In Francis Barker, Peter Hulme and Margaret Iversen, eds., *Postmodernism and the Re-reading of Modernity*, 46–65. Manchester: Manchester University Press, 1992.

———. 1996. *Fast Cars, Clean Bodies: Decolonization and the Reordering of French Culture.* Cambridge: MIT Press.

Ruedy, John. 1992. *Modern Algeria: The Origins and Development of a Nation.* Bloomington: Indiana University Press.

Ruscio, Alain. 1992. *La guerre française d'Indochine, 1945–54.* Brussels: Complexe.

———. 2001. *Que la France était belle au temps des colonies . . . : Anthologie de chansons coloniales et exotiques françaises.* Paris: Maisonneuve & Larose.

———. 2003. "Interrogations sur certaines pratiques de l'armée française en Indochine, 1945–54." In Claude Liauzu, ed., *Violence et colonisation: Pour en finir avec les guerres de mémoires*, 85–106. Paris: Syllepse.

Ruscio, Alain, ed. 1996. *Amours coloniales: Aventures et fantasmes exotiques de Claire de Duras à Georges Simenon.* Preface by Madeleine Rebérioux. Brussels: Complexe.

———. 2002. *La guerre "française" d'Indochine (1945–54). Les sources de la connaissance: Bibliographie, filmographie, documents divers.* Paris: Les Indes savantes.

Saada, Emmanuelle. 2007. *Les enfants de la colonie: Les métis de l'empire français entre sujétion et citoyenneté.* Preface by Gérard Noiriel. Paris: La Découverte.

Said, Edward W. 1992. "Interview with Edward Said," by Jennifer Wicke and Michael Sprinker. In Michael Sprinker, ed., *Edward Said: A Critical Reader*, 221–64. Oxford: Blackwell.

———. 1994a. *Orientalism.* New York: Vintage Books [1978].

———. 1994b. *Culture and Imperialism.* New York: Vintage Books.

Saint-Michel, Serge (script), and Dominique Fages (art). 1976. *Histoire du Togo: Il était une fois . . . Eyadema.* Paris: Afrique Biblio Club.

Saint-Michel, Serge (script), Alain Goutteman (script) and Jean-Marie Ruffieux (art). 2000.

De Gaulle, "le visionnaire," 1890–1940–1970. Colors by Yves Chagnaud. Paris: France Impact Promotion.

Saint-Michel, Serge (script), and René Le Honzec (art). 1994. *Histoire des troupes de Marine, tome 2, 1871–1931: Les bâtisseurs d'empire.* Paris: Mémoire d'Europe; Crépin-Leblond.

———. 1995. *Histoire des troupes de Marine, tome 3, 1931–95: Soldats de la liberté.* Paris: Mémoire d'Europe; Crépin-Leblond.

Saint-Ogan, Alain. 1995. *Zig et Puce aux Indes,* vol. 6. Grenoble: Glénat [serialized 29 March 1931 to 20 March 1932; first ed., 1932].

Salemink, Oscar. 1999. "Ethnography as Martial Art: Ethnicizing Vietnam's Montagnards, 1930–54." In Peter Pels and Oscar Salemink, eds., *Colonial Subjects: Essays on the Practical History of Anthropology,* 282–325. Ann Arbor: University of Michigan Press.

Sebbar, Leïla. 1985. *Les carnets de Sherazade.* Paris: Stock.

Sebbar, Leïla, and Jean-Michel Belorgey. 2002. *Femmes d'Afrique du Nord: Cartes postales 1885–1930.* Saint-Pourçain-sur-Sioule: Bleu autour.

Séra [Ing, Phoussera]. 1995. *Impasse et rouge.* Preface by Jacques Tardi. Paris: Rackham.

———. 2003. *Impasse et rouge.* 2nd ed. Paris: Albin Michel.

———. 2005. *L'eau et la terre: Cambodge 1975–1979.* Paris: Guy Delcourt.

———. 2007. *Lendemains de cendres: Cambodge 1979–1993.* Paris: Guy Delcourt.

———. 2011. *3 pas dans la pagode bleue.* Paris: Le 9ème Monde.

Séra [Ing, Phoussera], and Philippe Saimbert. 2001. *Les processionnaires,* vol. 1: *Le grand passage,* Paris: Albin Michel.

———. 2002. *Les processionnaires,* vol. 2: *Le jour du jugement,* Paris: Albin Michel.

———. 2003. *Les processionnaires,* vol. 3: *Ici-bas,* Paris: Albin Michel.

Sérullaz, Maurice. 1951. *Delacroix: Aquarelles du Maroc.* Paris: Fernand Hazan.

Servais, J.-C., and G. Dewamme. 1988. "Les voyages clos: Montagne fleurie." *Circus,* 125: 72–94.

Sessions, Jennifer E. 2011. *By Sword and Plow: France and the Conquest of Algeria.* Ithaca: Cornell University Press.

Sfar, Joann. 2003a. *Le chat du rabbin,* vol. 1: *La bar-mitsva.* Preface by Eliette Abécassis. Colors by Brigitte Findakly. Paris: Dargaud.

———. 2003b. *Le chat du rabbin,* vol. 2: *Le malka des lions.* Preface by [Mohand Saïd] Fellag. Colors by Brigitte Findakly. Paris: Dargaud.

———. 2003c. *Le chat du rabbin,* vol. 3: *L'exode.* Preface by Georges Moustaki. Colors by Brigitte Findakly. Paris: Dargaud.

———. 2005. *Le chat du rabbin,* vol. 4: *Le paradis terrestre.* Preface by Jean Giraud/Moebius. Colors by Brigitte Findakly. Paris: Dargaud.

———. 2006. *Le chat du rabbin,* vol. 5: *Jérusalem d'Afrique.* Preface by Philippe Val. Colors by Brigitte Findakly. Paris: Dargaud.

———. 2010. *Le chat du rabbin: L'intégrale.* Colors by Brigitte Findakly. Paris: Dargaud.

Shepard, Todd. 2006. *The Invention of Decolonization: The Algerian War and the Remaking of France.* Ithaca: Cornell University Press.

Sherzer, Dina. 1998. "French Colonial and Post-Colonial Hybridity: *Condition Métisse.*" *Journal of European Studies* 28 (1–2): 103–20.

Shohat, Ella. 1992. "Notes on the 'Post-Colonial.'" *Social Text* 31/32: 99–113.

Siblot, Paul. 1985. "'Retours à l'Algérie heureuse' ou les mille et un détours de la nostalgie." In Jean-Robert Henry, ed. *Le Maghreb dans l'imaginaire français: La colonie, le désert, l'exil,* special issue of *Revue de l'Occident musulman et de la Méditerranée,* 37: 151–64.

Sibran, Anne. 1999. *Bleu-Figuier.* Paris: Grasset.

Silverman, Maxim. 1992. *Deconstructing the Nation: Immigration, Racism and Citizenship in Modern France*. New York: Routledge.

Siné [Sinet, Maurice]. 1965. *Dessins politiques*. Paris: Jean-Jacques Pauvert.

———. 1992. *Le déshonneur est sauf: Dessins de la guerre d'Algérie*. Paris: La Découverte.

———. 2002. *Ma vie, mon oeuvre, mon cul!*, vol. 7. Paris: Editions Rotative.

———. 2004. *Ma vie, mon oeuvre, mon cul!*, vol. 3. Tournai: Casterman.

Sirius [Mayeu, Max] (art), and Xavier Snoeck (script). 1987. *La francisque et le cimeterre*. Marcinelle: Dupuis.

Slim [Merabtène, Menouar]. 1968. *Moustache et les Belgacem*. Algiers: Algérie Actualité.

———. n.d. "Le coup de l'éventail." Unpublished comic.

Slocombe, Romain. 1986. *La nuit de Saigon*. Paris: Futuropolis.

Slotkin, Richard. 1993. *Gunfighter Nation: The Myth of the Frontier in Twentieth-Century America*. New York: Harper Perennial.

Smith, Stephen. 1993. "La 'plus grande France' à la rescousse." *Libération*, 18 October, 3.

Smolderen, Thierry. 2009. *Naissances de la bande dessinée, de William Hogarth à Winsor McCay*. Brussels: Les Impressions Nouvelles.

Sommer, Doris. 1993. "Irresistible Romance: The Foundational Fictions of Latin America." In Homi K. Bhabha, ed., *Nation and Narration*, 71–98. New York: Routledge.

Sommer, Manfred. 1989. *Viet-Song*. Paris: Dargaud.

Spurr, David. 1993. *The Rhetoric of Empire: Colonial Discourse in Journalism, Travel Writing and Imperial Administration*. Durham: Duke University Press.

Staller, Jack. 1993. *Après la guerre*. Brussels: Editions du Lombard.

Stanislas [Barthélémy] (art), and Laurent Rullier (script). 1990. *Une aventure de Victor Levallois*, vol. 1: *Trafic en Indochine*. Colors by Christine Couturier. Geneva: Alpen Publishers—Humano S. A.

———. 1992. *Une aventure de Victor Levallois*, vol. 2: *La route de Cao Bang*. Colors by Christine Couturier. Geneva: Alpen Publishers—Humano S. A.

———. 1994. *Une aventure de Victor Levallois*, vol. 3: *Le manchot de la Butte rouge*. Colors by Christine Couturier. Geneva: Alpen Publishers—Humano S. A.

———. 2004. *Une aventure de Victor Levallois*, vol. 4: *La balade des clampins*. Colors by Dominique Thomas. Geneva: Les Humanoïdes Associés.

Stassen, Jean-Philippe. 2000. *Déogratias*. Marcinelle: Dupuis.

———. 2002. *Pawa: Chroniques des Monts de la lune*. Paris: Guy Delcourt.

———. 2004. *Les enfants*. Marcinelle: Dupuis.

Stora, Benjamin. 1992. *La gangrène et l'oubli: La mémoire de la guerre d'Algérie*. Paris: La Découverte [1991].

———. 1993. "La mémoire de la guerre d'Algérie chez les jeunes issus de l'immigration." In J. Barou, et al., *Mémoire et intégration*, 33–40. Paris: Syros.

———. 1997. *Imaginaires de guerre: Algérie-Viêt-nam, en France et aux Etats-Unis*. Paris: La Découverte.

———. 1999. *Le transfert d'une mémoire: De l'"Algérie française" au racisme anti-arabe*. Paris: La Découverte.

———. 2012. "Algérie-France, mémoires sous tension." *Le Monde*, 18 March.

Strömberg, Fredrik. 2003. *Black Images in the Comics: A Visual History*. Foreword by Charles Johnson. Seattle: Fantagraphics Books.

Tacconi, Ferdinando (art), Raphaël (art), Robert Bielot (script) and Pierre Dufourcq (text). 1978. *Histoire de France en bandes dessinées*, no. 24: *Vers la libération; Une France nouvelle*, September [Librairie Larousse].

Taraud, Christine. 2003. *La prostitution coloniale: Algérie, Tunisie, Maroc (1830–1962)*. Paris: Payot.

Tardi, Jacques. 1990. *Une gueule de bois en plomb*. Tournai: Casterman.

Tarek, Batist Payen and Kamel Mouellef. 2011. *Turcos: Le jasmin et la boue*. Preface by Yasmina Khadra. Cachan: Tartamudo.

Tenani, Mustapha. 1981. *De nos montagnes*. Algiers: SNED.

———. 1985. *Les hommes du djebel*. Algiers: Entreprise nationale du livre.

Thénault, Sylvie. 2012. *Violence ordinaire dans l'Algérie coloniale: Camps, internements, assignations à résidence*. Paris: Odile Jacob.

Thornton, Lynne. 1985. *La femme dans la peinture orientaliste*. Courbevoie: ACR.

Tian. 2011. *L'année du lièvre*, vol. 1: *Au revoir Phnom Penh*. Preface by Rithy Panh. Paris: Gallimard.

Töpffer, Rodolphe. 1994. *L'invention de la bande dessinée*. Edited by Thierry Groensteen and Benoît Peeters. Paris: Hermann.

———. 1996. *Le docteur Festus; Histoire de monsieur Cryptogame: Deux odysées*. Preface by Thierry Groensteen. Paris: Le Seuil.

———. 2007. *Rodolphe Töpffer: The Complete Comic Strips*. Compiled, translated and annotated by David Kunzle. Jackson: University Press of Mississippi.

Topin, Tito. 1987. "L'Orient n'existe pas." Review of Jacques Ferrandez, *Carnets d'Orient*. *Magazine Littéraire* n.n. (April): 101.

Tribak-Geoffroy, Nabila. 1997. "Carnets d'Orient: Jacques Ferrandez et l'histoire de l'Algérie, réalité ou mythologie." In Nicolas Gaillard, ed., *La bande dessinée: Histoire, développement, signification*, special issue of *Contre-champ* 1: 115–29.

Tristan, Anne. 1991. *Le silence du fleuve: Ce crime que nous n'avons toujours pas nommé*. Bezons: Au nom de la mémoire.

Tronchet, Didier (art), and Anne Sibran (script). 2003. *Là-bas*. Marcinelle: Dupuis.

Truong, Marcelino. 1984. "Sur le Fleuve Rouge." *Métal Hurlant Aventure* 5 (May): 16–20.

———. 1999. "Rencontre de Marcelino Truong." Interview by Philippe Dumont and Agnès Nguyên-Van. *Passions Viêt Nam* 2 (September): 4–6.

Truong, Marcelino, and Francis Leroi. 1991. *Le dragon de bambou*. Paris: Albin Michel.

Uderzo, Albert. 1985. "Valérie André." In Christian Philippsen, *Uderzo, de Flamberge à Astérix*, p. 79. Paris: Philippsen.

Vann, Michael G. 2009. "Caricaturing 'The Colonial Good Life' in French Indochina." *European Comic Art* 2 (1): 83–108.

Vann, Michael G., and Joel Montague. 2008. *The Colonial Good Life: A Commentary on André Joyeux's Vision of French Indochina*. Bangkok: White Lotus Press.

Vatin, Jean-Claude. 1985. "Désert construit et inventé, Sahara perdu ou retrouvé: Le jeu des imaginaires." In Jean-Robert Henry, ed. *Le Maghreb dans l'imaginaire français: La colonie, le désert, l'exil*, special issue of *Revue de l'Occident musulman et de la Méditerranée*, 37: 107–31.

Vaugeois, Charles. 2003. "Une guerre cruelle, 1954–62." In *La nouvelle revue d'histoire* 8: 27–35.

Venner, Dominique. 2003. "Les rivages amers. L'Algérie 1920–62." Review of *Les rivages amers*, by Evelyne Joyaux-Brédy and Pierre Joux. *La nouvelle revue d'histoire* 8: 62.

Verdon, Tony (script), and Perrin-Houdon (art). 1951–52. "Parachutés au Laos," *Bayard* 215–74, 14 January 1951–2 March 1952 [except nos. 225, 245 and 264, which have no episodes].

Verschave, François-Xavier. 2000. *France-Afrique: Le crime continue*. Lyon: Tahin Party.

———. 2001. *La Françafrique: Le plus long scandale de la république*. Paris: Stock. [1998]

Vidal, Guy. 1987. "Guy Vidal et les péchés de l'histoire." Interview by Thierry Groensteen. *Les cahiers de la bande dessinée* 77 (September–October): 84–88.

———. 2004. "Guy Vidal." Interview by Gérard Marinier. In *Ils ont fait la guerre d'Algérie: 40 personnalités racontent* . . . , vol. 1, 160–63. [Mâcon]: JPM Editions [1986].

Vidal, Guy (script), and Alain Bignon (art). 1982. *Une éducation algérienne.* Colors by Anne Delobel. Paris: Dargaud.

Vidal-Bué, Marion. 2000. *Alger et ses peintres, 1830–1960.* Paris: Paris-Méditerranée.

Vidal-Naquet, Pierre. 1983. *La torture dans la république: Essai d'histoire et de politique contemporaines 1954–62.* Paris: La Découverte/Maspero [1972].

———. 2001. *Les crimes de l'armée française: Algérie 1954–62.* Paris: La Découverte [1975].

Viollis, Andrée [Tizad, Andrée Françoise Ardenne de]. 1935. *Indochine S.O.S..* Preface by André Malraux. 9th ed. Paris: Gallimard.

Vittori, Jean-Pierre (text), and Jacques Ferrandez (illustrations). 2001. *Midi pile, l'Algérie.* Voisins-le-Bretonneux: Rue du monde.

Warnauts, [Eric], and Raives [Servais, Guy]. 1997. "La contortionniste," part 1. *A Suivre* 234 (July): 79–97.

Wasterlain, Marc. 1987. *Les aventures de Jeannette Pointu, reporter photographe*, vol. 1: *Le dragon vert.* Charleroi: Dupuis [1983].

Wazem. 1997. *Livre vert Vietnam.* Geneva: Papiers Gras.

Weeks, John. 2011. "Economics and Comics: Khmer Popular Culture in Changing Times." *International Journal of Comic Art* 13 (1): 3–31.

Willem [Holtrop, Bernhard Willem]. 2000. *Le feuilleton du siècle.* Paris: Cornélius.

Winston, Jane. 2001. *Postcolonial Duras: Cultural Memory in Postwar France.* New York: Palgrave.

Winston, Jane, and Leakthina Chau-Pech Ollier, eds. 2001. *Of Vietnam: Identities in Dialogue.* New York: Palgrave.

Wolinski, Georges. 2001. *Ma vie historique: Je montre tout!* Preface by Philippe Val. Hors série no. 14. Paris: Editions Rotative.

———. 2004. "Wolinski." Interview by Gérard Marinier. In *Ils ont fait la guerre d'Algérie: 40 personnalités racontent* . . . , vol. 1, 164–67. [Mâcon]: JPM Editions [1986].

Woodhull, Winifred. 1991. "Unveiling Algeria." *Genders* 10: 112–31.

———. 1993. *Transfigurations of the Maghreb: Feminism, Decolonization and Literatures.* Minneapolis: University of Minnesota Press.

———. 1997. "Ethnicity on the French frontier." In Gisela Brinker-Gabler and Sidonie Smith, eds., *Writing New Identities: Gender, Nation, and Immigration in Contemporary Europe.* 31–61. Minneapolis: University of Minnesota Press.

X, Dr. Jacobus [pseud.]. 1927. *L'art d'aimer aux colonies.* Paris: Georges-Anquetil.

Yeager, Jack Andrew. 1987. *The Vietnamese Novel in French: A Literary Response to Colonialism.* Hanover, NH: University Press of New England.

INDEX

counter-culture, 107

counter-*fait divers,* 118

counter-hegemony, 55

counter-history, 18, 119, 148

counter-narrative, 118

counter-violence, 14, 120, 178

"Le coup de l'éventail" (Slim), 20, 232n58

Le cousin harki (Boudjellal), 194–196, 201, 208–9

Le crabe aux pinces d'or (Hergé), 106

Crémieux decree, 232n59

Crépin, Thierry, 23, 25, 93–94, 120, 146, 234n1, 235n14, 238n53

crimes against humanity, 83, 112, 121, 127, 237n52

Croisière noire, 30, 243n17

Crumb, Robert, 146

CSEM (Centre Saharien d'Expérimentation Militaire), 153

cultural authentication, 80–81

cultural capital, 21–22

cultural formations, 5, 38–39

currency speculation, 84, 87, 114, 116

Daeninckx, Didier, 22, 118, 207, 209, 237n51, 237n52, 238n54, 239n8, 242n62, 242n63, 242n65

D'Algérie (Morvandiau), 14–15, 31, 143, 186–189, 216–218, 225n4, 226n23, 239n6, 243n15

Les damnés de la terre (Fanon), 94, 120, 193

Da Nang, 85

Dans la nuit la liberté nous écoute (Le Roy), 22, 133

Dans l'ombre de Charonne (Frappier and Frappier), 209

Dargaud, 157, 240n22

Daumier, Honoré, 39, 48, 227n11

David B., 153, 204–6

Debernard, Jean, 240n22

"Déclaration des droits de l'homme et du citoyen," 121

decolonization, 7, 9–11, 14–15, 17, 20, 30, 32, 35, 75, 77, 90, 127, 133, 139–140, 145, 147–148, 150–151, 202, 209, 213, 221, 228n18; arrested and partial 17, 26, 104

deconstructing and dismantling, 204, 210, 213

Decoux, Jean, 113

Defali, Djillali, 10, 209, 226n13

De Gaulle, Charles, 12, 15, 32, 54, 149, 155, 159–160, 185, 191, 194, 213, 238n54, 240n24

De Gaulle, "le visionnaire," 1890–1940–1970 (Saint-Michel, Goutteman and Ruffieux), 12

dehumanization, 133

Delacroix, Eugène, 17, 28, 40, 50, 54–56, 58, 62, 64, 67–71, 73, 75–76, 79–80, 157, 159, 182, 230n35, 230n37, 233n63, 233n66

Delavignette, Robert, 139

Delcourt, 242n2

Demain, demain: Nanterre, bidonville de la Folie, 1962–66 (Maffre), 207, 209

"Demain, dès l'aube" (Hugo), 201

La demoiselle de la Légion d'honneur (Christin and Goetzinger), 155, 157, 202

demonstrations: in Algeria (11 December 1960) by Algerians, 158; in Algiers (26 March 1962) by *Pieds-Noirs,* 185; in France against the Algerian war, 202; in Paris (17 October 1961) by Algerians, 22, 149, 203, 206–7, 209, 237n52; in Paris (1986) by students, 221; in Paris (8 February 1962) against the OAS, 209; in Sétif (8 May 1945) by Algerians, 10; in Vietnam, 114

Denon, Dominique-Vivant, 39

Déogratias (Stassen), 216, 218

Dernière demeure (Ferrandez 2007), 180–181

Description de l'Egypte, 39

deserts, 46, 52, 72, 81, 153–154, 165, 173, 176–178

Deshayes, Eugène, 234n66

despotism, oriental, 7, 43–44, 69–70

detective novel: 83, 119, 202, 207, 237n51, 237n52, 238n54, 238n56; hermeneutic of, 118–119, 164, 166

"Le deuil" (Alagbé and Stein), 239n6, 243n24

Dewamme, Gérard, 88

dey of Algiers, 7, 41, 44, 243n23

DGSE (Direction Générale de la Sécurité Extérieure), 118–119, 122

dialogism, 27, 30, 33, 91–92, 151–152, 158, 200, 208–9, 228n22, 240n23

diaries and journals, 25, 155–157, 162, 173, 178, 239n10

Studies in Comics and Cartoons

LUCY SHELTON CASWELL AND JARED GARDNER, SERIES EDITORS

Books published in Studies in Comics and Cartoons will focus exclusively on comics and graphic literature, highlighting their relation to literary studies. It will include monographs and edited collections that cover the history of comics and cartoons from the editorial cartoon and early sequential comics of the 19th century through webcomics of the 21st. Studies that focus on international comics will also be considered

Redrawing French Empire in Comics
  Mark McKinney